DEVON AND CORNWALL RECORD SOCIETY

New Series

Volume 62

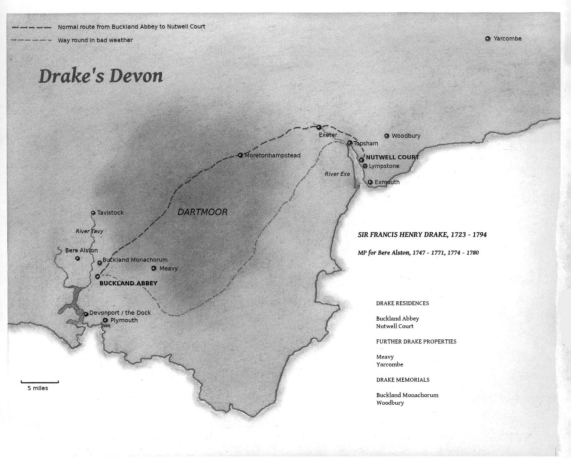

Frontispiece: Map of Drake's Devon. Design: Aziz Khan and Jonathan Hepworth

SIR FRANCIS HENRY DRAKE (1723–1794)

LETTERS FROM THE COUNTRY, LETTERS FROM THE CITY

EDITED BY

CHARITY SCOTT-STOKES AND ALAN LUMB

DEVON AND CORNWALL RECORD SOCIETY

THE BOYDELL PRESS

First published 2019

A publication of the
Devon and Cornwall Record Society
published by The Boydell Press
an imprint of Boydell & Brewer Ltd
PO Box 9, Woodbridge, Suffolk IP12 3DF, UK
and of Boydell & Brewer Inc.
668 Mt Hope Avenue, Rochester, NY 14620–2731, USA
website: www.boydellandbrewer.com

ISBN 978 0 90185 362 2

Series information is printed at the back of this volume

A CIP catalogue record for this book is available
from the British Library

The publisher has no responsibility for the continued existence or accuracy
of URLs for external or third-party internet websites referred to in this book,
and does not guarantee that any content on such websites is,
or will remain, accurate or appropriate.

This publication is printed on acid-free paper

CONTENTS

Illustrations

Frontispiece: Map of Drake's Devon. Design: Aziz Khan and Jonathan Hepworth

The editors, contributors, and publisher are grateful to all the institutions and persons listed for permission to reproduce the materials in which they hold copyright. Every effort has been made to trace the copyright holders; apologies are offered for any omission, and the publisher will be pleased to add any necessary acknowledgement in subsequent editions.

Acknowledgements

We thank the Devon Heritage Centre (DHC) for permission to publish the Drake letters (DHC 346M/F166–F485), and illustrations of Buckland Abbey and Nutwell Court by the Reverend John Swete (DHC 564M/F3 and 564M/F16; see *Travels in Georgian Devon*). We gratefully acknowledge the help over several years of the DHC staff.

We thank the Trustees of the Devon and Cornwall Record Society and the Boydell & Brewer team for supporting and overseeing the edition.

The project owes its inception, and significant initiatives along the way, to Dr Todd Gray. In 1993 Dr Gray came across the four bundles of letters in DHC 346M from Nicholas Rowe and William Hudson to Sir Francis Henry Drake, 5th Baronet. It was during his time as Chair of the History Section of the Devonshire Association (DA) in 2015–2016 that the Section, under the leadership of Alan Lumb, launched a project to transcribe the letters. During Dr Gray's year as President the transcriptions were completed, and in early 2017 a proposal for publication was submitted to the DCRS, with his encouragement. We are grateful for his continuing interest and support, and for his contribution of illustrations as well as written text to the introduction.

One of the initiatives that came to fruition during Dr Gray's year as DA President was the celebration of the Devon–Newfoundland Story that took place during the first two weeks of April 2017. A fortunate outcome of this celebration was a meeting with Professor John Crellin, a historian of medicine and Honorary Research Professor at Memorial University, Newfoundland. A concern with medical matters is a thread that can be traced through many of the Drake Letters, and we are grateful to Professor Crellin for his scholarly contribution to the introduction, and for numerous helpful discussions on the project as a whole.

This project was conceived as a collaboration between members of the DA. The transcribers Alan Lumb, Charity Scott-Stokes, and Dee and Mike Tracey have also contributed chapters to the introduction, alongside Dr Gray and Professor Crellin. Further members of the transcription team, whose work we gratefully acknowledge, were Marcia Babington and Irene Derczynska. Irene Derczynska also checked the transcriptions of the Hudson letters and helped to decipher problematic readings.

Charity Scott-Stokes checked two-thirds of the transcriptions, edited the letters, generated notes, bibliography, and index, and co-ordinated the introduction. Alan Lumb oversaw the initial photographing and transcription of the letters and subsequent circulation of the transcriptions. He checked one-third of the transcriptions, reviewed the edited letters and introduction, and was an active collaborator in the editorial process. We have tried to eliminate tiresome inconsistencies and repetitions between the different chapters of the introduction and ask the reader's indulgence for any that remain.

We thank Dr Sebastian Meier-Ewert, Jonathan Hepworth, and Aziz Khan for technical assistance.

ABBREVIATIONS

DA	Devonshire Association
DCRS	Devon & Cornwall Record Society
DHC	Devon Heritage Centre
Family and Heirs	E. D. Fuller-Eliott-Drake, *The Family and Heirs of Sir Francis Drake*, 2 vols (London: Smith, Elder, & Co., 1911)
FHD/Sir Francis	Sir Francis Henry Drake, 5th Baronet
ODNB	*Oxford Dictionary of National Biography* (2004) online
Travels in Georgian Devon	T. Gray and M. Rowe (eds), *Travels in Georgian Devon: The Illustrated Journals of the Reverend John Swete 1789–1800*, 4 vols (Tiverton: Devon Books, 1997–2000). This is a full edition of Swete's *Picturesque Sketches of Devon*, held in the DHC.

TIMELINE
1740–1778

FHD = Sir Francis Henry Drake, 5th Baronet

Crown, state, politics, society	Year	Drake family
War of Austrian Succession	1740	*FHD succeeds his father, Sir Francis Henry Drake, 4th Baronet; enters Corpus Christi College (informally known as Bene't College), Cambridge, and enrols at Lincoln's Inn*
General Election	1741	
Walpole resigns	1742	
Battle of Dettingen	1743	
War declared on France	1744	
Battle of Fontenoy	1745	
Defeat of Charles Edward Stuart, the Young Pretender, at the Battle of Culloden	1746	
Naval victories of Finisterre and Belle-Île; General Election	1747	*FHD elected MP for Bere Alston*
Treaty of Aix-la-Chapelle	1748	*Anne Drake, sister of FHD, m. George Augustus Eliott, subsequently Lord Heathfield, Baron of Gibraltar*
Westminster Election	1749	
	1750	*Francis Samuel Drake, brother of FHD, m. Elizabeth Hayman;* *b. Francis Augustus Eliott, son of Anne Eliott née Drake and George Augustus Eliott*
d. Frederick, Prince of Wales; William, Duke of Cumberland's hunting accident	1751	*b. Francis Thomas, first natural son of FHD's brother Francis William Drake*
	1752	*FHD appointed Ranger of Dartmoor Forest;* *Francis William Drake appointed Governor of Newfoundland (until 1754)*

	1753	*FHD appointed Clerk Comptroller of the Board of Green Cloth (until 1770)*
Death of Pelham; Newcastle ministry; General Election incl. Oxfordshire Election	**1754**	
Oxfordshire Election result declared; Earthquake at Lisbon	**1755**	*d. Francis Drake (cousin of FHD)*
Resignation of Newcastle; Pitt–Devonshire ministry; Beginning of Seven Years' War; Battle of Minorca	**1756**	*d. Henry Drake, brother of 4th Baronet; b. Francis Henry, second natural son of Francis William Drake*
Pitt–Newcastle ministry; Execution of Admiral Byng	**1757**	
2nd Treaty of Westminster	**1758**	
Capture of Quebec	**1759**	
Accession of George III	**1760**	*b. Anne Eliott, daughter of Anne Eliott née Drake and George Augustus Eliott*
General Election; Resignation of Pitt	**1761**	*FHD one of those sent to bring future Queen Charlotte to England*
War with Spain; Resignation of Newcastle; Bute ministry; Loss and recapture of Newfoundland	**1762**	
Peace of Paris; Resignation of Bute	**1763**	*Francis William Drake m. Elizabeth Heathcote*
Expulsion of Wilkes from House of Commons	**1764**	*b. Francis William Drake's daughter Marianne*
Dismissal of Grenville; Rockingham ministry	**1765**	*b. Francis William Drake's daughter Sophia*
Dismissal of Rockingham; Chatham ministry	**1766**	
d. Duke of York	**1767**	
General Election incl. Middlesex Election; French annexation of Corsica; Chatham's resignation	**1768**	*d. Lady Drake née Heathcote, widow of 4th Baronet, mother of FHD*
Middlesex Election affair	**1769**	

Grafton's resignation; North ministry; Messenger returns from Spain without King of Spain's answer	1770	
Henry, Duke of Cumberland m. Mrs Horton, goes abroad	1771	*FHD appointed Master of the King's Household;* *Francis William Drake succeeds FHD as MP for Bere Alston*
Duke of Gloucester unwell, abroad; d. Dowager Princess of Wales; Financial crash	1772	*d. Anne Eliott née Drake*
Boston Tea Party	1773	
General Election	1774	*FHD returns as MP for Bere Alston*
Battles of Lexington and Concord	1775	*George Augustus Eliott appointed Governor of Gibraltar*
American Declaration of Independence	1776	
Battle of Ticonderoga	1777	
War with France	1778	

INTRODUCTION

The letters at a glance

Sir Francis Henry Drake (1723-1794), 5th Baronet

• 1740 Succeeds to baronetcy
• Enters Bene't (Corpus Christi) College, Cambridge • Enrols at Lincoln's Inn
• 1747 First elected MP for Bere Alston (served 1747-71 & 1774-80)
• 1752 Appointed Ranger of Dartmoor Forest
• 1753 Appointed Clerk Comptroller of the Board of Green Cloth
• 1761 Among those sent to bring the future Queen Charlotte to England
• 1771 Master of the King's Household

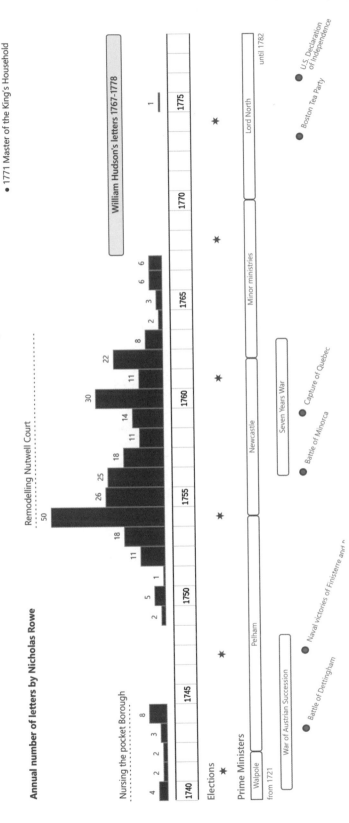

Annual number of letters by Nicholas Rowe

Remodelling Nutwell Court

William Hudson's letters 1767-1778

Nursing the pocket Borough

Elections

Prime Ministers

Walpole from 1721 | Pelham | Newcastle | Minor ministries | Lord North — until 1782

War of Austrian Succession | Seven Years War

Battle of Dettingham | Naval victories of Finisterre and ... | Battle of Minorca | Capture of Quebec | Boston Tea Party | U.S. Declaration of Independence

Figure 1. The letters at a glance.

1. General Introduction

Charity Scott-Stokes

1.1. The Letters

In 1957 a collection of Drake family papers was deposited in the Devon Record Office, now the Devon Heritage Centre (DHC), and catalogued as 346M. Most of these papers pertain to collateral descendants of the famous Sir Francis Drake, circumnavigator of the globe, who died without issue in 1596. The DHC introduction to 346M notes that the papers were deposited much as they had been assembled by the last member of this branch of the family, Elizabeth Douglas Fuller-Eliott-Drake, by marriage Baroness Seaton, in the early twentieth century. Lady Fuller-Eliott-Drake wrote a family history that draws extensively on the papers.[1] It has been a useful source of information for the current edition.

The edition comprises letters written during the period 1740–1778, and enclosed, perhaps since the late eighteenth century, in four neatly labelled folders. The time span falls within the reigns of two kings: George II (1727–1760) and his grandson George III (1760–1820). It includes the War of Austrian Succession (1742–1748), the Seven Years' War (1756–1763), and the beginning of the American War of Independence (1775–1783).

The letters were written from the environs of Buckland Abbey on the River Tavy, Nutwell Court on the River Exe, or London. Buckland and Nutwell were the Devon seats of Sir Francis Henry Drake, 5th Baronet, known as Sir Francis (see frontispiece). Of these letters, 282 were written to Sir Francis by Nicholas Rowe, a good friend of the Drake family who became the baronet's gentleman-overseer at Nutwell. A single letter to Rowe written by Sir Francis in 1740 has survived. Twenty-nine of the letters were written to Sir Francis by William Hudson, his London business agent, friend, and medical and scientific adviser. Hudson was a well-known London apothecary and botanist, and author of the acclaimed *Flora Anglica* (1762).

It is hoped that the publication of these letters will help to fill out the picture of the chief letter-writers and their addressee, of eighteenth-century electoral procedures, of Buckland and Nutwell, and of health and wellbeing in both London and Devon. They may also provide material for further specialist studies of topics ranging from parliamentary, social, and naval history to commerce and trade in native and exotic flora.

In this edition the letters are arranged in three parts, as far as is practicable in chronological sequence, which necessitates some deviation from the DHC numbering:

I   Letters 1740–March 1754, predominantly written by Nicholas Rowe, from Buckland and environs (DHC 346M/F196–F268);

---

[1]   E. D. Fuller-Eliott-Drake, *The Family and Heirs of Sir Francis Drake*, 2 vols (London: Smith, Elder, & Co., 1911).

II   Letters 1754–1767, and 1775, predominantly written by Nicholas Rowe
from Nutwell (DHC 346M/F269–F485);
III   Letters 1767–1778, written by William Hudson, from London and
environs (DHC 346M/F166–F195).

The surviving Rowe letters probably make up not more than one-third of those he
wrote. He mentions on several occasions that he customarily writes once a week
when Sir Francis is absent (e.g. F290).[2] Since Sir Francis seems to have spent not
more than four or five months in Devon in an average year, Rowe may well have
written some 1,000 letters in all, before his letters become infrequent from the late
1760s. The surviving Hudson letters are also a selection, rather than a complete set.

Such letters as have survived are sometimes incomplete; occasionally they are
little more than notes or fragments. It may be that the letters and parts of letters not
preserved were destroyed because they contained material which Sir Francis or his
heirs considered damaging to the family's reputation, or to their property interests.
The DHC introduction to 346M suggests that Lady Fuller-Eliott-Drake destroyed
many documents, particularly deeds and leases.

However, to the present editors it seems likely that Sir Francis made a positive
selection of the letters to be retained, for his own interest and use, and perhaps also
with his heirs in mind. They reflect his interests during various phases of his life, as
do numerous other documents in 346M that are not included in this edition. While
the single letter in the collection written by Sir Francis himself (F198) is incomplete, the part retained is concerned with matters of paramount interest to him:
the Drake family, and representation of the parliamentary borough of Bere Alston
(see Introduction, section 2). Main focuses in the Rowe letters are: parliamentary
representation of Bere Alston; patronage; the Drake family; Buckland Abbey and
Nutwell Court (see section 3), and further Drake properties; neighbours; tradesmen,
workmen, staff, and servants; and health matters (see section 5). The preponderance
of Rowe letters from 1754 to the early 1760s corresponds with phases of intense
activity on the Nutwell Court buildings. Main focuses in the Hudson letters are:
health matters; the royal family, affairs of state and parliamentary business; scientific
investigation, horticulture, and books; and personalities, friends and acquaintances,
and gossip.

Recurrent topics throughout all the letters include the weather, shipping,
travel, and transportation and communications by land and by sea. Human beings
and their vital helpmeets, horses, are not the only travellers. Sheep and cattle
are driven across Dartmoor, via Moretonhampstead, on the well-trodden track
between Buckland and Nutwell (e.g. F341–F343, F359–F360); and live ducks and
turkeys are sent from London (2–F167). Ships' crews on their return journey from
Newfoundland bring fish and whale blubber, and also live dogs and geese (e.g.
F325, F470, F471).

There are occasional annotations to the letters which Sir Francis probably
made himself, perhaps at the time when he was selecting and arranging those to
be retained (see especially notes to F196, F350, F382, F439, F440; **15**–F169, **22**–
F171, **28**–F175, **29**–F176). Strikingly, a marginal note from a Rowe letter of April

---

[2]   From this point on, the Rowe letters are cited as F196 etc., the Hudson letters as **1**–F166
etc., and all other DHC 346M documents by the full reference, 346M/F17 etc.

1758 has been retained, while the rest of the letter has been clipped off: 'Here is a report your Mother is very Ill, pray how is She' (F377). Was the body of this letter destroyed because it contained damaging material? Or was the left-hand edge with the marginal note retained because of pressing concern about Lady Drake's health, and the rest discarded as trivial by comparison? That material with potential for damaging the family's reputation was not necessarily destroyed is evident in the retention of Rowe's letters relating to troubles with the servants Joyce and her daughter (F442–F447), and Nanny (F463, F465, F469).

1.2. Sir Francis Henry Drake, 5th Baronet

Sir Francis was born in 1723, as the eldest child of Sir Francis Henry Drake, 4th Baronet, MP, and Anne, daughter of Sir William Heathcote of Hursley, MP. Sir Francis's health was delicate, yet he outlived his sister Anne and her robust husband, George Augustus Eliott, ultimately Lord Heathfield, Baron of Gibraltar. He also outlived his two younger brothers, who both rose to become admirals, and whose lives are more fully documented in biographical reference works than is that of Sir Francis himself. And he outlived his correspondents Nicholas Rowe, who was thirty years older, and William Hudson, who was ten years younger. He never married.

Sir Francis was educated at Winchester College, located not far from his uncle's seat at Hursley, and then for one year at Eton. In 1740, aged seventeen, he succeeded his father. In the same year he began his studies at Corpus Christi College (then generally known as Bene't College), Cambridge, and enrolled at Lincoln's Inn. The Rowe letters begin at this time. During Sir Francis's minority the parliamentary seat of Bere Alston was held for him by his mother's brother Samuel Heathcote (see Introduction, section 2).

Sir Francis became MP for Bere Alston in 1747, at the first election after his coming of age; he held the seat until 1771, and again between 1774 and 1780. He was appointed Ranger of Dartmoor Forest (1752–1794). He was also appointed to increasingly prestigious sinecures at the royal court: first Clerk and then Comptroller of the Green Cloth (1753–1770). Rowe rejoiced in the distinction accorded to Sir Francis when he was one of those chosen to accompany Earl Harcourt to the Elbe in order to escort George III's bride to London in 1761 (F432). Ten years later Sir Francis became Master of the King's Household (1771–1794).

There is a break in the Rowe letters from 1744 to 1749. Lady Fuller-Eliott-Drake suggests that letters may have been unnecessary during these years, given the likelihood that Sir Francis spent considerable time in Devon, following Rowe's advice and making himself familiar with election law and his own affairs, getting to know his constituents, and preparing for the 1747 election. He may also have travelled in Europe and have therefore been beyond the easy reach of letters.[3] It is also possible that Sir Francis simply did not keep Rowe's letters from this period. Indeed, he did not keep many from the years immediately preceding or immediately following the five-year break (see figure 1).

During the late 1740s Sir Francis formed long-lasting friendships with Jeremiah Dyson (1722–1776) and the poet-physician Dr Mark Akenside (1721–1770). Dyson was called to the bar at Lincoln's Inn. He was appointed Clerk to the House of

[3] *Family and Heirs*, vol. 2, p. 251.

Commons in 1748, became an MP in 1762, and gained many offices, eventually
becoming a Lord of the Treasury, Cofferer to the Royal Household, and Privy
Councillor. Sir Francis presumably made Dyson's acquaintance at Lincoln's Inn
and in Parliament, and met Akenside through him. In the 1740s and 1750s all three
were staunch Whigs. An ode addressed to Sir Francis by Akenside in 1752, on the
occasion of the baronet's failure to appear at a dinner party in London in early
November, makes comparisons between London and Devon (DHC 346M/F17; see
also p. 46 below). Akenside ironically muses on whether the Devon gentry have
discovered loyalty to the king and to the Whigs and have therefore become more
congenial companions than hitherto. Fifteen to twenty-five years later, there are
numerous references to Dyson, especially to his state of health, in the Hudson letters,
continuing until shortly before Dyson's death in 1776. Nor did the association end
there: a son, another Jeremiah Dyson, Under Clerk to the Green Cloth, was one of
the witnesses to a codicil added to Sir Francis's will in January 1793 (DHC 346M/
F845–F847).

During the years without letters, a very important Drake family event occurred:
the marriage in London of Sir Francis's sister Anne to George Augustus Eliott in
1748. At the time Eliott was an officer in the Horse Grenadier Guards, and had
already served in the War of Austrian Succession, notably at the Battle of Dettingen
in 1743 and the Battle of Fontenoy in 1745. From 1756 to 1759 the brothers-in-law
both had appointments at the royal court: Sir Francis benefited from his first sinecure
as Clerk of the Green Cloth, while Eliott was Aide-de-Camp to George II. The DHC
catalogue points out that 346M includes important papers relating to Eliott's later
career, during the American War of Independence, when he defended Gibraltar
during the siege (1779–1783) and was rewarded with the title 'Lord Heathfield,
Baron of Gibraltar'. Among the papers is a cordial correspondence between Sir
Francis and his brother-in-law, which is of great interest, but beyond the scope of
the present edition. Suffice it to mention that in 1779, notwithstanding the impending
siege, Eliott wrote to Sir Francis recording the dispatch of wine by sea, which he
would barter for cider, and regretting that Sir Francis and their friend William
Hudson were not with him to enjoy botanising in Spain, which was just as 'commodious' as in Wales (346M/F22; and **5**–F187).[4]

There are frequent references in the Rowe letters to Sir Francis's sister and her
family, often expressing anxieties for their health and welfare. We read of joint
expeditions of the brother and sister to Bath, for the restoration of their health, and of
the exploits, and wounds, of her husband. The Eliotts played a more important part
in Sir Francis's life than did the other family members, both in London and in the
country. Rowe records visits made by the Eliotts to Nutwell, and one by Sir Francis's
ailing cousin Captain Frank Drake and his wife (F272), but none by other members
of the immediate family. There is a reference in a Hudson letter to the Eliott family's
surprise that they did not hear from Sir Francis at their London home (**12**–F192). The
Eliotts' son was born in 1750 and Sir Francis made him his heir. This heir, the second
Lord Heathfield, erected fine memorials to his uncle as well as to his father in St
Andrew's Church, Buckland Monachorum.[5]

---

[4]   See also Introduction, section 4, p. 36, for botanising in the West Country and in Wales.
[5]   See p. 9 below.

With regard to other members of the family, the Rowe letters affirm that Sir Francis made the requisite financial provision for all his siblings, secured promotion for his brothers in the Royal Navy, and restored family harmony. He also arranged for his brother Francis William to become a freeholder in Bere Alston, and to replace him as MP during the years 1771–1774.

In reporting family news, knowing that he and Sir Francis were of one mind, Rowe makes no mystery of his shock at the early marriage of the youngest brother, Francis Samuel, in May 1750 (F220). However, mistrustful of the carriers of letters, and mindful, perhaps, of possible complications regarding inheritance, he is more circumspect with regard to Francis William's two natural sons, born in 1751 and 1756.[6] Rowe hopes that there will be 'no matrimony in the case' (F359). There was indeed no matrimony, and the mother of the two sons died young. Francis William married Elizabeth Heathcote, a first cousin, in 1763. Rowe hoped in vain that this marriage would produce a male 'representative' (F472); the couple had two daughters.

In the last year of George II's reign, at the mid-point of the Seven Years' War, Sir Francis was weighed down by personal sadness. From late August to December 1759 Rowe's letters reiterate messages of deep concern, sympathy, condolence, and hope for reprieve from melancholy. He never mentions by name the 'valuable person' who has died, but Lady Fuller-Eliott-Drake tells of a family tradition that Sir Francis was engaged to a Miss Knight of Plymouth and reproached himself for procrastinating until it was too late for a marriage to take place. Miss Knight's portrait, painted by Sir Joshua Reynolds, reported to be a friend of both families, hung at Nutwell Court.[7]

During her widowhood, Lady Drake chose to live in London most of the time, though not in close proximity to her eldest son. Sir Francis employed a bailiff to manage his share of the Buckland estate, where there was sometimes friction between his staff and his mother's. Several Rowe letters observe that mother and son neglected necessary maintenance and repairs to the Abbey (see Introduction, section 3). The absence of close relations between mother and son at the end of her life is strongly suggested by the nonchalant tone of two letters from Hudson dating from 1768 (4–F186, 5–F187). In the first, Hudson reports, among other things, that he has been to inquire about Lady Drake's health. In the second, he reports that he has made further inquiries, as Sir Francis requested, and heard that she had been dead some time. He goes on to discuss a few seeds enclosed in his letter, and to reflect on shared botanising expeditions.

Sir Francis was in full possession of Nutwell Court from the time of his succession in 1740 until his death, and both during his mother's lifetime and thereafter he often chose to spend time at Nutwell in preference to Buckland when he was in Devon. In 1754 he took Nicholas Rowe with him from Buckland to Nutwell, and entrusted to him the oversight of the estate, the building and landscaping projects, and the estate staff.

Sir Francis made extensive alterations to the Nutwell buildings, gardens and parkland (see sections 3 and 4). A man of science and the Enlightenment, he turned his chapel into a library, to house new acquisitions, as well as books that he brought

---

[6] See timeline, pp. ix–xi; see also DHC 346M/F29.
[7] *Family and Heirs,* vol. 2, pp. 294–295. We have not been able to trace the painting. Charles Duthie of Topsham History Group kindly drew our attention to an engraving of the painting by Samuel William Reynolds in the National Portrait Gallery.

to Nutwell from Buckland Abbey.[8] A late-nineteenth-century commentator, William Roberts, points out that Sir Francis Drake the great admiral was also a great bibliophile, and reports on the sale of several thousand volumes from Nutwell Court at Sotheby's in 1883.[9] Some of the specialist historical books, especially those on early navigation, fetched very high prices.

The letters provide ample evidence of Sir Francis's interest in the natural sciences, and in collecting. He collected books, botanical specimens, thermometers and barometers, medals, seals, and minerals, as is shown by a letter from the highly regarded Cornish clergyman and natural scientist William Borlase (346M/F21). This letter records the dispatch of a box of pillis seeds and three samples of Elvaen stones from Ludgvan in Cornwall to Sir Francis, at an address in Southernhay, Exeter, in September 1768.[10]

Sir Francis's position as Master of the King's Household, from 1771, will have required some attendance at court; yet the Hudson letters suggest that he found more time than usual to attend to Nutwell at this period, paying particular attention to the planting and cultivation of his garden (see Introduction, section 4). As previously mentioned, he arranged for his brother Francis William to represent Bere Alston as MP during the years 1771–1774.

The Rowe letters show that, in his early adult years, Sir Francis, like Rowe himself, had close social as well as political contacts in and around Buckland, Tavistock, and Plymouth. Some of these contacts were maintained after the move to Nutwell. In addition to professional advisers and estate staff, some friends and acquaintances from the Tavy made their way to the Exe. Mrs Carpenter, wife of the lawyer and accountant John Carpenter, visited for her health (F270), and Mr Porter, freeholder of Bere Alston, active in Plymouth Customs and Excise, and a good friend of the Drake family and of Rowe, rode to Nutwell for his health and spent some days there (F277, F279).

Rowe's letters attest that Sir Francis maintained working relations with neighbours at Nutwell: with Parson Lee of Lympstone, son of the attorney Lee of Exeter, alderman and mayor, an old friend of Sir Francis; and particularly with the entrepreneur Worthington Brice, who sent ships on annual whale-hunting voyages to Newfoundland and invested in prospecting for metals there. Sir Francis, whose two sea-faring brothers had both been in Newfoundland, supported him in such enterprises (F329, F330, F350n., F352, F353). There were contacts between Sir Francis's estate staff and the staff of other great houses on or near the Exe, such as Powderham across the river, and Mamhead (F286, F309, F310, F448, F451). Yet on the whole it seems that Sir Francis did not seek further social contacts in the Nutwell area. Akenside's remarks about Whigs cited above suggest that Sir Francis did not find congenial company on the Exe in the 1750s, and it seems that this did not change. Ten years later, Rowe assured him that his instructions were obeyed, and nobody was admitted to Nutwell house or gardens (F462).[11] This seclusion, and voluntary

---

[8] The conversion of the chapel reflected the spirit of the age. Across the Exe, at Powderham, the chapel was turned into a drawing room.

[9] W. Roberts, *The Book-Hunter in London* (London: Elliot Stock, 1895), p. 19; see also Introduction, section 4, p. 36.

[10] See also Introduction, section 4, p. 36.

[11] For the continuance of this tradition by several of his successors, see Introduction, section 4, pp. 37–8.

obscurity, sometimes resulted in a lack of understanding, or even downright hostility, on the part of Devon contemporaries, notably Polwhele and Swete (see section 4), and the denizens of Lympstone (F447).

In London, when not at court, Sir Francis seems again to have confined his social contacts to his immediate circle of family and friends. No mention of him has been found in the voluminous historical and epistolary writings of his sociable contemporaries David Hume, Tobias Smollett, and Horace Walpole.

The epitaph installed by Lord Heathfield in St Andrew's Church in Buckland Monachorum commemorates the powers of Sir Francis's mind, while acknowledging the frailty of his constitution, which prevented him from aspiring to great office:

In a vault beneath are interred the remains

of SIR *FRANCIS HENRY DRAKE BARONET,*

of *Buckland Abbey, in the county of Devon.*

Who died on the 19th of February 1794, aged 70 years.

His Descent was illustrious,

being lineally derived from the NAVAL WARRIOR of the 16th Century.

His natural and acquired endowments were such

That had the strength of his constitution been equal to the powers of his mind,

He might justly have aspired to the first offices of the State.

He was Clerk Comptroller of the Board of Green Cloth,

in the reigns of Their Majesties King George the 2d and King George the 3d;

and for more than twenty years immediately preceding his death

was Master of the King's Houshold.

The duties of which stations

he discharged with Fidelity to the King, and Honor to himself.

In Testimony of the respect due to his memory

His nephew, the Rt. Hon. FRANCIS AUGUSTUS *LORD HEATHFIELD,*

BARON OF GIBRALTAR, caused this Monument to be erected.

Above the epitaph, the word 'TRUTH' is inscribed on a horizontal slab. Above that again, a female figure, emblem of truth, is placing a garland round an urn, with seeds and flowers. A large magnifying glass at the bottom left of the relief is a further symbol of the pursuit of scientific truth.

Sir Francis chose to let the Drake baronetcy of Buckland become extinct at his death. He did not acknowledge the claim to inheritance put forward by his nephew Francis Henry Drake, sole surviving son of Francis William.[12] Nevertheless, this nephew chose to live as Sir Francis Henry Drake in Cheltenham until 1839, where he died without male issue. Two daughters predeceased him.

Sir Francis may not have been aware of the claim of another branch of the family, descended from a younger brother of the 2nd baronet. However, that something of both these claims was known in the early nineteenth century is shown in some

---

[12] See timeline, pp. ix–xi; and 346M/F29.

detail by the Reverend Thomas Moore.[13] One hundred years later, Lady Fuller-
Eliott-Drake commented in her private papers on the claim put forward in the
early twentieth century by American descendants of a younger brother of the 2nd
baronet (346M/F700). Such claims may be found in the twenty-first century on the
worldwide web.

1.3. Nicholas James Rowe

Lady Fuller-Eliott-Drake surmised that Nicholas Rowe was a grandson of the Oxford
graduate Joseph Rowe, vicar of Buckland from 1646 to 1683, and connected with the
family of the poet laureate Nicholas Rowe (1674–1718), who owned property at
Lamerton, not far from Buckland Monachorum.[14]

Rowe was a freeholder of Bere Alston, and was thoroughly familiar with electoral
procedure, including the property transactions that had helped secure the election of
a Drake baronet over several generations (see Introduction, section 2). He kept Sir
Francis fully informed about electoral proceedings, courts leet, and the individuals
involved. His thorough knowledge of electoral law and of the full range of Drake
property dealings, evident in the letters over many years in many different situations,
suggests that he had received legal training, in addition to the classical education
evident in his use of Latin quotations. He sometimes indulged in a flowery turn of
phrase, occasionally heaping mixed metaphors and literary and classical allusions
one on top of another. Sometimes he deliberately wrote in a manner comprehensible
only to Sir Francis.

An entry in Lady Drake's accounts for 1752 deducts payments by Rowe 'made
since he delivered in his Account' (346M/F511). This shows that Rowe was not only
a good friend of the Drake family but also on their payroll. In John Carpenter's
estate accounts with Sir Francis there are two entries for £5 5s 0d paid to Mr Rowe
at Nutwell, on 30 December 1758 and 17 October 1759 (DHC 346M/E63). Rowe
claimed expenses from Sir Francis's legal and business advisor, William Edgcombe,
for his travel between Nutwell and Buckland (F288). The mayor of Plymouth also
called on Rowe's services when charters were sought in 1753 (F234). Principally,
however, his expertise was put at Sir Francis's disposal.

In 1754, Rowe expressed pleasure in hearing that Sir Francis was making Nutwell
comfortable for himself, and wrote that he himself did not expect to see the place
again (F231). Little did he know that from that very year he was to spend most of the
rest of his life there. Sometimes he had to return from Nutwell to Buckland in order to
attend to Sir Francis's business affairs, in particular to locate counterpart documents
that nobody else could lay their hands on, relating to historic property deals, but
Nutwell became his principal residence for thirty years until his death in 1785 at the
age of ninety-three. His burial on 29 July 1785 is recorded in the Woodbury parish
register.[15] Notwithstanding his longevity, Rowe suffered from various ills, including
lameness and colic. He frequently mentions his health troubles, and expresses
concern also about Sir Francis's health (see Introduction, section 5).

---

[13] T. Moore, *The History of Devonshire from the Earliest Period to the Present*, 2 vols
(London: R. Jennings, 1829–1833), vol. 2, pp. 148–149.
[14] *Family and Heirs*, vol. 2, pp. 237–238.
[15] Joseph Rowe, vicar of Buckland Monachorum, had also lived into his nineties.

Whereas at Buckland and Bere Alston Rowe had found satisfaction and even pleasure in frequent business and social calls, close at hand and also in Tavistock, the Dock, and Plymouth, at Nutwell he seems to have sought solitude, as did Sir Francis. When gentry called in the early days, he did not see them. He intended to 'seclude himself from Spiritual and Temporal' and to be very abstemious, wishing to be 'pencioner not at Large' (F269), that is to say, to pay his own way.

When Rowe arrived at Nutwell, he continued his wonted activities on Sir Francis's behalf, inserting himself into negotiations on property, boundaries, and leases, legal proceedings, and manorial courts. An early preoccupation was with a footpath. Local people insisted on an ancient right of way from the river along the wood to the Topsham road. Rowe considered that a court of 'Substantial Neighbours' (F272) was required in order to stop such use of the footpath, and he pursued this over a period of several months. By late June 1754 he already had seven neighbours to hand, and hoped that Parson Lee of Lympstone might head the court (F274). However, Mr Ley, an Exeter attorney, did not consider this procedure advisable (F275, F276); it may have been on his advice that the footpath was blocked instead. Rowe does not mention the matter again until 1761, when he reports that young Farmer Horrell intends to write a letter to Sir Francis complaining that the planned Act of Parliament for re-routing the road by the wood would reduce the value of his property (F433).

Another early and continuing preoccupation for Rowe at Nutwell was Farmer Robert Coleman's lease (see F270, F288–F289, F291, F298, F300, F302, F304, F309–F310, F312, F314–F315, F317–F319). The farmer lived in part of Nutwell Court but desired to have a new house built for his own use only, and demanded the use of meadows that Sir Francis was unwilling to part with. The resolution of this difficulty required the skills of William Edgcombe, who looked after Sir Francis's affairs from Tavistock, and also of his ever-useful Buckland bailiff, John Channon, who was acquainted with Coleman. Both Edgcombe and Channon frequently travelled between the Tavy and the Exe on Sir Francis's behalf.

Rowe never wavered in his attempts to be of service to the 'Drake Interest' and to keep a vigilant eye on spending. He repeatedly asked Sir Francis to stop sending newspapers, which he considered an unnecessary extravagance (F270–F272, F274–F276). He tried to economise on postage costs by having post collected from Exeter, rather than delivered to Topsham, where he considered the cost excessive.

The unfamiliar tasks of overseeing the Nutwell estate and personnel, and the building and landscaping projects, taxed Rowe severely (see Introduction, section 3). For several years after his arrival, the house remained in disorder. Workmen were not always on hand when needed, their work was poorly co-ordinated, pipes burst, gutters failed, rats romped around the garden and in the house (F278, F280, F290), and a barn fell down. Wet penetrated everywhere, the drawing-room needed constant fires, the parlour woodwork was badly done, the brickwork was mouldy, and the chimney had to be taken down because of bad work (F290–F291). A broken pipe at the back door meant that there was no water in the house (F312). Work on the house stalled because of preparations for war, with press gangs arriving on the river; the workmen were frightened and disappeared (F307, F310–F314, F317). Rowe's gloom was deep during Sir Francis's long winter absences in London. The baronet's arrival for the summer months, during the parliamentary recess, always heralded a turn for the better.

Another great challenge for Rowe stemmed from the servants. Particular troubles arose with several individuals whose service with the Drake family had begun at

Buckland, and who had then moved to Nutwell: Sir Francis's first housekeeper at Nutwell Court, Betty Dyer, who wanted to emigrate to Newfoundland, and who had health problems (see Introduction, section 5); Betty's successor, Joyce, and her daughter, and Nanny; Sol, or Solomon, an all-round handyman in garden and park, and his wife, Hannah; and Sol's son Alexander, who went to London with Sir Francis, on Rowe's recommendation, and turned out to be an ungrateful servant and a fool (F228, F330). Rowe also regularly reported difficulties with gardeners, to whom he rarely gave a name. He was severely critical of Sol's and the gardeners' drinking habits.[16] The resourceful Buckland bailiff, John Channon, was particularly helpful when it came to finding accommodation in Buckland Monachorum for the troublesome Joyce in 1762.[17]

Rowe's extant letters became less frequent as he entered his seventies. Towards the end he writes of a great sadness that afflicted him: the loss of his dog, Duchess, who had been his companion. After 1767 there are no extant letters at all until 1775, when a final letter ends with a tranquil postscript, perhaps with some late solace for the loss of Duchess: 'Your Cat is very well, we Converse often Together' (F485).

The sale of books from Nutwell Court in 1938, after the death of Lady Fuller-Eliott-Drake, included three volumes of 'Letters of Nicholas James Rowe to Sir Francis Drake'.[18] The three volumes are presumably the three folders of Rowe's handwritten letters printed in this edition; no trace has been found of previous publication in book form.

As Rowe's extant letters decline, Hudson's begin.

1.4. William Hudson

William Hudson was born in the White Lion Inn, Kendal, and educated at Kendal grammar school.[19] He was then apprenticed to a London apothecary, whose practice he eventually took over. While still an apprentice, he won an important botanical prize given by the Apothecaries' Company. From 1757 to 1758 he was resident sub-librarian at the British Museum. He was elected a Fellow of the Royal Society in 1761. His Linnean description and classification of British flora, *Flora Anglica*, was first published in London in 1762. From 1765 to 1771 he was *praefectus horti* and botanical demonstrator to the Apothecaries' Company at Chelsea. In 1783 his house in Panton Street caught fire, and his collections of insects and many of his plants were destroyed, as were the materials he had assembled for a book on British fauna. In 1791 he became a member of the newly established Linnean Society. He died in 1793 and was buried at St James's Church, Piccadilly.[20]

---

[16] For Rowe's strictures on drink, see Introduction, section 4, p. 43; section 5, pp. 50–1.

[17] See 346M/F20; and notes on the letters.

[18] DHC FOR/B/2/164.

[19] This paragraph draws on the O*DNB* account of William Hudson's life. More information on sources is available in R. Desmond, *Dictionary of British & Irish Botanists and Horticulturalists* (London: Natural History Museum, 1993). None of the sources make any mention of Hudson's association with Sir Francis, of the letters to him, or of the bequest in Sir Francis's will.

[20] The O*DNB* article does not record the fact that Hudson's memorial disappeared when the graveyard was destroyed in the Second World War. The article lists a likeness of Hudson in the Linnean Society collection of engravings, but this cannot be found.

During the years when his letters to Sir Francis were written, 1767–1778, Hudson was initially *praefectus horti* at Chelsea, but the duties associated with this appointment became too time-consuming (**9**–F181) and led to his resignation. He was busy with his private medical practice, with meetings of the Royal Society, and with joint enterprises with fellow botanists, notably the young Joseph Banks. Banks had already written a Linnean description of the plants and animals of Newfoundland and Labrador, and joined Hudson as a Fellow of the Royal Society in 1766. It is in fact to an early twentieth-century biographer of Banks, Edward Smith, that we owe a snapshot of William Hudson during the early summer of 1768, during the first year of his extant letters to Sir Francis, and shortly before Banks set sail on the *Endeavour* from Plymouth with Captain James Cook:

> Another excursion was taken [by Joseph Banks] this summer, in the company of two companions. They spent a week or two in North Wales, mostly botanizing. William Hudson was one of this party; in all likelihood a very good comrade for the occasion. His social merits were high, the outcome of a tranquil but genial disposition. He had studied with an apothecary, and practised medicine. An acquaintance with Benjamin Stillingfleet, together with an ardent study of the Sloane Collections [in the British Museum], made him a botanist. He acquired a European fame by the publication of his *Flora Anglica* (London, 1762).[21]

Could it be that the second of the 'two companions' was the less gregarious Sir Francis? There are no letters from Hudson to Sir Francis between January and autumn 1768, and it is conceivable that they were together in Wales, with Joseph Banks, in the early summer months.

Be that as it may, there were clearly ties of friendship as well as shared scientific interests and business links between Hudson and Sir Francis. Although Sir Francis left most of his property and fortune to his nephew, the second Lord Heathfield, his lengthy and complex will begins with a straightforward bequest of an annuity of £100 per year to William Hudson, for the duration of his life (DHC 346M/F845–F847). In the event, Hudson did not live to receive this bequest; he died one year before Sir Francis, in 1793.

Hudson's letters provide ample evidence of the social merits and genial disposition noted by Smith, in which he differed so markedly from Sir Francis himself, and from Nicholas Rowe. He keeps Sir Francis up to date with what is happening in London. The two opening letters are good examples of his flamboyant style and panache. His comments on parliamentary business are informative and often entertaining. With society gossip, ghost stories, and lottery tickets he is in his element. Sir Francis and William Hudson shared a keen interest in lottery tickets, which are mentioned several times in the letters, as well as in a note probably added by Sir Francis (**15**–F169 note).[22] That Hudson hoped to appease Lady Luck by asking Mrs Otway, the coachman's wife, to buy a ticket, rather than buying it himself,

---

[21] E. Smith, *The Life of Sir Joseph Banks* (London: John Lane, 1911), p. 13.
[22] See also Bob Harris, 'Lottery Adventuring in Britain, c. 1710–1760', *English Historical Review* 133(561) (2018), 284–322, for the complicated eighteenth-century lottery marketplace, 'driven by both rational calculation and fantasy'.

demonstrates the incursion of irrational fantasy into the spirit of the Enlightenment, as does Hudson's susceptibility to the story of the Stockwell ghost (**17**–F177).

At the same time, he is a reliable purveyor of news about scientific publications (see particularly **12**–F192), an excellent source of botanical information, specimens, and seeds, and a tireless dispenser of remedies for physical afflictions, whether suffered by Sir Francis or by other members of the Nutwell household and estate staff (see Introduction, section 5). With wry humour he reports regularly on the health of Sir Francis's old friend Jeremiah Dyson, whom he regards as something of a hypochondriac. In September 1776 his hope that Mr Dyson is mending is not fulfilled (**27**–F188): Dyson died shortly afterwards. Section 5 places Hudson's discourse and recommendations in the wider context of eighteenth-century medical science.

2. Elections and Infrastructure

Alan Lumb

2.1. Working a Pocket Borough in the Eighteenth Century

At the beginning of the eighteenth century the political impact of the 'Glorious Revolution' of 1688 was still working itself out. Power had shifted to Parliament but the relationship between Parliament, the sovereign, and the ministry was not set out in any constitutional document. The Bill of Rights (1689) limited royal authority and gave Parliament control over money-raising and freedom of speech for MPs, although it was not until the Triennial Act of 1694 that real restrictions were imposed on the Crown.

The Triennial Act was intended to ensure there were regular sessions of Parliament and, by each lasting a maximum of three years, to limit patronage by the ministry, but, despite its good intentions, the Act brought serious unintended consequences. With a new government every three years, and additional ones when there was a new monarch, after 1695 there were ten elections in twenty years. A divided and rapidly changing society led to scurrilous leafleting and street mobs, though not in Bere Alston, where elections were conducted very differently. In the large centres of population, sweeteners and bribes proved costly where the seats were contested and led to constant election fever, talked of as the Rage of Party. One Whig clergyman wrote:

> The Number of Ale-Houses is increas'd near two thirds since the Triennial Act in most Corporations, to the great Corruption of the Age. An idle Fellow who cannot bring his Mind to live by his Labour, is sure, if he has a Vote, to procure a Licence to sell Drink; by this means his Neighbours are drawn in to be as idle as himself. Thus Drunkenness and Idleness march before, and Poverty follows close after, thorough [sic] the whole Parish.[1]

There was a growing belief that a longer period for each parliament would lead to greater political stability, yet, as Langford observes: 'An opposition which enjoyed no immediate prospect of an election had an interest in encouraging extra-parliamentary agitation, even violence.'[2]

After a period of Tory rule, in 1715 the Whigs gained an overwhelming majority. Once in power, supporting the Hanoverians, and with no constitution to limit Parliament's powers, their propagandists stretched every sinew to undermine the Triennial Act. In reality, times were very uncertain. Foreign governments needed to know that there was a stable government in London, and there remained the fear among voters that Stuart supporters would press their case in the 1718 elections. So for practical and political reasons the Septennial Act of 1716 was brought in to extend the existing government by four years and fix future ones for seven years. This

[1] O. C. Lease, 'The Septennial Act of 1716', *Journal of Modern History* 22(1) (1950), p. 42.
[2] P. Langford, *A Polite and Commercial People, England 1727–1783* (Oxford: Oxford University Press, 1998), p. 46.

allowed the Whig ministry to establish itself and to win a series of elections through good management and patronage. Such management meant that no ministry lost a general election for a hundred years after 1714. Overall it gave the impression of a period of calm and stability, despite there being many riots over local issues such as bread and food prices and the costs of new turnpikes.[3] In Bere Alston, as in many similar small boroughs, there were no direct parliamentary election contests in the eighteenth century, although there could be a subsequent appeal against an election – as there was against one Bere Alston result (see below).

Robert Walpole, as First Lord of the Treasury between 1721 and 1743, made an art of cultivating electoral interests. He built up a group of ministers from both parties to work with the sovereign. This gave the opportunity for personal advancement and the chance to pursue local interests. Patronage and pensions were skilfully used to create a ministerial majority. The Crown had more than a thousand appointments connected to the royal household. Many of these appointments were sinecures, but MPs were expected to vote loyally; Sir Francis only ever voted against the ministry once. There was effectively a one-party state from Walpole through to Henry Pelham and then the Duke of Newcastle. The Drakes were always in the Whig interest. Sir Francis entered Parliament in 1747; by 1752 he had attracted the attention of Pelham, who had taken over as First Lord of the Treasury, and he invited Sir Francis to join the royal household as a Clerk of the Green Cloth. As he was promoted to more senior positions, he came closer to the centre of government, for the sovereign remained a key political force.

As to the way local elections were organised in boroughs like Bere Alston, 'Local government units formed a jungle whose only rationale lay in history.'[4] There was much local variation in this jungle. In Exeter the magistrates elected their representatives, whereas in Plymouth the Admiralty nominated them. In some cases custom and practice were not well defined; in others the portreeve, the presiding officer, could be lax in his administration. At every election there were appeals over the results, many of which arrived at the Bar of the House of Commons.

Locally these elections were determined by courts leet, which originated in the manorial system and still survive in a handful of places in the 21st century.[5] In rural communities these courts had the authority to transfer property leases, establish standards in the sale of food and drink, maintain local paths and ditches, protect the integrity of common land, and punish low-level offenders. The portreeve ran the court and ensured that its decisions were carried out. He was aided by the steward as clerk, representing the lord of the manor. All the freeholders – burgage holders in the case of Bere Alston – were members and were bound to attend. They were annually sworn in as the jury. This gave them the authority to make legally binding decisions.

[3]   See section 2.2 below.

[4]   R. Porter, *English Society in the Eighteenth Century* (London: Penguin, 1990), p. 122.

[5]   According to the Wikipedia article on Spaunton, North Yorkshire: 'Spaunton is still the setting for a Court Leet. The court meets annually in October and decides on matters of encroachment onto the common land in the village and hands down fines to offenders. The full title of the court is *The Manor of Spaunton Court Leet and Court Baron with View of Frankpledge*.' This article draws on N. Rhea, 'When Sheep Were Big Business', Darlington & Stockton Times, 22 January 2016, https://www.darlingtonandstocktontimes. co.uk/news/14224382.when-sheep-were-big-business/, and G. W. Darley, 'Court Leet' (2004, rev. 2016), huttonlehole.ryedaleconnect.org.uk/about/court-leet (both accessed June 2019).

(It did not mean trial by jury: that was still evolving in the higher courts.) As we see in several of Nicholas Rowe's letters (F200, F202, F212), there were no more than twenty jurors agreeing who were to be the borough's Members of Parliament.

Burgage plots were an outcome of medieval town planning. The local lord of the manor, wanting to increase economic activity, would create a space for markets and fairs, thus drawing in people from a wide area. This was achieved by planning a main street widened in the centre with the land adjacent divided into long narrow strips measured as multiples of a perch (5 metres). These became known as burgage plots (from borough). Each plot would have a frontage to the market area, where a house or workshop would be built, while the land behind was used for crops or grazing. Burgage plots can be seen in several Devon villages today.

In Bere Alston, as in many other boroughs, burgage plots were owned by freemen, who, by virtue of a trade, were no longer in servitude. They paid a 'tenure' or rent, often conveying it for the duration of the election to another, entitling that person to vote. If the owner of a number of plots kept them to himself, there would only be one vote; if he leased them to tenants there would be several votes. The actual vote was by show of hands: in Bere Alston's case, in the open under a large tree in the middle of Fore Street. To succeed as a Parliamentary candidate the trick was to ensure that the chosen tenants were in one's interest, thus making it a pocket borough. It required some effort to learn the needs or hopes of the individuals in order to work on their behalf. By buying up burgage plots and taking as tenants those in one's interest, it was possible to guarantee the outcome of the vote. This is how local families could ensure that one of 'theirs' was elected. It is one of the main themes in the opening letters from Nicholas Rowe to Sir Francis, which begin by assuring the baronet that there is nothing to worry about: he just needs to complete his education and maintain links with the local freeholders.

> I'm Sorry Mr Harry Drake's application shou'd give you or Lady Drake any Uneasiness; I do assure you there is no Occasion for it. None but Good Dr Creed as I know of, is in his Interest, and He like the Æthiopian, can't Change his Hue. (F196)

Once the Members of Parliament were elected, the monarch chose a first minister and between them they appointed ministers from across the House. The two political parties, Tories and Whigs, worked very differently from today. They represented local interests rather than national policies. What would now be seen as national issues, such as education, transport, and poverty, were addressed spasmodically by private Acts of Parliament, hence there was a very uneven provision of, say, turnpikes (see below), which later generations would see as a wasted opportunity. What parliaments did do was raise money for wars and fund the political system.

As the potential of parliamentary power became understood more widely, the percentage of seats in which there were contests grew, as did the number of appeals against declared results. One of these was in Bere Alston in 1721, when Captain Philip Cavendish was returned at a by-election but one burgess holder, named Elford, claimed that the other candidate, Hon. St John Brodrick, should have been returned because the portreeve, Edward Elliot, a commissioner of excise, was not only barred from meddling in elections but had allowed unqualified persons to vote.

The appeal was upheld, Cavendish was unseated, and a resolution was passed which made it clear who had the right to vote:

> That the right of election for this borough is in the freehold tenants, holding by burgage tenure, and paying threepence per annum or more ancient burgage rent to the Lord of the Borough, and in them only.[6]

This held until the Bere Alston borough was abolished, with other pocket boroughs, in the 1832 Reform Bill. One imagines that Rowe had this appeal in mind when, in 1741, he wrote:

> that Mr Bray (who is Entirely in another Interest), was Chose Portreeve ... I won't expatiate Farther upon it, Than to Say if the Steward can Swear, or will any Person on the Jury he Thinks Fit, and admit Free Tenants who have not been presented by your Jury, you have no Remedy but Westminster Hall ... (F201)

To focus more closely on Nicholas James Rowe and the 5th Baronet, Sir Francis Henry Drake: in 1740 the 4th baronet, also Francis Henry, died unexpectedly of pleuritic fever, a painful chest condition. It is difficult to determine Rowe's relationship to the family but he was clearly very close and acted in a paternalistic way towards the 5th Baronet, who was still a schoolboy at Winchester College as Rowe's letters begin. If one accepts an account of life at Winchester quoted by Lady Fuller-Elliot-Drake, there was an emphasis on the struggle between Jacobites and Georgites and the 'degrees of social precedence'.[7] An education at Winchester and Cambridge was not one to make Sir Francis aware of the lives of ordinary people or of the details of local politics in Bere Alston, whereas Rowe, the older man, with a freehold in Bere Alston, knew at first hand the local levers of power.

At the time of the 4th baronet's death, neither his eldest son, still only seventeen, nor his two brothers were deemed eligible by the family to promote their interest in Bere Alston. George Drake lived in India, where he had business interests and rarely returned home, and Harry Drake was a pleasure-seeking spendthrift, who was seen as totally unsuitable to be an MP, although it was attractive to him as he constantly feared the debtors' prison, which if he were an MP he could avoid. (He never made Westminster but he did make the Fleet prison.) It appears that the family decided that the late MP's eldest son should continue the family's interest, once of age. In the meantime, it was agreed that Samuel Heathcote, brother of the dowager, should hold the Bere Alston seat for the remaining year of the then current parliament and stand in the 1741 election, continuing to hold the seat until his nephew was of age. Rowe, knowing that there were only about twenty burgage holders, reports that they were unanimous in voting for the Drake candidate, 'as I hope the Majority of your Father's Friends will always be to Serve his Son' (F200).

In the meantime Rowe urges his protégé to ingratiate himself with the local burgesses. Requests for patronage could have been made directly to Heathcote but

---

[6]   J. J. Alexander, 'Bere Alston as a Parliamentary Borough', *Transactions of the Devonshire Association* 41 (1909) 159.

[7]   *Family and Heirs*, vol. 2, p. 239.

Rowe, by involving Sir Francis, is promoting him and encouraging him to get to know the local community:

> My Humble Service waits on your Uncle and if you cou'd prevail on him to get Mr John Doidge made an Extraordinary Man at Plymouth, it wou'd be a Service to your Interest to let people See you can provide for your Friends … (F202)

Not that Rowe is over-impressed at the demands of these posts:

> You puzzle me to tell what Mr John Doidge is fit; what he desires, is a Tidewaiter at Plymouth but there is so much time on the hands of those people, which they generally Spend in an Ale-House … (F203)

And further:

> Mrs Bealey too has been Solliciting me to apply to ye all for a place for Her Husband, but how to describe his Qualifications – you can better than I … (F203)

In time, Rowe passes on requests for patronage directly to Sir Francis.[8] There are also a number of references in the letters to government posts in customs and excise at Plymouth. At a time when there was not a widespread civil service, these were sought-after appointments in the government's gift.

Despite Rowe's reassurances, he knew that the first election at which Sir Francis could be elected was that of 1747. Until that time there was, in the background, the unsettling presence of Uncle Harry, who clearly thought he should have one of what he believed were the family boroughs. He arranged a meeting at Cambridge with Sir Francis which is recalled in the one letter that survives from the baronet's hand (F198). Privileged students at that time did not live in hall but with their tutors. Uncle Drake invited himself for breakfast with the tutor to show that everything was 'proper' when he told Sir Francis that his father once had a numbers of boroughs that could be reclaimed. He also tried using a letter from Heathcote in support. When Rowe read this he responded scornfully, clearly thinking little of the chances of reviving the interests in the other boroughs (F199). Rowe continued to advise Sir Francis to contact local burgesses with a friendly word. On 19 May 1741, almost as an afterthought, he says that the 'The Election at Beer was Unanimous' (F200). Thus Samuel Heathcote was elected MP for the next seven years. Well before the end of that time, Sir Francis would have graduated and transferred his activities to Lincoln's Inn, in London. Rowe ends the letter by naming all those present at the court leet of 1741.

In October the same year, while updating Sir Francis on the new portreeve of another interest, who is offering a very loose interpretation of who can and cannot be a juryman, Rowe reminds the baronet of the decision twenty years earlier:

> I must Own I did not think anything of this kind wou'd have been attempt-
> ed, Considering what has pass'd. It Therefore Behoves you to look about

---

[8] See e.g. F225, F228, F231, F237–F238, F254–F255, F260, F263, F265, F267–F268, F271, F288, F296, F299–F300, F302, F307, F310, F315–F317.

betimes, to make yourself Master as Soon as possible, at least of Election
Law. (F201)

This anxiety was relieved a year later when the court officials were reappointed and
Rowe could report better news and continue to offer more encouragement for Sir
Francis to maintain contact with potential supporters. It was also important to watch
who inherited tenancies, to try to ensure that they were in one's interest, which is
why Rowe would keep Sir Francis abreast of these changes, even if he omitted the
details, as the postal service's security was widely mistrusted. Harry Drake was still
visiting, this time on a 'Party of pleasure':

> I don't hear anything about Boro's runs in his head now, unless they have
> a Cornish One in view, Being going There as they Say; Though I Fancy a
> More Material B[oro] do's or ought to take up his Thoughts. (F204)

The day of the next court leet came and farce ensued, according to Rowe's letter
written the following day (F213). We have a note (F212) of the court that met on
2 April 1744 and which dealt with several changes of tenancies. Dr Creed, vicar
of Buckland, arrived late, lost his temper and created a scene but without any
success. He had a tenancy in October 1742, as he is listed as a sworn juryman. At
this particular sitting of the court leet he arrived at the end of the meeting when
the 'presentments', the business of the meeting, were over. In order to have a vote
in the court, he needed to arrive at the beginning to be sworn in. By presenting his
nephew as a tenant, he was presumably aiming to gain another vote in Harry Drake's
interest. Perhaps he had a plan to gradually build up that support before the next
parliamentary election.

Lady Fuller-Eliott-Drake claims that 'July 2nd 1747 marked the accomplishment
of Sir Francis's long cherished desire to be elected Member of Parliament for
Berealston',[9] though it is difficult to see support for her view in these letters. Rowe
is constantly having to reassure, encourage, or cajole the young Sir Francis to visit
the borough more often, to get to know the burgesses, and to do what he can for them
with the help of his Uncle Heathcote. The record through the letters is incomplete, as
there are none relating to any of Sir Francis's election successes. It is reasonable to
assume, however, that he would have been in Bere Alston for these elections so there
would be no need to write. The only subsequent reference to elections is one leading
up to that of 1752, when anxiety rose again and further reassurance was needed:

> But good Sir, What can H[atch?] or W[ills?] do, if your Friends are True
> to you, which I Think you have no reason to Doubt of – Therefore I Think
> you need give yourself no Uneasiness. (F262)

Later letters offer no further insights into the politics of the borough. Rowe continues
to keep Sir Francis up to date on local matters but there do not appear to be
challenges to his nomination at subsequent elections.

These letters exemplify the eighteenth-century political system – a nationwide
oligarchy led by aristocrats and landed gentry. They show how the Drake family
achieved electoral success in one small borough, Bere Alston, where the two seats

---

[9] *Family and Heirs*, vol. 2, p. 253.

were shared between the Hobart and Drake families. Yet that success had to be managed. While the whole process seems to have been relatively calm and ordered, the election result could not be taken for granted as the tenancies could be taken by others who were not in the Drake or Hobart interests. There is no evidence of pamphleteering or rioting, just a little anxiety on the part of some. The tenants needed to know that their MP was on their side. Maybe Lord Hobart as lord of the manor had more opportunities to apply pressure on the tenants than the Drake baronet, who had to rely on maintaining a positive relationship with those in his interest. As a result, the Drakes were obliged to help not just individual burgesses but their family and sometimes their friends, which could amount to a large group of people. We do not know how many people lived in the borough: agricultural work was labour intensive; many households would have had servants. Yet labourers and servants, the majority in the borough, are almost invisible and had no parliamentary representation. At the time, this was accepted as the natural order. There was representation for the few, not for the many.

2.2. Roads, Turnpikes, and the Postal Service

During the period of these letters, turnpike roads linking Devon to London were gradually evolving. A national turnpike system was the major transport outcome of the eighteenth century and must have had a profound effect on the lives of our letter writers. It was an outcome rather than achievement, in that no central authority set out to construct the system; rather, it came about as the result of short radial roads, taking goods to local markets, being gradually linked to longer stretches, across the more rural areas.

Building roads meant that land had to be taken from landowners. To avoid costly local disputes, each initiative needed the protection of its own Act of Parliament. In Devon, new turnpike trusts included Exeter (1753), Devon and Dorset (1754), Axminster and Honiton (1754), and Ashburton (1754).[10] Roads did exist prior to the turnpikes, maintained by local parishes, but once the better-quality roads were built, lighter and faster 'flyers' were developed, halving travel times between major cities.

A letter from Rowe of February 1756 records Mr Porter's pleasure that the turnpike has been fixed according to Sir Francis's system (F333). This presumably refers to a Plymouth turnpike trust for which Sir Francis had some responsibility in Parliament. Mr Porter held a position in the Plymouth customs and excise.

Sir Francis travelled between London and Devon by coach or carriage, or on horseback. In addition to riding horses he kept coach horses (and cart horses) at Nutwell (F480–F482). His goods were sometimes sent by wagon or coach (F257, F312, F314, etc.; 10–F182, 11–F180, 13–F179, 21–F170, 23–F172, 25–F173), and sometimes by sea (F203, F277–F284, F289, F290, F294, F300, etc.; 21–F170, 22–F171). Mr Rowe travelled between Nutwell and Buckland on horseback, and suffered severely after one journey from 'a Flead Posteriors' (F381). At Buckland, he went on horseback to Tavistock, and probably to Bere Alston. He went regularly by boat to Plymouth and the dock. At Nutwell he travelled on foot to Exeter, and to the parish

[10] See M. C. Lowe, 'The Turnpike Trusts in Devon and Their Roads: 1753–1889', *Report and Transactions of the Devonshire Association* 122 (1990), 47–69; J. Kanefsky, 'Railway Competition and Turnpike Roads in East Devon', *Report and Transactions of the Devonshire Association*, 109 (1977), 59–72.

church at Woodbury. He sometimes complained of getting very wet on his travels. Mr Porter rode from Plymouth to Nutwell 'for his health' (F277). William Hudson undertook journeys on horseback to the north of England and Wales (**25**–F173, **26**–F174), riding his pony for not more than thirty miles a day.

Those who were obliged to travel by 'the waggon' suffered very uncomfortable journeys. When Sir Francis's gardener at Nutwell succumbed to a mysterious illness in May 1766, he told Rowe that 'if he had not Fear'd to have Dy'd in the Waggon going up [to London], he shoud have gone when first Taken Ill' (F475). Then, a little later, 'at Intervals he is very Sensible & Says he is not able to do your Business, so Desires to go Directly, & will trye to get up in the Waggon' (F477). It was not until the later part of the eighteenth century that the improvement in the roads, achieved through the coming of the turnpikes, and the development of lighter, faster vehicles, led to a less bumpy ride – and a better postal service.

At the beginning of the eighteenth century the poor roads had resulted in a very slow postal service. Throughout the century postal costs depended on distance and the number of sheets of paper used; as an envelope counted as one sheet, the letters themselves were often folded and sealed. The recipient paid for the letter. Postal costs were 'laid down in 1711 as a minimum of 3d. (the price of a good meal in a respectable inn or eating house) for the shortest journeys'.[11] MPs used their privileged position to frank communications for themselves as well as for family and friends. Sir Francis took advantage of this concession.

Outside the main cities there developed a system radiating from London to Edinburgh, Holyhead, Falmouth, and Dover. There were 'posts' about every twenty miles, where horses were exchanged and where the postmaster was required to have at least three horses available for use. Post-boys carried the letters between 'posts'. Buckland Abbey and Nutwell Court were near one of these major routes, Exeter being an important 'post' because of the bridge over the Exe.

Letters could be sent under another person's cover for security, or convenience. Thus Rowe asked Sir Francis to write 'under [Mr Porter's] cover' to Plymouth (F248), and 'under Alderman Lee's cover' to Exeter (F291). Rowe was critical of the expensive Topsham postal arrangements, and tried in vain to persuade the Exeter postmaster to keep letters in Exeter until called for by Nutwell staff (F270, F272). Latterly he preferred to use the Exmouth 'Carryer': 'as I receive & Send my Letters by the Exmouth Carryer, it is Sometimes 2 or 3 Days before they Come to my hands, But I am punctual in Sending answers to any of Consequence' (F461).

Writers were aware that, for 'reasons of State', letters might be read by postmasters, so they often wrote using a prearranged code. Such caution accounts for some of Mr Rowe's circumlocutions, abbreviations, and veiled allusions.

11 Langford, *A Polite and Commercial People*, p. 408.

3. Buckland Abbey and Nutwell Court: Buildings

Dee and Mike Tracey

3.1 Buckland Abbey

Buckland Abbey was founded in 1278 by Amicia de Redvers, the widowed countess of Baldwin de Redvers, 6th Earl of Devon and Lord of the Isle of Wight. It is perhaps not surprising, therefore, that the new abbey was colonised by an abbot and seven monks from Quarr Abbey, which had been founded on the island many years earlier by the first Baldwin Earl of Devon, who is buried there.[1] Buckland was the fifth Cistercian abbey to be built in Devon, after Buckfast (rebuilt as a Cistercian establishment in 1147),[2] Ford, now Forde and no longer in Devon (developed out of a very short-lived priory at Brightley, and completed between 1141 and 1148),[3] Dunkeswell in 1201, and Newenham, near Axminster, in 1246. It was possibly the last Cistercian foundation in England and certainly the most westerly. Amicia endowed the abbey generously, with a large outlying estate in east Devon and some 20,000 acres nearer to home.[4]

The Cistercians became a major influence on the religious and economic life of medieval England, but Buckland was a very late addition, and remained one of the order's more obscure houses. The property occupies an ancient site (an Iron Age earthwork exists to the east of the cloister area) in a sheltered cleave beside a small stream, on the eastern side of the Tavy valley. It lies between the village of Buckland Monachorum and the hamlet of Milton Combe. The Cistercian abbey was built to the traditional monastic plan, the abbey church and three ranges of buildings being grouped around the cloister, with its open central court. Ancillary buildings were further afield; they included a gatehouse, various parts of the home farm, and a huge barn, one of the largest medieval barns still in existence. All the buildings were of shillet, a local slate, quarried on the estate. The dressings were of Roborough granite, another local stone, which weathers to look like limestone.[5]

The nature of the site drainage dictated that the cloister be situated to the north of the abbey rather than the more usual south. The east side of the cloister range included the chapter house and, above it, the monks' dormitory. A section of medieval wall opposite the church indicates where the north wall of the cloister stood, and this contained the refectory. Outside the wall are two much-altered medieval buildings: Tower House was possibly the abbot's dwelling; Cider House

---

[1] R. Bearman, 'Baldwin de Redvers, Earl of Devon', *ODNB*.

[2] A. Emery, *Greater Medieval Houses of England and Wales, 1300–1500*, 3 vols (Cambridge: Cambridge University Press), vol. 3, p. 506.

[3] S. Heath, *The Story of Forde Abbey: From the Earliest Times to the Present Day* (London: Francis Griffiths, 1911), pp. 24–27.

[4] M. Mauchline, 'The Cistercian Foundation', in *Buckland Abbey* (Swindon: National Trust, 2014), p. 27.

[5] *Ibid.*, pp. 28–29.

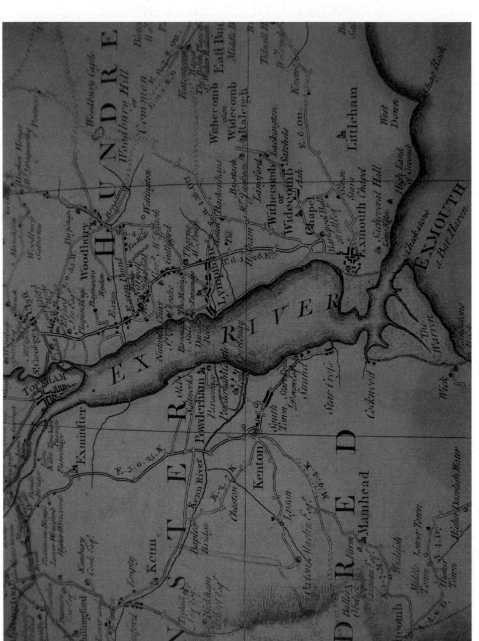

Figure 2. B. Donn, *Map of the County of Devon* (1765), Plate 7.

probably provided accommodation for the lay brothers. Nearby was accommodation for the masons, smiths, and carpenters who kept the abbey in good repair, as well as the abbey bake-house and brew-house. The present National Trust shop and restaurant were originally stables, converted in later monastic times to a guest-house or, more probably, the farm manager's accommodation. The great barn, which is very close to the church, has a superb arch-braced roof of the early fifteenth century. Pevsner dates the whole construction to this period,[6] but Mauchline contends that the barn was one of the earliest buildings on the site.[7]

With its strong endowment Buckland prospered initially, although it never had a large complement of monks, and there were only twelve, plus the abbot, by the time of the Dissolution. The abbey's revenues were then no more than £241 17s 9¼d, but the last abbot, John Toker, had 'been mindful of those of his own household' and, just prior to the surrender, had leased the rectorial tithes of Buckland, Walkhampton, Bickley, Sheepstor, and Bampton to his brother and two nephews.[8] In 1539 George Pollard of London was granted a lease of the abbey for twenty-one years but, more significantly, in 1542 Sir Richard Grenville was granted the reversion. He paid £233 3s 4d for the church, all the monastic buildings, the great barn, the home farm, and 568 acres of land. Hoskins considered that Grenville was probably responsible for the demolition of a substantial part of the abbey buildings,[9] although Hugh Meller thinks that much of the demolition did not take place until the early 1800s, when major changes were made for Lord Heathfield by the architect Samuel Pepys Cockerell.[10] Whoever is right, there is general agreement that it is Sir Richard's grandson, the more famous Sir Richard Grenville – he of the *Revenge* – who should be credited with much of the conversion that we see today. This is perhaps borne out by the fact that the date 1576 appears on the hall fireplace.[11]

What Grenville produced was 'an irregular Elizabethan mansion with a surprisingly tall and powerful tower'.[12] This is because the northern wing of the roughly L-shaped building is composed very largely of the remains of the abbey church: the tower, which is centrally placed over the crossing, and the nave and chancel, albeit with some reductions of roof height. The south transept was removed to let in more light, although the north transept did not disappear until some time after 1734, when it was included in the engraving made by Samuel and Nathaniel Buck. The nave became the basis of the great hall, which, although of considerable height, had chambers above and was not open to the roof – one of the earliest examples of this in the county. The present entrance to the building, which replaced an earlier one only in the twentieth century, is through a porch formed from the former north transept chapel. The chancel became a service room, with a large kitchen wing added to the south, and a grand staircase wing adjoining the site of the north transept. The staircase itself was rebuilt in the nineteenth century and again in the twentieth.

[6] N. Pevsner and B. Cherry, *The Buildings of England: Devon*, 2nd edition (Harmondsworth: Penguin, 1989), p. 229.
[7] Mauchline, 'Cistercian Foundation', p. 31.
[8] R. N. Worth, *A History of Devonshire* (London: Elliot Stock, 1886), p. 196.
[9] W. G. Hoskins, *Devon* (Chichester: Phillimore, 2003), 357.
[10] Hugh Meller, 'Tour of the Abbey', in *Buckland Abbey*, p. 6.
[11] Pevsner and Cherry, *Devon*, p. 227.
[12] *Ibid.*

There is still plenty of evidence of the church: from the outside one can clearly see a number of blocked thirteenth-century windows, and the roof lines of the transepts are visible on the tower. The crenellations on the north side of the chancel roof were licensed in 1336, when the French threatened the Plymouth area during the Hundred Years War.[13] Inside, the building is 'a curious mixture of medieval ecclesiastical details and later remodelling'. Pevsner is equally clear that it is the 'secular invasion of the church itself which makes Buckland Abbey remarkable – a sidelight on the attitude of Grenvilles and Drakes to the tradition of religion and piety'.[14]

By 1580 Grenville was apparently short of money, and sold the property for £3,400, via a complicated mortgage arrangement, to Sir Francis Drake, who made it his principal residence whenever he was in England, and from whom it eventually descended to Sir Francis Henry Drake, 5th Baronet, under whose stewardship it does not seem to have thrived.[15] Rowe's letters to Drake make remarkably few references to the buildings, but what he does say is rarely comforting. In 1750 the fountain was leaking and the plaster was cracked in the hall 'and will come down soon' (F219). The fountain seems to have been repaired, but what happened to the plaster is not revealed. Perhaps nothing, as when part of the dining room ceiling fell in four-and-a-half years later, it was mentioned almost as an aside, and there seems to have been no follow-up. This was a time when 'it rains in to all the rooms in the house' (F299).

Sir Francis did not live at Buckland and he did not gain full control of it until the death of his mother in 1768. Like him, she lived mostly in London, although not very close to her son either geographically or, it seems, emotionally. She left a gentleman farmer, referred to as 'the hine', in charge of the abbey, but neither she nor Sir Francis seems to have been anxious to pay for necessary maintenance and repairs. Rowe tried to stir them into action, but without any obvious success:

> As to this place, you know There has nothing been Done to the House, I mean that part which is inhabited, for a Long Time … if your Mother & you wou'd Rough Cast it, & paint the Sash-Windows at your mutual Expence, it might Save it; But the Hall Ceiling I fear will come down too – as to the new room, how the Cieling [*sic*] come to fall I don't know. (F302)

Some repairs were made – 'I fancy the pointing outside has in a great measure Lessen'd the Dampness' (F302) – but one gets the impression that both Rowe's and Sir Francis's efforts flagged.

Fortunately, the old house was made of sterner stuff, and survived until Sir Francis finally implemented an improvement and modernisation programme some fifteen years later. If the tenant who talked to the Reverend John Swete in 1792 is to be believed, Sir Francis was by then so

> attached to the place, that he generally past a month or two in the summer here, and … signified intentions, of adding to the Southern front a couple of handsome rooms – at present the apartments are uncomfortable and excepting the Hall, are rather mean than otherwise.[16]

[13] Worth, *History of Devonshire*, p. 195.
[14] Pevsner and Cherry, p. 227.
[15] D. Hart-Davis, 'Sir Francis Drake', in *Buckland Abbey*, pp. 39–40.
[16] *Travels in Georgian Devon*, vol. I, p. 153.

The future of Buckland was finally assured when the 2nd Lord Heathfield spent a substantial sum of money, mostly on restoration rather than significant rebuilding, early in the following century.

3.2 Nutwell Court

Before the Norman conquest, Noteswilla was held by a Saxon called Donne or Dunne, who still held it twenty years later, although in due course Henry I granted it to Geoffrey, lord of Dinan in Brittany.[17] Geoffrey in turn granted Nutwell to the Abbey of Marmoutier, for the benefit of the dependent Priory of St Malo at Dinan, but in 1272 Oliver de Dinan bought it back. There is an alternative view, that Nutwell came back following the suppression of alien priories,[18] whose assets were seques-trated repeatedly and for long periods over the course of the fourteenth century, culminating in the dissolution of around ninety smaller houses and granges by Act of Parliament in 1414.[19] However, the earliest known sequestration was in 1295, so, if the date of 1272 is correct, it must have been a straightforward purchase.

Oliver became the 1st Baron Dynham. In addition to Nutwell he held the manors of Harpford and Hartland, part of a large portfolio of Devon properties that the family built up over the centuries. It was during the ownership of Oliver's great-grandson John that there was the first mention of any building at Nutwell, when, in 1371, a licence was issued for the erection of a chapel, although it has been argued that there was a previous chapel, dating from the early fourteenth century, 'a date that accords well with the style of the remaining glass'.[20] Whether or not either chapel was accompanied by a house is unclear, although it seems probable. There was certainly some sort of dwelling there by 1458, when John's grandson, another John, died at Nutwell. Only a year later, the Yorkists were defeated at Ludlow, and it is said that the future Edward IV and Warwick the Kingmaker were hidden at Nutwell by John's widow until they could get a boat to France. John's son, yet another John, was created Baron Dynham in 1467. It seems that Oliver's barony was not hereditary, and that this was a new foundation. John Hooker, writing about 1600, said that 'it is reported that Nutwell was sometime a castle of defence', which is generally interpreted to mean a fortified house.[21] Risdon, writing perhaps a few years later, and probably using Hooker as his source, said much the same: 'Nutwell, sometime a castle; but when it came to the Lord Dynham, he altered it, and made it a fair and stately dwelling house.'[22] The listing description goes further: 'the house was rebuilt'.[23]

The 1st Baron Dynham of the second creation was also the last, and the male line ended in 1501. Nutwell, whatever its degree of remodelling, then found its way to John Prideaux, MP for Devon and a serjeant-at-law. After four generations the

---

[17] T. Hinde, ed., *The Domesday Book: England's Heritage, Then and Now* (London: Hutchinson, 1985), p. 84.
[18] D. M. Stirling, *The Beauties of the Shore* (Exeter: W. Roberts, 1838), p. 157.
[19] M. Morgan, 'The Suppression of the Alien Priories', *History* 26(103) (1941), 204–212.
[20] Historic England, Nutwell Court listing, 11 November 1952.
[21] Cited in Hoskins, *Devon*, p. 275.
[22] T. Risdon, *The Chorographical Description or Survey of the County of Devon* (Plymouth: Rees and Curtis, 1811; 1st edition 1714), 56.
[23] Historic England, Nutwell Court listing.

Prideaux also ran out of male heirs, but by then Nutwell had already been disposed of, although not before it had been fortified in the Parliamentarian cause in 1646.[24] In 1649 it was bought by Henry Ford, who was four times MP for Tiverton and who died at Nutwell in 1684.[25] A year after his death his executors sold the property to Sir Henry Pollexfen, who paid £6,318 for it in 1685. He was a great supporter of William of Orange, who rewarded him by making him Attorney General and Chief Justice of the Common Pleas, although verdicts as to his legal abilities are somewhat mixed. According to Pevsner, Pollexfen undertook further remodelling of the house.[26] Pollexfen's son, also Henry, married a daughter of Sir Francis Drake of Buckland, the 3rd Baronet, through whom Nutwell passed into the ownership of the Drakes. The Drakes, in due course, also lost their male line, with the 5th Baronet, the recipient of the letters published in this volume.

It was this Sir Francis who made major changes to the old property. These did not all meet with the approval of Reverend John Swete, but he wrote about the house with some affection in 1799, by which time its replacement was already in the process of being built.[27] Swete felt it necessary to comment because he was

> unwilling that so ancient and respectable a structure, so soon sharing the
> fate of its master [who had died in 1794], should be lost to the river which
> it once embellished, without a memorandum, or a vestige of what it was.

Swete characterised Nutwell as an 'ancient Gothic mansion, garb'd in a simple plain dress: the rough-cast or slap-dash of the country', which most pleased him when its

> predominant cast is grey, variegated with innumerable shades, which have
> been communicated to it by the effects of time, weather, smoke, not forget-
> ting amongst them all the inter-mixture of green, yellow and orange-tinted
> lichens. Such was the colouring of Old Nutwell.

He was also very taken with the beautiful views, especially that up the river to Exeter.[28]

Swete's description is useful in confirming that the numerous works undertaken by Sir Francis did not unduly affect the exterior of the mansion. That is not to say that they were all internal, nor that they were welcomed by all. Hoskins, albeit long after the event, was appalled: Sir Francis

> wrecked the fine medieval house with his 'improvements', demolishing
> the two-storeyed gate house with great difficulty in 1755–6, and cutting
> through the timbered roof of the fourteenth-century chapel to make a plas-
> ter ceiling.[29]

The gatehouse seems to have been one of Sir Francis's earliest projects, although, over three years before work started on it, Rowe, writing from Buckland, was 'very

[24] Worth, *History of Devonshire*, pp. 53–54.
[25] Stirling, *Beauties of the Shore*, p. 157.
[26] Pevsner and Cherry, *Devon*, p. 552.
[27] For a selection of Swete's watercolours, see figures 3–11.
[28] *Travels in Georgian Devon*, vol. 4, p. 147.
[29] Hoskins, *Devon*, p. 518.

glad you are making Nutwell agreable to you' (F231), which might or might not betoken a significant amount of work. It was, however, one of the more upbeat comments he made. Both Rowe and Sir Francis seem to have been great pessimists, and it is sometimes difficult to assess the true severity of the many problems they faced. Nor were matters helped by procrastination on the part of Sir Francis, possibly a natural trait, or perhaps occasioned by the pressures of his life in London. The gatehouse is a case in point. Rowe first asked for instructions, albeit somewhat obliquely, on 29 November 1755, a time, incidentally, at which the main house was 'in a Dismal Condition' (F326). By 6 January the following year he was holding out incentives: 'Nicholas ... Says it is now a Leisure Time, and that he cou'd do it much Cheaper now, than in the Spring' (F330). In February Sir Francis was worrying about the difficulty of removing the potential debris (F332), but he must have given approval, because by the twentieth of that month 'Nicholas is got below the upper windows of the gatehouse, yet much is Stil to come down' (F333). Within a week the bulk of the job was done, creating a new worry for Rowe about the possible effects of the wind on the now unprotected house (F334). Why Sir Francis decided to demolish the gatehouse is not known but, in an ironic touch that Hoskins might not have appreciated, some of its stones were later earmarked for work on the chapel (F376).

This second great desecration came a little later. There was some storm damage to the chapel in 1755 (F325) and 1757 (F376), which was repaired, and work was done on the wall in the chapel court in 1759 (F393). The next mention is not until July 1762, by which time work on the conversion to a library seems to have been well under way, accompanied by its fair share of problems. Bricks, lime, floor stones, scaffold boards, and workmen all caused difficulties, and the stained-glass windows suffered terrible damage, albeit accidental (F451). By the end of 1762 the major reconstruction work seems to have been pretty well complete, although there was still much finishing to do. By September the following year, however, work was being done on the floors and the chimney in 'the New Library' and the chapel was no more (F465).

Reverend Swete, as might be imagined, was far from happy with the treatment of the chapel, and on this subject he was at one with the later judgement of Hoskins. Swete's standing as a minister of religion was probably only partially responsible for his view that 'the magnificence of the ancient building' had 'undergone unwarrantable desecration', while the alterations 'do not constitute an uniform and accordant whole'. He was particularly incensed that only one original window was left, and that all the others were now 'plain and in a modern style: of such ingenuity, what man of taste can speak with approbation?'[30] Perhaps the answer to that is to concentrate on the end result. Polwhele's verdict was simply that Sir Francis had 'converted the chapel into a very handsome library'.[31] This time we do know that he had what seemed, to him at least, a very good reason. He was an inveterate collector of books, and he had recently moved a substantial number from Buckland. Perhaps

[30] *Travels in Georgian Devon*, vol. 4, p. 145.
[31] R. Polwhele, *The History of Devonshire,* 3 vols (London: Cadell & Davies, 1793–1806), vol. 2, p. 120, quoted in *Travels in Georgian Devon*, vol. 4, p. 145.

he also shared the family attitude to 'the tradition of religion and piety' which Pevsner thought so significant in the work at Buckland.[32]

When Sir Francis was not involved in wrecking and desecration, he still had more than enough to cope with. Although the completion of the new library towards the end of 1763 seems to have marked the end of his major alterations, it had been a long hard road. Work on the buildings was certainly under way by the time of Rowe's first letter after his move to Nutwell in June 1754 (F269), and it continued for the best part of a decade. While it was more than cosmetic, it does not seem to have been significantly structural. There were major problems: 'Sir, your House is now gutted, your Hall is a Barn, all the Timber & Floors over Taken down – The Beams all rotten, Cramp't with Iron in a Shocking manner' (F345), but, within three weeks, 'Your House ... is returning into its Forme again' (F348). Rowe noted that a 'Wall was 4 ft Thick' (F350), so at least parts of the structure were solid, and it seems clear from Swete's observations that the outside of the building remained much as it had always been, although it does seem to have had its stucco renewed. The work, nevertheless, was far-reaching. Barely a room was not tackled at some stage, and there are specific references to at least eighteen of them. Numerous outhouses also received attention, ranging from the coach-house (F473) to the privy (F428), from the brew-house to the dog-houses (F470). The materials used were also many and varied, including marble, brick, lead, slate, thatch, timber, lime, and sand.

One potentially very serious issue was flooding. Stirling waxed lyrical: 'This beautiful seat is sheltered on all sides by semi-circular eminences, excepting to the westward, in which direction it opens to the river Exe.'[33] But flooding was a continuing problem. In December 1754, there was a violent storm and 'Water cover'd the Bottome of the Parlour, & most of the Kitchen' (F296). A similar event occurred in March 1758, when 'the greatest Flood has been yet ... broke thro' the Wall from the Orchard into the pound House & Stable to Some Feet high' (F374). Nine years later, in 1767, repairs to the sea-wall were still necessary (F479).

There is no evidence that an architect was employed, and such indications as we have point to Sir Francis having been his own designer. Overseeing the work fell squarely on the shoulders of Nicholas Rowe, who seems to have been a reasonably amiable man, not always in the best of health, often beset by the inadequacies of the labour force, and perhaps struggling a little beyond his comfort zone. Masons, stone-cutters, tinners, plumbers, joiners, brickworkers, thatchers, and a variety of labourers, sometimes doing work that he did not understand, and too often conspicuous by their absence, would have been a trial for any man, let alone one into his sixties before work started, and with apparently very little relevant experience: 'I am a very poor Overseer, as I Fear you Think by the Blunders I make, but to my utmost I will do my utmost to Serve you in Everything' (F291). As early as June 1754 Rowe admitted that, in respect of the joiner, 'I don't Comprehend what he's about' (F270), and as late as August 1762 he declared that 'I can't understand what Ashlar work is' (F453). His lack of expert understanding was a recurring theme, as was the unreliability of supplies and suppliers: 'The Lime-Kiln is Stop't for want of Stones, so the Plaisterers can't go on, till they have Lime, nor Nicholas Lay the Floor of the Hall' (F368). He was also prone to consult Sir Francis about any number of relatively

[32] Pevsner and Cherry, *Devon*, p. 227.
[33] Stirling, *Beauties of the Shore*, pp. 158–159.

Figure 3. John Swete, *Buckland Monastery*, 18 April 1793.

trifling matters, which might indicate a lack of ability or confidence, although it seems to have been more a matter of tact and diplomacy. Rowe had a difficult job, and he seems to have tackled the problems along the way conscientiously, and to the best of his ability.

In 1794, some thirty years after completion of the work, Sir Francis died and bequeathed the estate to his nephew, the 2nd Lord Heathfield, whose approach was rather more destructive. The end result was very different: he created an almost entirely new house, to a design by Samuel Pepys Cockerell, who also did work for him at Buckland. Pevsner described the result as 'an exquisitely precise and austere neo-classical mansion', with a five-bayed front and two floors above a basement. He noted that from the east 'it is clear that all this is a remodelling of an older house', although there seems to have been precious little of the older house left.[34] The medieval chapel, desecrated though it might have been, was retained, but seems very much at odds with the rest of the 'austere' late Georgian structure. Hoskins had a somewhat cosier, although possibly less accurate, impression of 'a small and demure country house of the Jane Austen period'. He was, though, happy to think that 'the present house is perhaps some justification for all [the] destruction'.[35]

[34] Pevsner and Cherry, *Devon*, p. 552.
[35] Hoskins, *Devon*, p. 518.

Figure 4. John Swete, *Buckland Monastery*.

Figure 5. John Swete, *Powderham Church and Nutwell*.

Figure 6. John Swete, *Old Nutwell, Seat of Sir Francis Drake.*

Figure 7. John Swete, *Nutwell Chapel.*

Figure 8. John Swete, *Nutwell, West View.*

Figure 9. John Swete, *Nutwell, East View.*

Figure 10. John Swete, *Nutwell*.

Figure 11. John Swete, *Nutwell*, Seat of Lord Heathfield.

4. NUTWELL: PLANTING THE LANDSCAPE

Todd Gray

The Nutwell letters provide intriguing details on the development of the grounds as well as further insights into those at Buckland Abbey. The correspondence provides the most detailed information on an estate's plants and planting for any set of Devon letters. Uncommon plants and trees are shown to have been of particular interest to Sir Francis Henry Drake.

It is clear that Sir Francis had a keen interest in ornamental landscapes, and from London he routinely sent detailed instructions on the organisation of Nutwell's grounds. In 1793, a year before the baronet's death, a neighbour credited Sir Francis with being 'proficient' in botany.[1] It appears as though his interest in plants, and the study of them, was a considerable pursuit. This is borne out by manuscript notes penned by Sir Francis which were found in 1883 in his copy of William Hudson's *Flora Anglica*. Many important books from Nutwell's library had been sold the previous year,[2] and the annotations which were discovered show that Sir Francis had made considerable personal investigations into the identification and location of plants, particularly those in and around his two estates in Devon. Hudson's volume had been published in 1762 while Rowe was corresponding with Sir Francis. Moreover, in 1829 the latter would be posthumously recognised in John Pike Jones and J. F. Kingston's *Flora Devoniensis* as having toured parts of Devon with Hudson in order to record native plants.[3] He also corresponded about plants with William Borlase, the celebrated Cornish antiquary and naturalist.[4]

This edition includes a number of letters from Hudson. The correspondence not only confirms Sir Francis's interest in plants but also establishes that the two men were on friendly terms. Hudson lived in London and in his letters he referred to the botany expeditions with Sir Francis, as well as to sending him such plants as 'English' *Melica*, 'Welsh' *Cerastium*, 'Sea Pancratia', otherwise known as the sea daffodil (*Pancratium maritimum*), vetch (*Vicia*), yellow wood anemone (*Anemone ranunculoides*), spreading bellflower (*Campanula patula*), night blooming cactus (*Cereus grandiflora)*, heliotrope (*Heliotropium odoratum)*, gardenia, and jasmine, as well as varieties of *Plumeria*, *Gloriosa*, *Clitoria*, *Antholyza*, *Pentapetes*, *Asclepias*, *Leonarus*, and *Gladiolus*. Hudson also sent seeds from various sources in London and from across the country and beyond; in one instance they were acquired from

[1]   R. Polwhele, *The History of Devonshire*, 3 vols (London: Cadell & Davies, 1793–1806), vol. 1, p. 81.

[2]   See section 1, pp. 7–8 and 12, for this sale and for a further sale of books from Nutwell Court and Buckland Abbey following the death of Lady Fuller-Eliott-Drake.

[3]   *Bibliographer* 4(1) (June 1883), 15–17; T. R. Archer Briggs, 'Some Devonian Stations of Plants Noted in the Last Century', *Journal of Botany* 22 (1884), 168–174; J. P. Jones and J. F. Kingston, *Flora Devoniensis* (London: Longman &c, 1829), pp. 29, 54, 106.

[4]   DHC 346M/F21. In 1768 Borlase wrote regarding sending seeds of pillis, a type of oats grown in Cornwall. In the letter he mentions his friend 'Mr Hudson'. See also section 1, p. 8.

Jamaica. His correspondence refers to the death of a magnolia at Nutwell, to the survival of a *Hypericum*, to the employment of a gardener who formerly worked for Hugh Percy, 2nd Duke of Northumberland, and to Philip Miller, the Chelsea gardener. Finally, Hudson sent a list of books which he purchased for Sir Francis; these include a number of botanical titles.

Sir Francis valued the privacy that his estate provided. In July 1763 he instructed his servants not to admit visitors into either the house or the garden. Thirty years later the Reverend Richard Polwhele, who lived on the opposite side of the River Exe, recalled that Sir Francis

> was pleased to confine himself within the narrow circuit of his own grounds; averse from social communication and particularly inaccessible to men of talents and literature.[5]

In 1799 the Reverend John Swete, who lived at Oxton, also on the west side of the estuary, recalled that Sir Francis had been

> a strange compound of absurdity and of excellent sense! Though refined in his manners, and from his appointment at court versed in the fashionable world, he was yet one of the shyest of men! Very few of the principal gentlemen of the county had any acquaintance with him and not many knew him personally. When his attendance at court was dispensed with, he passed his solitary hours at his seat of Buckland or at Nutwell. Reports had classed him among the *Ancillarioli* and there is no difficulty in conceiving that a man thus shutting himself up from the world would at times want other amusements than his books and ornamenting his grounds.[6]

In his use of the Latin word *Ancillarioli* Swete was suggesting that Drake was given to 'wenching and low amours'. He was also claiming that Drake's activities in London were a release from his seclusion in Devon.[7] This evaluation of him in relation to gardening is interesting to compare with another given of him, where he was described as a 'silent, eccentric man'.[8]

In 1799 Swete tried to gain admittance to Nutwell's grounds. He had been allowed into the estate twice before but on this occasion was rebuffed by a servant whom he termed the 'dragon portress' at the gatehouse. The desire for privacy was inherited by the next generation: Sir Francis's successor was equally known for his solitude at home. Swete commented that Sir Francis's nephew also sequestered himself and wrote that no Spanish Don was more jealous of other men eyeing his wife than Drake's heir was of visitors viewing his garden.[9] This policy continued: thirty-one years later a subsequent owner corrected the text of an intended book on Devon by deleting the statement that Nutwell was open to the public. He wrote that it 'never

---

[5] Polwhele, *History of Devonshire*, vol. 1, p. 81.
[6] *Travels in Georgian Devon*, vol. 4, pp. 147–149.
[7] D. Hume, *The Philosophical Works of David Hume,* 4 vols (Edinburgh: Adam Black and William Tate, 1826), vol. 4, p. 427.
[8] History of Parliament, member biography for Sir Francis Henry Drake, historyofparliamentonline.org.
[9] *Travels in Georgian Devon*, vol. 4, pp. 147–149.

has been the case'.[10] One visitor, at least, to whom he did not refuse admission was Grand Duchess Helene of Russia in 1831,[11] but there are few contemporary travellers' journals which describe visits to Nutwell.

Yet another subsequent owner, Sir Thomas Trayton Fuller-Elliott-Drake, was noted in 1882 as having been eccentric and reclusive. A tale was told about him that year that:

> One of his peculiarities was a dislike to be seen; so he erected a splendid riding house approached by a concealed way; there he found horses ready saddled and bridled, but saw no one. The entrance to the parks and walks had high gates and spy holes, so that he could look through and see that the coast was clear before passing on. To secure greater privacy he paid $100,000 to get a road turned aside from his park and then erected a high brick wall for miles around it.[12]

However, he may not have been completely solitary: various hunts and local agricultural and horticultural society events were held at Nutwell in the late 1800s and these involved opening the grounds to the public.[13]

Nutwell's situation presented challenges for Georgian garden design. It lay on the east bank of the River Exe and in 1714 was noted as being 'very low by an arm of the sea, so as the high tides rise almost to the house. It is open only to the west being defended otherwise by little hills.'[14] Indeed, during the 1750s water flooded the gardens. Extensive parkland rises behind Nutwell to the main road from Exeter to Exmouth but the house's only prospects are across the River Exe to other estates. In this it has views of the skyline, which is punctuated by a ridge of high ground known as Haldon or Haldon Hills. The two belvederes, at Powderham Castle and Haldon House, had yet to be built, but the obelisk at Mamhead was already erected. However, to the south Joseph Drury would not build Cockwood House and embellish the landscape along that portion of the Exe for another two generations.[15]

Some features of the Nutwell landscape were hinted at in Rowe's correspondence, including the lawn, temple, terrace, walls, bowling green, canal, and pond. The last is still there. Others were recorded in some detail, including the building of a garden house of brick, and, with less detail, the digging of two water supplies, called octagons. The rebuilding of the house by Lord Heathfield, shortly after Drake's death in 1794, may have obliterated the works undertaken in the correspondence. There was also a fire in 1810 which destroyed outbuildings.[16]

[10]   Cited in T. Gray, *The Garden History of Devon* (Exeter: University of Exeter Press, 1995), p. 165.
[11]   *Morning Post*, 30 August 1831.
[12]   The *American* 1(5) (1 November 1882), 72. In the 1800s Nutwell continued to be a secondary home, with a residence maintained in London. In 1894 it was widely reported that Lady Drake announced plans to close the estate for three years and move to Demerara but she later denied that this was true: see *Portsmouth Evening News*, 15 December 1894. In 1885 she had spent the winter in Malta: *Exeter & Plymouth Gazette*, 12 January 1885.
[13]   For example, see *Exeter Flying Post*, 23 July 1879.
[14]   T. Risdon, *The Chorographical Description or Survey of the County of Devon* (Plymouth: Rees and Curtis, 1811; 1st edition 1714), p. 89.
[15]   T. Gray, *The Art of the Devon Garden* (Exeter: The Mint Press, 2013), pp. 161, 186–187.
[16]   *Taunton Courier*, 25 January 1810.

Sir Francis reformed his grounds in the 1750s and this included digging new plots, establishing a garden nursery, and putting in paths of either gravel or turf. Regular garden tasks comprised the watering of plants and trees, weeding, and planting trees in what was probably the parkland as well as in the 'wilderness'. In 1792 the Reverend Swete painted several views of Nutwell and these show a house with a lawn drawing up to its walls, while paths and walkways run through the overhanging woodland behind (see figures 5–11). It would appear from this that Sir Francis had been a follower of the newer garden style which embraced natural forms of nature in preference to the geometric lines and topiary prevalent in the early 1700s. It would have been these changes that Rowe was meant to oversee in the 1750s.[17]

Rowe informed his employer of various difficulties, such as the rabbits consuming the flowers in the shrubbery or the birds, flies, mice, and wasps eating the fruit. Rats were compared to an Egyptian plague and Rowe was even suspicious of earthworms. Perhaps the most informative garden references are those which mention the acquisition of plants. Some of these arrived in baskets. Trees were periodically transported from London. On one occasion there is a mention of 'flower roots'; on another, cantaloupe seeds were acquired from 'Mr Miller'. This is likely to have been Philip Miller, the aforementioned chief gardener at the Chelsea Physic Garden and author of *The Gardeners Dictionary*, which had been relatively recently published. In one letter, written in 1756, Rowe referred to having consulted Miller's dictionary in regard to the sowing of seeds from London (F336).

Plants arrived not only by wagon but also by sea. On one occasion in 1756 vines were brought in a ship from Gallipoli, and unloaded at Dartmouth. Four years later, two orange trees arrived at Nutwell from Dartmouth. It is unclear whether vines and oranges were brought from there by sea or transported on land.

It is also unclear whether the citrus trees were planted in pots and brought inside, in a glass house, or set outside in the open air. South Devon was particularly associated with citrus growing during the eighteenth and nineteenth centuries. There were local parallels for all these forms of planting at places such as Knowle, Mount Edgcumbe, Powderham Castle, Combe Royal, and the Moult.[18] It was also at this time that a few miles to the north, at Exeter, a gentlemen planted citrus trees outside against his cob wall. In 1761 a visitor reported to a friend that:

> I must tell you of a curiosity of 2 lemon trees in a gentleman's garden here. He has raised them from seed himself, they are growing against the walls & rails up like a peach tree and spreads a great way. At this time there is very large lemons as big as any Lisbon you ever saw quite ripe, some green and many blossoms. He finds himself in juice and has made presents and has had some that weighed 16 ounces. You smell them as soon as you enter the garden before you see them. He has a sash to draw them in winter.[19]

Sir Francis may well have heard of this successful fruiting.

It is perhaps not surprising that the correspondence shows that neighbouring estates supplied plants. Broccoli seeds, a plant then recently introduced into England

[17] *Travels in Georgian Devon*, vol. 4, pp. 147–149.
[18] Gray, *Art of the Devon Garden*, pp. 270–273, 312–315.
[19] Bedfordshire Record Office, M10/2/136.

from Italy, were sent in 1762 from the Powderham estate, which lies only two miles away across the Exe estuary. There are surprisingly few other references to the Courtenay family, other than the offer of an Alderney cow from the estate and the death of Lady Fanny Courtenay at Bath.[20] Two other gardens along the estuary also provided plants and this was done during changes of ownership; the plants were not acquired in a trade but the gardens were searched for interesting specimens and used as nurseries.[21]

Sir John Colleton's famed garden at Exmouth was one of these local sources. His family had held land in South Carolina from the 1600s and his son's estate there was called Exmouth. Sir John lived near Nutwell in the manor house at Withycombe Raleigh in Exmouth; he died in 1754.[22] Four years earlier, in 1750, a visitor had noted that Colleton

> had a garden full of curious plants chiefly from America ... He has the magnolia or lawrel-leav'd tulip [*Magnolia grandiflora* L. Poir] in blossom and also the Carolina sword-blade aloe; he has also the trumpet tree [possibly *Cecropia peltata*], the Carolina raspberry tree [possibly *Morus rubra*], the anemone tree, and Carolina kidney bean tree [*Wisteria frutescens*], the artichoke or orange myrtle [possibly *Citrus myrtifolia*], the flowers of which are in clusters and of a reddish cast, a beautiful turn cap'd Carolina Martagon [*Lilium Carolinianum*] which is red and white, the motle-leav'd tulip tree which seems to be only the occidental plane-tree, the serpentine euphorbium, the coat of which resembles the scales of a serpent, but it is very much raised.[23]

The year after Colleton's death, Rowe informed Sir Francis that plants from the garden were offered by the gardener of Thomas Hull, who lived at Marpool Hall, also in Exmouth. Four years later, Rowe continued to have a connection with the garden through the subsequent owner. Philip Miller had seen Colleton's magnolia and reckoned that it was the largest in England.[24]

---

[20] Powderham Castle also had a collection of unusual plants. In 1800 it was reported that the Norfolk Island hibiscus (*Lagunaria patersonia*) flowered for the first time at the castle. It was noted as being part of the viscount's 'collection' in H. C. Andrews, *The Botanist's Repository for New and Rare Plants,* 10 vols (London: for the author, 1797–1811?), vol. 4, unpaginated.

[21] One writer has misunderstood the relationship between the gardens as outlined in the correspondence: H. Meller, *The Country Houses of Devon,* 2 vols (Crediton, Black Dog Press, 2015), vol. 2, p. 723.

[22] 'The Colleton Family in South Carolina', *South Carolina Historical & Genealogical Magazine* 1(4) (1900), 336–337; S. Lysons and D. Lysons, *Magna Britannia,* vol. 6: *Devon* (London: Thomas Cadell, 1822), p. 560; The National Archives, PROB 11/811/401.

[23] J. J. Cartwright, ed., *The Travels Through England of Dr. Richard Pococke* ([London]: for the Camden Society, 1888), p. 102. The first magnolia to flower in Ireland was recorded in 1767 at Cashal in the garden of Thomas Matthews (*Bath Chronicle*, 8 October 1767).

[24] 'The largest tree of this kind, which I have met with in England, is in the garden of Sir John Colliton of Exmouth in Devonshire, which has produced flowers for several years': P. Miller, *The Gardeners Dictionary, 8th edition* (London: for the author, 1768; first published 1731), 'Magnolia', unpaginated. There may have been another early plant at Ebford, where Mr Lee, who was referred to throughout Rowe's correspondence, had a plant which was established by 1809 (*Exeter Flying Post,* 5 October 1809).

Colleton has been credited with introducing *Magnolia grandiflora* to England as early as 1722[25] and it was as late as 1911 that a large specimen of his *Exmouth* could be found on the site of his garden. The original tree has been thought to have been destroyed in 1794.[26] At Nutwell there was also a magnolia by 1759, there were some 'fine' magnolias forty years later when the Reverend Swete visited, and John Claudius Loudon recorded a *Magnolia grandiflora* standing at 25 feet high in 1841.[27]

In late autumn 1759, following a cold April, Rowe and Sir Francis corresponded on the use of mats for protecting magnolias from frost. Rowe pointed out that those planted at Powderham Castle and in Colleton's Exmouth garden had always been uncovered during the winter. Sir Francis was probably mindful of the destruction caused in 1739 when magnolias across England died from the cold weather. Few nurserymen sold magnolias immediately afterwards but they had become available in Exeter by 1779.[28] In addition, Rowe's correspondence noted that Nutwell had a raspberry tree by 1756; this may have been sourced from Colleton's garden.

Nutwell was also acquiring plants from Mamhead, the large and significant estate lying five miles across the estuary. The Ball family held the property from the sixteenth century until 1749 and it was well known that they had furnished the grounds with Mediterranean plants. In 1755 the estate was inherited by Wilmot Vaughan, 4th Viscount Lisburne, and Rowe noted his arrival in July 1756. For nearly 18 months prior to his coming, Sir Francis's gardener had been visiting the estate and procuring plants. In the midst of this plundering, by November 1755, the gardener at Mamhead was dismissed. Rowe wrote that he had 'pulled up all the flowering shrubs and flung them away' (F326). Nutwell's gardener filled up various parts of the garden with Mamhead plants and he continued to visit Mamhead after the viscount came into residence: the latter gave instructions to allow Drake's gardener to 'have anything there', which included not only seeds but trees (F286). In January 1758, for example, he visited to procure white elder.

In his letters Rowe chronicled that Nutwell had rowans, laurels, planes, and 'evergreen' (holm) oaks (*Quercus ilex*, 1755); Newfoundland (balsam) fir (*Abies balsamea*), larches, weeping willow, raspberry trees (possibly *Morus rubra*), strawberry trees (*Arbutus unedo*), cedars, and *Cistus* (1756); cypress (1757); black poplars (*Populus nigra*, 1758); barberries (*Berberis*, 1759); orange trees (*Citrus sinensis*, 1760); Weymouth pines (*Pinus strobus*, 1761); 'Spanish Nuts' and white fig (*Ficus carica*, 1762); myrtle (*Myrtus communis*, 1763); Scotch firs, otherwise known as Scots pine (*Pinus sylvestris*, 1765); and *Phillyrea* (1766). His letters also reveal that there were honeysuckles, roses, grape vines, tuberose (*Polianthes tuberosa*), and *Daphne mezereum*. Many plants were simply referred to as shrubs or wall plants.

Sir Francis was keen to hear about the progress of his vegetables, including Savoy cabbage, artichokes, and broccoli. He had soft fruit in the garden such as gooseberries, strawberries, and currants. Rowe informed him of the state of his

[25] *Exeter & Plymouth Gazette*, 7 January 1949.
[26] J. F. Chanter, 'Exmouth – Sir John Colliton', *Devon & Cornwall Notes & Queries* 11(1) (1921), 146, 209, 260–261; *The Magic Tree* (Exeter: compiled by NCCPG group, 1989), p. 69.
[27] *Travels in Georgian Devon*, vol. 4, pp. 147–149; J. C. Loudon, 'Notices of Some Gardens and Country Seats in Somersetshire, Devonshire and Part of Cornwall', *Gardener's Magazine* 19 (1843), 239.
[28] Miller, *Gardeners Dictionary*, 'Magnolia'; *Bath Chronicle*, 11 November 1779. Joseph Ford's nursery was near the new bridge over the Exe in St Thomas.

cantaloupes and melons, which were grown variously under glass, in frames, on mats, and in hot beds.

Fruit growing was continually reported. Drake had apples, apricots, cherries, figs (including white), peaches, pears (including Windsor and Bergamot), and plums. Rowe provided particularly good details on the growing of apples for use at the table or for cider making. He had Herefordshire grafts in 1758 and that same year acquired another four bundles of grafts for the cider varieties White and Red Styre, Foxwhelp, and Redstreak. Rowe does not mention local varieties such as the Royal Wilding (or Red Hill Crab) or Whitesour. Sir Francis was interested in fruit growing, although not as deeply as had been Sir Courtenay Pole at Shute.[29]

The Nutwell fruit trees were grown as standards in orchards as well as espaliers and wall fruit. There are many references to the latter, including in November 1754, when Rowe informed Drake:

> The Gardiner has Layd the Walk next the upper Wall, & is forward in that against the new Wall; he has planted Several Pears, but can't Find No. IX as directed by the paper you left him – But the Label Lay in the passage Window, So presumes you forgot it. (F290)

Introductions of another type, probably a consequence of the local connections with Canadian fishing, were also made to Nutwell. 'Newfoundland' geese were brought to the estate by 1755. These were possibly *Branta Canadensis*, which are now better known as Canada geese, but they may have been one of another seven types of Newfoundland geese. Drake's geese were at first confined to the chapel court but were afterwards kept during the day in the best garden in order for them to have access to water. Shortly thereafter it was noted that they had become tame, but there were concerns that the geese were picking at trees and might cause damage. This was confirmed weeks later: they were not only harming the trees but digging up the grass paths and the sides of the canal. Within a year there were plans to remove them to Buckland Abbey. In 1765 two Newfoundland dogs were also brought to the house. Rowe was apprehensive of them. He wrote:

> Your Newfoundland Dogs are Chain'd up & put in their Houses in the Court by the House Door, They are so Fierce, They are not to be Ventur'd Loose Till your Gates are secur'd, & some Door to the Drying Ground, as the Hedge is all Coming Down, and was They or Either of Them to seize any Person, they'd pull Them to pieces. Mr Lee's Dogs are Nothing to 'Em. (F471)

Rowe professed to be personally ignorant of gardening and in 1754 and 1755 repeatedly used the same phrase in relation to it: 'As to your Gardiner, he works, but I am no Judge how well' (F295); 'As to the progress your Gardiner makes, I am no Judge' (F311); 'as to artificial naturals, I am no Judge' (F314); 'as to your Garden

---

[29] T. Gray, 'Walled Gardens and the Cultivation of Orchard Fruits in the South-West of England', in C. Anne Wilson, ed., *The Country House Kitchen Garden, 1600–1950* (Stroud: Sutton Publishing, 1998), pp. 114–128; T. Gray, 'Their Idols of Worship: Fruit Trees and the Walled Garden in Early Modern Devon', in Stephen Pugsley, ed., *Devon Gardens* (Stroud: Sutton Publishing, 1994), p. 37.

I am no Judge, your Operator promises mighty Things' (F317); and finally 'As to your garden I am no Judge, Therefore may be mistaken, you'l distinguish presently whether I am or no' (F319). In 1754 he had expressed the desire to have Solomon's skills with plants but admitted 'I am a Stranger to Everything, but the Shrub, an Emblem of your humble Servant' (F277). In another letter of 1750 he wrote that 'For my part I am only a looker on, admiring the Wisdom of the present Generation, Tho' I don't understand it' (F221).

This did not hinder Rowe from expressing firm opinions on the estate's gardeners. One was described as being not only flashy and foolish but also a little too forward. Solomon, who had progressed from assisting the gardener to taking over his duties, was a married man, and his wife assisted in weeding. Six years later Rowe complained that Sol was a drunkard:

> Your Man Sol has been at Work all this week, & has done more in the Garden Than for several Past; had his been a Sickness acquir'd by any means but Drunkeness, I wou'd [sic] assisted him to the utmost, but Such a Debauch deserv'd none, neither had he any of me … (F449)

Moreover, he termed Sol's wife, Hannah, 'a vile strumpet'. Rowe was unsure whether his behaviour arose from stupidity or stubbornness but the consequence was that there was no garden produce.

In 1766 Rowe wrote with the news that a subsequent gardener was not only in a drunken state but had a more serious condition:

> Your Gardiner being Old, Poor, & in Distress I had a Compassion for Him, and wou'd not Trouble you with his bad Behaviour, as to Drinking, Being in hopes that he wou'd amend: as he kep't the Garden Clean & Stock't, hoped he would make up for what he had Done amiss. Mr Turney Thought as you wou'd be Soon Down, to Leave him to your Pleasure – But Yesterday Morning he Broke out into Madness, & So Continues; at Intervals he is very Sensible & Says he is not able to do your Business, so Desires to go Directly, & will trye to get up in the Waggon – He desires two Guineas to bare his Expences, & my Letter to you; in it I can't Say much in his Favour, only that when he did not Break out, he was up Early at his [Wor]k, but 3 or 4 Times he was out Late; Particularly last Friday night and Since then his insanity has appear'd – Whatever you intend by way of reprimand, or Otherwise, when he waits upon you, must be left to your Goodness – I fear some great Trouble attends Him. (F477)

Rowe added that the difficulties continued: he was concerned about Sol's presence at Nutwell. Other men were also employed in the garden, including Hercules Moore, and his son Thomas, whose main work lay in pruning and grafting.[30]

The Veitch family became involved at Nutwell following Sir Francis's death. This included producing a report on the plantations and woodland in 1819, in which John Veitch wrote that the planting was too thick and recommended thinning.[31] A storm in

---

[30] One of the subsequent gardeners was James Lawrie, who had died by 1839: The National Archives, PROB 11/1909/330.
[31] DHC 346M/E386.

1866 further reduced the number of trees, including well-established cedars.[32] Even so, Nutwell remained principally known for its trees. In 1805 the visitor William Bray wrote:

> We went in a chaise to see Lord Heathfield's at Nutwell, through lanes shaded by lofty elms, over Topsham Bridge. The house in a most beautiful dip, between swelling grounds, shaded by lofty noble trees, commanding the river Exe and the woods of Powderham and Mamhead on the opposite side of the river.[33]

Most visitors similarly complimented the estate for its trees.

Rowe's letters are littered with references to planting trees, and Sir Francis might well have been satisfied with the description of Nutwell made just over a century after his death. A writer in *The Garden* noted it as 'a delightful old tree garden'.[34] A tree associated with Sir Francis Drake stood at Buckland Abbey until 1929 and another at Northernhay in Exeter was known as 'The Lady Drake's Tree' in the early 1700s,[35] but the Drake family's lasting sylvan legacy remains the woodland at Nutwell that was replanted and nurtured by Sir Francis Henry Drake during the mid-eighteenth century.

---

[32] *Exeter & Plymouth Gazette*, 19 January 1866.
[33] Surrey Record Office, 85/2/5, p. 251.
[34] *The Garden* 54(1411) (28 May 1898), 449.
[35] DHC ECA, D1828; T. Gray, *Lost Devon* (Exeter: Mint Press, 2003), p. 134.

5. Healthways and Two Eighteenth-Century Devonshire Estates

John Crellin

5.1 Introduction

The disastrous effects of such eighteenth-century scourges as smallpox and other infectious conditions are commonly noted in general accounts of the 1700s. In contrast, the snapshots of health and illness found in the Drake letters focus more on self-limiting and chronic illnesses, albeit with hovering fears of life-threatening situations.[1] Thus Nicholas Rowe wrote to Sir Francis on 9 June 1752:

> I found [Mr Porter] a Bed under a Surgeon's operation; his Malady pro-
> ceeded from a pimple which rose in his seat after Riding, it turn'd to a
> Boil, which encreas'd to the Bredth of one's Hand ... (F226)

In weaving together excerpts from the letters with background notes, this account considers: home care and choices of practitioners; maintaining personal health; some specific medical conditions; and treatments. In so doing, a key consideration is an individual's approach to health, thus adding to the growing historical literature that focuses on patients' attitudes, beliefs, and practices that are not necessarily time-bound.[2]

Additionally, the letters from the apothecary William Hudson spotlight the intriguing transition of apothecaries to general medical practitioners, while those

---

[1] Short-term and chronic illness have not been ignored in the specialist history of medicine literature; for an example with a focus on south-west England in an earlier but not irrelevant period to the Drake correspondence, see A. Stobart, *Household Medicine in Seventeenth-Century England* (London: Bloomsbury Academic, 2016).

[2] A specific focus on patients, rather than practitioners, institutions, and medical science, accelerated after such publications as D. Porter and R. Porter, *Patient's Progress: Doctors and Doctoring in Eighteenth-Century England* (Cambridge: Polity Press, 1989); and M. E. Fissel, *Patients, Power, and the Poor in Eighteenth-Century Bristol* (Cambridge: Cambridge University Press, 1991). Various questions are asked about patients, some considered in a relatively recent review: M. Bashin, E. Dietrich-Daum, and I. Ritzmann, 'Doctors and Their Patients in the Seventeenth to Nineteenth Centuries', *Clio Medica* 96 (2016), 39–70. Particular interest exists in collections of letters written by patients to physicians requesting help by correspondence. However, such letters, while detailed, reflect measured editing and organisation, often with loss of spontaneity and context found in correspondence such as the Drake collection. For a contrasting accessible collection of patients' letters (to the renowned physician William Cullen), see The Cullen Project: The Medical Consultation Letters of Dr William Cullen, http://www.cullenproject.ac.uk/ (accessed July 2018). It should be added that, although the term 'patients' was well established and used in the eighteenth century, it is not always clear when the majority of individuals saw themselves as dependent, rather than seeing a practitioner as an adviser and extension of self-care.

from Nicholas Rowe prompt questions as to whether the quality of medical care and the impact of illness on business and society in rural Britain differed significantly from London and other growing urban areas. Even though Rowe's letters offer no specific answers, the context of a rural–urban divide, seen as a growing issue in the 1700s, should be borne in mind. It was even reflected in the opening lines of the poet-physician Mark Akenside's 'Ode to Sir Francis Henry Drake, Baronet':

> I.
>
> Behold! the Balance in the sky
> Swift on the wintry scale inclines:
> To earthy caves the Dryads fly,
> And the bare pastures Pan resigns.
> Late did the farmer's fork o'erspread
> With recent soil the twice-mown mead,
> Tainting the bloom which autumn knows:
> He whets the rusty coulter now,
> He binds his oxen to the plough,
> And wide his future harvest throws.
>
> II.
>
> Now, London's busy confines round,
> By Kensington's imperial tow'rs,
> From Highgate's rough descent profound,
> Essexian heaths, or Kentish bow'rs,
> Where'er I pass, I see approach
> Some rural statesman's eager coach ...[3]

5.2 Home Care and Choices of Practitioners

Nicholas Rowe's letters from 1740 to late 1775 reveal him as a close family friend of the Drake family, and, seemingly, a father figure to Sir Francis while serving him in countless ways at Buckland and Nutwell. Although he described himself as 'overseer', Rowe's unending responsibilities were primarily a labour of love, while he suffered from endless bouts of ill health.[4] He only occasionally mentioned medical practitioners, but, as with virtually everyone else, self-treatment was almost certainly part of his life. Similarities between his childhood home and other well-established families likely existed, including that of Sir Francis, whose mother, Lady

---

[3]   This is from the revised version of the ode, first published in J. Dyson, ed., *The Poems of Mark Akenside, M. D.* (London: Bowyer, 1772), 271–275, a volume edited by his friend and patron Jeremiah Dyson. Dyson noted (p. iii) that the version was from Akenside's own corrected copy, presumably from a 1754 version, now in the Drake papers (DHC 346M/F17). For an even earlier unpublished version (1750), see 'Ode to Sir Francis Drake Bar^t January, MDCC.XLIX. O.S.', first brought to light in R. M. Williams, 'Two Unpublished Poems by Mark Akenside', *Modern Language Notes* 57 (1942), 626–631. For invaluable context to the odes, see H. Jump, 'Mark Akenside and the Poetry of Current Events 1738–1770', DPhil thesis, University of Oxford (1987), pp. 155–170, 246–256. See also Introduction, section 1, p. 6, above.

[4]   'I am a very poor Overseer' (6 November 1754, F291).

Anne Drake, probably had basic medical knowledge, helped prepare those home medicines that were not purchased, and may well have provided some medical aid to estate workers. Perhaps, too, she passed on medical skills to young Francis.[5] In later years he offered advice to various individuals.[6] Rowe once told him to be his 'own Physician and use those Lenitives, you wou'd prescribe to another' (8 February 1760, F401);[7] and, in the 1770s, the London apothecary William Hudson advised Sir Francis about treatment for certain individuals (see section 5.4 and the appendix below).

Self-sufficiency and self-care only went so far, and a variety of practitioners with diverse educational backgrounds could, depending on taste and fees, be consulted: for instance, physicians, apothecaries, surgeon-apothecaries (commonly apoth-ecaries known for particular skills/reputations in practical procedures but rarely major operations), surgeons (specialists), chemists, druggists, 'mountebanks' (often referred to as quacks), midwives, and 'wise' women, maybe from neighbouring towns or villages.[8] Individuals like Rowe and Sir Francis, unconcerned about fees, could limit themselves to consulting physicians (that is, those with a university MD). Rowe himself attended John Huxham (1692–1768) of Plymouth, not only when residing at Buckland, a half-day or so journey from Plymouth, but also when he was at Nutwell nearer to Exeter. Although Huxham acquired questionable standing

---

[5] While historians of early medical recipes (medical and culinary were commonly included in the same volume) often point out a female lineage for passing on information, contem-porary resources indicate considerable interest among men. See E. Leong, 'Collecting Knowledge for the Family: Recipes, Gender and Practical Knowledge in the Early Modern English Household', *Centaurus* 55 (2013), 81–103. It is likely, though not certain, that the Rowe and Drake households owned an eclectic collection of medical recipes, commonly entered into a single volume, as by the Arscott family at Tetcott, for example, fifty or so miles away (see Wellcome Library MS 981). This includes a cancer treatment from 'Dr Huxham of Plymouth', dated 1743 (fol. 164). (See below, pp. 48, 53–4, 57, 58–9, 63–4, for Huxham.) For discussion of the preparation of home medicines based on a recipe book, see E. Leong, 'Making Medicines in the Early Modern Household', *Bulletin of the History of Medicine* 82 (2008), 145–168. It is unfortunate that not more is known about the relationship between Sir Francis and his mother; there is no indication of a close relationship in later years.

[6] Sir Francis developed a herb garden at Nutwell. Rowe wrote in 1754: 'I saw Mr Ned Chute, who Says he can procure you any Phisical Herbs, & will very readily Do it, if you'l please to Let Him know in writing the Sorts, & in the proper Season' (F276).

[7] It is plausible to suggest that such lenitives (laxatives) were mild ones administered to ensure a general 'cleansing' of the stomach and bowels that, for some, was as much part of maintaining health as treating an illness.

[8] These terms raise the problem of the loose, inconsistent way in which they were used by practitioners and others, including in print. Irvine, in considering rural Suffolk, emphasises this especially with regard to surgeon-apothecaries (S. Irvine, 'Surgeons and Apothecaries in Suffolk: 1750–1830', PhD thesis, University of East Anglia (2011), pp. 72*ff*). In some instances, use of such a title reflected a special area of interest, e.g. surgery among surgeon-apothe-caries; most of them, however, undertook few major operations, their 'bread-and-butter' practice covering venereal and skin diseases, a wide range of localised infections (e.g. ulcers), accidents, and sprains, for which see also I. Loudon, 'The Nature of Provincial Medical Practice in Eighteenth-Century England', *Medical History* 29 (1985), 1–32. The multiplicity of practitioners has been considered by innumerable medical historians and viewed as part of a growing medical 'market place'. Amid a now considerable literature, see M. S. R. Jenner, and P. Wallis, eds, *Medicine and the Market in England and Its Colonies, c. 1450–c. 1850* (Basingstoke: Palgrave Macmillan, 2007).

as a self-centred individual who constantly drew attention to himself, his medical abilities went unquestioned by Rowe, as when he wrote:

> Dr Lavington has Shewn his grateful regard to his deceas't Friend to the last; I wish he had Sooner Taken his Advise & not Conceal'd his Weakness from Him. Dr Huxum did his Utmost – all too Late. (4 December 1753, F246)[9]

Huxham was an interesting choice of practitioner with a growing national and international reputation through his medical publications; moreover, as indicated below, he frequently emerges, if only tangentially, in the Drake story.

Sir Francis's physicians are not documented in the letters. However, during his early years and when he was in Devon, it was probably Huxham. Rowe wrote in February 1755: 'I have seen Dr Huxam who very Cordially Sends you his Compliments & Thanks for your kind Remembrance' (F307). It is also reasonable to assume that, during much of his time as a parliamentarian in London, Sir Francis consulted Mark Akenside until the latter's death in 1770, perhaps because of a close friendship between them, partly reflected in Akenside's odes to Sir Francis.[10]

Like many wealthy individuals, Sir Francis, in addition to consulting physicians, was not averse to advice from apothecaries (or surgeon-apothecaries), whose

---

[9]   That Huxham did achieve the confidence of his 'professional brethren' and public esteem, perhaps aided by changing his religious affiliation from Dissenter to the established Church, was the judgment of William Munk, known as a generally careful compiler of physician biographies (W. Munk, 'Biographica Medica Devoniensis; or Collections towards a History of the Medical Worthies of Devon', *Western Antiquary* 6 (1887), 258–262). Munk also indicates the reputation that Huxham's publications brought him. The negative characterisation of Huxham has been emphasised more recently by W. Schupbach, 'The Fame and Notoriety of Dr John Huxham', *Medical History* 25 (1981), 415–421. Schupbach does not accept the view of R. M. S. McConaghey, 'John Huxham', *Medical History* 13 (1969), 280–287, that the primary negative statement about Huxham is not authentic. It may be that Huxham's concerns with medical investigation reflected the influence of his time as a medical student at Leiden, when the renowned Herman Boerhaave had tremendous influence. The deceased lawyer John Edgcombe was evidently a close friend of Rowe and Sir Francis (see *Family and Heirs*, vol. 2, p. 269). The Dr Lavington mentioned was probably Andrew Lavington (1716–1782), who practised in Tavistock for many years: see *Munks Roll: The Lives of the Fellows of the Royal College of Physicians (1861–)*, vol. 2, p. 143, available at munksroll.rcplondon.ac.uk (accessed July 2018).

[10]   See above, n. 3. *Family and Heirs*, vol. 2, p. 296, identifies Akenside in Rowe's reference to 'the Dr your good Friend' (4 September 1759, F389). Shortly after Sir Francis entered Parliament (1747), Akenside focused on developing his medical career. One letter from Akenside to Drake has survived (dated 27 October 1757, 346M/F18), opening with 'My dear friend'. It is primarily concerned with political matters, but also comments on the health of their mutual friend and Akenside's patron, Jeremiah Dyson. Sir Francis's literary tastes are reflected in his rebuilding of the Nutwell Court chapel as a library, and in his constant collecting, evident in Hudson's letter of March 1771 (12–F192) with its list of natural history and other books he bought for Sir Francis. It would be remiss to omit mention of the scholarly interpretation of a homosexual relationship between Akenside and Dyson, hence a possible factor in Sir Francis's own character. However, evidence is tenuous and twenty-first-century attitudes cannot be extrapolated back to the 1700s. For a critical review of some literature interpreting the homosexuality of Akenside, see R. Dix, *The Literary Career of Mark Akenside* (Madison, NJ: Fairleigh Dickinson University Press, 2006), Appendix 3. For an introduction to Akenside's medical career, see R. Dix, 'A Newly Discovered Manuscript Dedication by Mark Akenside', *Medical History* 53(3) (2009), 425–432.

core education was through apprenticeship. In fact, he developed a multi-layered relationship with the apothecary William Hudson, covering medical advice, supply of medicines, and business and personal affairs, and as a confidant in London gossip.

Although it might be easy to dismiss Hudson as a mere apothecary, the mid-eighteenth century had seen the virtual end of many decades of tortuous relationships between physicians and apothecaries, with the emergence of the latter as essentially the country's general medical practitioners while they continued to run their apothecary shops and dispense physicians' prescriptions. Hudson typifies this, although he was more than a common-or-garden apothecary and probably escaped long-standing criticism of apothecaries who, while practising medicine, left dispensing in the hands of apprentices and assistants, thus opening themselves to charges of mistakes and inferior-quality medicines.[11] As a highly regarded botanist and naturalist (elected a Fellow of the Royal Society in 1761) with an extensive knowledge of gardens, Hudson helped with a variety of plantings for developing the grounds at Nutwell. He was well connected in London society, with seemingly a substantial medical practice. He noted in a letter of autumn 1768: 'I have been a good deel hurried for this week past having patients out of Town where I have been obliged to go every day' (4–F186).[12]

One of his patients, Jeremiah Dyson, the friend and patron of Mark Akenside and a well-known parliamentarian, followed the pattern of consulting apothecaries *and* physicians, one of the latter being the eminent physician William Heberden, another friend of Akenside and likely of Sir Francis too. Heberden is of peripheral interest to the Drake medical story as a reminder of variations in prescribing, sometimes to suit the social standing of the patient. For instance, not long after Heberden had denounced the celebrated, expensive medicine mithridatium as valueless, Hudson prescribed it for Sir Francis.[13]

Given that, as one historian has noted, apothecaries/surgeon-apothecaries were, during the 1700s, consulted by a wide range of the public even for relatively minor

[11] The criticism increased during the stormy relations between physicians and apothecaries towards the end of the seventeenth century. While fading thereafter, it was ultimately an indirect factor in many apothecaries closing 'open' shops, and turning to consultation and dispensing: see J. K. Crellin and J. R. Scott, *Glass and British Pharmacy 1600–1900* (London: Wellcome Institute of the History of Medicine, 1972), p. 3.

[12] Biographical notices of Hudson view him primarily as a botanist, with cursory mention of his role as an apothecary. See the entry in the *ODNB* and contemporary notes by R. Pulteney, *Historical and Biographical Sketches of Progress of Botany in England*, 2 vols (London: Cadell, 1790), vol. 2, pp. 351–352. The rising eighteenth-century social status of apothecaries has been noted by various authors: see, for instance, P. J. Corfield, 'From Poison Peddlers to Civic Worthies: The Reputation of Apothecaries in Georgian England', *Social History of Medicine* 22(1) (2009), 1–21; J. G. L. Burnby, 'A Study of the English Apothecary from 1660–1760 with Special Reference to the Provinces', PhD thesis, University of London (1979). For comments regarding the early seventeenth century, see also D. Levitin, '"Made up from Many Experimentall Notions": The Society of Apothecaries, Medical Humanism and the Rhetoric of Experience in 1630s London', *Journal of the History of Medicine and Allied Sciences* 70 (2015), 549–587.

[13] Mark Akenside was also involved in Dyson's health care. Heberden castigated mithridatium, with its long history of a sovereign remedy, in *Antitheriaka: An Essay on Mithridatium and Theriaca* (n.p., 1745), with such comments as: 'destitute of all its celebrated virtues is forced to take refuge in that of a diaphoretic, which is commonly the virtue of a medicine that has none' (p. 10). It is unlikely that Hudson was unacquainted with Heberden's work and the many other critiques of the preparation.

ailments, one might anticipate that Sir Francis arranged for a local apothecary to provide necessary care of estate workers.[14] However, no evidence for this has been found for those employed for specific or seasonal tasks, nor even for two long-time workers for whom Drake likely had some moral, if not legal, responsibility, namely Sol, an estate factotum in the development of the Nutwell grounds and garden, and the housekeeper, Betty Dyer, both of whom appear to have had some independence in decision-making, perhaps because of past connections with the Drake family.[15] Once Dyer had to plead for Sir Francis's benevolence to deal with her long-term leg problem, said to be made worse by long periods of standing:

> I have been under the surgenes hand allmost this 9 munths who says if I stand and walk on my leg as I now am oblidged to do I shall never be well. I have a long bill to pay and he very well deserves more then I am capable of paying him. I have wrought harder in your honner's service ...
> (28 January 1757, F356)

Dyer went on to indicate that, owing to her lengthy service to Sir Francis, she was in 'great danger of making my self uncapable of service any more and then I must be very unhappy having no other way of getting my living'.

Subsequent correspondence is silent on the matter, but Dyer remained until around 1759, likely with financial help for medical expenses and with the assistance of a maid.[16] Maybe at times she did not help herself by irritating Rowe, who, it seems, had a generally poor opinion of servants: 'There is no Sense of Gratitude in Servants' (16 January 1756, F330).[17] He certainly had little sympathy for Sol's medical problems, which he attributed to excessive drinking: 'Had his been a Sickness acquir'd by any means but Drunkeness, I wou'd [sic] assisted him to the utmost, but such a Debauch deserv'd none, neither had he any of me' (10 May 1762, F449).[18] Rowe did, nevertheless, recognise that Sol's wife, sometimes staying

[14] See Loudon, 'Nature of Provincial Medical Practice'.

[15] For a customary legal and moral responsibility to provide medical care for servants, see C. Crawford, 'Patients' Rights and the Law of Contract in Eighteenth-Century England', *Social History of Medicine* 13 (2000), 381–410. But there is at least one instance where Rowe suggests Sir Francis's likely 'preventative' help: 'Sol's Boy is now at Home doing nothing; if you wou'd be so good to Take the Boy, it wou'd be Saving him from Ruine & want' (9 February 1753, F236).

[16] Rowe wrote on 21 July 1758: 'Betty Dyer is as She was, has Taken Phisick again, wants your Leave to go down to See Her Relations once more, will be wanting but a week' (F380). Economic difficulties impinging on health undoubtedly beset other workers on the estate. For instance, Rowe wrote to Sir Francis that 'Your Man Solomon is Still with Hannah, She came here yesterday to Complain he has nothing to help Himself & is, as She Says, Dying of a Dropsy, having not been able to work these Five weeks' (7 January 1763, F460).

[17] Thus Betty Dyer's insistence that Rowe's directives came from Sir Francis himself possibly frustrated Rowe. Dyer also once complained when Sol's wife was expected to stay in the house (2 June 1754, F269). Later, after Sir Francis had intervened over wages, Rowe felt obliged to write to him: 'I am Sorry she continues in her obstinacy' (16 December 1757, F370). For another comment on servants: 'I am very Sorry Alexander is such an ungrateful Fellow, But servants are all so; his Relation here [Sol] wou'd be I fear the same, had he any Pretence' (21 July 1758, F380).

[18] At times Sol's behaviour, presumably linked to drinking, evidently caused Rowe angst. Aside from unscheduled absences, one occasion was: 'Sol return'd last Friday Evening from his mad Expedition to Buckland; the Butcher to whom he Sold the Bullocks, came here a

at Nutwell to work at weeding, was valuable in helping him limit his habit.[19] It is unclear whether Rowe felt that generally living away from his family contributed to Sol's drinking, or even to episodes of 'apoplexy', for which Sir Francis, maybe with the advice of a practitioner, provided Sol with 'Powders' (name and composition unknown). Rowe once reported: 'I have given Sol the Powders you Sent, who Takes 'Em as you direct. He has no Fit since you went' (14 May 1756, F336).[20]

If Rowe was less sensitive over health issues suffered by those working on the estates than in his feelings for Sir Francis (see below), it likely reflected character-istics ranging from his uncomplimentary views of servants, placing them among the 'vulgar' as distinct from the 'better sort', to his own sense of self-sufficiency,[21] the latter evidently laced with stoicism, as over his own bouts of colic (see section 5.3), and with a fatalist attitude more evident as he grew older ('whilst we think we Stand Secure, we may Fall'; F222).[22] Perhaps stoicism, even though he openly complained about and sometimes wallowed in his ills, was at play in what must have been one of fairly frequent accidents that interrupted work on the Nutwell estate:

> Last Saturday forenoon I unaccountably Fell into the Tank at the End of the Orchard, which brings in the Water to the Garden; had the Tonkin been in, I must inevitably have been Drown'd, and tho' there was no Water, I sunk so Deep in the Mudd, That I cou'd neither move hand nor Foot, & shou'd have been Suffocated (21 January 1757, F354).

Rowe went on to indicate that it was mere chance that he was rescued:

> Else I might have Layn God knows how Long as I cou'd not help myself. I am much Bruis'd & my head hurt, But God be Thanked no Dislocation nor Broken bone, a Mercy I hope I shall always remember with Thankfulnes.[23]

Monday to Enquire after Him, and threatens to Trouble Him about the Bargain, 'tis well your Service protects Him, or he'd be in a Scrape, But if your Reprimand don't restrain him from Drinking, he'l be fit for nothing' (25 February 1757, F360).

[19] 'What I wrote you about Sol was upon great Reason, But I hope he'l repent & Reform – But as he has little victuals and Less Drink, when he gets any given, he uses it to Excess, & I fear unless he has his Wife to keep him Regular, He'l break out again' (13 February 1756, F332). Life was not easy for Sol's wife; Rowe had written earlier: 'As to Sol, I hope he won't offend so again, and as his Wife's Stay will be Short, as he Says, Betty Dyer will Dispense with Her, But it can't be Convenient for her Long, nor for Them neither, as the Woman Leaves 3 young Children to a Nurse – Indeed the Weed is much over-run in the Gardens, & she Clears it apace' (June 1754, F272).

[20] With reference to Sol's apoplexy or fits, Rowe wrote: 'Sol & the Tinner [have b]een Both Ill Since their Return, the [1st wi]th An apoplex, the Other with the Rheumatism, But he's now Digging Gravel' (8 November 1754, F292).

[21] For the social distinction of the vulgar and the better sort, see for instance the letter of 6 June 1754 (F270).

[22] Another comment reflecting acceptance of fate followed an unspecified 'accident': 'There, you see how soon & by what small Instruments a Humane Creature may be demolish'd – Even a bare Bodkin may do the Business' (15 May 1752, F224); similarly, ''tis quite indifferent to me where the tree Falls' (9 February 1753, F236).

[23] Rowe was not silent about the accident: 'My Fall has so Disorder'd me, That I am uncapable of anything, my head is so Jarr'd, which disables me from Writing my Back still Bad, and I have Scarse a whole part about me, which must be an apology for Sending you Such Scraps as the Enclos'd' (28 January 1757, F357).

Since uncertainty was a constant feature of medical care, it can be assumed that, along with growing wealth and increased consultations with practitioners, numerous occasions of false hope of a cure existed. Rowe, however, perhaps appreciated the limitations of medical knowledge when he once mused: 'But I hope in God I Shall get over it, as the Weather grows Warmer without the Help of any Physitian, who can give no Relief to me. I am my Own Doctor' (18 February 1757, F359).[24] And another time Rowe was under the 'Care not Cure of two Honest Chirurgeons', probably surgeon-apothecaries (17 December 1758, F381).

If a patient's particular outlook – perhaps religious faith, stoicism, or fatalism – helped to frame the way that he or she understood and coped with particular conditions, then care and treatment could vary. Particular idiosyncrasies could be significant, accounting for choice of, or mistrust of, practitioners. Jeremiah Dyson was perhaps one such patient. In 1771 Hudson told Sir Francis about Dyson's 'hypochondriacal symptoms' (16 November 1771, 15–F169), while later implying that Dyson imagined them:

> Mr Dyson came to Town yesterday morning in order to see Dr Heberdon and returned this morning. He is very well and indeed as much so as he will be, could he be brought to think so, but unhappily he has taken a different turn and finds out complaints which don't exist, and distresses himself so much that I only wonder he is so well as is. He is dissatisfied with himself and everybody else – indeed he makes himself truely miserable. (20 July 1775, 25–F173)[25]

5.3 Maintaining Personal Health

Rowe's approaches to maintaining health seemingly followed well-established, common-place knowledge, though, given his education, this was probably reinforced or adapted from reading popular medical books. Thus, in following long-standing views linking health to the effects of the environment on individual constitutions, he made clear the need to avoid or mitigate inclement weather, fatigue, alcohol, and certain emotions, while pursuing friendships and exercise.[26] That he did not refer to

---

[24] Although Rowe provides no clear indication that religious belief was a *significant* part of his approach to health care, it must be said that, for most people at the time, religious faith continued to be inextricably linked to their health, ranging from sin as a cause of disease to interventions from God in a 'cure'. God could work through nature, but physicians, long held to have assisted God, were increasingly accepted as having the primary role.

[25] I have used the word 'imagined' for 'complaints which don't exist'. For changing meanings of hypochondriasis from a somatic disorder to one of the mind, see R. Noyes, Jr, 'The Transformation of Hypochondriasis in British Medicine, 1680–1830', *Social History of Medicine* 24(2) (2011), 281–298. The History of Parliament member biography for Dyson, historyofparliament.org (accessed July 2018), outlines Dyson's parliamentary career and notes health issues. Mark Akenside also offered early evidence of Dyson's long history of ill health in his letter to Sir Francis (see n. 10): 'Dyson has [been] very poorly ever since you left us, with a very troublesome sort of Arthritis vaga & other bad complaints.'

[26] In all likelihood, Rowe was in tune with the thinking of Huxham, although not from reading the '3rd Volume of Dr Huxum' that he could not find in the spring of 1756 (F335). This was Rowe's only reference to a medical book, one that may have belonged to Sir Francis. Reference to a third volume is unclear, as only two volumes of Huxham's *Observationum de*

equally well-known advice on, for instance, diet and sleep was probably because such matters did not arise when corresponding.

The weather

Rowe constantly noted the weather – cold, storms, heat – when it affected farming, the development of Nutwell gardens, building work, and travel arrangements, as well as the 'inconstancy and inclemency of the seasons' that, as many physicians advised, had to be guarded against to avoid a spectrum of health problems.[27] Cold temperatures were considered by practitioners and the public alike to be avoided as much as possible since they were linked to numerous ailments. Rowe once complained: 'It is very Rough Cold weather here, & very Unseasonable & Unhealthy, I hope you take Care of Catching Cold' (15 April 1743, F204). His physician, Huxham, in upholding this view, supported a long-standing belief that cold suppressed regular perspiration, resulting in the retained 'perspirabile' becoming 'acrid'; this could then lead to such conditions as 'pass under the general name of scorbutic, as well as more immediately of catarrhs, squinzies, peripneumonies, fluxes, colics, &c, which are notoriously the effects of suppressed perspiration'.[28]

Rowe found cold weather an exceptional burden, once admitting that he needed to take care of his 'carkass' after his 'old Companion the Cholic did not Relish the Severe Turn of Weather, or my getting a Cold in the Snow gave me Some particular Twitches' (15 February 1754, F261). Other specific frustrations were 'an Easterly wind for Some Days, the Glass at Set Fair But very Cold', which added to his other discomforts (lameness was mentioned from time to time) by causing 'a Violent pain in my Back which is Scarse Tollerable!' (10 December 1756, F352), and, a short while later, cold compounded his troublesome pain: 'the very Cold Weather pinches me much, I was never so sensible of Winter Before' (7 January 1757, F353). Yet another *cri de coeur* arose when

> a Chil, which I never Felt before, added to a dead pain in my head gives me more uneasiness than the general pain in & Thro'out – There, warm Weather may do, what I am Sure the Cold do's not. (4 February 1757, F358)

Aēre et Morbis Epidemicis had appeared, in Latin, by 1756. Other publications were single volumes. An occasional incidental remark from Rowe hints that Huxham made clear the importance of attention to careful living, for instance: 'Thomas Reed is got over his late Disorder for this Time, But Dr Huxum Says he must be very Careful' (8 March 1751, F222). Huxham's investigative mindset and study of the environment with respect to disease may have been stimulated during his medical education at Leiden, where Herman Boerhaave had a tremendous influence on the many students who went there.

[27] George Cheyne, *Essay of Health and Long Life, 9th edition* (London: Strahan, 1745), p. 179. Elsewhere Cheyne notes 'injuries of the weather' (p. 100). His book was one of the popular guides to health at the time; the ninth edition is used here, as being contemporary with Rowe's concerns.

[28] Huxham became renowned for his systematic recording of the weather over many years, along with the concurrent outbreaks of disease. He noted the concept of suppressed perspiration a number of times, this quote being from *Dissertation on the Malignant, Ulcerous Sore-Throat, 3rd edition* (London: Hinton, 1759), p. 16. It was written in the context of wondering whether the outbreaks of ulcerous sore throat (for which see below, section 5.4) were associated with weather patterns. For an overview of the concept of blocked pores, see E. T. Renbourn, 'The Natural History of Insensible Perspiration: A Forgotten Doctrine of Health and Disease', *Medical History* 4(2) (1960), 135–152.

Unsurprisingly, Rowe reminded Sir Francis (forewarned is forearmed) about the potential dangers of inclement weather. 'Very melancholy wet Weather' (10 July 1752, F230) was a particular concern for him, since he felt that it could foster or exacerbate 'lowness' of spirits. He worried constantly about Sir Francis falling into this more serious and debilitating state than temporary melancholy associated with an unhappy or sad occasion: 'for Godsake no Such Melancholy imaginations as to yourself' (16 January 1756, F330) and 'That you so Soon in Life shou'd have Such Frequent uneasinesses is very Melancholy indeed' (22 July 1757, F368).

Rowe clearly appreciated that a melancholy state, a not unfashionable condition at the time, had various degrees that today would be interpreted as ranging from exogenous to endogenous depression. The physician George Cheyne, in his successful book *The English Malady or a Treatise of Nervous Diseases of all Kinds* (1733), indicated that 'foreigners' thought that such conditions as 'nervous distempers, spleen, vapours, and lowness of spirits' characterised the country.[29] Among predisposing factors, he noted the variable weather and moist air. It is plausible to surmise that Rowe – in line with the views of Cheyne and other physicians – considered that a person's constitution was a predisposing factor behind low spirits; hence Sir Francis, apparently a silent, shy and introspective man, was vulnerable, perhaps made more so by his rather sedentary duties as a parliamentarian.[30] Rowe once told Sir Francis of the apparent concerns of Dr Huxham:

> I heartily wish you a perfect Restoration, which I wou'd not have you Despair of; you have youth of your Side, But must Relax – Dr Huxam always Says when I see Him, you must Lessen your assiduity. (10 January 1755, F302)

Rowe added that the next time he expected Huxham to admonish Sir Francis for sitting and reading so much that he may 'Fix a weakness in his Bowels which may be very Dangerous: I'l get him to write you a Line of Admonition, I won't Say of Advice, as you'l know their Secret'.

Undoubtedly Rowe constantly worried that melancholy, perhaps precipitated by family crises and illnesses, could cascade to other health problems:

> Your melancholy Letters give me the greatest Concern, for Godsake Take care of yourself, or you'l Destroy your Health – the only pleasure of my life is your Welfare, & these Turns determine the whole … (6 December 1759, F394)[31]

---

[29] G. Cheyne, *The English Malady or a Treatise of Nervous Diseases of all Kinds* (London: Strahan, 1733), p. i.

[30] Linking individual health with different individual constitutions was of long standing and widely accepted in the eighteenth century. An example, recognising melancholy constitutions, is N. Robinson, *A New System of the Spleen, Vapours and Hypochondriack Melancholy* (London: Bettesworth 1729), p. 22. It is possible, though perhaps unlikely, that Rowe read Cheyne's *The English Malady*, which included a case that could have reminded him of Sir Francis: 'A Knight Baronet of an ancient family, by keeping bad hours, in attending upon the business of the Parliament, and living freely about town, had so worn down his constitution, that he ran into habitual diarrhoea' (p. 277).

[31] Rowe also wrote: 'Your melancholy Letter quite Turns me! For Godsake Endeavour to Support yourself – I am very unfit to advise – But I hope God will Give you ability' (14

Friendship

Rowe's concerns about Sir Francis and his constant encouragement and support were what he undoubtedly viewed as cardinal features of friendship: 'I always had the Tenderest Sentiments for you, Fix't in the most Faithful Friendship' (16 January 1756, F330). It seems that he considered faithful friendship in the same way as people today argue that friends can contribute to healthy lifestyles. The physician George Cheyne hinted at this when noting that moderate drinking promoted 'friendship comforting the sorrowful heart, and raising the drooping spirits, by the chearful cup, and the social repast'.[32]

Writing on 27 February 1740 to young Francis, then a student at Cambridge, Rowe was glad that his Winchester 'School Fellows' were with him, for 'that Early acquaintance Carrys a Friendship with it as lasting as Life, and often very useful' (F197). Eighteen months later he commented: 'I am Glad to hear you got to London, Tho' not well, yet it's better to be among your Friends, when you are so' (15 October 1741, F201). Yet Rowe also encouraged Sir Francis to keep in mind that friends were needed as much for political as for social support:

> Your Friends [in Bere Alston] Seem for the Generality untainted (except the Rotten Member, who by the Bye is in a very bad State as to his Health) yet your presence and acquaintance with 'Em, you'l Find more & more Necessary. (3 April 1744, F213)

Another time he wrote: 'the Majority of your Father's Friends will always be [unanimous] to Serve his Son' (19 May 1741, F200).

Exercise

Amid Rowe's advice on maintaining health, he once described exercise as a 'fine Medicine', while opining 'I wish I cou'd use it; I hope you will find the good Effect, as I wish you Everything Agreable' (24 December 1754, F300). And, in response to Sir Francis's low spirits, he advised him to 'Take Every Method to raise 'Em, Exercise & agreable Conversation' (8 July 1757, F367). Essentially, the same advice was repeated a number of times: 'For Godsake Take Care of yourself, and Don't Let your Spirits Sink; I hope when the good Weather Comes you will Ride much, Exercise do's great Things' (18 February 1762, F444); 'Pray Take Care of Yourself, Use Exercise, & See your Sister Often' (20 August 1763, F463).[33]

Fatigue

Did Rowe think that over-strenuous exercise could undermine health? He was, after all, concerned with the deleterious effects of fatigue when occasioned by lengthy and tiring journeys: for instance, 'I am under Such Concern for you, Least the Fategue of the Journey in such Bad roads & Weather on this Melancholy Occasion, & the

---

September 1759, F391). The sense of cascading problems also emerges in relation to fatigue (see below).

[32] Cheyne, *Essay of Health and Long Life*, p. 51.

[33] William Hudson also noted exercise as part of the care of Jeremiah Dyson's hypochondriacal symptoms: to go out every day, to exercise and to take a preparation of bark (16 November 1771, **15**–F169). Later Hudson again referred to Dyson's use of the bark, seemingly as a tonic (January 1772, **17**–F177).

uneasiness Thereon shou'd have any bad Effect' (7 November 1760, F423), and, a year later, 'I am under great Concern about you; Fear your Fateguing Journey & your Other Avocations affect you too much' (10 December 1761, F435).

It is reasonable to suggest that Rowe's basic concern was that fatigue would foster bodily weakness, a potential harbinger of cascading medical problems. Weakness, then, had to be nursed carefully:

> For Godsake Take Care of yourself, Don't Trouble yourself, now you are
> so weak, to Write, only once a Week as usual but 2 Lines how you Mend,
> Which I heartily pray to God you may ... (6 March 1757, F362)

It is likely that he was especially concerned about fatigue precipitating Sir Francis's melancholy:

> I ... hope you won't Fategue yourself with such quick Journeys – your
> great Uneasiness I trust Time will aleviate, & give a Turn to your Spirits:
> the pain of the Mind is the Worste of Maladys – pray God Send you Relief.
> (26 October 1759, F392)

A 'vice'

One further aspect of lifestyle merits comment: the abuse of alcohol, a growing medical and social problem in the eighteenth century. Rowe clearly had concerns over how Sir Francis fared while he was a student in Cambridge. He subtly delivered a 'message' when writing encouragingly:

> I am Charm'd with your Reflection on that Contemptible Vice, it destroys
> more than the locusts of Ægypt, and has Marr'd more bright Genius's than
> Mahomet's paradice ... Silenus is more a Beast, than the Ass He's put
> upon. (27 February 1740, F197)[34]

Another early letter indirectly emphasised the dangers by commenting on the position of tidewaiters at Plymouth who had too much time on their hands, 'which they generally Spend in an Ale-House' (5 November 1742, F203). As already noted, Rowe was later less than sympathetic toward Sol's health problems, which he associated with excessive drinking.

5.4 Some Specific Medical Conditions

Even if individuals felt they were healthy, uncertainties and worries were rarely far away, certainly for Rowe. Even mild feverish conditions might be harbingers of fatal outcomes. On one occasion he expressed relief on hearing that a fever had left Sir Francis, who should therefore have little to 'fear' (10 August 1759, F386). Perhaps,

---

[34] Silenus, described variously as a companion or tutor to ancient Greece's wine god, Dionysus, was commonly depicted in the seventeenth and eighteenth centuries as inebriated while reclining on a donkey.

in this instance, the worry was over 'ague', a term used loosely for intermittent and other fevers.[35]

Some of the other feverish conditions faced by those living in south Devonshire were listed on the title page of Huxham's book, *An Essay on Fevers, and their Various Kinds, as depending on Different Constitutions of the Blood: with Dissertations on Slow Nervous Fevers; on Putrid, Pestilential, Spotted Fevers; on the Small-Pox; and on Pleurisies and Peripneumonies.*[36] Huxham, as already noted, correlated weather conditions over many years with outbreaks of 'epidemic fevers' in Plymouth or nearby.[37] High mortality rates were not uncommon, though in some contexts Huxham blamed improper medical care: often misuse of the basic treatment of bleeding plus 'small beer and a purge', owing to what he felt was misdiagnosis and failure to tailor treatment to the individual.[38]

Smallpox undoubtedly generated particular fears. Rowe noted one family tragedy: 'William Wills our host at Beer is dead of the Small Pox, his Wife, Daughter and her Husband too' (20 February 1755, F308). Fear existed not only about fatal outcomes, but also with regard to a legacy of disfiguring pock-marks among survivors. Rowe once remarked: 'Mrs Elliot runs much in my Mind, I shall be very glad to hear she has got well over, a young Woman dreads Disfigurement almost as much as Death' (14 April 1758, F378).

An informative letter to Sir Francis from his lawyer John Carpenter, written shortly after the last of the Rowe letters, merits comment. Carpenter was a close observer of the health scene and possibly acquainted with Huxham's writings, since he commented on two conditions discussed there. The letter reveals the enigmatic puzzle that he and others faced over the apparently random outbreaks, at a time of diverse views on contagion and anti-contagion, well before the modern understanding of germ theory.[39] One condition, the 'sore throat', was almost certainly the 'malignant, ulcerous sore throat' (in most cases likely to have been diphtheria), on which Huxham had published a separate book in 1757:[40]

---

[35] For an earlier concern, 'I am very glad to find that you have got the better of your disorder, which I understood was an ague till then' (15 April 1743, F204). While the term 'ague' commonly indicated malaria, it also covered any condition characterised by hot and cold sweats and shivering. The incidence of malaria in the region at the time can only be guessed, but the River Tavy, with marshland and rich fishing water, is within walking distance of Buckland, while Nutwell is on the east bank of the River Exe.

[36] J. Huxham, *An Essay on Fevers, and their Various Kinds* (London: Austen, 1750). A second edition appeared the same year.

[37] The first of two monumental volumes on the subject was published in 1739: *Observationes de Aëre et Morbis Epidemicis* (London: Austen, 1739). English translations appeared in 1759 and 1767.

[38] For basic treatment, see Huxham, *Essay on Fevers*, pp. 100, 101. With regard to smallpox he wrote positively about the value of inoculation against smallpox that became popular from around the 1740s (see, for instance, p. 133). Its use in Devonshire has not been explored. I. Maxted, 'John Huxham's Medical Diary: 1728–1752', *Local Population Studies* 12 (1974), 34–37, made an initial attempt to correlate Huxham's published data with records in burial registers.

[39] For context, see M. DeLacy, *The Germ of an Idea: Contagionism, Religion and Society in Britain, 1660–1730* (Basingstoke: Palgrave Macmillan, 2016).

[40] Huxham indicated he had first met the condition in Plymouth around 1750, though it had been in nearby towns a year or two earlier: see *A Dissertation on the Malignant, Ulcerous Sore-Throat* (London: Hinton, 1757), pp. 2–3. Rowe indicated in 1753 that Huxham, evidently

We have had the sore throat very rife in this Country & they had also at
Honiton, Payhembury & that neighbourhood when I was there, but Yarcombe & its Neighbourhood or Nutwell or the Country to the South of
Honiton & Exeter had then known nothing of it. It has been very fatal at
Plymouth & some other parts South of us to Children, but I have heard
of no grown person fail under it, nor do I now hear of any person but one
farmer … From thence I hope 'tis on the Decline & will soon leave the
Country. Buckland has had it for some time but is now I learn entirely rid
of it, and no grown person or Child (as my Servant who is one of the parish
tells me) has miscarried in it. We have I thank God happily escap'd it, & I
hope your Honour may soon without Danger venture into the Country. (22
June 1779, DHC 346M/F487)

The second condition noted by Carpenter, the 'slow nervous fever', came to be
commonly diagnosed as typhus, the one-time scourge of prisons ('gaol fever') and
crowded living conditions:[41]

A slow nervous fever has been very prevalent also in this Country & has
carried off several, but is now entirely gone from us. My Eldest Daughter
had it but happily recover'd it & has been perfectly establish'd near a
Month.

Carpenter added that he believed that the cold showery May weather 'was the real
Cause of those Disorders'.

Colic/Devonshire colic
Aside from fevers, Huxham took a special interest in what he called Devonshire
colic ('cholick' or 'cholic') associated with drinking cider.[42] Some details of what
became the cider controversy underscore the scourge, especially among Devon
workers, and the dilemma created for cider producers such as Sir Francis.[43]

---

studying the disease at the time, did not think 'the late Sore Throat was so Contagious as
imagin'd', and that 'the Malignancy is much abated' (9 February 1753, F236).

[41] That is not to say that all cases of 'slow nervous fever' were typhus. For relevant discussion,
see D. C. Smith, 'Medical Science, Medical Practice and the Emerging Concept of Typhus in
Mid-Eighteenth-Century Britain', *Medical History,* Supplement 1 (1981), 121–134.

[42] Huxham's account of the Devonshire colic was first published in his *Observationes Aēre
et Morbis Epidemicis* as 'Opusculum de Morbo Colico Damnoniorum Anno MDCCXXIV'.
For background, see R. M. S. McConaghey, 'Sir George Baker and the Devonshire Colic',
Medical History 11(4) (1967), 345–360; I. Maxted, 'Cider and Eighteenth-Century Evidence-
Based Healthcare: a Devon Pamphlet War' (1996), *Exeter Working Papers in Book History*,
http://bookhistory.blogspot.com/2007/02/cider.html (accessed September 2018).

[43] Cider, mentioned a number of times in the correspondence, was produced at Buckland and
Nutwell. Rowe once noted: 'I was at Buckland yesterday & Tasted the Medyat Cyder, which
I believe may answer your Expectation. Your Mother's Servant Says there is about a pipe of
That, and another of Credling, a Hogshead of Each he believ's may be good, But the other Two
Fines Slowly; I Fancy He's no Critique in Cyder' (9 February 1753, F236). When production
started at Nutwell is not clear as new orchards were being developed. Among many issues
over cider, Rowe wrote on 9 December 1763: 'You will greatly oblige your Constituents, in
your Endeavours about the Cyder affair' (F466). This referred to Bute's Excise Bill (1763)
taxing cider. Whether Sir Francis, given his constant support of the Government, voted against

It has already been noted that cold could exacerbate Rowe's own colic. He was not silent on this 'old Enemy' that often 'roughly treated' him; for instance: 'Having had for Some Time & Still Continuing Some Severe Fits of the Cholick, prevented my acknowledging the Receipt of your Letter Sooner, and I am now forc't to do it by Spurt' (3 January 1752, F223).[44] However, his complaint was unlikely to have been the Devonshire colic, as Huxham hinted that this resulted from drinking large quantities of new cider by the 'lowest sort of people' and that he saw 'no one seized with it, that abstained from apple drink and diet'; moreover, he noted that it did not attack people of the better sort, who lived elegantly, 'for they (as the fashion is) despising cheap things, scarce ever tasted the apples'.[45] Furthermore, Rowe does not seem to have complained about the wide range of symptoms that followed what Huxham described as an 'excessively tormenting pain [in] the stomach, and epigastric region'.[46]

It is unlikely that Huxham's account, only available in Latin until 1788, had much, if any, impact.[47] However, concerns over cider changed dramatically in 1767, with a publication by the Devonshire physician George Baker (later Sir George), then developing a fashionable practice in London. Baker vigorously critiqued the view of Huxham that the colic resulted from cider's acrid quality (from an acid salt).[48] He argued that the cause was lead poisoning; his support for this included analogous symptoms, analytical chemical evidence of lead in samples of Devonshire cider, and testimony that lead was used to fill fissures between the large circular stones of apple-grinding mills (as well as one instance of a mill with lead lining), and in cider presses.[49]

---

the Bill is unclear (see www.historyofparliamentonline/org/volume/1754-1790/member/drake-sir-francis-henry-1723-94 (accessed June 2019)).

[44] Rowe complained of his colic multiple times: for example, 'very Roughly Treated for Some Days past by my old Enemy the Cholic' (3 February 1753, F235); 'I am so freequently attack't by the Cholic, That I give but a Little regard to anything' (9 February 1753, F236); 'I have had the Cholic so Bad I cou'd not Come in 'Till now' (29 January 1754, F258); 'As my perregrinations grow too many for me, & the Cholic too, unless your Commands require it, I will Lye by for a Little' (1 March 1754, F265); 'You must Excuse what's amiss, For added to my Lameness, I have been so Severely attack't with the Cholick, That I scarse know what I write' (16 July 1756, F347).

[45] See J. Huxham, 'A Small Treatise on the Devonshire Colic which was very epidemic in the year MDCCXXIV', in The Works of John Huxham, 2 vols, (London: Bent, 1788), vol. 1, pp. 5–51. Huxham mentions the 'lowest sort', and the fashion of despising things (p. 14), and those who are not 'very elegant and careful in their diet' (p. 5). He first noted an outbreak ('epidemic') in 1724, though he elsewhere recorded outbreaks during the 1740s: 'The colic, arising from drinking too freely of new-made cyder, with a violent flux, was troublesome to a great many' and 'Numbers laboured under a cyder-colic, generally attended with a diarrhoea, by means of which it as soon removed. For a colical disorder very seldom torments those persons that are laxative; at least this disease soon gives way to anodynes' ('Observations on the Air and Epidemic Diseases', in Works of John Huxham, vol. 1, p. 87).

[46] Huxham, 'Small Treatise', p. 5.

[47] For the first English version, see n. 45.

[48] Huxham justified his work as based on observation ('experience without which all speculative reasoning about things is vain'). See Huxham, 'Small Treatise', p. 25; for the 'acrid' nature see, e.g., p. 22.

[49] G. Baker, An Essay, Concerning the Cause of the Endemial Colic of Devonshire (London: Hughs, 1767); also published in extended form in a series beginning Medical Transactions 1 (1968), 175–256.

While Baker's experiments and arguments were influential, he faced some credible challenges from cider producers and others, especially from Devon, who recognised the high incidence of the condition. It was said, for instance, that Baker relied on minimal testimony, and that the limited cider samples he had had analysed were not typical of ciders from other mills and presses.[50] Sir Francis, too, made efforts to defend the Devonshire product, at least as judged by William Hudson's analyses on what may have been Buckland or Nutwell cider:

> we have tryed the Aple Juice. It acts very slowly upon lead for after stand-
> ing two days it won't colour. The Iron did a little. So that from the small
> quantity of Lead about the presses and its acting so slowly upon it are
> sufficient proofs that the colick does not arise from it. (Autumn 1768,
> 3–F183)

Hudson went on to suggest that any objection could be removed by using tin as he did not find any dissolved in cider after standing for a week. Perhaps, too, he sided with Huxham's views that the condition was partly associated with drinking large quantities: 'should no Lead whatsoever be used in the making the Cyder that they will find the distemper just the same provided they continue to drink the crude juice'.

Given the variations in cider equipment, a conclusive evaluation of the conflicting evidence and opinions put forward is unlikely. Nevertheless, it is noteworthy that accounts of Devonshire colic were fading by the early 1800s. Although it cannot be entirely discounted that this was due to changes in production, it is perhaps relevant that Baker's interpretation fed into existing public fears of metal toxicity in foods, while shifting drinking habits also need consideration.[51]

---

[50] F. Geach, *Some Observations on Dr Baker's Essay on the Endemial Colic of Devonshire* (London: Baldwin, 1767). For comments on Geach and other Devonian defences, see McConaghey, 'Sir George Baker'. McConaghey, however, accepted Baker's evidence as convincing despite its small sampling and (as Geach made clear) considerable variability in mills and presses. See also T. J. Peters, L. Payne and N. J. Level, 'The Life and Times of Francis Geach MD, FRS (1730–1798), Senior Surgeon to the Royal Naval Hospital, Plymouth (1778–1798)', *Journal of Medical Biography* 23(2) (2015), 63–73. That Huxham and Geach knew each other (see, e.g., Huxham's presentation of some of Geach's surgical cases: J. Huxham, 'Two Remarkable Cases in Surgery, by Mr. Francis Geach, Surgeon in Plymouth', *Philosophical Transactions* 53 (1763), 231–237) does not seriously undermine Geach's cogent response.

[51] Contemporary fears of various poisons, including copper from copper vessels, was fostered by a number of publications from the 1750s onwards. See J. Robertson, *An Essay on Culinary Poisons* (London: Kearsly, 1781). If lead was the culprit in many cases, detailed consideration needs to be given to the seasonal nature of outbreaks of complaints, how far symptoms match acute and chronic poisoning, and other sources of lead (e.g. lead-glazed vessels, addition of lead acetate to sweeten cider, water supply) apart from the equipment used. Alternatives were highlighted by a Barnstable physician, James Hardy, for whom see H. A. Waldron, 'James Hardy and the Devonshire Colic', *Medical History*, 13 (1969): 74–81. For a full account, see also J. R. Childs, 'Sir George Baker and the Dry Belly-Ache', *Bulletin of the History of Medicine* 44 (1970), 213–240; R. Charlton, *An Inquiry into the Efficacy of Warm Bathing in Palsies* (Oxford: Clarendon Press, 1770), with a section on 'A Palsy of the Hands from the Cyder Colic', pp. 73–81.

5.5 A Variety of Treatments

Although, as noted, Sir Francis may not have helped estate workers with consulting a practitioner, he probably provided advice and medicines. A large domestic medicine chest, maybe one of those commercially available by the mid-1700s, was a probable standby, typically containing conventional medicines.[52] However, many of these competed with expanding numbers of enticingly advertised proprietary (loosely called 'patent') medicines, many of which gained considerable popularity.[53]

One such commercial preparation, Dr James's Fever Powder, prospered amid criticisms. Hudson, for one, indirectly hinted at problems when writing to Sir Francis about the premature death on 17 September 1767 of the Duke of York, a younger brother of George III. After ten or twelve days of a 'Milliery' (miliary) fever, the Duke insisted 'upon taking Dr James's Powder, which accordingly he did & it had its usual effect'. Possibly, Hudson felt this led, a day later, to 'the Eruption [that] struck in & fell upon his bowels and brought on a mortification in his stomach & bowels' (20 September 1767, 1–F166).[54]

Baths

Another aspect of treatment straddling self-care and practitioner treatment, at least for the wealthy who could afford the travel and meet living expenses, were visits to what had become fashionable mineral water spas or to the increasingly popular sea-water bathing resorts. While the value of such practices was not without controversy, they were recommended by many physicians for treatment or recuperation. Rowe reports that Mr Edgcombe 'has had Dr Hucksom, who advises the Bath, where He must go, as soon as he has Strength, But at present he isn't able to ride, nor to go out of his room' (25 May 1750, F220). Many people went of their own accord to their favourite place, maybe to a local spa. Rowe once remarked that he hoped that Sir Francis could visit 'that you might have the Benefit of Bathing' (22 July 1757, F368), though quite possibly this referred to sea-water bathing. Mrs Carpenter's relatives brought her to Nutwell and hoped that 'Bathing in the Salt-water will be of Service to Her – She's a very Weak Woman!' (6 June 1754, F270). Otherwise, favoured spas included Bath: 'Shou'd be glad to hear your Sister Elliot received Benefit from the Bath' (January 1759, F383), and 'I have your Favour from Bath, I hope your Sister's Company & your own Endeavours will Divert if you can, aleviate your Disagreable' (11 February 1760, F402); Buxton: 'I hope Buxton will made [sic] an agreable alteration in your Mama' (21 July 1758, F380); and Malvern: 'I wish Malvern may Mend your Mother' (29 June 1759, F385).[55]

---

[52] Such chests were replenished by an apothecary, chemist, or druggist. For this alignment of self-care with conventional practice, see J. K. Crellin, 'Domestic Medicine Chests: Microcosms of 18th and 19th Century Medical Practice', *Pharmacy in History* 21 (1979), 122–131.

[53] Much has been written on this expansion: see A. Mackintosh, *The Patent Medicine Industry in Georgian England* (Basingstoke: Palgrave Macmillan, 2018).

[54] The self-administration of James's Powder, an antimonial preparation, adds detail to an account of the Duke's death in the *Gentleman's Magazine* 37 (1767), 493–494. Some of the early controversies are noted in J. K. Crellin, 'Dr James's Fever Powder', *Transactions of the British Society for the History of Pharmacy* 1(3) (1974), 136–143.

[55] It is tempting to speculate whether, by the 1770s, the same level of enthusiasm persisted, given increased questioning of, for instance, the fashionable elements of certain spas. See

Hudson's Medicines
Turning to medicines for the estates, while many were likely obtained from
Plymouth or Exeter, Hudson sent some, at least those with supply problems, from
London. They are considered next, partly as a reminder that availability and costs
commonly shape treatment. Hudson's advice on treatments follows. It is given at
length not only to indicate that Hudson was far from insignificant in the health care
activities of Sir Francis, but also as an addition to the already noted issue of apothecaries becoming essentially general practitioners at the same time as running shops.

> I could not send you a Peice of Guaiacum Wood as it is difficult to get ex-
> cept from the Turners who ask much more than the whole of the Shavings
> come for. (20 July 1775, **25**–F173)

It seems unlikely that Sir Francis wanted the guaiacum, a popular extremely hard
wood, for carpentry, as Hudson indicated that the shavings were used in preparing
medicines. Since the sixteenth century, the wood (or its resin) had been regarded
as having specific value in treating syphilis and skin conditions. What persisted,
however, was a reputation as a mild diaphoretic (for increasing perspiration/sweat),
as well as a stimulating or strengthening medicine for the stomach, intended to ease
digestive disorders and remove toxins.[56]

> I shall not be able to send you the Pulv. Contrayerv. C. till next week ...
> I am promised a share of a small quantity of the true Root brought from
> Portugal, for I have not at present more than 4 oz left of the old sort. What
> this kind they have brought I don't know but if I have it I find I must pay
> for it very dear, after the rate of 500 per Cent, but there is no remedy.
> (Spring 1772, **18**–F185)[57]

Various formulae existed for the pulvis contrayervae compositus (compound powder
of contrayerva), though Hudson likely followed the simple one of the *London
Pharmacopoeia*.[58] The contrayerva root – Sir Francis presumably knew that his
illustrious ancestor, the first Sir Francis Drake, was given credit for introducing the
root into England from Peru in the early 1580s[59] – had become increasingly popular

---

the attitudes expressed in *The Expedition of Humphry Clinker* (1771) by Tobias Smollett, an
author whom Sir Francis likely followed as a bibliophile, well versed in the comings and
goings of London society.
[56] W. Lewis, *The New Dispensatory* (London: Nourse, 1753), p. 135. This publication is
used here and below as a successful reference book of the time, critically compiled, and
representative of what many accepted as relatively standard practice amid much variation in
therapeutics.
[57] See also a further Hudson comment, 'Contrayerva except the bastard kind is likewise
scarce and Russia Rhubarb more than either' (late summer 1774, **24**–F191).
[58] Lewis, *New Dispensatory*, p. 454, for pulvis contrayervae compositus, noting the simpler
formula of the *London Pharmacopoeia* compared with that of the Edinburgh College.
[59] John Gerarde's popular herbal must have helped spread its reputation. He quoted Clusius,
who stated that Sir Francis Drake had, while in London, given him roots with the report that
they were held in 'high esteeme amongst the Peruvians'. Clusius named the root *Drakena
radix* or 'Drakes root': see J. Gerarde, *The Herball or Generall Historie of Plantes (Enlarged
and Amended by Thomas Johnson)* (London: Norton & Whittakers, 1633), p. 1621.

by 1700 as an anti-poison (alexipharmic) and diaphoretic, a reputation that accounted for continued usage for treating virtually any feverish condition.[60]

> I have only sent you half a Pd of Bark as it is so extravagently dear and likely to be much more so if some don't arive soon. (late summer 1774, **24**–F191)

By the mid-eighteenth century, the bark, or Peruvian bark (to become generally known as Cinchona bark), already had a history of use in treating fevers, notably 'intermittent' ones such as agues (commonly malaria; quinine was later isolated). The bark's bitterness and astringency also lay behind its reputation as a tonic and strengthener of the stomach, hence its use for gastro-intestinal disorders.[61]

Hudson's advice for Sir Francis's patients
Sir Francis, as already noted, provided medicines for some individuals when he was in Devon. Sometimes he requested Hudson's advice (medicine by correspondence). Two examples are included here, while further advice is included in an appendix for those who have a special interest in this subject.

> In regard to the person you mention, I think you had best give him a Dose of Rhubarb or two, and then give him Two tea Spoonfulls of Tincture of Bark in a Cup of Strong Camomile Tea with some Ginger in it twice a Day, and drink Ginger tea for common drink to half a Pint … (19 December 1772, **22**–F171)

Hudson went on to indicate ways to make this palatable to 'get the better in a great measure of his indigestion', namely to add to the 'common drink' two spoonfuls of brandy as a 'punch', or to add just one spoonful of brandy, and sweetener to taste, as a common drink instead of wine.

Without any information about the patient or symptoms (apart from a digestive upset), little can be said of the potential value of the regimen, save that, for many practitioners, the approach was basic for a variety of conditions. The use of a laxative (rhubarb) was to ensure that the stomach and bowels were devoid of putrefactive material or toxins, while a tonic (stimulant), such as the bitter tincture of bark, could 'strengthen' the stomach, and the carminative action of chamomile tea and ginger could help with flatulence. One senses, too, that efforts to tailor treatment to suit the preferences of a patient were often a significant part of successful care. Given the desire for palatable preparations, one wonders whether Sir Francis used or recommended Huxham's Tincture of Bark, not only because of past associations with the physician, but also because the preparation quickly developed a widespread reputation that persisted into the twentieth century.[62]

---

[60] Lewis, *New Dispensatory*, pp. 117–118.

[61] *Ibid.*, pp. 178–180.

[62] A version of the formula was included in the early twentieth-century *British Pharmaceutical Codex* (London: The Pharmaceutical Press, 1923), p. 327. With regards to its reputation, it is perhaps relevant that, in 1750, Huxham said that he had used his Tincture successfully for many years in 'intermittent and slow nervous fevers, but also in the putrid, pestilential and petechial', and that he himself had ordered it 'to be kept in these Parts [in the shops of apothecaries, chemists, and druggists], as an officinal medicine'. His formula comprised Peruvian

> As to the Person you mention, the best thing to be done is Poulticies of
> bread and Milk and the skin to be oil'd with a Feather to prevent the Poul-
> ticies sticking as greasy things do very seldom. With ulcers of that kind he
> should keep his leg up as much as possible and at the same time, if much
> inflamed, hold it over the steam of warm-water, the water should not be
> too hot – and the steem should be confined by a Cloath thrown over the
> Leg &c at the time of steeming it, and then to apply the Poulticies. His
> body should be kept open – but I doubt if you will be able to heel them
> intirely ... (17 December 1776, **28**–F175)

This advice is quoted at length to illustrate, as an example, the detail often given for
a treatment regimen, detail that, with knowledge of the time and trouble taken, might
well contribute to a patient's comfort, which was part of a good practitioner–patient
relationship. At the same time, Hudson made sure not to raise hopes too high by
warning about over-expectations of a complete cure.

Hudson's personal advice to Sir Francis
This is noteworthy, not only for the detail (although still requiring some knowledge
on how to compound the suggested medicines), but also for the repeated advice to
take 'Mithridate' (mithridatium), as in the following example (for two others, see
the appendix):

> I ... am sory to hear your Bowels are so indifferent. I would advise you to
> try bark in small doses, about ten grains, and some Nutmeg – and Mithri-
> date at night while the laxness continues, but the Bark I would continue
> twice a day for a Month (17 December 1776, **28**–F175).

For the 'indifferent' bowels, suggestive of irregularity, the bark (administered as
a powder with ground ginger to help mask the bitterness/astringency) served as
a mild tonic/stimulant or strengthener. Mithridatium, also recommended, was a
multi-ingredient medicine with a centuries-old reputation as a general antidote to
putrefactive or other poisonous material. However, only the wealthy could afford
the high cost of the genuine product, which serves as an example of a medicine that
maintained a following despite criticism that it was essentially ineffective. Hudson's
many connections in London society, evident in his letters, helped him acquire
notable patients, some living outside London, including, as noted, Jeremiah Dyson,
who followed the pattern of consulting both physicians and apothecaries.

---

bark, orange peel, saffron, cochineal, and spirit vini Gallic (French brandy): see Huxham,
Essay on Fevers, p. 122. Whether or not Huxham's influence did lead to it being 'kept' in
many shops is impossible to say, but the formula appears in one manuscript formulary that,
plausibly, was connected with an apothecary shop, perhaps in Devon, and in use in the 1770s
(one added date in the manuscript is 1 August 1776). To the formula labelled 'Tinct Cort[x]
Peru by Doctor Huxham', a note was added: 'to be given in intermittents when the bark
in substance will not sit with the patients' (Wellcome Library MS 7365, fol. 84). A puzzle
remains with a crossed-out heading on the title page (first leaf): 'Huxham's Tincture of
Bark'. This is repeated beneath ('Huxham's Tincture') almost as a doodle, suggesting that
it was uppermost in the mind of the writer. Also written crosswise is 'Taunton Devonshire',
maybe Church Staunton/Church Stanton, in Devon until 1896, when it transferred to Somerset
(Taunton was, and is, in Somerset).

5.6 Conclusion

Although no generalisations can be made from the snapshots offered in this account, examples emerge of an individual's characteristics and other factors (from repeated drunkenness to serious accidents) that, in one way or another, might shape approaches to maintaining health, choices of treatment, and relationships with a practitioner. Both Rowe and Sir Francis, unlike so many in the country, had the means to consult physicians, or any other practitioner. Although they seemingly had confidence in and maybe a close relationship with a physician, other practitioners were consulted. Indeed, consulting multiple practitioners – sometimes both a physician and an apothecary for the same illness – was probably not uncommon, the apothecary occasionally apparently serving as assistant physician. Rowe's comment that limits existed to what any one practitioner could do was a good reason to drive many to obtain further opinions; he himself once had advice from two 'honest chirurgeons'. Perhaps he accepted living with chronic bouts of colic, albeit not without constantly feeling that he knew more about his ailment than any practitioner. And perhaps he agreed with a sentiment from another eighteenth-century patient that the physician 'found me very well; for me I was still feeling sick'.[63]

Rowe's attitude also raises questions about the roles played by stoicism, fatalism, and religious faith in health care, for his letters offer a sense that such characteristics helped him deal with his problems, though he still complained and blamed illness for his dilatoriness. It is tempting to suggest that stoicism and faith had greater priority among those without ready access to a practitioner, or who had concerns over fees even when paid over time or in kind.[64]

In the eighteenth century, a good many home medicines continued to be prepared inexpensively from locally gathered herbs, although, as noted, economic and commercial shifts were accelerating change in self-treatments. While there had long been a permeable interface between home and conventional medicines, the century saw the nature of home medicine being tipped increasingly toward medicines prepared in house by apothecaries, chemists, and druggists, all of whom also sold the widening number of popular patent medicines.[65]

---

[63] See M. Louis-Courvoisier and A. Mauron, '"He found me very well; for me, I was still feeling sick": The Strange Worlds of Physicians and Patients in the 18th and 21st Centuries', *Journal of Medical Ethics and Medical Humanities* 28(1) (2002), 9–13.

[64] On the fees of a country practitioner, see, for example, I. Loudon, 'Nature of Provincial Medical Practice'; and more generally, A. Digby, *Making a Medical Living: Doctors and Patients in the English Market for Medicine, 1700–1911* (Cambridge: Cambridge University Press, 1994).

[65] It is hard to determine the tempo of change toward commercial medicines, commonly assumed to be slower in rural areas where wild-crafting of herbs was relatively easy (though see Mackintosh, *Patent Medicine Industry*). On the one hand, ready-to-use well-established and new packaged medicines with authoritative claims enticed even those with limited means. On the other hand, traditional usages had their protagonists, and many examples of what are generally referred to as folk treatments persisted in Devonshire and elsewhere into the twentieth century. Some practitioners, too, took particular interest in traditional remedies, perhaps in the belief that they were unchanged over time, and hence essentially empirically tested, or they recognised the therapeutic value of a patient's belief in a treatment (the power of the mind in health care). For an example of a country recipe possibly of interest to an Exeter surgeon (as it was included in a volume of recipes, some of which were associated with him): 'a country-man troubled with the tooth-ache was persuaded by another to rub his tooth with helleboraster; [unfortunately] he unwittingly rubbed all his teeth on that side, and

Although the letters are silent on self-treatment, whether traditional or commercial, it is hard not to believe that Rowe, especially with his multiple ailments, did not try various treatments in his search for relief, if not cure. Perhaps, too, since Rowe and Sir Francis were unmarried, the housekeepers had a role in preparing, even suggesting, remedies, if only simple decoctions and tinctures; Betty Dyer, for example, acquired a still, or maybe a replacement (2 July 1754, F275). On the other hand, it is possible that, by that time, Sir Francis was offering treatment – one imagines even to Rowe.

The growing eighteenth-century appreciation of a rural–urban divide was noticed earlier in quoting Akenside's 'Ode to Sir Francis'. Regional remoteness, lengthy travel times, and ill health could impact on, but were not barriers to, trade and business dealings, though whether this was any more significant than in urban settings is difficult to say.[66] Likewise it is difficult to assess whether or not the overall quality of medical care differed substantially from that in large towns and expanding London. The Rowe and Hudson letters throw no light on this, but equally nothing suggests any difference from rural practice in, say, Suffolk from 1750 to 1830, which one historian has viewed as 'quality medical practice' provided by country practitioners.[67] Indeed, the letters to Sir Francis offer constant reminders of links with Plymouth and Exeter, where a number of medical luminaries and growing hospital facilities in the eighteenth century were significant in encouraging the local spread of information on new practices and treatments. Moreover, medical influences from London infiltrated via various personal relationships, as seen with Sir Francis and Hudson.[68]

To conclude, albeit with the risk of inappropriately injecting present-day health-care values into the past, the impact of an individual's character and idiosyncrasies on healthways, appreciated in the eighteenth century, remains relevant today

---

presently allmost all those teeth fell out. Therefore if you will try this medicine defend all the other teeth with soft wax' (Wellcome Library MS 7073, fol. 48).

[66] The matter of the cumulative impact of ill health on society and business is beyond the scope of this discussion, except for the following note. Leaving aside the obvious disruptions owing to high mortalities from infectious disease outbreaks, it is impossible to assess with confidence the local effects of self-limiting illness, especially without, for example, modern statistics on days lost at work. Moreover, the letters lack specific detail. Nevertheless, given Rowe's many references to passing ailments among workers (added to personality issues as with Sol and Betty Dyer), disruption to the smooth running of the estates must always have been anticipated. Rowe included in a report to Sir Francis about a land agreement: 'provided Mr Hendra Bewes is in a very good state of health, for all hangs on that' (23 March 1743/1744, F210). For a specific example of the challenges offered by rebuilding and development of Nutwell: 'The want of Water still Continues, & it's now Found out That there's a hole in the pipe, which the Plumber's Man did not Find out, for the Master was then Sick, and you observ'd he made so Quick a return, That you did not know of his being here, 'Till he was gone; in Short the Fellow did not understand his Business: the Master has promis't to Come out' (2 July 1754, F275).

[67] Irvine, 'Surgeons and Apothecaries in Suffolk', pp. 300–301.

[68] Influences probably also came via other members of the Drake family. Hudson wrote to Sir Francis: 'I saw Dr Thomas today who told me that Lady Drake is very ill. He was out of Town when she was taken ill and so they sent for Dr Addington; but from Dr A's account of her Thomas thinks she will not be able to get over it and I don't find that Dr Addington has much hope' (20 September 1768, 4–F186). Anthony Addington (1714–1780) was a successful London physician: see *Munks Roll*, vol. 2, p. 198, available at munksroll.rcplondon.ac.uk (accessed July 2018).

as it similarly affects, for example, a patient's compliance with prescribed treatments.[69] That is not to say that outside influences do not continue to have a role: perhaps a new fashionable treatment that, because of slow dissemination into rural areas, could contribute to short-term rural–urban differences in health care.

5.7 Appendix

Three additional examples of Hudson's advice for Sir Francis's patients

> I have this day sent you the Tea, cinnabar of Antimony & extract of Hemlock as I should think she should continue it a little longer & to Purge her two or three times with salts or any other purging medicine and wash (with bran & water strain'd or thin water gruel) the sores twice a day. (Autumn 1768, **3**–F183)

The 'tea' presumably referred to China tea. The other items (cinnabar of antimony – a varied composition at the time, but generally mercuric sulphide – and extract of hemlock) were sent to continue an existing treatment. Depending on dosages (not noted), the cinnabar of antimony was used as a diaphoretic (as Hudson probably intended) or as a purgative action, but this is covered by laxative salts or analogous medications. The poisonous extract of hemlock was becoming fashionable (though not without controversy) by the late 1760s; it was used externally or internally for treating tumours.[70]

> I should think the first thing to be done for the woman is to let her have an Issue cut at the knee & then to give her a dose or two of Hiera Picra or any warm Opening medicine so as to get two or three stools & then give her some Pills prepared with equal Parts of Gum Ammoniacum & Soap, twelve Pills to be made out of a dram, and to take four night & morning for three weeks. (20 September 1768, **4**–F186)

The use of an 'issue' – a deliberate cut into the skin in which was inserted one or more issue peas (often wooden beads) to induce the promotion of pus – was a fairly standard treatment for inflamed joints, as well as for other actual or presumed inflammatory areas. Sir Francis may well have performed the procedure. The 'hiera picra' (a common name for a preparation of the purgative extract of aloes) was part of the standard 'purifying' of the stomach and bowels, to be followed by pills of a mild laxative.

> you might give Mrs B some milk or flower of sulphur, which will take off the effect of mercury sooner than anything else I know. She should take a sufficient quantity night & morning so as to give her one or two stools a

---

[69] For eighteenth-century recognition, see E. Perman, 'Samuel Tissot: Patient Compliance in the 18th Century', *Hektoen International: A Journal of Medical Ethics* 3 (2011), https://hekint. org/2017/01/30/samuel-tissot-patient-compliance-in-the-18th-century/ (accessed October 2018).

[70] For aspects of the controversy, see J. K. Crellin, 'Anton Störck (1731–1803) and British Therapeutics', in E. Lesky, *Wien und Die Weltmedizin* (Vienna: Böhlau, 1974), pp. 27–31.

> day, and to discontinue it a few days before she begins her Pills again; if
> she can go into a tub of Warm Water twice in a Week it will then be giving
> this method a fair trial and by opening her pores the mercury will be less
> liable to affect her mouth. (16 November 1771, **15**–F169)

The use of mercury preparations was widespread for a variety of conditions covering
syphilis, skin conditions and as a purge, especially on the presumption that it
removed bile. Side-effects were well known, including, as apparently in Mrs B's
case, excessive salivation and perhaps sore gums. Hudson offered suggestions to
ameliorate the effects.

Two additional examples of Hudson's advice to Sir Francis himself

> I received the favor of yours and am sory to hear you are so indifferent
> – if your purging continues I would encourage it by taking a few grains
> of Rhubarb, and repeat it occasionally and take after it is gone off twenty
> grains of Mithridate with ten of Contrayerva – and the contrayerva with-
> out the Mithridate in the morning – if you are feverish with your Rhuma-
> tism two or three drams of Mindereri Spirit with the above … (16 January
> 1770, **8**–F189)

In addition to the rhubarb to help clear the bowels (although according to dosage it
might have a constipating effect), the alexipharmic and diaphoretic reputations of
mithridatium and contrayerva were viewed as cleansing the blood. The Mindereri
Spirit (also known as Spiritus Mindereri or Liquor Ammoniae Acetatis) was viewed
as an esteemed deobstructant and diuretic for febrile inflammatory disorders.[71]

> I am sorry to hear you have got so troublesome a complaint. I hope it will
> not be of long continuance – I would advise you to take a dose or two of
> Physic such as will give you two or three stools and to rub your Loins
> with some volatile liniment and to keep a flannel to them – and likewise
> to take some contrayerva with some weak whey to promote a gentle Per-
> spiration. If the contrayerva & Physic does not relieve your Pain I would
> then advise you to take two drams of oil of almonds or olive & ten grains
> of salt of Hartshorn and some mint water with a little sugar and to take it
> three times in the day – and if restless ten or twelve drops of Laudanum
> added to night draught or you may take twenty grains of Mithridate. I hope
> soon to hear you have got rid of your Pain – without any further aid … (6
> January 1778, **29**–F176)

There is precise detail in this recommendation, with a reminder of the diaphoretic
property of contrayerva, and, if pain is not relieved, to take almond or olive oil,
maybe with the thought of softening the stool, and spirits of hartshorn in mint water
as a carminative to relieve flatulence. That the laudanum (tincture of opium) was to
aid sleep almost suggests that the mithridatium was superfluous but could be seen as
an added, expensive safeguard with which Sir Francis was comfortable.

---

[71] Lewis, *New Dispensatory*, p. 296.

Editorial Method

Our aim has been to print the letters in chronological order. This has involved some deviation from the DHC numbering. In the DHC numbering the Hudson letters precede the Rowe letters, whereas in fact they follow on from them chronologically. For this edition, the Rowe letters are printed first, and identified by the DHC number (F196, etc.). They are followed by the Hudson letters. The DHC numbering lists a dozen letters dated by Hudson, followed by the undated ones, in random sequence. For this edition, the Hudson letters are identified by a chronological number 1 to 29, established either from Hudson's dating or on internal evidence, followed by the DHC reference number (1–F166, etc.).

Dates have been standardised in the format day/month/year. A date given by the correspondent is placed at the beginning of the letter, even when the writer placed it at the end or in the margin. Putative dates are enclosed in square brackets.

The opening and closing salutations of the letters are sometimes compact in the originals, evidently at times with a view to saving space, but they may also be elaborately spaced over several lines. In this edition, the spacing of the opening salutations is standardised, and closing salutations are usually printed in no more than two lines, followed by the name. Some items are notes, or extracts, rather than complete letters, and may lack an opening or closing salutation.

Postscripts are a striking stylistic feature, especially in Nicholas Rowe's letters, and are retained as such. They follow the edited letter, even when they are added in the margin or intertwined with a closing salutation in the original. Nicholas Rowe's signature appears in the original as ligature 'NRowe'; it appears in the edited text as 'N Rowe'.

Square brackets are used to enclose:

1. editorial restoration of damaged text, interpretations, and additions;
2. modern equivalents of unfamiliar words, unfamiliar spellings, or familiar words with unfamiliar meanings, within inverted commas;
3. translations of Latin quotations, within inverted commas, except for Latin tags in common use (such as *in statu quo*), which are not translated;
4. a question mark, indicating a doubtful reading, doubtful sense, or doubtful expansion of abbreviation;
5. *sic*, added, sparingly, to readings where a reader might reasonably suspect an editorial slip.

Irretrievably damaged or illegible words for which no restoration is suggested are indicated by an ellipsis (…). Words deleted in the original are not shown in the edition, unless referred to in the text. Interlinear and marginal additions or corrections in the original are silently adopted in the text. Slips of the pen, repetitions of small words, and missing letters at the end of words (especially frequent in pronouns, where, for instance, 'the' may occur for 'they') are silently corrected.

Roman font is used for the main text, italic font for titles of books, newspapers, journals, Latin text, and ships. Manuscript underlining for emphasis and for scientific terms is retained.

Abbreviations, including superscript letters, are silently expanded. Similarly, initials for place names and proper names, both given names and family names, are silently expanded (where known) on their first occurrence in a letter, but left as initials if they occur again in the same letter.

Paragraphing is lightly modernised. Punctuation is lightly modernised, including the use of apostrophes. However, the writers' characteristic use of a dash '–' to mark a break between phrases, sentences, and even paragraphs is retained.

Word division is retained as in the original in compound nouns, but standardised in adverbs and pronouns, such as 'today' (often 'to Day' in the original), no-one (often 'no One' in the original), and 'anything' (often 'any Thing' in the original). Otherwise, original spelling is maintained, with variations characteristic of the eighteenth century.

Capitalisation is modernised at the beginning of paragraphs and sentences, and for days of the week. Otherwise, original capitalisation is maintained as far as possible. It is often difficult, especially in Nicholas Rowe's handwriting, to distinguish upper- and lower-case letters, particularly in the case of 'S/s' and 'O/o'.

THE LETTERS I

FROM NICHOLAS ROWE TO SIR FRANCIS HENRY DRAKE, 1740–1754 (DEVON HERITAGE CENTRE 346M/F196–F268), WITH ONE (F198) FROM SIR FRANCIS TO NICHOLAS ROWE

F196

Buckland, 20 February 1740

Sir

I Troubled you with a Letter Some time go, which I hope came Safe to your Hands; I have now only to let you know, that Lord Hobart's Entertainment was last Wednesday, when your Sister's & Nephew's ['kinsman's'] Letters were Read, and Receiv'd with an Unanimous approbation; I'm Sorry Mr Harry Drake's application shou'd give you or Lady Drake any Uneasiness; I do assure you there is no Occasion for it. None but Good Dr Creed* as I know of, is in his Interest, and He like the Æthiopian, can't Change his Hue –

I am with great Respect, Sir
Your most obliged and Humble Servant
N Rowe

When you have Read the Enclosed & my Lady, be pleas'd to Send it to the young Gentleman.**

If you wrote a Word or two to Mr Edgcombe & Mr Wyatt, 'twou'd be not amiss.

* Mr Harry Drake's application was for the position of MP granted by Lady Drake on FHD's behalf to her brother Samuel Heathcote. Dr Creed, the vicar of Buckland Monachorum and a freeholder of Bere Alston, was a frequent cause of trouble.
** The letter was to be forwarded to Samuel Heathcote.
Added on reverse, possibly in FHD's hand: 'Mr Rowe. Feb:20.1740.'
Added in pencil: 'to Mr Heathcote.'

F197

27 February 1740

Dear Sir

I Received your Favour of the 15th with much pleasure, it being always one to me to hear of your Welfare, which None more Sincerely wishes – Whenever your Studys will permit, a Flight from Bennet College will be very agreable here –

I am very Glad you have Some of your Winchester School Fellows with you, that Early acquaintance Carrys a Friendship with it as lasting as Life, and often very useful – I am Charm'd with your Reflection on that Contemptible Vice,* it Destroys more than the Locusts of Ægypt, and has Marr'd more bright Genius's than Mahomet's paradice – the Fatal Effects I'm at present too Sensible of: I'm perswaded you know how to preserve the proper Decorums with the Young Gentleman you hint at, Though his Taste is Disagreable to you, as I pray God it always may – Silenus is more a Beast, than the Ass He's put upon.

Mr Edgcombe and the Majority of the Beer [Alston] People are your Friends; I'm Sorry your Uncle Harry attempts to make a Schism among 'Em, as I am that he has occasion to be put on such measures. I hope you'l Soon be Enabl'd to Act for yourself, you'l then Distinguish who are for, or against your Interest – In order to that, may Alma Mater infuse that Light, which no false appearances may be able to Extinguish; may you reap all the advantages of a generous Education, may it raise you to a Sphere becoming yourself, and Family; and agreable to the Interests of Both.

I am Dear Sir

Your most affectionate Humble Servant

N Rowe**

* See Introduction, section 5, p. 56.
** On reverse, possibly in FHD's hand: 'Mr Rowe. Feb:27.1740. / Mr Rowe's Letters / From 1740 to 1751.'

F198*

London, 3 March 1740

Dear Sir

My omission is so great that I really have plea to make. I informed Mr Edgecombe** that you wou'd give him a Perusal of my Letter to you, which I have not yet sent: The information I wou'd give Mr Edgecombe, is of my Uncle Drake's application to me. Last Wenesday [sic] was Sen'night I was surprized with Intelligence Mr Heathcote gave me of Mr Drake's proceedings, & not half-an-hour after the receipt of this news I had an additional surprize with notice of his being at Cambridge. He waited on my Tutor the next Morning where I breakfasted with him. After breakfast he broke Silence with Saying he thought it proper to speak before my tutor least people shou'd imagine he said anything improper to me, I answered him that I thought that Method was very proper.

He then said that he cou'd inform me (if I were not as yet acquainted with it) that upon my father's coming to his Estate he had in his power the election of one Member at Plymouth, Plymton, Dartmouth, Totness, Tavistoke which interest was now lost, but if my interest at Beer was placed in the hands of a person who had interest with the superior powers, those boroughs might be reclaimed. I told him that I had Entrusted my interest with a person whom I thought most worthy of that trust, & one whom I was confident wou'd make a proper use of it.

He then shew'd me Mr Heathcote's letter on my Father's death which you read. He ask'd me whether he had not sufficient grounds for his application to me, when he had received such a letter from Mr Heathcote. I told him I thought that letter was nothing but what common civility required, that he said he would make no application, yet did not say that he wou'd refuse a pressing offer from my Mamma: there were some things that dropt that wou'd exagitate Mr Row ... ... respects to all my f ...***

* For this letter, the only one from FHD to Rowe, see Introduction, section 1, pp. 3 and 4.
** John Edgcombe, a freeholder of Bere Alston, advised the Drake family on legal and business matters, especially with regard to property.
*** The concluding salutation has been excised.

F199

Buckland, 8 March 1740

Dear Sir

I have your Favour of the 3rd and Thank you for what you mention of the Conference at Cambridge – Nothing can exagitate me, but an attempt on your Interest, and when my honest Endeavours are Misrepresented; I only wish you was able to undertake yourself, what can't be so well Effected by another. The Interest in Boro's, if Ever, so many, was lost long ago, and don't look Feazable, that they may be so Easily Recover'd; you may now Judge how practicable such Schemes are and whether from Such Means, it is probable matters might be reinstated; as you are best able to Conclude from your present Choice: These are Tender Topics for me to touch on, your own good Sense makes no Doubt the proper Distinction.

If you write a Line or two to Mr Serle it would not be amiss, But for anyone Else I don't see there is any immediate Necessity – Unless you have a mind to touch up your Cousin the Quondam Admiral, Now General, or that you can recover the Dr from his Ingratitude &c &c.

I have Seen Mr Wills Since you wrote Him, he is perfectly your Friend; Mr Bealey expresses the Same, and I have no Doubt but of a very Few – Mr Corket Convey'd his Lands some time ago to Mr Wyatt, the Letter you Directed to Mr Cokeet, I suppose you meant Him, was Sent to Mr Wyatt, as Mr Edgcombe & I thought 'twas meant, Tho' I understand Since you had wrote to Him before –

Wou'd you have a List of the Beer Votes?

I cou'd wish you had all in my knowledge, for fear of the Irresistable Fate of All Things –

None Wishing you more Sincerely Well Than Dear Sir

Your most affectionate Faithful Humble Servant

N Rowe

I thank you for the Reason. But the Reason of all is – ambition.

My humble Service to your Good Uncle.*

* The uncle referred to in this, and in several more letters of the 1740s, is Samuel Heathcote, as above (see F196, note).

F200

Nutwell, 19 May 1741

Dear Sir

I have your Obliging Letter, which I shou'd have answered Sooner, But the hurry I have been in prevented me; as to your writing to me, there is no need of any apology, whenever you Do it is a pleasure to me, But pray don't Let it Interrupt the more Necessary – your Studys – That my Dear will be your assistance, when I & all your Freinds may be Remov'd: as I don't know how Soon it may be my Case.

As I have Ever faithfully watch'd your Interest, So I wou'd willingly give you all the Lights I can & personally; in order to it I have Sounded your Mama & Uncle, who are both Willing you shou'd Come down in the Vacation for a Month, of which, before the Time, I will be more particular –

The Election at Beer was Unanimous, as I hope the Majority of your Father's Friends will always be to Serve his Son; on the other Side are the Names of Those,

who did on the late occasion; for the Rest I'l Defer it, 'Till I see you; when I will
in the most explicit manner Impart to you my heart, and make you Master of
Everything I can.

    Your Uncle & his Lady went hence a Sunday, pray Write to him, he is your Friend,
As is Dear Sir
Your most Faithful
N Rowe

For the Last, I can only Say *[Dul]ce Ridentem* ['gently laughing']

[on reverse]:*

9 May 1741

William Morden   )
Samuel Heathcote   ) Esqrs

John Edgcombe   portreeve

Nicholas James Rowe	Thomas Wyatt	John Rich	Thomas Reed
John Kemp	William Corter	George Edgcombe	
Robert Worth	John Sangwin	Richard Corter	
John Wills	Anthony Porter	Robert Kelly	
William Bray	William Bealey	Thomas Cummin	
John Doidge	John Reed	Abraham Searle	

Your Mama Sends you her Blessing, your Bro' Samy** his Love, Mrs [Porter] her
Service, she's as Fat & Sweet as Ever; Mr Porter who wrote this presents you his
best Services, he's much your Friend, very honest, and above Temptation. Your Bro'
Samy go's with him tomorrow morning to Plymouth to be Settled in the School
There.

* This list of those who voted in the Bere Alston election is a useful point of reference. Most
of those named reappear at least once, requiring patronage at the workplace or charitable
support.
** FHD's younger brother, Francis Samuel.

F201

Tavistock, 15 October 1741

Dear Sir
    I am Glad to hear you got to London, Tho' not well, yet it's better to be among
your Friends, when you are so. I wrote you the 6th to Nutwell from Tavistock, &
Enclos'd it to Mr Grey at the Post office; which I hope he Sent you before you left
that place.
    I therein acquainted you that Mr Bray (who is Entirely in another Interest), was
Chose Portreeve; & that Parson Hurle was put on the Jury, at least I aim'd at doing
it, For I was so blind I cou'd not read what I wrote. Mr Edgcombe having promis'd
to write you the State of the Case, I won't expatiate Farther upon it, Than to Say
if the Steward can Swear, or will any Person on the Jury he Thinks Fit, and admit

Free Tenants who have not been presented by your Jury, you have no Remedy but Westminster Hall, and shou'd They multiply upon you in this Manner, and a Dispute Ensue, you can have no Relief but in St Stephen's Chappel.*

I must Own I did not think anything of this kind wou'd have been attempted, Considering what has pass'd. It Therefore Behoves you to look about betimes, to make yourself Master as Soon as possible, at least of Election Law.

I hope you will think the Rest worth your while & Find it so – not knowing what may happen, you shou'd always be present at the Choosing the portreeve to keep your Friends together, and tho' you are not of Age, to let 'Em know how soon you shall – For if these Things are done to a green Tree, what may be done to a Dry.

Keep the Trust of the Parish Lands, as long in your Self as you Can, and Don't let Complaisance draw from you, what you have a power to keep – I wish more was in my power.

None can have a greater Inclination to Serve you Than Dear Sir
Your most Faithful
N Rowe

My Humble Service to your uncle.

I hear Mr Wills's Friend Andrews is made an Exciseman, to be sure Mr Wills will thank Mr Heathcote for it.

* See Introduction, section 2, pp. 16, 17–18, for appeals in Westminster against the outcome of an election.

F202

Buckland, 8 October 1742

Dear Sir

I am glad to hear you all got up well – your Fellow Traveller's name I'm told is Gambier [?], a Change-Broker, I hope he carry'd on the agreable to the Last.

Mr Wyatt's new place of Master Corker prevented his being at the Court so the Jury Chose William Bealey for Portreeve, who to be Sure will act agreeably.

This is the last Electing Court till you will be able to act yourself; I hope you will think Early of your Interest, & Exert yourself, it will be an Encouragement to your Friends to give you their assistance –

The Doctor behav'd very well,* Everyone was Civil to him, and I hope God will open his heart, to do you Justice.

Mr Spry was at the Court, he will be of Age next January. I need not Tell you he has lands in Beer nor add how necessary it is to keep Fair – shou'd he Come to Town, before you leave it, Cou'd not you Contrive to See Him? He's somewhat <u>particular</u>.

As I wish you very well, Take the Liberty to give you these hints, which I don't Doubt but you'l Improve.

I am Dear Sir
Your very Faithful Fr[iend] to serve you
N Rowe

I herewith Send you a Copy of the presentments That you may See the manner of it.

My Humble Service waits on your Uncle and if you cou'd prevail on him to get Mr John Doidge** made an Extraordinary Man at Plymouth, it wou'd be a Service to your Interest to let people See you can provide for your Friends, Since nothing is done for Them Elsewhere.

Mr Edgcombe will be at Yarcomb a Monday next.

You See Mr Kemp's Heir presented, wou'd it be amiss, if you gave Him a Hint about getting their Fines levy'd, you see how Parson H[urrell] gains upon you.

Borough of Bere Alston

To wit a Court Leet Law day & view of Frank pledge of the Burrough aforesaid held at the house of John Maynard within the said Burrough for the Right Honourable John Lord Hobart Baron of Blickling & one of the Honourable order of the Bath Knight, this fourth day of October in the Sixteenth year of Our Soveraign Lord, George the Second, by the Grace of God of Great Britain &c and in the year of Our Lord 1742, before Nathaniel Carpenter, Steward

Names of the Jury

John Creed Dr of Divinity	John Doidge
Thomas Hurrell Clerk	John Rich
Francis Drake Esquire***	Thomas Rich
Nicholas James Rowe Gentleman	William Corter
John Edgcombe	William Bealey
Abraham Searle	
John Sanguin	
Richard Corter	
Anthony Porter	

We present all those that Owe Suit & Service at this Court & have not appear'd.

We present Mr William Bealey to be Sworn Portreeve for the year Ensuing.

We present Mr Roger Hurrell to be admitted Tenent or Free Burgess for the moiety of a Dwelling House & Lands which he has purchased of the Rev Mr Thomas Hurrell who lately purchased the said Lands of John Bampfylde Esquire –

We present the Death of Mr John Kempe, late a Tenant or Free Burgess & his Lands to be descended to his Daughters: Elizabeth the Wife of William Burnaford, Mary the Wife of Mr Peter Burnaford, Alice the Wife of George Grills, and Susanna the Wife of George Edgcombe –

We present Thomas Wills & William Moysey to be Sworn Bread Weighers & Ale Tasters for the Year Ensuing –

We Continue all former presentments not amended.

Sign'd by the above Jurors

* Dr Creed, as above (see F196, note).
** John Doidge, a needy freeholder of Bere Alston, on whose behalf requests are repeatedly made.
*** The jury member Francis Drake is a cousin of FHD.

F203

5 November 1742

Dear Sir

As I had given you an account of Bere Court in my Letter of the 8th past, I forbore answering yours 'till now; That the Books you desir'd are sent in a Box with some things for your Mama, of which Mr Porter will advise –

You puzzle me to tell what Mr John Doidge is fit; what he desires, is a Tidewaiter at Plymouth but there is so much time on the hands of those people, which they generally Spend in an Ale-House, a place that has been his ruine, and which He's too fond of Still: All that I can Say is, that his Circumstances require some assistance.

Mrs Bealey too has been Solliciting me to apply to ye all for a place for Her Husband, but how to describe his Qualifications – you can better than I – only this I know, that you stand much the Fairest to be his Heir – as to his being Portreeve, 'twas the Desire of Mr Wills & as Mr Wyatt was not there, it was also very Agreable to Him: it is Strengthening the Band, neither cou'd it be in a better Time.

Mr Edgcombe lately inform'd me That He had wrote up that Lieutenant Drake* was willing to sell his Right to you in his Tenement at Yarcomb, and that your Uncle had wrote Him, He willing to treat for you, if I approv'd of the Terms. That's a Compliment in no measure belongs to me, But as I wish you and your affairs very well, may venture to Say, that you may give him for his Life ninety pounds which is at £15 a year 6 years' value (if you are Satisfy'd a Gentleman in his Situation runs no Risque). The Estate is valu'd in the Survey Book at £20 a year, and his Father gave your Grandfather for 3 lives £200 in 1713, which at 12 years' value is between £16 & £17 a year; if he lives to come back it is much better for you than anyone Else, becaus when you come of Age, you may set a full Estate in it. He cannot fill it up at present, nor ever Seems Likely, till he has received his Wife's Fortune.

He is order'd into the Streights on Board Admiral Mathew's Ship the *Neptune*, he went away last week, has left his affairs in great Confusion – he has made over all his Estates to Mr Edgcombe, with a power to sell this & his Right to the Lands in Beer to you. If 'tis thought adviseable to buy the Yarcomb, get the other first Settl'd, 'twill come the Easier; for No-one but you, I am perswaded, wou'd buy his Right in Yarcomb as it now stands – You will be pleas'd to Communicate this to your Uncle, who I hope is Better, pray my humble Service to Him, & excuse my not writing to Him, I wou'd give Him as Little Trouble as possible.

I am Sir

Your most Faithful humble Servant

N Rowe

Your little Mare has been very Bad in a Cold, is far from Well, the Hine takes great Care of her, and Mr Serle is the Dr.

* FHD's cousin Francis Drake, as above (see F202, note).

F204

15 April 1743

Sir

I am very Glad to find by your Letter That you have got the Better of your Disorder, which I understood was an ague 'till Then. It is very Rough Cold weather here, & very Unseasonable & Unhealthy, I hope you take Care of Catching Cold, as I do that you will Come down Soon in the Summer, which will be for your health & Service –

Mr Strode was at the Court at Beer last Monday, and was Taken Tennant. I forbare Expatiating in this manner, But when I see you, what I observ'd, will be more particular in –

The 'Heirs' of Mr Kemp were presented, and two of Them Taken Tennant. But Parson Burnaford & his Brother were not There on account of the Death of one of his Children, But the next will be There. There were some very Trifling objections made, which Show plainly &c &c. And that they were not a little Startled at the Number 4.

I was at Mr Edgcombe's a Saturday to See the Parties Execute, they were all Extreme Hearty, and if you desir'd Mr E to return Them your Thanks I think it wou'd not be amiss. As to Dr Creed, I heard (had his Nephew Peter Come a Sunday as he Expected) he wou'd have been at the Court too, But for what End I know not.

Your Uncle Harry Drake call'd here about a Forthnight ago, But I did not See Him. He and one Mr Peirce with whom he is, went Then for Exeter in order to proceed Directly for London, But Mr Porter told me a Monday, That to his great Surprize they were Come back to Plymouth again. They are upon what they call a Party of pleasure, I don't hear anything about Boro's runs in his head now, unless they have a Cornish One in view, Being going There as they Say; Though I Fancy a More Material B[oro] do's or ought to take up his Thoughts.*

I heartily wish [you well] and am Sir
Your most Faithful Humble Servant
N Rowe

* Perhaps a facetious reference to the King's Bench Prison, a debtors' prison close to Borough High Street in Southwark. In due course, Harry Drake spent time in another debtors' prison, Fleet Prison, on the opposite side of the Thames.

F205

22 July 1743

Sir

I have your Favour of the 14th and hope you are perfectly restor'd to your health –

As to Comb Farm,* I thought as the Times went, it was more for your advantage to abate the Rent, than keep it in hand at so great an expence, & small return – Mr Edgcombe was of the same Opinion, and I presume the Reason why he han't answerd your Letter is that he waits till th'Assize to enquire into the Man's Character & Circumstances.

I am Oblig'd to you for Communicating the Enclos'd, I Always had a mean Opinion of the Man,** and nothing but the flagrant Injustice I knew he did you (Being the unhappy Occasion of his having it in his power) cou'd have induc'd me to have taken any notice of him; I hope he'l perform what he promises without any

Equivocation, or &cs – And Cease to deserve the Epithet, he so Charitably Confers on me – I pity the Wretched Man, whose late sickness wou'd not amend, and treat his suggestion, as he Deserves Himself, with Contempt.

Mr Bealey too ought to do Some things, which I hope he'l Comply with, when you require them of him: a Trust without a proper Explanation, you See Everyone is not to be Trusted with, and none Ought. I have Done my best to serve you, But if you or your Friends Disapprove of my Conduct, you have my hearty Concurrance to Disavow any part of it, if you find it for your Service so to Do; and upon that Supposition, you'l have a good Foundation to Correct by your Own, what you shall find amiss in mine; and may your affairs & Actions meet with the Success I sincerely wish you.

Far be it from Me ever to propound what might be Expensive to you, I thought what I propos'd might be for your Advantage, without that disagreable Attendant; But Since you and your Friends are of a Different Opinion, I have no more to Say.

What I hinted to you here, I imagine can't properly be Done but by a personal application from yourself. Things of that Nature can't prudently be trusted to Writing – as no-one who is your Friend can't Think but it is highly Necessary for you to be at Michaelmas Court at Beer.

Just after, I humbly think, will be the fit Time to propose it to Everyone; and no honest Man, I am perswaded, will refuse it.

I am with Esteem Sir

Your very Faithful Humble Servant

N Rowe

Lord Hobart,*** 'tis Said, has given Beer Living to One Mr Snow, who you'l find a more Artful Man than his predecessor.

My humble Service to your Uncle, poor John Doidge greatly Wants your assistance. Mr John Wills is a Sollicitor to get his Friend the Excise-Man restor'd, he Complains much He has not the *News* duly; if you was to write Him a Line, That you think of Him, it wou'd affect him much.

When you address your Friends, as the good Dr professes so much Regard, try to get Both from Him, to prevent any Future Temptation; For if you wou'd have my Opinion of the Man, and his Letter, I think He is not so Constant in anything, as his Malice; Therefore a Fit of the Bottle, or a Fit of the Brain may turn all his Canting professions to the Same performance your Father met with from Him, which was to deceive him to the Last.

* Combe Farm was part of the Nutwell estate.
** The trouble-maker Dr Creed, referred to again in the postscript to this letter.
*** Lord Hobart, subsequently Buckingham, was lord of the manor: see Introduction, section 2, p. 21. Hobart and FHD controlled Bere Alston's two parliamentary seats.

F206

Buckland, 5 August 1743

Sir

Whatever your Friends or you think I know not, But Still your Interest is at Stake – I have Labour'd in the Vineyard, whether you or They may approve it. This I know, that I have acted uprightly, and can Say with Samuel (tho' upon a greater Occasion) 'Whose ass &c'.

I hope for your own Sake, you won't Take impressions, but where you find Them well grounded, there Fix 'Em; whether they proceed from a Spiritual or Temporal Intimation – So much for Eclaircissements.

Now young Gentleman, for so I may call you until the twentyeth Instant, For St Paul you very well know, has made the Distinction much Better than I can – I wou'd only Touch tenderly, and with Respect, That your Situation requires some Thought, not the narrow Notions of a Pedagogue, not a Fellow of a College, nor an acquir'd Dr in Degrees; your good Sense I know has Learnt to look meanly on 'Em, as you do on the Buttery Roll ['College wine-store'] – But still a modest & a Learned Man has your private Distinction.

I wou'd only add that Business must be your Early Care – That Mr Pollexfen by will gave his Estate, which lineally Descends to you, your Father prov'd it, according to the Form of Law, But that probate I have heard him say, He Could not recollect in whose hands it was Left. One Mr Harper of Lincoln's Inn pass't his Bill for him, as an Agent, whether he or Sir William Heathcote has it, it is highly necessary it shou'd be in your possession. You will, I don't Doubt, make the proper Enquiry about it – For what is in my Custody as knowledge you may always Command my best Information (not withstanding any Suggestions to the Contrary),

as I am Sir
Your most Faithful Humble Servant
N Rowe

I write with a Labouring hand, it shakes, & it's Time to Shut up.

I have not heard from Mr Edgcombe since I wrote you.

F207

27 January 1743/1744*

Sir

Though I am very Badly Able to Do anything at present, yet I can't Deferr any longer letting you know my Surprize at what you write about – I know he** do's all that can be – the Fault don't ly on his side. The Misfortune is, That everything turns out Bad, and Miracles can't be wrought. All the Favour I ask is, that as I am Concern'd in several Things with Him, all matters may be adjusted cooly & fairly, and let his accounts be made up to Lady Day, which shall be done here too – and then let Everyone do as they Please: But I wou'd have them maturely to Consider, Before any precipitate Resolution is Taken, it will else be too late, For when a Diffidence is once shown, No-one will act afterwards; and the Crisis (which Things are Reduc'd to) may Confound the whole, if not nicely observ'd – I'l answer he's an Honest Man, and I too well know, what the Consequence wou'd be to differ with Him – In short, things are so Envelop'd, That it is not for Either of your Interest, to make any alteration at present, which I can very Easily Explain at a proper Time, this way it is not. So Beg you'l with my service Intimate This, as my Thoughts, which I am sure will be Found right – and Further, I wish I knew where to mend it.

As to the Deeds you mention, Michaelmas Court will be Time Enough, so your Brother may bring 'Em, when he comes up.

But as to Mr Spry, that's at a Stand, as you han't Thought upon One to Succeed Him –

There are many Things to Say & Do, which I hope for your Own sake, you'l Think of – There's John Doidge, Thomas Rich Continually pressing; & I hear Mr Wills's Friend is *in Statu quo* – Captain St Lo is order'd to Portsmouth, only waits a Wind, I have got Him to take Mr Searle's Son, he has made John Blanchard's Son in Law his Carpenter's mate. Cou'd a Warrant for a Bomb ['sailing ship with mortars mounted'] be got for Him, 'twou'd give a Lustre to the Little Corps – Captain St Lo has been very obliging Besides; a Line or two from you wou'd be kindly Taken – There you know Best.

I am Sir
Your most Faithful humble Servant
N Rowe

I will only take the Liberty to add That neither the person at Plymouth you nam'd, nor the Other wou'd advance *sine qua* ['without anything'] – 6d. But wou'd enhance the Reckoning – by the Choice I perceive they are not known, Tho' they wou'd <u>be Trusted</u>.***

* The letter-writers sometimes use 'dual dating' for the period 1 January–24 March. According to the 'old style', the new year started on 25 March; according to the 'new style', it started on 1 January. The changeover for the start of the year, especially in letters, began earlier than the full transition from the Julian to the Gregorian calendar, which was not implemented in England until 1752. When there is 'dual dating' in these letters, the second date is the one applicable for modern reckoning, based on the Gregorian calendar.
** John Edgcombe, the Drake family legal and business adviser, as above (see F198, note).
*** One of Rowe's veiled references, in which he mentions no names.

F208*

19 February 1743/1744

Sir

Your Letter of the 5th came not to my hand 'till last post – Tho' the Lady, nor the Lord [?] don't immediately return you Some Answer, I wou'd not give it up, But Try 'Em again, I shou'd Think with regard to what's past, They wou'd make such an Easy Acknowledgment –

As to Mr M– [?] I'm very sorry he wou'd not oblige you as to the Com[mon?] P[lace?] Books of your Grandfather, I hope He has what you ask'd besides –

Mr Porter's Notions, I'm perswaded, proceeded from the highth of Gratitude & Respect – that same Word (Court) is what all Expect, tho' in Diminutive power; whether in this Case you don't Think it worth your While, you are the Best Judge; But as your Friends wish you well, you must put a Favourable Construction on their sanguine Hopes, Tho' you disagree with 'Em –

I wrote you an answer to what you Desir'd, with my Thoughts impartially, But you don't Say you Receiv'd it.

I heartily wish you well, may God Direct you in Everything, & inspire you with such Sentiments as may be Conducive to your Interest, and the Support of That you are now Entitl'd to, which will require your Thoughts and a sutable application.

I am Sir
Your Faithful Humble Servant
N Rowe

I presume you've alter'd your mind about the Wear ['weir'], But you & your Mother conjunctly might make a good advantage of the Fishery, which now yields nothing – But I don't pretend to advise anything, Least it Shou'd be Thought an Expencive project – However, there are Times & Seasons for Everything.

* Again, a deliberately obscure message, with no spelling out of names.

F209

13 March 1743/1744

Sir

I have answer'd your several Letters, am now to acquaint you, That Luce* is Dead. You know how the Affair about Him is, I humbly Think you shou'd write to Mr Edgcombe about it, least as it has been Kept a secret, any of his Relations shou'd Claim &c at the next Court, which is the 2nd April. Mr John Doidge has apply'd to your Uncle to succeed him as a Tide-Waiter at Saltash, But I fear the Gentlemen for that Boro' have got it.

Parson Peter Creed, I hear, intends to attend next Court to be Taken Tennant; his good Uncle may harden his Metal, But such alienations may be of Dangerous Consequence to your Interest – For suppose anyone Else should Do so too – upon an equal Right, any one may.

I hear there was an attempt made for you at P[lymouth/Plympton?]** – tho' without success, and that your Uncle Harry, who was then there, appear'd in it. He is in a gay Equipage, a Valet & a brace of Geldings – Bills & Cash in poco ['a small amount']. Being advis'd to the Sea Air for his Health, He thought his Native the most proper; He has been to Visit the good Dr – and is now at Meavy with Mr Buttal with the Plymouth Hounds. He talks of Coming here, But I have not yet Seen Him.

The Times are Trying, pray God Direct you, and Guard you against all Attacks.

I am Sir

Your most Faithful Humble Servant

N Rowe

The Vessel that Carry'd up your Books was Cast away in Bigberry Bay on her Return.

* Luce was evidently a freeholder or tenant in Bere Alston. For FHD's potential claim on Luce's land, with relevance to voting rights, see below, F213. For FHD's payment of £30 for Luce's 'interest' and the suggestion that he should pay the same for the sailor Hatch's 'interest', see F253.
** For Plymouth and Plympton as two of the boroughs where Harry Drake sought to re-establish Drake control, see F198.

F210

23 March 1743/1744

Sir

I have your Letters of the 12th & 15th. I think you are very Right to apply to Lady K [?] again, the House is Down & of no Value, the thing itself tho' to you of some Consideration, can be none now to that Family, I shou'd therefore Think for what's past, They won't refuse it you –

I think Mr Edgcombe, as the Times go, has made a good [ba]rgain with Mr Bewes for you, provided Mr Hendra his Uncle is in a good State of Health, which Mr E Told me he now is, For that was the Objection 5 year ago, when Mr B was in Treaty with your Father at Nutwell and not on account of his age, For he is not an old Man. Mr E acquainted me some Time ago upon what Terms he had agreed with Mr B if you approv'd of it – It's true those Estates are Tyth-Free, But your Grand-Father, nor Father never Rais'd their Demands, and as the Times go, it won't Bare to begin now, But hereafter you may Do as you Please, only Consider you get rid of Estates in hand, which upon Seing your accounts you won't find to have Brought you in much –

Newhouse Reserv'd Rent	£ 1.
Undertowne ———————	–. 18. 9
Beefparks ———————	1. 10. –
	3. 8. 9

Now as no allowance is made for these Rents, you may reckon it at 13 years' value for the Estates in hand, & 8 for the Revertions, so That I think, as I am perswaded Mr E wou'd in no Case Deceive you, my Entering into the affair, wou'd Look as if you doubted of Him; But you may put it upon this, provided He is perswaded Mr Hendra Bewes is in a very good State of Health, for all Hangs on That. In anything you Think me Capable of serving you, you are always Sure, But one wou'd not Create Jealousys, when there is no Occasion.

Mr Heathcote has wrote Me, That Mr Wills's Friend is provided for; I am very Glad you intend to write Mr W of it, your Correspondence with your Friends is highly ingaging, and you'l Find what an Effect it will have.

I have troubl'd your Uncle with Letters in behalf of John Doidge to be a Tidewaiter at Saltash in the room ['place'] of Luce but fear as I wrote 'twill be *re intecta* ['a clear matter']. I hope you have received my Letter as to Luce & Peter Creed, as the Court Draws nigh – Mr Bealey had oblig'd me to write to Mr Heathcote to be a Salt Officer at Plymouth. Thomas Rich is always Teazing me too – I am Sorry you'r at Such a Distance from your affairs; if your Health requires it, I am sure your Interest do's, to be more Conversant in this Country than you have Hitherto Been –

I have Such a Disorder in my head that Disables me from Everything – I wish you may pick out my Confusion –

I heartily wish you well & am Sir
Your very Faithful humble servant
N Rowe

Your Brother Samuel is now here, But the Sooner He was Settl'd elsewhere the Better. He presents you his Service.

Your Uncle Harry I have not yet seen.

F211

Buckland, 30 March 1744

Sir

Understanding by your Mother That you are at London, I give you this Trouble.

I have Troubl'd your Uncle with several Letters about John Doidge & William Bealey – Your Friends seem to Expect some Notice to be Taken of Them. You are the best Judge in what manner it is to be Done, Since they Expect it from you, and their importunitys must have Some Countenance shown 'Em – John Doidge is with me almost Every Day, I wish you wou'd write to Him & Mr Bealey yourself.

The inclosed to Captain St Lo I shou'd beg your Uncle's Frank for,* and if you wou'd write Him a Line in Favour of John Blanchard's Son-in-Law Lean (who he made his Carpenter's Mate at my request) to get Him preferr'd to a Warrant as there is a Likelyhood of War, it wou'd be very obliging to your Friends, & I Dare say the Captain wou'd pay a Due regard to it.

Your Mother seems to be much Displeas'd with Mr Edgcombe, for what I know He can't help – Whatever her Reasons are I know not, But this I am sure of, that for many Reasons, which I shan't mention here it is in no wise prudent to Differ with Him; shall I say *Sate* ['enough'] as Things stand.

If you think it worth your While to do anything about Dr Creed & his Nephew, I hope you have wrote Mr Edgcombe, Becaus I Expect They'l make the Attempt a Monday. I hope likewise you have wrote to Him about Luce's affair at Beer. Your being Frequently There is of the last Consequence to your Interest, it can't be Done by a 2nd Hand now.

I am Thus Free as I wish you well & am Sir
Your most Faithful Humble Servant
N Rowe

* Rowe is requesting that Samuel Heathcote should cover the postage for this letter, 'free franks' being a perquisite of MPs. See Introduction, section 2, p. 22.

F212

Boro' of Beeralston
To Wit a Court Leet &c held for the said Boro'
2nd Day of April, Year 1744

Names of the Jury

Nicholas James Rowe Gentleman	John Sanguin
John Edgcombe	William Bealey
Francis Drake Esquire	Joseph Grills
Abraham Searl	Richard Corter
John Wills	William Corter
William Bray	Robert Kelly
Anthony Porter	
John Doidge	

We present all those that Owe Suit & Service at this Court & have not appear'd.

We present Mr William Bredall to be admitted Tennant or Free Burgess for Lands within the said Boro' formerly the Lands of John Anthony which the said Mr Bredall Lately purchased of Sir Francis Henry Drake Baronet.

We Continue all former presentments not amended.

F213

Buckland, 3 April 1744

Sir

I have your Favour of the 27th past –

Yesterday was the Court at Beer, Enclosed is a Copy of the presentments.

It was not Thought proper to present Luce 'till next Court, when you wou'd produce your Title to his Lands.*

After the Jury had Concluded the presentment, and all but 2 or 3 Sign'd their Names – Dr Creed Bolted into the Room with his Nephew, and Tender'd his Deeds to the Jury.** We Told Him as we had Finish'd the presentments & sign'd 'Em, He was Come too Late, however He insisted to have Them receiv'd, But being rejected, went Down to the Court Room, and Tender'd the Deeds to the Steward, and fell upon Mr Edgcombe in a most scurrilous Manner, and after the most abusive Language offer'd to Strike Him, upon which the new parson of Beer, Mr Snow, who is a Justice of the Peace, being present, Commanded the peace – The good Dr was very Insolent to me too, But that I disregarded; Mr E did not spare Him, However Behav'd Extremely handsome & Zealous for you – The Dr is a very Bad Man (to speak it in the softest Manner), a Hardn'd Wretch, in Contempt with all Mankind, and the More so if possible, for his yesterday's Behaviour, where he Show'd his Iniquity, & Ingratitude in the most Flagrant Manner to the Astonishment & Detestation of all – yet I cou'd perceive a pleasure in some Faces.

No Doubt Mr E will write you more particular – to Crown the whole, the Vile Wretch got Drunk & Behav'd like a Beast. Such Eclaircissements tho' acted in Such a vile manner, yet it puts people upon Thinking more than they otherwise wou'd, and more in Favour of Themselves – John Doidge is no Doubt capable of Doing the Duty of a Tidewaiter, But how far he'd be regular I can't say, & less for Thomas Rich. As to William Bealey, whatever his Circumstances may be, he's more pressing, & his wife too, than if they weren't worth a groat. I wish you wou'd write Them yourself –

Mr Tapson, tho' so old, was at your Court, and Declar'd openly he wou'd Serve you & Your Family as Long as he Liv'd. At this Juncture if you wou'd write Him, & Take some Notice of his Sons tho' unknown, it wou'd be vastly agreable to 'Em. His place is Insdon near Ashburton.

As Mankind grow more & More Deprav'd, they must be the more attentively Observ'd. Your Friends Seem for the Generality untainted (except the Rotten Member, who by the Bye is in a very bad State as to his Health) yet your presence and acquaintance with 'Em, you'l Find more & more Necessary –

Lord Hobart, Mr Snow told me, is Soon Expected Down.

I shou'd not wonder if this vile Dr offer'd Him all his pretentions, the Steward Seem'd to be very obsequious to Him.

I don't Doubt your Endeavour to prepare yourself for all Events, & I pray God assist you – I had almost Forgot to Mention it, But your Friends were yesterday very full of an address, and That you wou'd get one Drawn & sent down which They desire you, with the Members, wou'd present to his Majesty. This they desir'd me to Communicate to you, and are in full expectation of an answer.

I am Sir
Your most Faithful Humble Servant
N Rowe

I am very Sorry your Mother is so Dissatisfy'd with Mr Edgcombe.

I am Sure 'tis without any Just grounds, He being not only a Faithful Servant but a Friend to the Family in General –

Your Brother*** comes up in the Coach next Monday and indeed it is high Time he shou'd be fix'd Somewhere, where more Effect might be produc'd, than from the Country, which he seems to be Above –

* For Luce's death, see F209.
** See Introduction, section 2, p. 20.
*** Francis Samuel had completed his schooling in Plymouth.

F214

29 April 1744

Sir

I have Both your Favours: as to the first, I only answer'd the Request of your Friends, by intimating to you what They Desir'd, without any Intension of your meeting with Tiberius' Compliment for a late address.

As to the other, I don't See what greater proofs can be given of your Side of an Agreement, than so perfect a Complaisance – But as you know so well how to distinguish between Absolute & Conditional, it is not for me to Enlarge – I know of no Lands in Treaty for there, perhaps the good Dr as he has bragg'd may make a Tender of His, where he will be received with open arms, But let his ignorance and Ingratitude Carry Him where he will, if you Exert yourself, He can make no Title to 'Em –

As to the Monoculus ['one-eyed creature'] [?], his affairs are indeed Dubious, But there is more upon it already, than anyone wou'd give, unless the Jacobites* have Hopes, & Make high purchases – if you wou'd but know your Friends, you wou'd soon Fix Such an Interest in 'Em, That No-one cou'd remove, which is worth your Thought.

I hope you have Try'd again, or will, Lady K [?].

I am Sir
Your very Faithful Humble Servant
N Rowe

All the Redstrake Cyder, which was made, is Sent up to London and by this Time got up; it was little above a Hogshead.

* Fears regarding Jacobite uprisings were well founded: the Battle of Culloden took place the following year.

F215

27 January 1748/9

Sir

I shou'd have acknowledg'd your Favour Before But indeed I am quite out of Frame, & unfit for anything –

Your Father has been now Dead 9 years; I shou'd hope, as I wish, That all Family Difficultys will be soon Determin'd, and that amicably too, as we know not how soon it may [be] out of our power –

As the Demands on you have & may be suddain, & uncertain when, you will do well to be provided against all Events, and I am glad it is now in your power, keep it so.

I hope your Brother* has got well over his Trial, the Country have it That He is to have the *Unicorn*, a new 20 Gun ship Building Here. I wish it may be so, pray my service to Him –

The long wet & stormy Weather has Try'd the old Monastry, the House & Barn require some Repairs – the Head wear ['weir'] has been Try'd by the Floods.

I congratulate you on your popular Favours at T[avistock?] –

Captain T Williams I hear nothing of, But I have had a Melancholy Letter from his Brother, which I am not able to answer. He says He has wrote you too, But of That you are the best Judge –

Old Kelly** has been Bad some Time, He talks of Disinheriting his Grandson & selling his Lands, by which I Fancy He won't Live long. I Query whether He can do it, But if you think proper you may Let Mr Edgcombe try to see his Title, & give him your Orders.

The Compliments of the season attend you all, I hope you have your health as I wish you – *multos & Felices, vive & vale* ['many and happy years, be well and prosper'].

I am
Your Faithful Friend to serve you
N Rowe

I hope you have received the silver.

* FHD's brother Francis William was tried and found not guilty after losing his ship: 'On 29 January 1748 he was posted captain of the Fowey 20, seeing service in the West Indies under Rear-Admiral Charles Knowles during the Austrian War of Succession. His command was wrecked on the Florida Keys on 27 June 1748, but at the subsequent court martial held in England he was acquitted of any blame regarding her loss, it being put down to an unknown current': see R. Hiscocks, 'Francis William Drake' (2016), https://morethannelson.com/officer/francis-william-drake/ (accessed June 2019).
** Kelly is one of the Bere Alston freeholders listed in F212.

F216

14 December 1749

Dear Sir

I shou'd answer your Letters, & Do a great many Things more Regularly But indeed I am not able, the Days are Come in which I must Say I have no pleasure in Them –

I am truly Sorry you have had no Success in the pursuit of your health, I heartily wish it you & Everything that's agreable, pray pursue all Methods Conducive Thereto –

As to your Pheasants, I Fear they won't answer your Expectations here, as Things govern – you mistook me, or I was wrong in Writing. Benjamin put but 6 of the Hens & 1 Cock in the Hall-garden, one of which (the Hens) has been kill'd, not known how, or Own'd. The Garden is Secur'd as to the Cats, But then the Doors are Frequently open'd about the Cyder so that nothing is to be Depended on. *Statu Quo nunc* ['as things stand at present'] all the Other Pheasants, Cocks & Hens, are in the gardens, Pidgeon-House and Pond.

The Place you mention behind the Stable, they Say, is not to be Done as you mention, But the Gutter-Holes are Stopt where the Water runs –

Solomon this morning Found One of the Cocks half Eat by Something, whether Hawk or Vermin is not Known, For Both Frequent There, and Mr Hine makes great Complaints of the Havock They do in the gardens & I hear has wrote about it –

What your Cousin the Captain has wrote you about the Plantation in the Padock seems the most feizable, But I Fear without a proper person's care, all won't Do.

I wish I had had your Sentiments about the Counterparts sooner, Becaus such management has not <u>a Counterpart</u>.

I am truly Concern'd for your Brother Samuel. His Uncle Harry Drake shou'd be a Light to Him to avoid Those <u>Breakers</u>. There, if you pay Him, you've done your Part, But I Fear the Blood of the Nelsons is not Extinct.*

I am very Truly
Your affectionate Friend
N Rowe

I have not Seen Mr Edgcombe since you went & have Kept the Memorandum till I see Him – as writing on Such Things is uncertain.

Since my writing the above Solomon brought in 2 Cocks & 2 Hen Pheasants Kill'd by Something.

I have Sent up for the Captain to Consult what to do.

Yesterday was very windy & last night very wet, what can be done but Take 'Em in, & where to put 'Em, I know not.

* Rowe is evidently concerned that Samuel is running up debts, like his uncle Harry Drake. 'Blood of the Nelsons' may possibly refer to John Nelson (1653?–1734), merchant, entrepreneur, privateer, land speculator, and political activist in New England and Nova Scotia, who also had some involvement in fisheries controversies in north-eastern America. See *ODNB*, *Dictionary of Canadian Biography*, and *American National Biography*.

F217

7 January 1749–50

Sir

I am Sorry to find by yours That the Admiral* is in so Declining a way – the Torid & the Frigid Zone Few can Temper –

There, we are all Bound for the Same Port, Tho' varied are the Courses Steer'd to it, yet By & Large they all point to the Load Stone.

As to Ascents, I know but of Two.

Boniface wou'd make no Scruple to Squeez Wax again, But Cupid must be more tenderly Toutch't – *quod non est Notum non est Factum* ['what is not known is not done'], must be a Syllogism –

You will have many occasions to reflect on my Soliloquys at parting, a Knowledge in middle Life wou'd insensibly make an Interest, where Remainders are Contingent, and That's the mark you must aim at. I hope there is not the immediate Danger you apprehend, cou'd we foresee it there wou'd be no Difficulty, But to be arm'd against Everything that may happen, as if it wou'd happen, is a Caution necessary in your Situation – all that I can Say is that *propria persona* ['the proper person'] <u>must</u> be Found out to answer your Purpose. I must own Frankly I know None I cou'd rely on: as you have wrote to Mr Edgcombe – He may probably recommend Some.

I heartily wish you health & many happy new years & am Sir
Your True Friend
N Rowe

As the three fold Cord may be too Soon divided, pray Think Favourably.

Pray has anything been Done about Hatch – old Hatch – <u>is Just gone</u>.**

You ha'e near Lost poor Tom Reed, But he is recover'd it's to be hop'd, tho' the Death of his Wife had almost Done his Business. I wou'd not alarm you, But wrote to Mr E.

He said He wou'd Take care about the needful – Suppose you <u>wrote</u> to Honest Tom Reed a Line of Comfort, I'm sure He'd Take it in a very grateful sense –

I have sent Mr E the Conveyances from Mr Spry & Mr Tapson to the Captain for his Determinacion.

* Probably Admiral Philip Vanbrugh, as in F233, F240.
** As becomes evident in subsequent letters, the sailor Hatch had a claim in Bere Alston.

F218

9 February 1750

Sir

Your Brother the Captain* Surpriz'd me with a visit last Sunday S'ennight at night & return'd (on an Express that one of the Indiamen under his Convoy was safe at Falmouth) to Plymouth at one in the Morning; But came again the next Day, But after a Boat or two to Plymouth Left this Place on Wednesday last. Whether he is gone or no I can't Say – It was very Providential <u>very much so</u> (Such Stormy weather we have had of Late) That he put in, or rather gain'd this port; in all Humane probability, He might else have been Lost – He's an honest young Fellow, who tho' he has Seen the World abroad, wants to be better acquainted with that at Home – A perfect Harmony between you Two (which I heartily wish) may be a great means Thereto, I need not mention to you the obligation. His health is better than I expected, and wou'd be more so, if He'd use the means.

Your Brother the Lieutenant in expectation** was with Him here, He's an object of great Compassion! Lord, what can He do without your assistance – You must overlook his weakness, I intreat it of you – Natural affection pleads Strongly for Him, & moral Duty commands it: as God has given you better Sense, I'm persuaded on Reflection you've better Sentiments, than I can pretend to inculcate – To Save a

Soul from Death has a great Reward; and to save a Brother from destruction carrys a great Satisfaction here & a greater hereafter – I've talk'd to Him roundly, He pleads Necessity & promises better Things – Think, I beg you, of a Brother on the Brink, pull Him back, and He may Live to thank you in a better manner, than I can Express – As I love you all, and wish you well; Nothing but That cou'd induce me to give you, or myself this Trouble.

Multos & Felices vive & vale ['Many and happy years, live well and prosper']

* Francis William Drake.
** Francis Samuel Drake.

F219

3 April 1750

Sir

I am Sorry I can't write you as I would, I am now Sensible I shou'd have Exerted more than I have, But I find now it's past, and so will Everything; I can but Repeat, I wish you well.

By the assistance of your Cousin the Captain I have Got a Carpenter who has undertaken to right the Pallisadoes, & I believe will do it to your Liking, and in the Expence too, but he can't go upon it 'till Whitsuntide, being pre-ingag'd in Church-Work, which he can't put off – 'tis Edgcombe of this parish, who formerly wou'd have undertaken it and I wish now, it had then been done –

I have Talk'd to Penkivel the Mason, who lay'd the Fountain's bottome at first. He Says part, if not all, must be Taken up, will engage to Stop the Leeks Effectually, But then the pipe is broke that plays the Jet d'eau & the Boy is Defective – you know how Things are, a Little may be Done, but all in general is in Decay – and I am Sorry to Say the management is so Raw, to call it no worse, that there's little Encouragement to be Explicit; and the misfortune is the greater, that it is not Thought so; But Time will too Soon Convince, Tho' nothing Else will.

If omitting coming to an Election on the first proper oppertunity be not a Deviation from the T[est] act,* then doubtless the Customary Day of Election is Best. But that Surely you can be better inform'd of where you are; Mr Edgcombe Seem'd to think it may be Deferr'd 'till Michaelmas Court as it is an Unusual Thing; the Case requires your best Attension.

I am Sir
Your very Faithful
N Rowe

I'm truly Sorry for your unthinking Brother Samuel. *Facilis Descensus* ['the descent is easy'] &c.

Your Father had Two Hynes, broken Farmers of Small Estates, which were Treherne & Widdecomb. Your Mother Remembers their Management. They were Small Beer Flat, this is bottl'd – I won't make any Inference the Case is Similar, as I fear the Consequence will be, with far greater Oppertunitys – So much for the Serjeant, the Lieutenant carrys the Considerable, but whether he'l prove like the man's Nightingal, *vox* ['a voice and nothing more'] &c his Conduct will Show – Such are the Props of the Falling Driory [?].

You Talk'd of painting the parlour &c, it is at present the general Rendezvous of the Hine & all sorts of his Companions, which won't Sute with your Intended Decorations, and I had almost Forgot to let you know, that much of the Plaistering in the Hall is crack'd & will come down soon, which will be no Small Delight to your Coming in.

Tho' there has been much Stormy Cold Weather of Late there is a Likelyhood of much Fruit in the Gardens & Orchards.

I hope you'l be so good To appoint your Captain your Engineer for the Reason I mention'd to you, For I can't bear the Thoughts of a Negative from your Present Officers –

We cou'd not get the Materials 'till today, as Tarras & Lime & Clay, and I ventur'd to open the Fountain; the Masons have Found out the Leak, which is by the Waste-pipe, so I hope the Expence won't be so much, as was imagin'd, nor the Bottom new Lay'd as was at first Fear'd –

As to making the Palisadoe's Tops Strait & plain, it will Look Very odd, & the Expence to make 'Em all alike, as they will be done Stronger won't much enhance your Charge which in the Whole will be much less than I imagin'd, or I believe <u>you Do</u>.

Here's another Objection occurs when the Rails are Repair'd, if some Method is not found out to Keep the Horses from being Hitch't to 'Em, they'l be Soon broke again. Now there are a parcel of posts Which with a Single rail might be Fix't under the great Trees, which wou'd prevent it.

* The Test Act of 1673, amended 1678, was a test of eligibility for public office retained throughout the eighteenth century.

F220

18 May 1750

Sir

When Mortality is the Subject all Resentments Subside.

I am truly Concern'd for Mrs Martyn & her Unhappy Daughters,* made so by a Freedom which Parents can't Justify, nor Trustees – I am Sorry it is not in my Power to assist 'Em, neither can I presume to reccommend; But surely the Subject is very Moving.

The present situation of things here give [sic] no Encouragement to improvements: a Chimney Piece to a Smoky room: and old Wainscot wou'd be no Decoration: a Dark green Stuff to hide the Defects, when the Sun Shines, is all the Place will Bare. The Highth of the Windows is 8 ft, Bredth 6 ft – what is wanting, is so much, That unless a Thoro' repair was to be, Everything to remain *in Statu quo* you'l Think Best, and 'Twill carry it! Excuse – For was you to See, it wou'd be Enough!

Poor Mr Edgcombe has been very Ill, I fear he has a bad Stamen; There, like the Burn't paper, one Spark go's out after another Till –

I heartily wish you Success in Everything and am Sir

Your very Faithful

N Rowe

I hear your Brother Samuel is marry'd, & I Fear Marr'd!**

Your Brother William's Government I don't Think any preferment under a Commodore.

If you have a good offer for Stancomb, you'd certainly agree with B[?] or C[?].

Your Horses & Mares answer well. But your Pheasants I fear will come to Nothing, what do you propose to do with their Eggs? They rise High in Number but no young.

25 May

This Letter shou'd have gone last week. I went a Wednesday to See poor Mr E – and found Him a very weak man. He has had the Yellow Jaundice, & Rheumatism; and Since, a Violent Cholick, which had near Carry'd Him off, and Still lys in his Bowells; They Say he is much Better than He has been, But I think Him in a very Indifferent way, so do's Dr Lavington – He has had Dr Hucksom, who advises the Bath, where He must go, as soon as he has Strength, But at present he isn't able to ride, nor to go out of his room: He desir'd me to present you his Service, & to let you know he was not able to write you – Have desir'd his Brother to write you how he is by this Post.

They wou'd not alarm you, But they fear'd He wou'd have Dy'd last week – I wish you wou'd write to Him.

I have Consulted a very good Mason, who says the Chimney must all be Taken down, to prevent its Smoaking, it not going up Direct, and it wou'd (as it now is) Stain any Chimney-piece presently.

Captain Rodney has been Here some Time, & Expects your Brother in Every Hour.

* Cousins of FHD.
** Rowe evidently enjoys the word-play, yet there is no evidence in the letters that Francis Samuel's early marriage 'marred' him.

F221

7 December 1750

Sir

Captain Drake I presume has inform'd you That the Trees are Come – Mr Snow's Gardiner was here a Wednesday and planted some in (by Guess) as Hayman did not send an account of the Sorts. For what is Done I referr you to the Enclos'd – The Reason why the London Trees last sent were Planted in Lady's Garden, was becaus They Look'd Best; the Pidgeon-House Garden will Take But Six – so Places must be Look'd out for Eight. Mr Snow's Gardiner Thinks the Wall by the new-room door will Take 4, 2 against the Best Chamber in the Bowling Green & 2 where the Heath Bird is Kep't – He promis't to Come here today to Set what there is ground prepar'd for & order about the Rest. I cou'd wish you had Fix't Everything Before you Went, Becaus you had made provision but for 16 pear-Trees, and There is 28 Sent, so your Plan is quite Vary'd, but not Here. For my part I am only a looker on, admiring the Wisdom of the present Generation, Tho' I don't understand it.

I am Sir
Your Faithful
N Rowe

The Horses are all sick Here & Everywhere, But none dye as I hear.

The Trees from Nutwell Pheasant Court look the Worste: They all come well.

F222

8 March 1751

Sir

I had yours of the 19th past in Time, But as I have nothing material why shou'd I Trouble you –

The Trees came to Horowbridge last Teusday, had not the Man at the Inn sent a Messenger on purpose the next Evening to acquaint They were There, They might have Layn there I don't know how Long, no Letter having Come about 'Em. The number is 10 pears, 6 plumbs, 4 Cherrys – the pear Trees very Indifferent, 2 much Hurt, They seem to have been Long out of the Ground. As there is no Directions where Each sort is to be planted, I have sent to Mr Snow's gardener to do as he Shall See proper – The Trees already planted Seem to do well, Tho' here has been very Wet Stormy Weather, a long Time.

Thomas Reed is got over his late Disorder for this Time, But Dr Huxum Says he must be very Careful; whilst we think we Stand Secure, we may Fall; what Mr Edgcombe has done I know not, But a prudential Caution is best at all Events.

I am Sorry to See what I do – But what do's that avail!

I am Sir

Your very Humble Servant

N Rowe

15 March

I intended This as Dated but was prevented.

Since Mr Snow's Gardiner has been here, who don't seem to like the Trees at all, He has planted 18 of 'Em in the 6 Borders in Lady's garden, so there are but 2 for that Long Bed in your pond-Garden which is 130 ft Long, But the Season is too far advanc'd for any further Plantation this year. Continual wet, which kceps the Lent Tillage very backward.

F223

3 January 1752

Sir

Having had for Some Time & Still Continuing Some Severe Fits of the Cholick, prevented my acknowledging the Receipt of your Letter Sooner, and I am now forc't to do it by Spurt –

I desir'd the Captain to acquaint you That the Trees were Come, Tho' they did not by Horro'bridge, where I sent twice, but by Mr Edgcombe from Tavistock. The Baskets were made by Hayman's direction and planted by yours & his by Sol, who by such plain orders can doubtless do anything of this Kind as well as Mr Snow's – The Trees are planted as in Course in the list from the Necessary House to garden Door – & the Remaining two are put where you directed. They came very well, the Burd de Roy ['pear'] is pretty Large, the Rest very Small.

The Duke of Cumberland's late accident,* and the Repeated Breaches so quick after Each other must be very affecting to the King and to all well-wishers –

There, who is without their Trials – I therefore hope as I wish, That all Family affairs may be amicably adjusted –

Sir I have forgot the Languages I had once a Smattering of, I have almost Forgot my Own – But I hope I shall to the End be able to make a Right Construction of *Memor & Obliviscor* ['I remember and I forget'] to the most Extensive Definition.

I am glad you got up well in the bad weather, and that This will find you so. Here has been a Share – Devonshire can't be Term'd the Ejypt of this Isle, yet part of November was very good to put the Wheat in, or Else I don't know what They wou'd have done in these parts: and now is Frosty & Fair.

Solomon has planted one of the Squares in Lady's garden with Dutch Currance from Grills as you directed Him –

The Cyder ly's ready at Lophill for a Boat to Carry it to Plymouth; the Cask wou'd not hold quite 5 Dozen of Bottles, I think 4 & ½ .

I am with the Compliments of the Season Sir

Your very Faithful

N Rowe

Mr Kelly is under great Concern he has not heard from his Grandson & as he's a very worthless Chap *E[he]u* ['Alas'] how &c &c.

* William, Duke of Cumberland, a younger brother of George II, had a bad fall from his horse while hunting at Windsor on 21 November 1751 (reported, for example, by Baron George Bubb Dodington, in H. P. Wyndham, ed., *The Diary of the Late George Bubb Dodington* (Salisbury: E. Easton, 1784)).

F224

Buckland, 15 May 1752

Sir

Your Favour was very Agreable to me, to hear of your Welfare is always so, and was I able & had anything worth writing, it wou'd be very agreable but *tempora mutantur* ['times change']! I am very glad to have from yourself, That you have got over the accident so well – There you see how soon & by what small Instruments a Humane Creature may be demolish'd – Even a bare Bodkin may do the Business.

I am very glad matters are Concluded so agreably between ye, and hope Everything will continue so –

I have not seen Mr Edgcombe but heard from Him about a month ago in General That the affair was Settl'd – I have wrote to Him about the Beer people by Mr Snow's direction Fishing,* as do those at Maristow, and Land their nets on Beer Side by his Encouragement. As you have Seen the Lease, and no Doubt Consider'd it & advis'd Thereon, you will order accordingly. For if they proceed in so frequent a Manner, 'Twill much prejudice the Fishing above. Few Salmon have been Taken as yet, and Fewer will for the Future.

Your Brother the Captain was here about 6 weeks ago; he Tasted the Wine, which is prick't, he agrees it is no Madera, & that he was impos'd on. He advis'd to put some Brandy into it, which is done, but I fear even Brandy won't Save it – He has left some Bottles of Madera for you, & said He wou'd Endeavour to get you some that was good.

Your Brother the Lieutenant came up here last Week for some Sheep he had bought of the Hine, the only Time I have seen Him since his return from Eastward and once before; as to his Request I am no Judge, but for Godsake overlook his imperfections, and do what you can for Him; I hope he'l atone for his past Indiscretion – It Seems to me as if Both wou'd Want you.

I can't Say I in any Shape like Lady Drake's rural management, the Victualling Contract was pretended ['presumed'] an advantage, as the Fat Cattle cou'd not be Sold any other way – The Barton was very Commode for the partnership, what allowance was made for it I know not – As I have been so odly Treated, I can say no more; But Consequences will Show.

Here is a good Show of Blossome, and Stands it as yet; your Plantations hold very well, considering the Weather we have had; one Figg dead & 2 or 3 of the pears look suspicious; there is Some Wall Fruit. Mr Moor when he Comes will give you a better account, he seems to me to be the Best has been here, & I hope will answer your Expectacions here & at Nutwell.**

There are several Pheasants about the Barton and Neighbourhood, But those within the Walls are much diminish'd by the bad weather – I'm Endeavouring to raise two Broods – Mr Tremayne has had Some Eggs – Love & Jealousy has drove away Several (Even the old Cock is gone) and Some have been kill'd by Fighting.

I am much oblig'd for your kind Enquiry after my health; I am determin'd never to trouble anyone with my Infirmitys, but This I find daily, that 60 summers are attended with 600 Inconveniencys, to which I humbly submit: Cou'd the Reflection be but so well digested; But *hic Labor, hoc Opus* ['here is travail, here is work']! There the black horse, if he don't gallop, I am Sure he Trotts.

I heartily wish you health & happiness – may you Find out this Scribble, which I am lost in, a Craizy head & a Crack't –

I am with true Respect, Sir

Your very Faithful

N Rowe

The Mare you sent here seems a very likely One –

The *Torrington* sail'd last Monday.***

The wind has been here for some Time past at N.W. Cold & much Rain Last Week – this, very Fine Weather, Wind at E. & by S. and now, I have Tyr'd you & I am Sure myself.

---

* For disputes over several generations over fishing rights on the Tavy, and litigation ongoing for forty-three years, eventually decided in FHD's favour in 1750, see *Family and Heirs*, vol. 2, pp. 163–168. See also F225, postscript, and F228.

** This is the first of numerous mentions of the pruner Hercules Mo(o)re, who was active at both Buckland and Nutwell.

*** HMS *Torrington* was a 44-gun fifth-rate ship launched in 1743.

F225

19 June 1752

Sir

I have the pleasure of your obliging Favour, which I found here at my return last Sunday Evening – Sorry I am to hear of your Disorder, pray Take care of yourself – how insignificant in Comparison are the Complaints of an old Fellow broke with age &c, and the incidents attending 'Em: if it thus happens to a green Tree, what must be the Fate of the Drye? –

It is no Compliment to tell you, That you are the hopes of your Family & Friends; And that Providence has plac'd you where you are for valuable Considerations; it behoves you therefore to be doubly regardful of yourself for that Reason.

I wrote you from the Dock of your Brother's Ilness; he Sail'd last Friday, & I wish the Sea air may recover Him; it was a great surprize to me in the manner it was Told, and it yet affects me –

Mr & Mrs Wyatt took great care of me, and so did my old Friend Mr Batt, with whom I very agreably spent 3 or 4 Days in renewing the Varietys we have met with, & reflecting on our own Alteracion: I need not Tell you he was your Father's particular Friend, That he has a great respect for you; in Discourse it fell in, that the nearest Relation he has (next his Brother) is an Excise-man in London, of whom he gave a very good Character; he very modestly said he had no pretence to ask any Favour of you; but I know it will very greatly oblige Him, if you wou'd get his Kinsman made a supervisor. I refer you to the Enclosed, for your information, which I had from Mr Batt.

As to your Brother Samuel, you are very Good; your Brother William Left nothing behind for reasons no doubt He has acquainted you –

Neither Dean Swift, nor Narcissus, I take to be Dangerous Men; the one may raise your Few Liberty Men, & the Other may head 'Em, but they can't Drain the Liffy.* I hear nothing of Them, neither do I believe you will.

As for S– [Sol?] he's *omni presenti* ['for all present'], and wou'd not Take your intended gift as a Favour – Your Gardiner Moor has not been here yet, there has been a blast in your Orchards, however there is yet Some Fruit.

Mr Wyatt, an Israelite indeed, & Mr Batt send their Compliments, as did Betty Dyer her Duty; she came here last Munday.

Lord Hobart is very fond of the Water, he has 2 Boats from Port Elliot (a pinnace & a Wherry) and a Sailing Boat from Salt-ash, with which He often Entertains Himself. When Mr Batt brought me up a Sunday in his great Boat we Saw the Fleet. On Midsummer Day his Lordship has a Revel on Beer-Down.

A Shift for the Maids, Breeches & Hat for the Men, but no Wrestling or Cudgels for fear of Bruises.

Mr Snow has Stop't Fishing, but can the Maristow People land their Net on Beer Side, Mr Edgcombe says yea – Qu[estion]: But Few Fish to last year.

As for myself, I fancy I have been in Medea's Kettle – a high Flow from this late flutter; but I expect an Ebb accordingly. I am very much oblig'd for your kind offers, you have been very Good already – I can't give you any further Trouble – I have that little Regard to my Insignificansy now, That any agreable is quite Lost to me – However I am much Thankful.

I heartily wish you Health & Happiness.

I am Dear Sir

Your very Faithful and Oblig'd
N Rowe

I am very Glad the affair between ye is finish'd, I hope amity is fix't, and That it will Continue.

Mr Snow has Sent here for Salmon Several Times (but try's first if there are any at Maristow) since Lord Hobart has been with Him – Pray how is the affair as to your reserv'd rent on your Fishery settled, there was an arrear? I wish it mayn't +++++ [*sic*]

* Narcissus Marsh was provost of Trinity College Dublin during Swift's time there, and author of a manual of logic recalled in the fourth voyage of *Gulliver's Travels* (see 'Jonathan Swift', *ODNB*). Rowe chooses this elaborate way of saying that he sees no immediate Jacobite threat from Ireland.

F226–F227 [2 small scraps of paper]

I Forgot to tell you That in my ramble I went to Plymouth on your Brother's intimating to me, that Mr Porter was Ill. I found Him a Bed under a Surgeon's operation; his Malady proceeded from a pimple which rose in his seat after Riding, it turn'd to a Boil, which encreas'd to the Bredth of one's Hand; it was Fomented 10 Days ago, & yesterday I sent to know how he did, & I had Word, That he was Just got down stairs & look'd very Bad – *sic variis modis* ['thus in various ways'] &c.*

There has been much rain this Week, particularly Wednesday night & yesterday Morning when there was the greatest & Highest Flood I ever saw, all Terrace Meadow, & Causeys Cover'd – The Wear ['weir'] stands it, only a Breach in your Bent which is Lifted up surprizingly; one of your Hatches is Carry'd off, But your Hatch little Hurt as yet can be perceiv'd, & I hope 'twill be soon Repair'd – Many Salmon are gone up – The Water rose 8 ft above the ground.

They have been but Twice with Salmon to Exeter for you. Yours went yesterday with 2 Horses. Hard Showers this morning, I hope no more Floods.

* See Introduction, section 5, p. 45.

F228

5 July 1752

Sir

I am very much oblig'd for your last Favour. I imagin'd you had heard of your Brother's Ilness immediately from Himself, and That He had acquainted you with the Reason why he did not Leave anything for you; it was owing to some Information given at Portsmouth.

Mr Batt will be much oblig'd for your Regard to his Relation.

I presume if your Mare has Oats about a Week before you Send for Her, which you will order accordingly. As to Alexander, no Doubt you may have Him to bring Her up, But as he now Stands in a Man's Stead, I cou'd wish you wou'd Hint that to the Hine, when you have the Lad up; But he's a near Chap, & it being a Busy Time, He'l Expect you pay for a Man in his Room ['place'].

As to the Maristow people's Fishing, & Mr Snow's Conduct thro'out, is too long to trouble you now; when Hear more particularly you'l be able to Judge better than from my Information. I wish the late breach in the Wear ['weir'] han't Injur'd the Fishing, Few having been Caught Since.

I am Sorry you have not found the Benefit from your Journey as you Expected, I hope you will.

I was to see Mr Edgcombe Some time Since who was not well; I don't like his frequent Disorders.

I congratulate you on your Promise of those Lands, I need not Say any more. I wish your Friend the Dr may have Success.*

The Weather has been very uncertain of Late, it now promises better, & I hope the Hay will be Sav'd well.

I exert myself much, was you to know all you'd Say so, But I find there's no Fence against a Flail, nor Frailty.

I am more & more sensible of my Decline, I don't Wonder at it, and Expect accordingly.

I heartily wish you Health & Happiness & am Sir

Your Faithful & oblig'd

N Rowe

The Glass has long Continu'd at the Changeable point, & tho' yesterday was very Fair, it rains today, which shows the Weather is not Settl'd. God send Better in his good <u>Time</u>.

* Dr Mark Akenside?

F229 [2 scraps of paper]

Mr Burnaford with his Compliments begs you wou'd Let your Servant buy for Him a pair of Temple-Spectacles for between <u>60</u> & <u>70</u>, and as Clergimen read their Notes at a Distance to have the Glass accordingly.

Moor the Gardiner came here a Sunday, He'l finish today – The Trees you have Sent do very well, and I think whatever may be Suggested, He manages Them so Too.

Several have had Fruit on, Some Still hold it: I mean your new planted Peaches; the Espal' Cherrys had Some Blossome & one of your Pears (a Burd de Roy).

F230

10 July 1752

Sir

Mr Ryder has made a Demand of £9 odd money for Chief Rents due to Him on the Meavy Estates.* I desir'd Mr Edgcombe to acquaint you with it as a matter fit to be Look't into.

I am sorry your Friend the Dr has lost it.

Moor went away a Saturday morning. I think has done the Trees very well.

It is very melancholy wet Weather, as bad as last year.
I am Sir
Your very Faithful
N Rowe

You will be so good to Frank the Enclos'd.

* There was Drake property in Meavy. Rowe returns to Mr Ryder's demand, and its history, in several letters.

F231

17 July 1752

Sir

I am always glad to hear of your Welfare, your Favour of 7th gave me an addition.
Mr Edgcombe, I hear, is very well again –
As to Moor's pruning, what He has done here Seems very well, as to Nutwell I can say nothing – all your Espalier pears are in a very good Way, Except that in your pidgeon House garden, which Moor Says will recover; it had a bad root, & was hurt in Carriage.
They Sav'd the Hay in your great Meadow last Week Tollerably well, & this Week your Clover.
St Swithin was rainy in the Forenoon, which adds to the Superstition of the Common People – But as you rightly observe, this Country has its Share of Rain –
Mr Burnaford will, I know, be much oblig'd, as will Mr Batt with your kind intensions to his Relation.
Your Mare is very well, & will be order'd as you direct, & Mr Serle will Trim Her if you approve of it.
I am very glad you are making Nutwell agreable to you, I heartily wish you long to Enjoy it with health and happiness, But I have Something within me, which Tells me I shall never See it again   I have made Essays, But Find what I shan't Trouble any one with.
I have had many Complaints Formerly about Baron's Management, but with all his Faults, I have never seen his Fellow since – Here's a large Field for Expatiation, But I Forbear –
But Few Fish Since the Flood; that wants your looking into, when you Come down, as I doubt ['fear'] Mr Ryder's Demand* Requires it.
Sol has grafted Several Trees with what he had from Moor, & More I wou'd say, was I able, But Tho' I Fail in Every other particular – I shall never in approving myself,
Sir,
Your Faithful
N Rowe

Poor Mr Porter is Still very Bad.

* There is evidently a link between Mr Ryder's demand and the fishing dispute (see F224).

F232

24 July 1752

Sir

The old peach & Nectarine Trees have most of Them Fruit upon 'Em, Even those Two which Moor Remov'd. I am Sorry your Trees at Nutwell Fail so, I don't know, & so can't Comprehend the Reason, But can't tell how to think it is the Man's Fault, from what He has done here.

The weather & the Birds destroy'd all the Cherrys here before they were Ripe, so that I gave over making any Chery Brandy, but upon your Direction I have desired Mrs Porter to make you some. The Hine sold the Cherrys here to a man for £4 and he did not make 10s. of 'Em for the above Reason.

Mr Porter I hear is much Better.

If the Weather Continues Fair, the Hay here will be over next Week, but it did not Change here so soon as you mention, and as to the Clover, I mistook a part for the whole, all not being Saved till yesterday.

My Letter to Lady Drake was about Mr Ryder's Demand, to let Her know, I was entirely unacquainted with it – It is for 23 years Chief Rent for Durance [in Meavy] & Greenwood. Bennet Blanchard Says he paid 6s. a year 'till He was forbid, and that becaus your Family had a Demand of that kind on his, as I know not how Either are founded, have desired Mr Edgcombe to Inform you what He knows of the Matter. As he is very well again, I presume you have by this Time heard from Him –

I wish my account in this or anything Else cou'd Contribute to your Information, But as I have confounded myself, I shall Everyone I correspond with, which I wou'd not willingly Do to you,

As I am Sir
Your very Faithful
N Rowe

Mr Chancellor Fursman call'd here yesterday with Mr Burnaford, he go's for Exeter to morrow.

He desir'd his Compliments & hoped you wou'd Do Him the Honour to let Him wait on you, to the Bishop.

As I write my Letters many Days before I send 'Em There must be many Inconsistencys (particularly This which was wrote a Teusday) and a Wednesday it rain'd most part of the Day, all the Clover not Sav'd till yesterday in the Evening, and the Grass cut in Middle & Terrace Meadows too much to be Tended at once; But your Mother's [Hine?] is for Wonders at a Cheap Rate, But I know who pays.

F233

Dock, 8 December 1752

Dear Sir

I have yours of the 5th, no apologys are Necessary in no Shape, you have nothing to ask, or Fear, you won't Desire anything from Me, But what is the only Thing I have to fear, your Welfare, which I am tenderly wrap't up in. There is but One object more, Should you Both Fail, Garrick never Fain'd a Stronger passion in *Lear* Than I shou'd Fall by.

Your Brother I came here to See, But Miss't Him; I will inculcate in the best manner I can. The woman I have Seen,* She deserves a Better Fate, we're all Sprung from Adam.

As to the Ordnance, Plymouth is too, too Considerable to be a Dupe to any Board, Either to Irish assurance or Staf Stupidity – M[ayor?] thinks so too. 'Tis your own Fault if Portsmouth may be in Favour again, Plymouth must. The good Commodore may Live,** and Baulk the present – pray be Civil to Captain Rogers &c &c Tomorrow I scettis [?] B—r.

As to your Suddain Visit, I don't see any ocasion for it, unless it is to give me Fresh pain in parting; you know I do Everything for you & can *Sine Cura* ['without obligation'].

Betty Dyer I have Seen & Comes to you on any Terms, we must Take Care of Her.

And now, *non Consanguiniis, non Successoribus sed Tibi Soli* ['not for relatives, not for successors but for you alone'], no Extacy of Virgil *sic vos non vobis fertis aratra Boves* ['thus you oxen draw the plough not for yourselves']. I'd be no Drudge but to you; Palinurus may nod, But I hope not Fall over Board. I have Lately had a narrow Escape, least a Worse Thing happen to me I will Do so no more.

I am as always
Your most Faithful
N Rowe

Pray write to Mr M[ayor?].

Poor Thomas Wyatt, & wife are Ill, so is Porter & his. Both Honest & True, pray mind Them.

Caution John Edgcombe not to be Religious over much.

Apology to Mr Townshend to Whom I Enclose this.

I'l see at Candlemas, God Willing I won't be knock't on the Head for Nothing, But when I See you may Tell you God's Truth & plasibly ['placeably/feasibly'?] too perhaps possibly Too.

* Samuel Drake's wife, who was shortly to find favour with Lady Drake.
** A further probable reference to Commodore Philip Vanbrugh (see F217, F240).

F234

Buckland, 3 January 1753

Sir

The Mayor's Agent wrote Him That you Told Him, you had all their Charters, upon which He desir'd me to Look, if I cou'd Find 'Em, as it wou'd save 'Em much Expence; I have accordingly been Several Days here, But can find none. I went once before, and met with an English Copy, which I let Mr Mayor have.

Mr Bastard's Lady is much indispos'd with the Reigning Cold, as Dr Huxom told me last Sunday Evening. He assures me if you much Lean to read and write, it will produce a Contraction in your Bowells, to which He imputes your present Disorder; and which He hopes you'l Endeavour to prevent by a necessary precaution: He Expresses a great Regard for you, I wish you would write Him.*

Sol's Boy, who is 14 years of age, your Mother's Hine has dismiss't. Was you to take Him for 7 years by Indenture (for otherwise I wou'd not advise, as his Father is a proud Coxcomb, and wou'd Spoil Him, was he Free) he'd make an admirable Servant, useful to you on many accounts; and when you are in Town, Farmer Coleman** might improve Him in Husbandry: He can read & write.

Mr Reynolds the Painter is gone to Town; He has Drawn Several pictures at Plymouth, I think very Well. He intends to wait on you; it Looks as if He wou'd Turn out a Vandike, at Least to Family Pieces. Cou'd not you Trust Him as to a Copy of your Ancestor, without requiring it to London.

From Whiteford I write This *Solus cum Sola* ['alone with the only one']; the Palatine, I am told, is no obstruction; I must come to London to Talk with you gravely *inter nos* ['between ourselves'], But Beauty without a Blemish wants no Inducement, but to See & be Subdu'd. A Certain person intimated Something, which I very well understand and you are Sure of me, But there, Inclination is all & I shan't interfere in That, only to wish you well.***

Tavistock, 6 January

Sir

I lay last night with Mr Edgcombe; he is not so well as I cou'd wish Him. He has wrote you of Wat Pyke's Catastrophe [?], He Turn'd out the Wretch, I always took him for – I'm perswaded you'l Take care of the Writ, and you may rely on your Friends.

I saw poor Mr Pyne this Morning. He seems in a very Declining way, Tho' he Flatters Himself He's Better: They Say his Lungs are Touch't; Be his Disorder what it will, he don't seem to be long Liv'd; He is not able to preach & I Fear never will again; you have his & Mother's Compliments with their Thanks for your intended Favour.

Plymouth, 9 January

Sir

The Mayor I Left Sick of the gout this Morning &c

Exeter, 11 January

Sir

I Din'd this Day with the Mayor, Mr Lee. He'l write you Soon. *Non magna Loquimur Sed vivimus* ['we do not talk much but get on with things']. I may probably Leave you a Legacy – My Love, if I live & whilst I Live, that is yours absolutely – The rest to time a Custom ... Shall break ... *Sonares inter nos* ['sounding between ourselves'] –

Mr John Ley the attorney is gone to London, is to be heard of at Mr Samuel John's in Lion's Inn. I need not Tell you he's a useful & valuable man & may be so in both Cases.

Your Portreeve was here today, I have taken Care to get him Sworn; as also by Mr Saunderson, Mr Leif's late Clerk, who acts for the undersheriff, to get the precept, when Sent down, Forwarded to Mr Edgcombe, and I shall (God willing) punctually attend at Beer –

Mr Chancellor & my Cousin Snow send their Compliments. Mr Short sends his & desires me to acquaint you that he has Enquir'd about the Papers you Directed at Saltash, But can hear of none.

Counsellor Jeffery has been Sounding me whether upon an application to make Exeter a free port, you wou'd appear in their Favour? I bid Him Try; & must Desire you to find this Scrawl out.

Adieu

* See Introduction, section 5, p. 47.
** Farmer Coleman was the tenant of the Nutwell home farm.
*** This is the first of several references to a beautiful lady who, in Rowe's opinion, would merit FHD's attention.

F235

Plymouth, 3 February 1753

Sir

I have your Favour of 30th past, But have not had That you mention directed to Buckland, a place I don't like to visit *in Statu Quo nunc* ['in its present state']; neither do I believe Some People will always approve those measures They seem now so Fond of; *Experientia docet* ['experience teaches'].

I went yesterday to Dock, but did not See your Brother,* He being gone abroad ['out']. He told me the last Time I saw Him, That He Expected his Captain from London in a Fortnight, & That They shou'd sail in a Month. I think your Reasons Convincing, and Shan't Fail to inculcate Them as opportunity offers; Certainly to be at Sea is much better than a Guard Ship, for more Reasons than One –

I have aquainted the Mayor with what you Directed. He is much out of Order; Tho' hardly out of the gout, has an attack in his Loins, is often ailing.

I have had a Letter from Betty Dyer, That She got Safe to Nutwell, from Whence no Doubt She has wrote you –

I have been very Roughly Treated for Some Days past by my old Enemy the Cholic, which makes me write This with some Uneasiness.

I am Sir
Your very Faithful
N Rowe

Mr Mayor Sends his Compliments, so do's Mr Porter.

4 February

Sir

I yesterday Saw your Brother, who is Convinc'd of your Favour Towards Him & Entirely resigns Himself to your better Judgment.

In the gaity of my mind I Desir'd your Servant to procure me Several Things. I am Since & so Often Disorder'd, That the Days are Come wherein I have no pleasure in Them: So that I wou'd Desire nothing may be done in it as I am perswaded I shall have Little Occasion for Them or anything Else.

* Samuel Drake, who had been serving on a guard ship for some time.

F236

Dock, 9 February 1753

Dear Sir

Your Favour of the 21st past Mr Edgcombe was so kind to Send me. I don't Think He's so well as I cou'd wish Him; I have not Seen Him, since your Re-election at Beer, Tho' I heartily wish Him, The health He seems to Want, as he's a very Honest Man, and your Zealous Friend.

As to your humble Servant, Ceremony is quite over; whatever I write you, is with a good Intension, But expect no diversion from your momentous Avocation, unless you think I can be of any Service to you. So you are but well, That's enough for me.

I am so freequently attack't by the Cholic, That I give but a Little regard to anything. I have more Shoes &c Than I expect to Use. What I mention'd besides was intended with a View to your Service, but as there is not immediatly any Further Occasion, I am Sorry I mention'd anything about 'Em; Superfluitys was never my Taste, So I cou'd wish I had never given you any Trouble at all –

I very lately saw Dr Huxum; He don't Think the late Sore Throat was so Contagious as imagin'd, but be it as it will, the Malignancy is much abated. I am very much oblig'd for your kind regard; but 'tis quite indifferent to me where the tree Falls; Fall I know it will, perhaps Sooner than may be imagin'd, I hope not at Beer.

I had Some reason to believe a Journey to London might be of Some Real Service to me in a particular Case [?]; to you am Sure it wou'd [be] no prejudice. But I respite every Consideration, to your better digested Sentiments.

Sol's Boy is now at Home doing nothing; if you wou'd be so good to Take the Boy, it wou'd be Saving him from Ruine & want.

I was at Buckland yesterday & Tasted the Medyat Cyder, which I believe may answer your Expectation. Your Mother's Servant Says there is about a pipe of That, and another of Credling, a Hogshead of Each he believ's may be good, But the other Two Fines Slowly; I Fancy He's no Critique in Cyder.

Mr & Mrs Wyatt Send their Compliments, the poor Woman has been at Death's Door with the Rheumatism, but is now on the Mending Hand. Mr & Mrs Porter do the Same tho' often ailing – As to any P in particular [?],'tis as indifferent to me as Pensilvania, unless you think Otherwise.

Dr Huxum is always repeating his great Desire to Hear from you –

The Mayor is in high Hopes from Mr Pratt &c – One Mr Carly, an Attorney & Common Council Man, is Soon Coming to London about, I believe, that affair. Shou'd He wait on you, I know him very well, & can assure you, He's much Confided in by the powerful There: He's a Sensible young Fellow.

I have lately Seen your Brother, his Captain is expected Down Next Week, & They expect to Sail very Soon after; He Seems much Resign'd.

I am with Respect Dear Sir

Your very Faithful

N Rowe

Mr Mayor & Mayoress Send their Compliments General & Natural & Yours.

F237 [a short note]

One Thomas Campbell, a Seaman belonging to his Majesty's Ship *Sunderland*, was Sent on Shore in the Long Boat in the West Indies, and happening to Straggle from his Companions in the Country was Seized by the Indians, and the Boat went on Board without Him; and the Captain Run Him.*

This man is Considerably indebted to a poor Woman of Plymouth, who is without hopes of Recovering her Debt, unless his R̲. can be taken off, which is most humbly Requested.

* Registered him as absent without leave.

F238

Plymouth, 16 February 1753

Sir

Gazets inform Country Puts in Politics Which otherwise They wou'd not know, & it is no great matter whither They did or no – The nominacion of the Sheriffs has put it out of Dispute, That There will be no new – [?]

Whether inquisitive Enquiries have, or may be of Service, Time must Show. To know Who's who, and What's What, require different Senses. Parade with Property are Ostentatious Proofs of Power; But a Property with plainess, and a Fix't Interest go a great Way with middling People, & generally Prevails; a real Power & a Seeming Power have a Certain distinction, which is soon Seen thro', & There I Leave it: you are to Judge of the Rest, as you Find it or may Think it Worth While to go Further.

Several People have a great Respect for your Family, & you in particular; a Natural Interest is General, and is not to be Confin'd –

The inclos'd comes from a Tenant of yours at Meavy, Mr Pike the Deputy Town-Clerk; if you can assist Him in the affair, by the means of the Comptroller of the Navy, who is the Man must do it, you'l oblige a very Honest Fellow, who is much your humble as is

Sir

Your very Faithful Servant

N Rowe

Mr Mayor sends his Compliments.

F239

Plymouth, 8 May 1753

Sir

Your Brother the Captain was paid off last Saturday, and went Directly from the Dock to London, where I suppose by this Time you have Seen Him – I am Glad he's Clear of his Ship, as I believe He is too; you know best, But the Sooner He's Employ'd the Better (*variis Causis* ['for various reasons']); I won't presume to say Further.

Mr Mayor go's for London to morrow, He shou'd know best Why. Some Think he had better Stay; I won't pretend to determine for Another, But am Sure was it my Case, I wou'd not go Just now, and I hope for his Own Sake He won't Stay Long – What his views are, Time or you may Discover – perhaps on Pegasus's Wings we Soar, with Icarus we Sink for want of proper Cement, which Some too presumptuously Think They know the Secret of –

Your Brother* was admitted at Beer Court for Spry's Lands, and poor Harry Mildron's death was Simply presented *Sine Hæredibus* ['without heirs']. Seneschal ['the steward'] *non est Socrates* ['is not Socrates'].

Your Brother Samuel sail'd last Thursday night for Nova Scotia with a brisk wind at E. – Which has Continu'd ever Since. They have been long Kept Here: Whatever is past can't be Recall'd; He behaves very well now; pray Regard Him; I hope his Future Conduct will Merit your Favour; Tho' he can't retrieve the Lapsus, which will Stick by Him, He knows it, & must wear the Garland. If it prooves a Crown of Thorns, He must make it as Easy as He can; I wish I cou'd Contribute to it.

When you have Leisure I shou'd be glad to Hear from you How, When & Where! Till then I am as always

Dear Sir

Your Faithful

N Rowe

Mr Veal has got a Certain Body in a Cleft Stick. Qu[estion]? Whether Ignorance or Obstinacy has had the predominancy – That They want; Oh what do They Want? why, a Friend.

* FHD's brother William.

F240

Buckland, Whitsunday, 6 in the Morning

Sir

I came here yesterday – I am *Seges ubi* ['a field where once stood'] &c.

For my part, this place is a Sinker, to see &c. – So I shall dwindle into my Former Stupidity. I can't bare to Look over anything, so the Enclos'd must Supply your Expectacions. Your last gives me great Anxiety; if Such Things happen to a green Tree, what will become of the Drye! –

I have Tasted the Cridling Cyder; it is Fine but not so Sweet as you may Expect; it will be Sent to Mr Porter as you Direct, the first opportunity.

I saw Mr Veale lately, he is much your humble Servant.

Mr Bastard's Lady is in a Dangerous Way, & Commodore Vanbrugh* near his Dissolution – Captain Rogers Flatters Himself.

I saw Mr Moresh yesterday Morning at his vil. If we don't Love I imagine we Fear, and at Least an appearance might be made no wise to your Disadvantage, But *quot Homines Tot Sententiæ* ['as many opinions as men'].

Am now going to Tavistock; if anything Occurs There, will Close with it; as to Mrs Willesford, farther your Orator Sayeth Not – If your Relation can be of no Use this year, I am Sure He'l be of None the next – and I wish I had not given myself so much Trouble to so Little purpose, But *ex Nihilo Nil Fit* ['nothing comes of nothing'].

Tavistock, Monday Morning

Mr Edgcombe Sends you his Compliments; He Seems much to Break, which I am truely Sorry for, yet I hope I shan't Dye in his Debt.

Cake is Still Living, But Sir – Littleton has got a promise of the Place to Strenthen his O– Interest as to P [?] – *si non Optandum, nil agendum, dic mihi & Taceo* ['if not wanted, nothing shall be done, tell me and I shall keep silent'].

Whiteford, Teusday Evening

I am Just come here to relax a Little after T[avistock?] Confinement. The Lady Enquir'd after your Welfare in a manner peculiar to Herself. I wou'd not have you See with my Eys, But wish you wou'd with your Own; if Vertue, Humility, and Good Sense Join'd with natural Beauties, have their Charms, I think I have Seen Such an object, Tho' it is *rara avis* ['a rare bird'] –

I hope Soon to See you & am as Ever
Dear Sir
Your Faithful
N Rowe

If you wou'd Send a Copy of the Jews Bill you'd oblige.**

* Philip Vanbrugh (1681–1753), Commodore Governor of Newfoundland.
** The Jewish Naturalisation Act of 1753, repealed in 1754 after public outcry.

F241

Thursday Evening

I sent for the Captain & have got all the Pheasants out of the Gardens where they were into the Hall-Garden, I think the Number is 21 Hens, & 34 Cocks.

I referr to Him, For I am not able to be Exact in anything – He tells me good Mr Edgcombe is out of Order, if I am able God Willing I will see Him tomorrow – may He Live for your sake, *Si amicus honestus Semper erit mihi bonus amicus* ['if an honest friend he will always be my good friend'] –

Friday 15

The Spirit is Willing but the Flesh is weak, I find myself not able to go to Tavistock, my Head is too giddy to ride.

F242

Buckland, 20 July 1753

Sir

I came here last Saturday Se'n night from Plymouth and have had a violent Cold ever Since, which still hangs heavy upon me –

Your Favour of 3rd did not come to my hands 'till Monday night last, Mr Edgcombe having sent it to Plymouth, imagining I was There –

Ah, Sir Francis, I'm gone past redempcion, and upon Conviction too! I cou'd wish some Cornish Hill to cover me – oh Kit-Hill! If my Politiques are so unsuccesful too, good night <u>Nicolas.</u> I have had a great Flow of spirits, they begin to Flagg too; Nothing violent I find is Lasting; if I can be of any service to you, I shou'd desire a Continuance a little Longer; Else, n'importe.

As to this decay'd Place, I don't see what can be Done to it, but cutting weed &c. The House, oh the House! What can be Done to That – There, I'l get it as Clean as I can.

Mr More was here, They say, near a Month since, and I think your Trees are Tollerably well, Considering the Blaste & Drought, But some Rain the Week past, which has refresh'd Everything much, and this Week's Fair Weather has given a Dispatch to the Hay which lay in a Doubtful Manner.

Poor Buckland! I fear They won't make a Pipe of Cyder this season. I will acquaint Mrs Searle in general of your kind Intensions, But not particular, Least she shou'd Blabb: poor Mrs Willesford will break her Heart, Tho' I can't say, she had a Foundation: I don't hear the Man is Dead – is not the Stripling very Young for Such a Thing? There, you know Best.

Mr Mayor & Mayoress came to Tamerton last Saturday; I saw 'Em a Sunday, They're in great affliction for the Death of One of Their Children.

I wish I han't gone too far near the Water, I know to my Sorrow I have over the Mountain as you call it; and it shou'd be the [Fa]te of all old Quixotes, There's no putting Teeth in a Horse's head, that has lost 'Em.

Your Mama's hine is much out of Order, But Some Cherrys are left, & I've sent to Mr Porter for Some Brandy. A good Deal of Last year's is left, and I've put Some Fresh Fruit to it.

I am told there are Some young Pheasants on the Barton, Tho' I have not seen any.

The Bishop dines with the Mayor today at Plymouth. There has been a Confirmacion & Visitacion. The Discourse of the Country is, That Mr Short is to have Mr Snow's Daughter, a Confirm'd Havage ['scold'].

I wish everything agreable to you where you are and every Happiness with Health to attend you.

I am Sir
Your Faithful
N Rowe

Wou'd you be so good to Excuse & Forward the Enclos'd.

F243

Tavistock, 27 November 1753

Dear Sir

At Lane-Head this Day at 2 o' Clock I heard of good Mr Edgcombe's Death. I Forc'd myself here, But God knows how I shall get Back – Poor Will, with Whom I now am, is under the greatest Concern (as well He may) not only for his Loss, but least He shou'd not answer your Expectations – He will do his Utmost, and I am Sure is to be Depended upon – Pray Comfort Him, being under great Diffidence, & Distress.

As to the Parson, That's now at an End.
I am as always Dear Sir
Your most Faithful
N Rowe

Mr William Edgcombe sends his Duty.
  John Carpenter must now be in Angl[sey?].
  Pray Let me hear from you – I am now under a Difficulty as to an Order.

F244

Tavistock, 30 November 1753

Dear Sir

I am not myself: you must Excuse Inconsistanceys. Poor John Edgcombe's Death Confounds me – Pray don't let it have the Same Effect on you – We shall daily miss Him, But must provide against all Events – He is Lamented universally, and Justly, as an able & Useful man is gone – He han't Left his Equal nor anything like it in this Country – In your affairs I have Lost my Right Hand – I can say no more –

His Brother is a very Honest Man – Time & Business do's great Things, He shan't Want ['lack'] my aid, poor as it is: pray Write Him, He'l want your Support, which I have Taken the Liberty to Tell Him, He may be assur'd of; 'Twill give Him a Reputation in the Eys of the World: I need not add –

I am very Glad to hear you got up Well, before this hard Weather. Frost & Snow much a Teusday night, Such as has not been Seen in this Country for many years, & Still very Severe – The Country cover'd Thro'-out.

I am Sir
Your most Faithful
N Rowe

Pray Let me Hear from you as to W. I saw no-one There, But I heard W must not Think to engross Both – But C must & will have one. [?]

F245

Buckland, 2 December 1753

Dear Sir

By the over-Forwardness of the Postman at Tavistock, who sent it away before I came, I had it not yours 27th November till Last night, That I got Here –

For Godsake keep up your Spirits. To a Gentleman of your good Sense, 'Twou'd be impertinence even to propose Consolation. You have Losst a Valuable Friend, & Useful Servant, One That had an affection for your Person, and an inviolable regard for your Interest: But then you are to thank God he did not Dye in your Minority, *nec Donec* ['nor until'] –

Mr William Edgcombe is made sole Executor, all his affairs & Effects left to his Management, particularly the House at Tavistock, his Lands, of which He has made you Trustee, and after Family Legacys, Has made him residuary Legatee; so that everything is *in Statu quo*: But the Man is gone! I truly Lament Him, So do's Everyone, But what do's it avail –

I wrote you by Teusday & Friday's post from Tavistock – As to your own private affairs with the Deceas'd, They'l be honourably regarded by his Brother, So you need be under no Concern as to that Particular: neither can I for that reason Think of anything to advise in this melancholy Juncture: I very Sensibly Miss the Man for your sake, and Shall always respect his Memory as a Faithful Friend – But as I may & must Soon Follow Him, God knows how soon, For God's sake Dear Sir Francis make yourself thoro'ly acquainted with all your affairs, & Thank God you are so well able – you may depend on my Faithful aid.

I am very Glad you got well up to Town before this hard Weather; it began to Thaw last night Just as I got here, But as it Continues Cold & the Weather glass don't Fall, I Fear 'twill freeze again.

I will go in Friday or Sunday next again to Tavistock, Tho' 'tis no Small Force upon me, if I am able, For the shock & the ride have not a Little ruffl'd me. I will upon all Occasions inculcate everything I am able with the young Man. He's very honest, as his poor Brother always pronounc'd; He must Endeavour to imitate, what he can't Come up to. There, he han't left his Fellow –

Pray Take care of yourself & Believe me to be

Dear Sir

Your Faithful

N Rowe

Your Mother's Hine has been out of order Ever Since I went away almost, & has kept his room this week & more. If she neglects the present Offer, it mayn't happen again.

F246

Buckland, 4 December 1753

Dear Sir

I receiv'd your Favour of 27th past from William Edgcombe. I truly Sympathize with you even in Tears, I don't know I ever Drop't more for the nearest or Dearest, Tho' that is not my manner of Showing Concern. *Manet mente* ['he remains in our mind'] &c, I shall never Forget the Man, having long prov'd Him & allways found Him Faithful – We never value rightly Our Friends, 'till we have lost Them – I have thought Our late Friend greatly broke (we observ'd it particularly when he met you at Westbridge*) yet not so near his End – We deceive Ourselves with flattering Ideas; Still we are not to grieve as without hope. May my End be like his; He dy'd as he Liv'd an honest Man, well within as he declar'd, Just before his Senses left Him; would to God I had seen Him before he Dy'd: *variis Causis* ['for various reasons'] – Poor Man, his diffusive good nature carry'd him too great lengths for unworthy Objects: Even his last Effort was forc't from him by gross Flattery, even to a Doubt: But it was his Superabundant Generosity, which press'd him so far, That upon reflection he disapprov'd, as I am perswaded he wou'd (even his last request) had I but once Spoke with him. There, with all his Foibles he han't left his Fellow! Universally Lamented & Respected – a Sensible ['deeply felt'] Loss to this Country.

Your kind Intension as to a Monument is Like yourself, it will do honour to you, and Justice to the Man, who deserv'd it of you; and it will be a lasting Memorial of your Esteem – your Sentiments of him will add Lustre to his ashes; I will Obey your

Commands – His Relations will Take it, & it will be a lasting honour to Them – That such a Man belong'd to 'Em, who had such a Friend. William Edgcombe receiv's general respect for his good Brother's Sake; He's honest, & I hope will Endeavour to deserve it; I tell him he must Study to imitate what he can't come up to; I give Him all the Salutary hints I am Capable of.

And now Sir for myself, ever the least of my Care, I am vastly oblig'd for this proof of your Friendship, which shan't be flung away; you know me – I am naturally grateful, you shall always find me, as I have Ever been, affectionate to your Person & Faithful to your Interest; But I Fear I shan't grace your Reccommendation, as I doubt ['fear'] it comes too Late for an Eclat. Yet to the Last I will approve myself
    Dear Sir
    Your True Friend to serve you
    N Rowe

Dr Lavington has Shewn his grateful regard to his deceas't Friend to the last; I wish he had Sooner Taken his Advise & not Conceal'd his Weakness from Him. Dr Huxum did his Utmost – all too Late.

I will if able go to Tavistock Either Friday or Sunday next, when I will write you again –

The Hine Still continues Ill, sure your Mama <u>will Think</u>.

* Westbridge, Tavistock.

F247

Buckland, 7 December 1753

Dear Sir

I have wrote you so many Letters on the melancholy Occasion I am quite Exausted – I have Intimated your kind intension to William Edgcombe, who will acknowledge the honour done Them in a proper manner: Tavistock's now very Disagreable to me, But when Occasion, will Force all I can, at present I am not able –

Thomas Cummin I hear is so poor That he has Sold his few Household goods for Bread, & must soon Come to the Parish; when that's the Case, the Officers will be Trying about his Land: did you Order Baron to advance Him a small subsistance this hard Weather it wou'd Save you a Public Declaracion – They say he can't last Long; Neither can I any more, But That I am with Respect
    Dear Sir
    Your Faithful
    N Rowe

Mr Stapleton has been here, and put in the Trees from London, and Moor – Those you Enquir'd after are right as to your Plan.

The Hine still continues Ill, Sure I'd ne'er have a Gentleman & an Invalid, The vanity of the Coxcomb is Superlative, more fuss & state than your Father.

Alderman Phillips at Plymouth is Dead, now if ever for Mr Porter.

I Forgot to mencion That Mr Edgcombe has by his Will devis'd his Lands in Beer to his Brother William in Trust &c.

F248

Tavistock, 14 December 1753

Dear Sir

Your Favour of 11th gave me great Satisfaction, as I fear'd you might not be Well – the Bill Enclos'd I have receiv'd, which I Thank you for, and That and all my Life shall be apply'd to your Service –

You may rely on the Person you mention, and if you Think it for your Service the Persons you mention will attend you in the Holy Day Week.

I shall go to Plymouth next Week, when I shall Settle it so with Mr Porter, That if you have anything particular to Communicate, let it be under his Cover, for Some Reasons.

I observe all your Hints and will pursue Every Thing for your Interest – As to a H [Hatch?] or any Little h, we'l Endeavour to arm against 'Em. I'm sorry to hear People are so Weak to make lofty Elevations on Shallow Foundacions, Such openness can't be Dangerous.

Pray Take Care of your health; mine tho' insignificant, I shall the more prize as Devoted to Your service.

I am as always
Your Faithful
N Rowe

Mr William Edgcombe Sends his Compliments. Pray write Him; 'Twill support him in Every Shape.

F249

Tavistock, 28 December 1753

Dear Sir

I have your Favour with the 2 Enclos'd Letters. I think you gave yourself too much Trouble with the Modest Man who makes himself too Significant without any pretence – H [?] & W's [?] Successor don't know your power, or don't Consider it, But you do, God be Thanked, and I hope will Let 'Em know it in a proper Time – previous to any Future Essay. I will Lay by Carefully the Two Letters; But must repeat, the attempt on the Cutter wou'd be Constru'd a Breach, a Flagrant One –

I am glad you have alter'd your Mind as to Coming Down; there can be no Occasion, for your giving yourself a Trouble or Risque this Weather – I'l Watch the Beacon, but such False Feint Fires can give no Alarm, it only Shows, & very unpolitickly at this Juncture, what They wou'd be at.

I'l Trye the Sailor, he's a sad Mortal; I've Seen Him & have a Scheme, which I'l Trye him with again and as I advance acquaint you if I Succeed.*

I'm glad your Mama is come to her Senses. I've seen Baron & settl'd with Him as to Cummin.

Alexander has brought down the Bay-Horse without being Sent for, by a Mistake; I'l send Him back next Monday without the Horse, which I'l Take Care of. I've agreed with Him for £5 a year; the Lad is so modest he wou'd Entirely rely on your goodness, But I Follow'd your Order; you'l please to Order him up, or as you please.

Chancellor Fursman has been very Ill; I wou'd Willingly See Him, so shall go up the Middle of next month with Mr Edgcombe for a Day or Two to Exeter; if you have any Commands to Nutwell we will Execute 'Em; a Line under his Cover to Exeter at that Time will Come to hand –

William is perfectly honest & you may rely on Him, *Cætera probatur* ['as for the rest he has been tested'].

I am greatly oblig'd for your kind Declaracions. I shall never Encroch upon 'Em, But always approve myself
  Your Faithful
  N Rowe

* The sailor, in this and the following letters, is Hatch, who had some claim to property in Bere Alston.

F250 [slip of paper which had been sealed into a letter]

A Lady at Whiteford desires a paper call'd the *World*, or Adam Fitz Adam. Wou'd You be so good to order it Her (by Callington) you'l oblige Her &c, and if it is not too much the newspaper once a Week to Come to Tavistock, Friday's post, your Friends asking it of me.

F251

                                     Buckland, 30 December 1753

Dear Sir

I Think you do my black Cozen [?] too much Honour by so Large a Correspondence, I look upon him as the Man did on the Nightingale, *vox et præteria Nihil* ['a voice and nothing more']; however, Such Fils de Fortune get into the Saddle, when their Betters walk on Foot. You may Shorten Matters, when you please, without a Parson or his Clerk. Whenever I have the Pleasure of Seing you, we may be more Explicit.

Upon Second Thoughts, I will keep Alexander here, 'Till you order how He is to Come up to you.

An Extreme hard Frost, I am very Glad you did not Fategue yourself with an unnecessary Journey.

I heartily wish you many happy new years, pray Take care of yourself.

I am as always Dear Sir
  Your Faithful
  N Rowe

I wrote you last post from Tavistock.

William Edgcombe with some management may Do, But *Fratres non Sunt Similes* ['the brothers are not alike']; I miss the Man daily, But as it is irretrievable, We must not Despair.

Pray Excuse the bad paper, writing this at Searle's.

F252

Buckland, 4 January 1754

Sir

I hope you'l Excuse the liberty I took for the Lady, I can refuse Her nothing; did you but en passant hint it to Mr York, I know it wou'd greatly oblige Her.

Mr J Wills is much Concern'd for the Foolish Conduct of the Cutter; Says he cou'd have prevented it, had he known it in Season – the Cannon has assum'd the Direction of the Affair, But you have it in your power to Defeat it, For there is an Encroachment on your Land, & Therefore it is Doubly so, in Such Chaps to inter-meddle in purchases, which ought to be resented.

Next Week I will Trye the Sailor again, if I can bring my Scheme to bear, will acquaint you of my Success –

You will let me know how Alexander is to Come up to you, & When: the Bay horse has such a Cold, he must be kept in at nights.

Many happy new years!

I am Sir

Your Faithful

N Rowe

F253 [brief note on slip of paper]

Luce had £30 & Such a Place for Conveying his Interest.*

The Sailor is very Poor, the Mortgage is £10 besides Interest, wou'd you give £20 more –

Unless he Complys with Some Certainty, wou'd you get the Place for Him?

I Think it is a great Boon to trust Such a Chap *Sine qua non* ['an essential condition'] – But John Doidge can't hold the Place, He's worne out, and can't do the Duty, as he has wrote you.

I will Trye the Sailor once more; if I can't prevail I will Leave Him to you. But J D Should not be Superannuated Till he is Fix't, least the place shou'd be Catch't up by the Plymouth People.

Pray what is the Price of Bacon's *Abridgment* 3rd Volume?** Question, if a 4th.

* For Luce's death, see F213. The bargain made with Luce is referred to again in F254.
** Mathew Bacon, A *New Abridgment of the Law,* 5 vols (London, 1736–1766).

F254

Plymouth, 30 January 1754

Sir

The Sailor is a Sad Contemptible Fellow, not worth the Assiduity you Express. However, by Mr Porter's assistance will get him to be an Extra Man in the Port, and Endeavour to Fix Him, where he may work to his Trade too, There not being Constant Employment in that Capacity – and Then upon a *quantum Meruit* ['however much has been earned'], if you Think it worth your While to get John

Doidge Superannuated (who desires it, & Seems in a Bad Way) That the Chap may succeed Him. I'l Trye to make a Luce's Bargain.

Pray where are the Deeds, which were Lodg'd with your Brother to no purpose?

Your Mama has acquainted me, That She has hir'd Channon. The Hine still Continues *in Statu quo*; I shou'd have Thought, he wou'd have declar'd his inability But the Fuss is made with Him here, is not to be had Else where so I don't wonder.

I am with my best Wishes

Yours

N Rowe

I have Desir'd Mr Porter to write you about the Organ, Mrs Parsons Taking much State upon Her as to her Spouse – I Fear I can't now undertake the Exeter Journey.

You'l please to Order about Alexander.

F255 [small slip of paper]

Richard Corter's Son John is a Journeyman Shoemaker in Tinker's Alley near Leicester Fields; if you show'd Him by your Servant a Little Countenance, it wou'd be taken by his Father as a great Favour, who is a very Honest Man.

The Regard you have been so good to Show J Corter has much oblig'd his Father, who is a very honest Friend.

F256 [small slip of paper]

Robert Stevens has built part of his House on part of the Lands of Hogeson & Webb. The House part of said Lands adjoining to Stevens's is Falling down. Whenever Rebuilt, that part of Stevens's House which Encroaches may be pulled Down.

F257

Buckland, 20 January 1754

Sir

I was lately to see Sir J Rogers, who Seems in a panic as to his being Sheriff, But I met with Him at a Neighbour's, Mr Treby, who Told Him, Mr Taylor of Denbury will be the man, by what Authority I know not.

The Squire has been very Ill, was in some Danger, but it Terminated in the Gout; He talks of going to Town next Week, is on the Fox chase as usual; I saw his Brother the Captain with Him, a Jolly young Fellow, Who no wise relishes the Fille de Joy, nor the Steward King, who was there Likewise.

Channon came here in Cog last week with one of the Lakes to see Cattle; I met Him, but Took no Notice of Him & He did the Same; the Hine Continues *in Statu quo*, and no Likelyhood of an Alteracion, Therefore the Sooner a Change was the more for your Mother's Advantage, But your humble Servant Says nought.

The Weather has been so Bad, That I cou'd not Send Alexander away; He is breaking the Colt, you order'd for Sol, and Takes Him up with Him to Nutwell; She is so gentle, He might ride Her to London, if you approv'd of it, But She will never be Fit to draw, being too Little, But Serve She wou'd for a Hackney, if you had any

Occasion for Such a One in Town; if not, He may Leave her behind, and Come up by the Waggon, which I think is the only Way, as he has no great Coat; He has bought a pair of Boots, & Leather Breeches, having wore out what He had; you will be so good to Consider Him for it, he's a very Tractable, willing Lad, I hope he'l please you – You'l please to order how you'd have Him to Come up, as I am no Judge.
 I am Sir
 Your Faithful
 N Rowe

You'l excuse me as to Mrs Prowse and order me as to the Sailor.

F258

Buckland, 22 January 1754

Sir

 I had not your Favour of the 12th 'Till Last post. I am oblig'd for the *World* to Whiteford, and agree with you as to Mr York; But Ladies are so pressing in their affairs, That They won't be Deny'd – There, They are Coming to Town next Month, And I wou'd not have you Surpriz'd, Shou'd one of 'Em be her own Sollicitor –

 But I ask pardon, & will Trouble you no more on Such Subjects.

 I made an Essay last Sunday Sen'night, to trye my ability, as far as Sir J Rogers's, But the Weather was so bad Monday & Teusday, and my Spirits so Low, That I cou'd not undertake the Journey to Exon, and a Certain Diziness attends me, That makes me Diffident of Travelling alone – I am Sorry however I did not go, or That I Said I wou'd.

 Mr William Edgcombe being at Nutwell I presume answer'd your Expectacions as to Coleman, and to be Sure took particular Care of poor Betty Dyer, who I imagine was in no Small perplexity: your Being down in March, I shou'd think as you probably will bring Company with you.

 That Alexander's riding up the Colt may be of Some Use in the Journey Down, he go's to Nutwell with Her to Morrow, There to wait your Orders how you wou'd have Him Come up.

 As John Carpenter can't so well be Spar'd from Home at the Juncture, I am now going in with the Several Deeds you Direct, will Stay whilst They are Engrossing, which Shall be Done by Himself in a Snugg Manner, & I will take Care, They shall be Sent to you as Soon as possible, & will desire Alderman Lee to Forward Them to you.

 As to Grills, he is very poor; you will Order Him by William Edgcombe Some small gratuity for his Second Signing.

 I am with Respect Sir
 Your Faithful
 N Rowe

Tavistock, 29 January 1754

Sir

 I have had the Cholic so Bad I cou'd not Come in 'Till now, the Deeds for your Executing Shall be Sent you This week, I am now going Back.

 Hope in this Change of Weather you are well –

Mr William Edgcombe & John Carpenter Send their Compliments, I don't Doubt But They'll be yours obsequiously.

The glass has been Some Days above Fair, and yet a Continual Fogg all Day, with a Mist, & rain in the night, which is very unusual. And now a Deep Snow & Hard Frost.

F259

1 February 1754

Sir

Since my last I have Seen the Sailor again, and Talk'd roundly to Him, But Still find Him intractable; He Says 'Twou'd break his heart to Sell what he never Bought, and Shou'd he have a Family (which he may) He has nothing else to Leave them; I obviated That by a long Lease &c, Then he intimated a Sort of a Curse if ever he parted with &c. To this I reply'd He might, as he ought, keep his own Secret; upon this injunction we parted, to cooly Think it over; He had this further Fetch, That he wou'd Lay Himself under any Obligation as to his Fidelity – In Short, he is more than I cou'd have imagined Sçavant pour Soimesme ['knowing well what is to his own advantage']: all That I can Think Further, is to let Him Strut with his present Feather, 'Till necessity brings Him to a Different way of Thinking.

As to Grills, will Trye with William Edgcombe to get him to do what you desire – There's another of the Significants, Such Chaps too well know the Unum. It was the late Mr Edgcombe's opinion, and it is mine, to do all at once with Such People, For 2nd applications make 'Em the more untractable; and for Divisions by an act of God, Especial Care Shou'd be Taken, That They are never united again. I wish in this Case it had been so – a Future Caution won't be amiss: I know he'l expect Something, for this piece of Service.

The Weather is very Severe, an Extreme hard Frost, and much Snow on the ground. Alexander can never bring up the Colt now. There, he is at Nutwell, waiting your Order.

The Hine mends but Slowly; He, I hear, Says he is to be Discharg'd, and That Sol has given it out so in the parish; I Think the Fellow was much to Blame, as it will make the Man quite Indifferent, But in Short I Think Him of no great Service.

I am Sir
Your Faithful
N Rowe

Here is a report go's about That your Brother Samuel is Dead. The Deed is Drawn by William Edgcombe to him, But we'l respite the Execucion, 'Till I hear from You – The 3 Deeds to Colonel Elliot, Sir Thomas Heathcote, & his Brother go tomorrow by the Carryer to be Forwarded to you by Justice Lee from Exeter – No Letter by this post.

F260

Buckland, 8 February 1754

Sir

I have your Favour of 31st past, Mr William Edgcombe Sent it out by his Servant; I hope you have received the Deeds. Counsellor Jeffery was so kind to Send me yours under his Cover, which I have acknowledg'd the Receipt of.

I am glad to hear your Brother Samuel is well, the Report of his Death has given me some Trouble; I hope he'l Live to merit your Favour.

As to the Sailor, all my Efforts have prov'd ineffectual; money won't do – As John Doidge desires to be Superannuated, if you Think it worth your while to get Him to Succeed, on Condicion &c I will Trye again – But if he was to chew the Cudd a Little – However, I will do as you Direct.

I have got a Cold, the general Effect of this hard Weather, But I hope I shall be able to go in next Week, when I will Trye by Mr Porter what can be Done, Tho' I think there's too much Fuss with the obstinate Fool: I will observe the Razures you mencion when I receive the Box.

I Think you are Right as to Hatch. *Potestas prudentia, ut amor, omnia vincit – nunc aut nunquam* ['power with wisdom, like love, conquers everything – now or never'].

I am as always Dear Sir
Your Faithful
N Rowe

Pray Take care of your Health. I hope Everything will answer your Desires.

F261

Buckland, 15 February 1754

Sir

I have your Favour of the 5th, am infinitely oblig'd to you for your kind Concern – My old Companion the Cholic did not Relish the Severe Turn of Weather, or my getting a Cold in the Snow, gave me Some particular Twitches, But I Thank God 'tis Somewhat abated; I have indulg'd myself more on that account Than Ever I did in my Life, & I am as Sensible of your goodness as if I made use of any, and Thank you as much; But an insignificant Carkass isn't worth so much Consideracion; however I will be more Careful for the Future, Especially as you Desire it.

The Weather is quite Chang'd Since Saturday, a Thaw & Foggy rain ever Since.

The Sailor's Deeds I have Received, will Let Him alone a little, Believe 'twon't be amiss. He's an Etourde ['stupid man'] with an oddity not very Common, to abound with Evasions – But I'm pritty Sure he won't Wander.

Thank you for the Spectacles, which I shall be very Choice of, agains I want 'Em.

As to your Conference, the Loftiness must proceed from the Lightness of the Scale, which you can preponderate, and That They are too Sensible of; So a Few airs may be indulg'd: But I Think to ingage Posterity is a note above Elah ['too high-pitched']. There, your good management wants no Hints; Only I humbly Think no pragmatical Intruder with one Ticket at his Breech Shou'd like the ape be always Looking to it: no Jack Daw among the Rooks; To Week minds it may be a Sort of an awe, Tho' despis'd by Common Understanding.

As to your h. [?], if he had Common Modesty, he wou'd not presume to make Himself a party in the affair, But he has the Randome Eclat, which carrys him thro', Tho' with Contempt; yet Such *e promptiis* ['visible at once'] carry too often a Sway with Better Understanding. I Fear his Magnificats Sway too much on Softness: But with me & the School Boys *hic non est Littera* ['here no letter is visible'].

As I write in a Little uneasiness you'l Excuse my Enlarging, But be assur'd you may Command me in Everything in my power.

I am with Respect Sir
Your Faithful
N Rowe

Mr Docton's being nam'd Sheriff gives a little amusement: is it not a Mistake?

Sir

Since my writing the above I received yours with the 2 Letters & your answer Enclos'd, which I will Lye by as you Direct – the Expatiations, or Explanations don't alter my opinion of the Man – Only I Think you do him too much Honour, by being So Explicit; as Do's Somebody Else in making Him a party, which if I ken right, can't be of any Service, But the Quite Contrary.

F262

Buckland, 18 February 1754

Sir

Mr William Edgcombe brought me yours of 14, and I have Conferr'd with Him as you Direct, But good Sir, What can H[atch] or W[ills] do, if your Friends are True to you, which I Think you have no reason to Doubt of – Therefore I Think you need give yourself no Uneasiness.

What has pass'd between you & Lord B[uckingham?] I don't presume to be any Judge of, But This I know – That you can Command *Ambo* ['both'], and That He must know too – so That when the Time Comes to do what you shall Think best, & not to alarm your Friends in the mean Time – William Edgcombe is very honest, Says you may rely on Him & the Lamertonians, & I Think you may rely on the Monachorums &c.

I am Sir
Yours Entirely
N Rowe

F263

Plymouth, 18 February 1754

Sir

After Edgcombe's Departure I have again Thought Over your Letter. I'm astonish'd at your Fear, Where no Fear is – Had I been *in Statu* ['on the spot'], I wou'd have Convinc'd you & all the Alphabet That – But as you sent the Letter I cou'd not but Communicate; was he not Honest, I wou'd not have Done it – But let it not be mentioned in Gath, nor Whispered in the Streets of Ascalon – That Snow fell in Winter – I wanted to Trye whether your young Fellow wou'd bear Dipping

– He answers, tho' awkwardly, That he is Staunch – Surely a Black Jaundice, nor a Christaline in the Ey, nor a Low Sneer in the lowest Dreg, a Corrupter of Corrupted Scandalls of the priesthood have any influence on your Humble Servant; I Shou'd hope it has none anywhere Else.

But to be plain These – show, what inclination Prompts without Power – Your Ancestor gave 'Em an Instance with not ½ D° [?] – I don't advise a Breech, But Bullying without the where-with shou'd be answer'd with a Shot <u>point Blank</u>. Your Prudence with your Coolness may Do it by Surprize – If Mr Fuller brings in a Brown, why mayn't a T—n mortify as well as a Wod—. I don't pretend to Dictate, But leave it to Better Judgments.*

I am
Semper Idem ['as ever']
N Rowe

You will Order Mr William Edgcombe Settle with Lady Drake's Steward the Hine's account before He Goes.

I have Just Seen Mr Porter & Hatch. Do you Think of Fixing Him in Doidge's place, Be so good to Let me know – Mr Porter Sends his Compliments.

* An extreme instance of Rowe writing in a manner fully comprehensible only to FHD.

F264

Tavistock, 22 February 1754

Sir

I have your Favour by this post; you know so well how to act, I need not advise, But There's an old Saying to make peace, Sword in hand; There can be no occasion for more Recruits I humbly Think; if there was, I dare Say Voluntiers might be Found without beat of Drum: I don't care for Retorts, but Such might be made as These, That a long continu'd Complacency at so <u>Cheap a Rate</u>, when Such Favours are so much Esteem'd, not to be acknowledg'd, wou'd be call'd Ingratitute, not where they have been conferr'd.

J Grills has Convey'd as you Desire, and I'm perswaded all your Friends are Staunch – I can Say no more.

Mrs Prowse go's for London a Monday next & I am you may imagine –
Yet I am Sir
Yours Entirely
N Rowe

F265

Buckland, 1 March 1754

Sir

Mr Porter wrote me last Week That he had received a Letter from you, about John Doidge's Superannuation and Francis Hatch's Succeeding Him; now the Fellow is Such an odd Wretch That I can't Fix Him, and whether you think it proper to confer this Favour on Him, before He has Conform'd to measures, or keep it in petto ['close to the chest'], 'Till you Come down; or get Mr Porter to trye Him or whether I shou'd go in to Him again, or how, I Leave it to your Determination.

I cannot Think there is any occasion, as you have now added 5 to the number, to Encrease: for 5 is more Than I can anyway make out in Favour of – Let 'Em be as lofty as Sarum Spire.

Mrs Prowse & Miss Archer went for London yesterday, when I took my Leave of 'Em; They have taken one Mr Griffyths' House in Great Queen Street Westminster on the Park-Side: I wou'd not pretend to Say further, But I know your Compliment of Service wou'd be very kindly Taken –

Mrs Prowse is much oblig'd for the *World*, But as she is gone into it, Begs to give no further Trouble of Sending any more.

As my perregrinations grow too many for me, & the Cholic too, unless your Commands require it, I will Lye by for a Little. I have Occasionally Seen all your Friends who are Entirely So as I am

Sir
Your Faithful
N Rowe

I am now going to Tavistock where I will acknowledge any Letter I shall receive from you.

You'l Excuse the Trouble of the Enclos'd.

Tavistock, Friday a noon

Your Favour of 26 past, I have received and will answer it particularly next Week. I Think your Showing the great Light [of] your Power quite Right – For the Rest you do well in Endeavouring to gain as much as you can, Though you don't Want it – As you Talk of Being Down the Middle of April, pray Contrive it so, as to be at Beer at the Court 21st, That you Pay the Rents & Fix Everything.

William Edgcombe Sends his Compliments; when you write anything par[ticular] Let it be in an Enclos'd paper, But your Letter so General That I may Show it if necessary; But I shou'd rather Reserve Essentials, Till I have the pleasure of Seing you.

F266

Plymouth, 15 March 1754

Dear Sir

The Weather has kep't me here 'Till now, But tomorrow God Willing I will return to Buckland, and a Sunday go to Tavistock to see if that post brings anything particular from you.

The Shock, which the Universal Loss gives at this Critical Juncture, so affected me by the unexpected Surprise, That I don't know What I wrote you last post from hence.* This place have so grateful a Sense of the late Gentleman's goodness to Them upon all occasions, That They are Determin'd religiously to Comply with his Reccommendation, That Walton Bridge, shall not be Borne down with any Freshot: Lord Barrington without any Trouble will be the Other.

As for what Concerns Yourself, no Delemma can interfere – for T[avistock], Mr Bland** & Alderman Dickenson are to be the Men, and one of 'Em is expected There today or Tomorrow.

As to the Sailor, he's so Dirty a Fellow That I can't Trouble you Just now any Further, Than to let you know, Tho' he has no Shoes to his Feet, nor Cloaths to Cover

Him, He is Determin'd never to part with <u>but half</u>; if you will risque the place on That Condition, with some Gratuity besides, you will Let me know.

An undivided Thing may keep him by management – So I'll Trouble you no more about it: Mr Porter Thinks he can Do much, so I'll let Him trye, But I'm Tyr'd with the Fellow – I hope when matters are Settl'd, you'l Come down as you propose, in the mean Time I am as always

Sir
Your Faithful
N Rowe

Mt Wyatt & Mr Porter Send Their Compliments; So do's the Mayor of Plymouth who is a very <u>honest Man</u>.

Since my writing the above Mr Porter has done more than I could, he has Fix'd it with Hatch, if you approve of the Terms which He'l write you by this post.

* Henry Pelham, 1st Lord of the Treasury and Chancellor of the Exchequer, quasi Prime Minister, died on 4 March 1754.
** Thomas Brand, MP for Tavistock, was a friend of the Duke of Bedford, who held the Tavistock interest.

F267

Buckland, 22 March 1754

Sir

I had yours of 19th brought me this morning and yours of 12 & 14 out of Time sent here; as matters here at present are Quite out of Tune, unless I go myself to Tavistock, I can't depend on my Letters, and of Late I have not been able, as I have a great Cold, which has Stuck by me Long.

This and your Soon Coming down has Occasion'd my not writing before – and now I can only Say, That there are no Deeds in the Sailor's power, but he is certainly heir at Law to his Grandmother, and after his Grandfather (who holds by the Curtesy of England during his Life) Sole heir in revercion. You was so Desirous to have the Thing perfected at any rate, as I could not, Mr Porter made an agreement with Him to Convey to you His right in revercion after his Grandfather, reserving to himself an Estate for Life, and a Lease for 60 years: Consideracion, 20 Guineas, without Taking notice of the Mortgage to the Captain, which is out of the agreement –

Mr William Edgcombe is now at Exeter at the Assizes; I will go in tomorrow & Talk with Him, if return'd. But I shou'd Think, as your being here will be so Soon, it wou'd be Better to respite it, 'till Then, when it wou'd be done more to your Satisfaction. But that I submit, and as you order, it shall be Done; If you write by the Return of the Post, Mr W E will soon Draw the Deeds, and I dare Say the Fellow will rely on your honour as to the place; But I admire John Doidge has not wrote you about his Superannuacion, having Settl'd it with Him 3 weeks or a month ago: will Call on Him in my way to Tavistock. I have nothing further But That

I am Sir
Your Faithful
N Rowe

Sunday morning

Sir

This I Thought to have Sent as Dated, but was Prevented, as Everything here is in an odd Way – But Friday night as I was going to Bed, the Sailor brought me a Letter from Mr Porter, with yours to him Enclos'd, and yesterday I called on John Doidge to know what was the Reason he had not wrote you as he had promis't me: Said he had Thought over the matter, & cou'd not take the oath, For tho' his Estate was mortgag'd, yet he hop'd he had £10 a year Left; But I found out what his aim is; he wants to have some allowance from the Person who is to Succeed Him – Such Libertys are Taken at this Juncture!

I Think matters must be respited, 'till an Expedient is Found out.

F268   [small note]

John Doidge is very Poor. He came to me after This – to desire you'd Consider Him as an object of Charity, & wants an allowance from his Successor.

Tavistock, Sunday 8 at night

Mr William Edgcombe not returned from Exeter; will get Draughts made and wait your order.

THE LETTERS II

From Nicholas Rowe to Sir Francis Henry Drake, 1754–1775 (Devon Heritage Centre 346M/F269–F485), with two (F355, F356) from Betty Dyer to Sir Francis, and two (F434, F441) from John Channon to Nicholas Rowe

F269

Nutwell, 2 June 1754

Sir

I am glad to hear by your Favour from Bridport That you got well There; I hope this will Find you so in Town –

Your Directions to Betty Dyer & Sol I have Communicated to Them & They will be Comply'd with.

There was a Fine Rain Most part of yesterday & this morning, so no need of Watering.

Mr Brice has finish't the Garden-door and painted it with Turpentine.

The Fence at the end of the Canal is done too, but I Think not high Enough.

Sol is gone down to fetch up his Wife to weed in the garden, Says he has your permission, But Betty Dyer Thinks it will be very inconvenient for her to be in the house and Expects your Order before She admits her –

Sir John Davy & his Sisters came here the Day you went away, & Saw the House, But not me, For I intend whilst here to seclude myself from <u>Spiritual</u> & Temporal –

In what manner I am to be here, you'l intimate to your Housekeeper; pray Let it be as Pencioner ['paying costs'] not at Large, For I intend to be very abstemious.

I am Sir

Your very Faithful Servant

N Rowe

I sent you by Wednesday's post Two Covers, wherein were 3 Letters, 1 for yourself, & 2 for the Captain. 1 to Each was Charg'd; that to you I cou'd not Contest, unless you'd return the <u>Cover.</u>

The Farmer* says he has reserv'd a Pipe of his best Cyder for you, desires to know if you'l please to have it, Else he'l Dispose of it; you shall have it as he sells the Same Sort.

* Robert Coleman, tenant of Nutwell home farm.

F270

Nutwell, 6 June 1754

Sir

I have your Favour of the 1st Past, and am very Glad you got to Town well & <u>so Soon!</u> –

I hope as the Flock was so Large, Few Scabby Sheep were among 'Em; and if the Shepherd bides among 'Em, 'Twill be the more agreable too.*

The Joiner wants your Orders to rip up the Floor in the upper Closset over the porch, Says the Boards being of the same Colour with those in the new Buildings-Chambers, They'l do better Than new: Says you gave Him Leave to Take away the Wainscot There too. I Desire you'l please to order a Crown a Week for his Brother's Subsistance. As I don't Comprehend what he's about, so I can't Say anything further than That he & his Brother come Every Day.

Mrs Carpenter came here this week, as she Finds Dyets herself ['makes her own arrangements for food'], I hope it won't be Disagreable, as her Stay will be short, and you'l Thereby highly oblige her Brother, & Son, who came to Take care of Her & is return'd – They hope Bathing in the Salt-Water will be of Service to Her – She's a very Weak Woman!

The Tinner** & Sol have been absent 4 Days in a visit to their Wives; the Former go's on with the guttering, and the Latter has Brought his Wife; He says her Weeding in the Garden will be of great Service, she is to stay about a Month.

The Melons are very Prosperous, & Everything.

The Farmer has not brought in any Stones yet to the Meadow. I have sounded Him, & Find him not Inclinable to renew his Term here; I don't Think it prudent, to press Him; when you come down, 'Twill be Time Enough for you to Determine –

As to Taking away the Way from the Water-Side thro' the wood, I Fear you'l Find Some Difficulty among the Vulgar; I made an attempt by Forbidding some that were Coming out of the gate from the green by the House, which They did not Relish at all; Said 'twas an ancient Path, & never Forbid – I will hear what the Better Sort Say to it & Let you know; But my Leg still continuing Quear, must defer it a Little.

I am much oblig'd to you for the *News*, But as it is very uncertain as to the Farmer's going Fridays, the Topsham post bringing it, wou'd be too Expencive, unless it was directed to Alderman Lee's; upon the Whole the Trouble & Expence is more than my Curiosity deserves, & I am as Thankful without.

There has been Fine rain here Several Days, yet the want of Water Continues; if you'd please to Send Down a Force ['force-pump'] 'twou'd be of great use, as the Water sometimes comes down very well to the House.

I am very Sorry your Brother Sam is adrift, I hope he won't ground on Deal-Beach.

I am Dear Sir
Your very Faithful
N Rowe

Betty Dyer begs your Orders as to Sol's Wife's being in the House, <u>or not</u>.

* FHD evidently travelled with companions, and is here referred to as their 'Shepherd'.
** Stephen Philips, active at Buckland and at Nutwell. He also represented Sir Francis's interests at the Tavistock Stannary Court (see F289, F292).

F271

Nutwell, 14 June 1754

Sir

Having nothing particular to Write must refer [you] [to] [enclo]s'd mem.*

[I] [hop]e when Hatch has receiv'd this further proo[f of your] Generosity, He'l Endeavour to merit in Some measure your Favour by his Future Behaviour.

May this Find you well as I wish you.

As to the *News*, I beg you will give yourself no further Trouble.

I am with Truth Sir

Your very Faithful

N Rowe

Betty Dyer Desires me to acquaint you That more Blankets will be Wanted when you Come down:

a Dripping pan, a pestle & Mortar.

* See F273.

F272

[undated]

Sir

I have your Favour of the 11th Instant.

As to the *News*, I must repeat my request to you not to Send it, as it costs 4d. a Time to the Topsham post for bringing it: I got Farmer Coleman last Friday to call at the Post Office at Exeter & to desire their Letters directed <u>Here</u> might be kept <u>There</u>, 'Till Call'd for. The Clerk very saucily refus'd it; Mr Lavington was not There, But to avoid any Further Trouble – pray Sir don't send any more; and as to your own Letters, if you write on the superscription 'to be Left at the post House, 'till <u>Call'd for</u>', I hope they won't presume to send Them by the Topsham Post.

As to Sol, I hope he won't offend so again, and as his Wife's Stay will be Short, as he Says, Betty Dyer will Dispense with Her, But it can't be Convenient for her Long, nor for Them neither, as the Woman Leaves 3 young Children to a Nurse – Indeed the Weed is much over-run in the Gardens, & she Clears it apace.

There are a Few of the Cedars come up, the garden has been Water'd, But as there was a Fine rain a Sunday, Though none Since, Everything Flourishing.

The Joiners come duely, & Early & Stay Late, But as their Work at present is about Conversion of old into new I can't so well Judge of their performances. They are fitting the Window Spaces & Shutters in the Chamber over the great Parlour, which is near Done, & the Wainscotting round the Room; They have got Lead for the Sash Weights. The plaisterers have done the Sides once, and are filling up the Tops & Sides of the Sash-Frames outside – The Joiner is not in immediate Want of Work, so there is no hurry as to your Determinacion about pulling up the Boards in the Closset, which it's a pity to do, 'Till you pull down the porch, as a few new ones will do – I will observe when They are absent: the Elder Joiner has been again Enquiring, whether you have order'd Some weekly Subsistance for his Brother: my reason of mencioning, whether you had given him an unlimitted order to Take up Deals, was becaus I hear there is a Bill with Andrew Parker, perhaps larger than you imagine.

They have brought 50,000 Slatts But no Raggs which is a pity, as they may be Wanted; Nicolas has put Them at the upper End, where the Dung-hill is behind the Stable, which he Says is the Safest place – As Soon as the plaistering is Drye, he'l give it another Coat.

As to the guttering, Shall be able to give you a particular account in my next.

I have Talk'd about the Stopping the Way to the Wood &c. It is much approv'd of as a general Good, But was it not so, They say to oblige you, They wou'd readily Come into it; the Difficulty will be to pick out a number for a Jury of the Substantial Neighbours, & I Fear a greater to keep the Rabble out.

My avocations E. or W. are to Serve you, So you may Command to Either
Sir
Your Faithful
N Rowe

21 June

My Mistake of post Days. I intended this by the Last –

About noon a Wednesday last Captain Frank Drake with his Spouse came here, Both Surprizingly well from what I expected; They went in the Evening for Exeter in their Way to Plymouth – and Thereabout to stay for health.

Parson Lee complains Farmer Coleman don't pay him according to your Order, wonders he don't hear from you.

F273*

Whether you allow the Joiner to fetch Deals from Topsham without your order.

The Mortar in the garden The Mason says belongs to Him and Fetches it away accordingly.

The Chesnuts come up now.

Nothing yet appears in the Boxes in the Chappel-garden.

The Melons do very well in the Frames, but Those growe too big in the Hand-Glasses.

No Rain for some Days, Hot & Drye, so the Trees must be Water'd.

Small Show in the new Orchard.

The guttering go's on Well, but no Judgment can be made, 'till the great gutter is Finish't to the Head next the Lane.

The gate is put up by the Nursery according to your Direction.

The grass grows finely in the Meadow.

The paleing outside the garden put up as far as the Bridge, the Rest will be Done as Soon as Mr Brice has more Stuff.

* This is the memo referred to in F271.

F274

[undated]

Sir

I have your Favour of the 18th Instant.

Nicholas Shall Take away no more of the Mortar, the Joiner shou'd have your Order about Deals, I Think he ought not to fetch any without it.

I sent Sol to Topsham with Mr Brice's Boat but Captain Pyke is not Come in, neither is there anything at Exeter or Topsham for you – He is Expected in every Day; When they are brought home, they shall be open'd as you Direct.

Upon further talk with Mr Brice, he Says They can easily make up a Jury – Shou'd not Parson Lee be at the head of the Inquest? I have Thought of 7 as inclos'd: the Thing may easily be accomplish't, if you'l be at the Expence.*

Here is no Water; a Force ['force pump'] will be of great Service, but I Thought it wou'd not Cost a Quarter so much.

As to your Operators here –

The Joiners come duely, but the Windows are not Finish'd above Stairs; the 2 Doors in the Drawing room are; For my part, I am not a Judge of their performances. There, you will, when you See what's Done, when you Come down.

The Tinner has been hindr'd helping to get in the Slates, and breaking the hedge to bring in the Stones to the gutters; he is gone almost thro' the great ones & has Fill'd up the upper ones –

Sol is clearing the Weeds in the Borders; There has been rain several Times, so no need of Watering.

Parson Lee did not Cut his Meadow 'till Monday last, & Sol says yours won't be fit, 'till the middle of the next Month; I believe There will be a good Share.

Your having a Gardiner will certainly be more Regular –

The Mare is Sound –

Pray Sir, Send no more *News*; it is not worth your Trouble & the Expence.

I am glad your Brother Sam is provided for; I wish the Captain was too, Familys require assistance. Sol wants Matts for the Melons; all Thrive in the garden & I hope he'l be Diligent.

The Farmer desires I'd Transmit you the Enclos'd,

And I am Sir

Your Faithful

N Rowe

I believe I shall get the Plot of Farmer Coldridge, will Let you know in my next.

* The jury would need to be made up in order to carry forward the scheme to prevent local people from using the way by the wood, first mentioned in F270.

F275

Nutwell, 2 July 1754

Sir

I have your Favour of 26th past; as the Post-people at Exeter Continue to Send the Letters by the Topsham post I beg you wou'd not order any more *News*; indeed Dear Sir, it is not worth the Expence –

Mr Brice is very Zealous about the diverting the Way; I have no Doubt as to any you mention, But <u>Both Horrells</u>, as They make the Wood their Constant Road: Suppose you was to Write to Parson Lee to mencion the affair to his parishioners; he Likes Such applications – I have a notion that the 3 Farmers Coldridge, Coleman and Wheedon are fit Persons, as they are Sufferers by the people going over their Ground – Smith & Witherell are unable to attend, being Layd up. I have got a Violent

Crick in my Back, But will Trye tomorrow to go in to Mr John Ley, and Let you know his Sentiments.

There is much Fruit on the Wall-Trees, and some pears & apples on the Espaliers, and <u>one</u> of the Latter on the upper-most Tree next the Canal; your young Trees.

As to Captain Drake & Spouse, They much Surpriz'd: They were very Full of his Wonderful recovery, no Conversation particular. He is *Idem* ['the same'], Talk'd of Writing to you, and That he intended to ask Mr Sprye for the use of his House at Walkhampton.

The Mare Seems very Sound, Sol is bringing Her gentle, she is Horse-ward So She's kept in, as She broke out often; I believe She'l prove a good One, and fit for your Use.

There are several Melons. Some Large now.

The Joiners Seem not to have much to do. Next Week, They'l go about the Windows in your Room, if Nicholas comes this.

The Leads that are Left in the Meadow, now the upper gutters are fill'd, are wheel'd by John Coleman to the Middle Gutters, where Earth is Wanting; if you have any Objection to his being Employ'd, you will order accordingly, But 'tis a Pity the Tinner should be Taken off from Digging, which is his Excellency.

The want of Water still Continues, & it's now Found out That there's a hole in the pipe, which the Plumber's Man did not Find out, for the Master was then Sick, and you observ'd he made so Quick a return, That you did not know of his being here, 'Till he was gone; in Short the Fellow did not understand his Business: the Master has promis't to Come out.

Betty Dyer Says a Still wou'd be very useful.

Buckland Fishery has been very Backward 'till last Week, when They Took as many salmon as weigh'd 270 lb. This Channon wrote Coleman by Stacey who brou't 'Em to Exeter to sell.

I am Sir
Your Faithful
N Rowe

No rain here these 10 Days. Sol has Water'd the Trees. Very Different from you.

Exeter, 3 July

Sir

I have Seen Mr Ley, He Thinks the Movement on your Writ shou'd be respited, and by this post He'l give you his reasons, to which I referr you.

Yours
N Rowe

F276

Nutwell, 5 July 1754

Sir

I made a Shift to Walk to & from Exeter a Wednesday. I chose not to be Explicit, referring you to Mr Ley's Letter, and Shall only now add, That by Suing out a Writ *ad quod Damnum* ['appropriate to the damage'], you seem to admit a Right, which you ought to deny, and by barring up the Ways to the Wood & green, you'l maintain and in Time Confirm – But this I submit to better Judgments. The Lawyer is very much your humble Servant, & Seems mighty Zealous, That his patron & you should have a Neighbourly Correspondance. He's an artful Man & has his Views, but Still may be Useful –

I saw Mr Ned Chute, who Says he can procure you any Phisical Herbs, & will very readily Do it, if you'l please to Let Him know in writing the Sorts, & in the proper Season –

I met Alderman Lee at Northay, who very respectfully Enquir'd after your Welfare.

It rain'd at my return in the Evening, & Seems to portend more – it has been very Wet in the West.

Poor Betty Dyer is very much out of Order with a Cold.

Nothing particular Since my Last.

I am Sir
Your faithful
N Rowe

Since my writing This Mrs Searle call'd here in her Way to Powderham.
No Rain Since.
Pray no more *News*.

F277
Nutwell, 12 July 1754

Sir

I have your Favour of the 2nd.

I have heard nothing of your Things yet, by Captain Pyke; when he comes will make the Enquiry you Desire, and Let you know What he Says; perhaps he was assign'd to Some other Port First.

As to the Path, if Mr Ley's System is the Cheapest, & the Safest too, I hope 'twill answer your Expectation; the paper was only a List (I thought) of people for the Inquest; I omitted Sending it, as I was not quite Sure of all of 'Em.

The Joiner has Fetch'd sixteen 12ft Deals; he's Still mighty Fond of unflooring the Closset, but for a few Deals and a little Want of Colour, 'tis a pity!

The Several Things you mention Coming, & the Force, shall be Enquir'd after in Time; the Water is a Mysterious Thing, Sometimes Comes, oftener Stops; the Force will be of great use, But the broken Pipe must be mended.

I have inform'd the Joiner of the Several particulars you mention – the Painter Searle is going to take Searl's youngest Son; his Wife came up about it, So you'l oblige Them Both by Employing Him, & I Think Him a very honest able artificer. When Nicholas has filled up over the Sashes outside, the painter Shall begin as you direct There, and the Windows in your Room shall be Then Done.

The Fruit on the Pear Espalliers which you Saw Stands, So do's the apples, and only one on the young Trees next the Canal; I wish I had Solomon's Skill in plants (not Our Solomon), how happy shou'd I be in your Correspondence; But I am a Stranger to Everything, but the Shrub, an Emblem of your humble Servant, who Dwindles Daily.

Betty Dyer is much Better, and will attempt the Still; & get a Dripping pan of the Latin order as you Direct.

The Wall Fruit continues prosperous, only the 2 Trees which you observ'd before you went away.

If Water can be got in the next Field (which the Tinner Says can) Farmer Coldridge Says the Hop yard is at your Service on any Terms you Please.

The Chancel at Woodberry Church, they Say, is much out of Repair; the priest Vicars have Soon a Meeting, They Talk of presenting it. Dear Sir, have no Dispute with the Jack Daws.*

There are about 10 Hogshead Tolerably Good, wou'd you have Them repair'd, as there is a prospect of apples (Tho' not here!)

As to the Tinner, he go's on well; the ground on the Middle gutters shou'd be Levell'd as he go's, as the ground soon grows hard.

The Enclos'd I received from Channon; 'tis no recent Complaint, as I have before Told you of my assuming Kindred; Sure *ex post Facto* ['retroactively'], 'Twon't be So Soon Forgot, But he's one of the head Longs; Yet I hope Softness won't be Over-rul'd by the Toss of a hoop, nor an Empty Cannon. *Tempus fugit* ['time flies'], But whilst the Mill is going round, Some are giddyed, and Vainly Think, like Sancho, They are really Governours; You must Trye to Dissipate the imaginary Delusion, the Man with the long nose is not immortal.**

Captain Drake & his Spouse have Taken up their Quarters at Wilcox's at Buckland.

Mr Porter came here a Wednesday, a ride for his health.

Yesterday Sol began to Cut the Meadow; Fine weather, so Drye, That the Night before he Water'd the Garden –

Captain Pyke came in yesterday, tomorrow they will go for your Things; He did not Leave this port much above a month Since, so he cou'd not have had Them so long as you mention, will Enquire into it; pray Excuse all my Blunders, my head being very Disorder'd.

I am Sir
Your Faithful
N Rowe

Some rain last night.

* A reference to the vicars choral of Exeter Cathedral, who held St Swithun's Church, Woodbury, from the later medieval period.
** The man with the (false) long nose is the disguised squire of the Knight of the Mirrors who frightened Don Quixote's squire, Sancho Panza.

F278 [part of a letter?]

[undated]

The gate in the Wood next the Road is broke down; if That was stop't up, & a Door plac'd There, as you Said, Intended; a Strong pale Gate in little Culverhays next Sea-Lane, another at the White-Style in the Green next the Water-Side, That wou'd Stop Foot-passengers and in case They attempted to break any of 'Em Down, a Reward offer'd on a Discovery, wou'd awe 'Em from any Such attempt, & a prosecution, if any were So hardy, wou'd Effectually Stop any further attempt of that kind.

The Rats begin to Visit the Garden, I wish your Melons may Escape 'Em.

A large piece of the great Barn is coming down, it must be Stop't for the present.

The Rats abound in the house too.

Now the Meadow at Combe Farme is Mow'd, 'tis Easily Seen how by Guttering it may be remedy'd – The Tinner Talks of leaving Some part of the Gutters open, 'Till you come down, in relation to the Conveying the Water into the Garden, and to go to Combe Farme, unless you'd have Him go on the Hop-yard at Scotts.

I have Seen the Colts at Combe-Farm; They are in good Flesh, the Brown Colt will make what They call a pretty Hackney; The Sorrel Mare grows, But will be onely Fit for a Drudge.

Captain Hunt, who brought down your Sash-Frames, has been with the Farmer for the Freight; Says He has no Orders from you to pay it; shou'd he not have your Orders for That, & What Other Things you may Send?

F279

Nutwell, 19 July 1754

Sir

I have your Favour of the 9th.

I have heard nothing of Mr Ley.

We have had Continual Fair Weather, Till last Teusday & Wednesday – It took poor Sol when he had half made his Rick.

However yesterday proving Fair he wou'd have Finish't it, and I Think very good Hay, But a Shower at 2 put a Stop.

Betty Dyer is recover'd; She presents her Duty, with her greatest acknowledgments for your Notice; as to Boarding your Gardiner, She will in obedience to your Commands Trye to accomodate Him, but Fears as She is only Herself, That she Shan't be able to Carry it on –

There are Several Melons in the new Frame. Sol will remove the Frames with the Cedar plants into the Shade; There are Some Come up.

Captain Pyke has nothing for you, which I wonder at. He Says he never heard about Carrying anything for you.

As to Captain Pearse, Mr Brice has promis'd his assistance, if There's notice in due Time.

The painter will be here to Work next Week; he has been here to See what is to be Done, your Directions Shall Then be Observ'd.

The glazier will Finish the Windows in your Room tomorrow; The old glass looks little Better Than what was There Before –

I was at Tiverton and Talk'd with Mr Heathfield, about the Sale of his Estate; he Seem'd to intimate That his Son, if he did Sell it, Expected a high Price, So I press'd it no Further.

Mr Porter Return'd home today, Said he wou'd write You.

I am very Sorry you've had a Touch in your Back, But very glad it so Soon Left you; it's a very odd pain, and held me Long, I Thank God it's gone –

I heartily wish you health, & am Sir
Your Faithful
N Rowe

The late rain & Wind has Beat down the Corn much.

F280

Nutwell, 26 July 1754

Sir

I have your Favour of the 16th with the Enclos'd Account of particulars Sent by Captain Pearce; when he arrives, will Endeavour to get the Things out as you Desire. Two boats will Scarse Bring all.

I wish the Canon may observe his Injunctions.

Sol Sav'd the Hay well a Saturday, & has Thatch'd the Rick; it has been Catching Weather Since, Broad Meadow not so well.

The Wood gate next the Road is mended; I have Talk'd with Mr Brice about the Paled gates; he Says he has Stuff by Him fit for the purpose, and They can be Soon made, So thinks it best to Deferr making Them, 'till you come Down, as They may be done to your Liking.

When the Painters come, if Such a Fence is Thought Necessary in the garden, Sol may make one; But it is to be hop'd, They won't Venture, as no Fruit will be ripe Enough to Tempt Them.

The Badness of the Weather has Kept Mr Searle from coming out, having Sent Some of his Things.

The Glazier has done the Windows in your Chamber; he Says you Order'd him not to mend any of the Windows, 'Till you come down; the Stormy Weather has broke Several pains [*sic*], 'Tis pity They are not Stop't from going Farther.

The Rats are so numerous, That ginns wou'd be of Service to Take 'Em.

As to the progress of the Joiners & Tinner, I am no Judge, further than That They are here Duely.

I hope Sol will for his Credit Cleanse the gardens of Weeds great & Small against you Come down; the Showry Weather makes 'Em Encrease daily.

Nicholas has not begun the Head yet, But is hewing the Stones in Order to it.

I am very much oblig'd for your kind offer, But can't Trouble you for anything now.

I am Sir
Your Faithful
N Rowe

Betty Dyer is quite recover'd, & Mr Porter went away Better.

There has been rain & very Stormy Weather Ever Since Sunday afternoon, The Corn much Beat Down, & much hay still to Save. The poor Farmer has not Sav'd Broad Meadow, Tho' Cut Monday Sen night.

F281

Nutwell, 29 July 1754

Sir

I have your Favour of the 23rd with the Enclos'd which I will Lay by Carefully; the Sire ought in gratitude to have Done it Long Ago; I am Glad you have accomplish't it at Last, & in so agreable a manner. Certainly the Lady [?] had a great hand [in] it, you See Sir Francis what a handsome young Fellow can Do.

Sol & the Farmer's hay too are now Sav'd. I wish your Rick of old Hay in broad Meadow was at London, as it Sells so well.

Betty Dyer will Endeavour to accomodate the Gardiner; her Fear is He won't Like Her provision – pray Sir when he comes down, how is your pleasure, as to the Cropps Sol has put in?

The Glass looks much Better in your Chamber Windows now it's Clean. There is a Visible alteracion in what you have Ordr'd There.

I wish you an agreable Tour to Blenheim; Fair Rosamond* no Doubt Eat Venison at Woodstock; the Fair in Queen-Street wou'd I dare Say Like it as well, now it belongs to his Grace of Marlboro.

As to Mr Heathfield, he's a Tradesman, But very Respectful; I only went a Fishing; if you Think of going Further, I will See what he's made of; This you may be Sure, he'l make as much as he can of the Estate.

The garden has been much rufl'd by the Windy Weather; the Wet has made the Trees very Exuberant, they Want much to be Lay'd back; the Fruit Stands well; and the Ridge of Earth for the new Border has been Turn'd & Turn'd again, is now very Clean; John Coleman has been about it off & on Ever Since you went away. The Pails outside the garden Wall are Finish't.

The Joiners Come Early & go away Late, between 5 & 6 in the Morning and about 7 at night. This I know; But don't so well what They Do, as I don't Understand Such Sort of Work. That you'l Soon See yourself, as you know what you order'd Them to Do.

I am oblig'd to you much for your kind regard, I Bear up Surprisingly Considering Everything.

In Every State I am Sir
Your Faithful
N Rowe

Your Things are Found at Last in the Ware-house at Exeter, as by Enclos'd.

They are now Sent for today.

* Fair Rosamond, mistress of Henry II, heroine of ballads and folk tales.

F282 [slip of paper]

[undated]

The Wharfinger at London writes to Captain Pyke (who brought the Things) and Directed his Letter to Captain Pyke at Topsham; now no Captain Pyke Living There, the post people at Topsham Sent the Letter to Captain Pyke at Limpston, and he being abroad, the Letter lay Till his Return, which was but last Week; he gave last Friday the Letter to the right Captain Pyke, who lives at Exeter, and he immediately went to the Ware-house at Exeter, where all the Things were Found. This is the Case.

But the Captain, who brought Them, or the Ware-house Keeper at Exeter, That They gave no Notice, Even to your Friend Alderman Lee, who is an Owner (in part) of Captain Pyke, is the Occasion of all the Trouble!

F283

2 August 31 July 1754

Sir

I intended to have Sent the other Letter as Dated, but upon further Thought respited it Till I had Seen in what Condicion the Things were –

The Farmer Fetch't Them in his Cart a Monday, viz 2 Cases in which were the 2 Grates, the hearth-pace, and the Bundle with the Fenders, Tongues &c. They are a little Rusted, but in much better Condicion Than cou'd be Expected Considering how Long They have Layn. There are 2 Fenders, & but one Set of Tongues &c.

I have given the Joiner the Plan of the Stairs and let him know your pleasure as to the Rest. He is now about your Bed-Chamber.

The painters came here a Monday last. They are now painting the great Parlour, which the Joiner Says Shou'd be first Done, That it may be the Sooner Drye; the Windows outside, They Say may be Done at any Time.

Nicholas the Mason promis't to go on this week with the head Wear ['weir'] in the Canal; has not yet begun it.

I am Sir
Your Faithful
N Rowe

Captain Pearce is not yet arriv'd as I hear.

F284

Nutwell, 2 August 1754

Sir

Captain Pearce Came over the Bar Last Wednesday, and yesterday your Things were Brought from Star-Cross in 2 of Mr Brice's Boats. Sol & the Farmer went Down to help – All is Come well and Every Thing is unpack't as you Directed, Except the Cases with the Glass, & that with the Paper, which do's not Seem to have Taken wet.

I have not Further to Trouble you, But That
I am Sir
Your Faithful
N Rowe

Fine Harvest Weather.

The Boxes with the Glasses and Wax-Candles are not open'd. They are not mortic'd Locks.

The painters will have painted the great Parlour once over tomorrow night, as it must Lye & Mellow; Mr Searle Says it won't be Fit for a 3rd Colour these 3 Weeks.

F285

12 October 1754

Sir

I am very Sorry you had Such Rough Weather to Bridport; we had no Thunder nor lightning, But a Smart Shower about 11, the rest Fair & windy; But last night about

7, Just as the Boy got home it began to rain, & did so very hard most of the night; it is now Fair but very Windy, and the Glasses rise.

The Tinner is not return'd; the gutters all Draw, but that next the Wood. When he Comes, will Let you know of his progress, and his opinion of the gutters.

The Gardiner is gone to Exeter about the Trees you order'd; he Took up the plug in the Canal to prevent overflowing; He wants to know if you wou'd have the Hamper of Pears & apples you order'd to be Sent by Land or Water.

The plumber's Bill, & That for the Terrace, you gave no order about.

I hope you'll have better Weather to Town and That this will meet you well There.

I have only this further to Trouble you, That Mr Lee thinks you had better Trye your 4 Tenants' Cyder, 2 or 3 Hogsheads from Each, to See which is Best, which will be an Encouragement to Them.

I am Sir
Your Faithful
N Rowe

The Enclos'd came yesterday.

The Joiner is very pressing to know your pleasure about the Bill he gave you for His Brother.

Nicholas has not been here, Since you went away; will Send to him tomorrow, & to the glazier to put in the Glass in the Window in the Little room.

F286 [added on separate sheet]

[undated]

Your Gardiner has been at Mamhead. Mr Vaughan has wrote to his Servant to let yours have anything There. He brought from Thence Seeds of Several Sorts, and is to have Trees at the proper Season.

F287

Nutwell, 18 October 1754

Sir

I hope this will meet you well at London.

Betty Dyer wants to know how you wou'd have your Box Sent, by Sea or Land.

The painter wants a Gallon of Turpentine; your pleasure shou'd be known, as you Left no Orders about Him.

The Tinner Return'd a Monday noon; he has put 1 man to work, all he cou'd get; has Seen the Steward, but miss't him at Moreton, being gone to Tavistock, to give notice of his holding a Court at Plimpton next Teusday Seven night, or at Tavistock – when he must attend; the Steward gave him information how to fix the Bounds, So he has done it anew, Says the Work promises very well, and he has been Ever Since about it; That is, going to & fro' – Wou'd it not be proper, That Mr William Edgcombe Shou'd See how they proceed, and give you an account of it – As to the Tinner Stephen Phillips, when he has done the guttering in the Meadow, what wou'd you have him go about? He Says you'd leave in writing what he was to do, But you left nothing with me –

Wou'd you have Sol to level the ground?

The Painter has not Finish't the great Parlour yet; the Joiners are about the Bed-Chamber in the new Buildings.

Nicholas I have Sent to, and will again; the Joiner much wants him.

I have likewise Sent for the Glazier, to put up the Window in the Little Room.

Stephen Phillips will have Finish't the gutters in the Meadow tomorrow night, but to level the ground will Require more Time – He Thinks, if you approve of, to dig the Gravel in Wet Weather, and to do the gutters at Combe Farme when Drye Weather, and wou'd know whether he is to dig the gravel by the Day or the Load. Under is his account, which desires to know how you wou'd order him to be paid.

I am Sir
Your Faithful
N Rowe

Due to Stephen Phillips for 88 Days work to the 19th of October inclusive at 1s. 6d. a Day	£	s.	d.
	6.	12.	0
Paid for a Shovell you gave him	0.	2.	0
	6.	14.	0
Received of you	2.	17.	0
Remains due	£ 3.	17.	0

F288

Nutwell, 22 October 1754

Sir

I have your Favour of 17th Instant; in my next I will particularly answer it –

Only now, as Mr Edgcombe is going away, I Take this oppertunity to let you know, That he having made Some Bargains at Yarcombe wants Some Counterparts, which he can't have but by me, So I must go down, when you Think proper. Tho' my Travelling Days Seem to be much over, I will Endeavour to Serve you as Long as I can – As I desire nothing but on that account. I've Taken of Mr Edgcombe 5 Guineas as going to & Fro' may occasion Some Expence.

Sol is helping the Tinner to Level the gutters in the Meadow; as the Farmer don't Seem inclinable to take a Further Term it will be for your Interest, to Secure what the Tinner has done – The Rubbish, which came out of the Foundation of the 1st new Wall, which lyes in the Orchard, will be very handy to fill up the Vacancys, which you'l order about; For I wou'd not Take Solomon from the Gardiner, who Says he wants him much to assist about the Walks he's now Doing; you'l Likewise Order what you wou'd have the Tinner to do first, and who is to pay him.

I am Sir
Your Faithful
N Rowe

I hope you won't Forget writing to Commander Rogers about young Thomas Wyatt.

F289

Nutwell, 25th October 1754

Sir

Enclosed is the Mensuracion you directed.

The Joiners are Still putting up the Wainscot in the Bed-chamber, & Nicholas is filling up the Noggings ['brickwork in timber frame']; when you determine the Joiners going, their Chest Shall be Sent by Sea, as you Order.

The painter has finish'd the great Parlour, is now painting the gallery, but for want of the White Lead from London is at a Stand. I propose to Send for Some from Exeter, unless the Vessel comes today as She is hourly Expected.

The Farmer's Expectations are so Large as to a House, and so peremptory as to the rest, That I don't know what to Say, but must referr you to the paper Mr Edgcombe Sent you.

Your Box was Carry'd to Exeter a Teusday.

The Carpet shall be carefully pack'd up, & Sent by Sea directed as you Order: But as Mr Kingman don't Expect any Ship this Fortnight will respite the preserv'd Peaches, and the hams, Till we know if he has any for you.

I have Talk'd with Farmer Watts about the Bog you mention; Says he can't part with it, as it is the only watering place he has, But there are Several poles which you may have if you please.

The Boat won't Lye in the Coach-house, being too long, So they were oblig'd to put her under the gate way; I hope no harm will come to her, as the Situation is very inconvenient.

I am very Glad you got so well to Hursely & so Soon, as I am That your Brother knows his Destiny – Mr Porter wrote me lately, That he was not yet come to Plymouth but daily expected; I wish Him a good Voyage.

The Gardiner is about the Walks, There has been very Fine Weather, Ever Since you went only a little rain a Wednesday; Stephen Phillips go's tomorrow Evening so as to See what his Brother is doing, and to be at the Stannary Court at Taverstock a Teusday next; I hope you have wrote to Mr Edgcombe about Him, & about his Brother's working, what Mr E is to advance him, as he must be Supply'd. At Stephen's return he Shall go about the gravel; you will order about its being brought into the garden; in the mean Time he & Sol must do what They can about Levelling the gutters, which shou'd be Done I Think out of hand.

As I must go down about these Counterparts for Mr William Edgcombe, whilst the Weather is good 'twill be Best, so Expect your Directions.

Can't the Gardiner then go to prune the Trees at Buckland? But how to get There! That's the Question puzzles.

I am Sir
Your Faithful
N Rowe

Christophers has Trimm'd 5 or 6 Hogheads and Believes he may pick out as many more.

Sol Says Some of the Pipes are good, wou'd Trye two of Them.

As to the value of Cyder, none of your Tennants will Sell under 10s.

The Stuff from t'other Side the water I wou'd not advise, but to buy it of <u>Them</u>. You will Let your pleasure be known <u>in Time</u>.

Mr Brice is return'd & has bought a Ship at London, 340 Tun. I have Talk't to him about the Enchroachment of the Key, and he is willing to make you any acknowledgment.

F290

Nutwell, 1 November 1754

Sir

As I can be of Little Service here but as a Journalist, I shall Continue, Tho' I dont hear from you, to let you know weekly what Occurs.

After Several Times Sending after the White Lead from London the Painter got it by going in on purpose to Exeter a Teusday; he lost Two Days for want of it; Things by Sea are very uncertain, Especially this time of the year, and I shou'd Think it might be had near as Cheap in the Countrey: He's now painting the gallery.

The Joiners have not Done the Bed-chamber yet, Nicholas has Layd one Coat of plaistering.

There was much rain & Wind a Wednesday at S.E. and it beat much in in [*sic*] the new Buildings, which with that wind They Say it always will, 'Till the outside is Stuckow'd.

The mice much abound in that part, I wish They don't attack the Paper.

The Gardiner has Layd the Walk next the upper Wall, & is forward in that against the new Wall; he has planted Several Pears, but can't Find No. IX as directed by the paper you left him – But the Label Lay in the passage Window, So presumes you forgot it.

The Casks are Trimm'd, and They'l amount, Pipes & Hogsheads, to 3 Tun; it will be Time now to Look out to fill 'Em. 10s. Seems the price; wou'd you Trye all your Tennants?

The gutters in the Meadow Seem to draw very well, But it is a pity They are not well Secur'd & the ground Levell'd; I wrote you to know whether Sol shou'd Do it.

The rats abound, you Said you'd Send Some ginns.

Wou'd you have the Carpet Sent directly, or Stay till it's known whether Mr Kingman's people bring you any hams, and So Send all you order'd by Sea at the Same Time.

The Tinner is not return'd, Though He went away a Saturday last, as I wrote you.

The Joiner is going about the Parlour today; He wants to know your intensions about him, Says he'l write you for your particular Order –

The little room on the great Stair Case is Floor'd, the windows shou'd be glaz'd; the room by the long Garret is.

I shou'd Think Nicholas might Contrive Some way to prevent the rain beating in thro' the Tops & Sides of the Sashes in the new Buildings; when he comes about the Parlour, which I hope will be a Monday, as I shall hasten Him, he Shall Trye.

It is now very Calm & Close, inclining to rain, Tho' both Glasses rise.

I am Sir

Your Faithful

N Rowe

F291

Nutwell, 6 November 1754

Sir

Your Favour of 26th past Came not to my hands 'till late Friday night Last. Next Morning I communicated your Orders to the Joiner & Painter; the First has done Some Jobbs since and, as he Says, he can't go without his Tools, he must Stay Till he can get a Passage to go with Them; a Vessel is Expected to Sail Every Day, when the Carpet & what you Order'd besides, Shall be Sent.

Nicholas is doing the Parlour Chimney, was Forc't to pull it down from Top to Bottome, the Wall very Loosely put Together, a very odd Job –

Sely will acquaint you about it when he gets to Town.

I got Parson Lee to view it; hopes you have Receiv'd his Letter. Begs whenever you Favour him with any Letter, you wou'd please to Send it under his Father's Cover.* He will pay the Painter the Guinea Extraordinary, when he go's away; he will Soon have done the Stair Case.

The Gardiner has planted 44 Elms & 22 Firrs. They are Small, as I wrote you, and the Fence is Finish't, is now going about Pruning the Trees.

We had last week two or three Days Smart Frost, now moderate –

They have brou't In 135 Horse Load of Gravel, can bring in no more, 'Till Christmas, the Farmer having all his Tillage to do. I Think as you do, he's a very Pradmatical Fellow in his Demands, But yet I wish you might Let your Estate. When you have Sent your Resolution to Mr Edgcombe, he will best Treat with Him; as I Choose to avoid Talking to Him, Least he should Think, I had Some Design upon him.

I had a Letter from Mr Porter, who writes the Case for the Writings is Come to Plymouth.

My Lameness (which I don't know what to make of) Still Continues, & a Weakness which greatly dejects me; So That I am much Confus'd.

I am Sir

Your Faithful

N Rowe

The gutter which I wrote you about, has been open'd, and is Choak't up from one End to th'other, being onely with Pebbles, So they are making One, which must be Cover'd, Nicholas Says, or the House will be much injur'd, as it's Fludded Every Rain; I'm oblig'd to have Sol to help the Tinner, or 'twou'd never be Done; your Gardiner is much offended at it, Swears like a wretch, how can it Otherwise be Done?

My Dear Sir Francis

I am a very poor Overseer, as I Fear you Think by the Blunders I make, but to my utmost I will do my utmost to Serve you in Everything.

It now rains, yesterday there was a good Fire in the Drawing-Room, the workemen Say always in Damp Weather there shou'd be a Fire in that room; pray your Directions, That Betty Dyer may <u>not Err</u>.

The parlour makes a Dismal appearance, Nicholas Says his work will Strengthen the Wall, which was very Bad, Seley Says the Timber work is so too; his Brother is Discharg'd ['account settled'], and he must Continue plaining the Boards for the

Floor, 'Till he go's; as that must be Done, they will be Better for Drying; I Shall hear today when the Ship will Sail, he can't go Before.

* Parson Lee's father was the attorney Alderman Lee of Exeter.

F292

Nutwell, 8 November 1754

Sir

Though I have not heard from you Since yours from Hursely, I hope you are well.

The Tinner did not return 'till Saturday last at night, he tells me he made good your Bounds at the Court at Tavistock, Tho' much oppos'd by Parson Richards the Minister of Calstock, who has a Share with Mr Sprye in the late Justice Elford's Boundings. You must be call'd next Court again at Tavistock which will be 19th Instant. Mr John Carpenter was there for you, who I presume will give you an account what was Done; I Fancy he'd do for a Steward of the Stannary Court. But after all this Trouble no Lead as yet, and the prospect is for Copper. Your Book of the Stannary Laws wou'd have been of Service There.

The Joiners have Taken up the Floor in the Parlour, which is all rotten, & the Timbers under and all the Wainscott on the windows-side. There was a great Deal of Water on the ground. Nicholas has put a Second Coat of plaistering, Tho' the first was not quite Drye, in the Chamber; and will Soon Come and do the Chimney & brick the Floor. But Sely tells me they are quite out of Work as he has wrote you, and to know your Intensions about him & his Brother.

The Tinner has Try'd the Place in Clift Close & Finds the gravel as on Mr Brice's Side – He is willing to digg it at 1d. a Horse Load, and Farmer Coleman will Carry it at the Same price; you will Signify your pleasure about it, as to Both.

The Storme last Wednesday Se'nnight did much Damage westward, particularly on the River Tamar; Dartmoor was so Bad That he had much ado to get to Moorton, & in two Days here. Sol was Sent for by his Wife, & the weather was so Bad, They made a Week of it; you will please to observe I gave Solomon no Leave.

I hope you'l Soon order about the Joiner, I wou'd have had him plain the great Parlour Floor, But Says he had no Orders from you, & I'm Sure I wou'd interfere without 'Em in no Sort, Tho it's a pity he has no Employment.

The painter is priming the new Work in the Bed-Chamber; he don't Seem to have much more to do, you will Send your directions about him too; he Says there is paint Enough left to do thrice the great Stair-Case if you approve of it.

I mistook about the Casks; There were no pipes Trimm'd, only 10 Hogsheads. It is high Time you shou'd Determine about the Cyder, as pounding will be soon Over.

I am Sir
Your Faithful
N Rowe

The Bay horse Stray'd from the green last Saturday & has not Since been heard of; he will be Cry'd in Exeter today, and Shall be in the neighbouring Parishes next Sunday.

Since my writing This, the Horse is found; he was Taken up at Topsham, a Saturday night all over Dirt, at the Post House Stable Door, where he us'd to be Sent,

So 'tis Suppos'd Somebody rode him & Turn'd away Thereabout – The green is no Secure place, must See & Secure the Wood gates & keep him There anights, or put a Lock on One of his fore-legs, or keep him in the Stable – For the Newfoundland Crew, when They come home I fear will make free with Him, perhaps ride him quite away – The Farmer paid 4s. 8d. for Crying him & Keeping.

Sol & the Tinner [have b]een Both Ill Since their Return, the [1st wi]th An apoplex, the Other with the Rheumatism, But he's now Digging Gravel –

There was much rain yesterday and the glasses fell from Fair to rain.

F293

Nutwell, 15 November 1754

Sir

I have wrote you by Every Friday's post Since you went, But have had no Letter, since that from Hursely. I hope you are well.

The Joiners are at a Stand as I wrote you, and the Painter will have Finish't in a few Days, unless you will have him paint the great Stair Case, as I wrote you.

Nicholas will have finish't the Plaistering in the bed-Chamber today; as to the Old parlour, Says you have given him 'till Christmas to alter the Chimney &c.

Your Gardiner is preparing the Walk for the gravel: I don't pretend to understand his profession; There, you'l See what he has done, & Judge Accordingly; I hope, as He is Sensible ['aware'], you know what he ought to do, he'l behave Accordingly – He has Taken up of Rowe the Ironmonger at Exeter Several Things, without any Direction from me; I Think, as I have Told Him, he ought to have your Order, before he Takes up anything; Some hint from yourself wou'd not be Amiss –

The Tinner is guttering at Combe Farme, 'Till your Determination is known, whether he is to dig the gravel by the Day, or Horse-Load.

You will Send your Order about the Cyder You'l have, what Quantity, and from Whom.

I have been very Lame by a hurt in One of my Feet, and had a narrow Escape by a Fall over a gate.

I am Sir
Your Faithful
N Rowe

F294

Nutwell, 22 November 1754

Sir

I have yours of 12th Instant, & have Communicated your Directions to Mr Lee about the Joiner's Brother; They are planing the great Parlour Floor; They & the Painter seem now to have near Finish'd; Your Finall Directions about Them, will be very Soon Wanted.

The Gardiner & Sol are preparing the Walk for the Gravel; as it is very Fine Weather, will be ready for it this Week.

The gutter is Stop't up, which carrys the Waste Water from the Kitchen, So that it comes into the House; Nicholas has open'd Some part of it, Says he fears 'tis Chok'd up to the End.

If you don't Soon Order what Quantity of Cyder you'l have, They'l have done making.

Mr Kingman's Ships have brought no hamms, nor goose-Eggs. How will you have the apples & pears Sent? By Land or Water.

As Soon as I hear of a Ship bound for London, will Send the Carpet as you Order'd.

The Tinner Return'd from the West yesterday noon, proposes to Stop the Work this week 'till Spring, becaus the water comes into the Shaft; Says Mr Edgcombe will give you an acount what was done at the Court, he being There.

As the Farmer can't Carry the gravel 'till tilling is Over, which won't be 'till after Christmas, Stephen must go to Combe Farme Guttering 'till Then, unless you Order Otherwise.

    I am Sir
    Your Faithful
    N Rowe

I have been Lame this Fortnight, & Still Continue so.

F295

Nutwell, 29 November 1754

Sir

    I have your Favour of 19th Instant; am very Sorry you are out of Order, hope this will find you well, pray Take Care of Yourself.

For my part I have been Lame Some Time, & Still Continue so, to my great Mortification.

The Cyder they Say is very good, 10s. a Hogshead at the Pound's mouth, as I wrote you, and if I hear nothing from you by this post to the Contrary, will Take up Two Tun of your Tennants, as They will have Done, before I can hear from you again and then 'twill be too Late.

As to your Gardiner, he works, but I am no Judge how well; the Walks that are done, Look even, but the Turff is very Bad; he Talks next Week of begining to prune The Wall-Trees; The Leaves don't fall yet; the new Wall Takes Water much – I am very unwilling to give my Opinion of what I don't pretend to understand, But if he had a Little more Steadiness, it wou'd not be amiss – There, if he pleases you in the management of your Trees, That I suppose is the Main – The Elms are but Small, the best he Says he cou'd get.

You have never Said whether you'd have the pears & apples Sent by Land, or Water.

Nicholas came a Wednesday about the Parlour; he begs pardon for not Coming before, apprehended you did not intend to do it so Soon. I Let him know your Directions, so hope he'l be more punctual for the Future: He and the Joiner is about it, but I can't yet understand their Intensions; but fear 'twill make a Breach in all the rooms, I hope you'l Send particular Directions, what you wou'd have Sely to do; he Says he has wrote to you to know, whether you wou'd have him Floor the parlour, and what Sort of Windows you'd have put in, as he can't fit the Wainscot 'Till he knows; he is now out of all work but This; you will therefore Send your immediate Orders; The Sleepers I presume must be had of Mr Brice, and Stuff for the Window Frames.

The Painter has had Orders from his Master about the Stair-Case, which he'l go about, as Soon as he has done the Middle room; I wish your plaining the great parlour don't hurt the painting; Betty Dyer must make Fires very often. She has begun, it has been Frosty, but all Damp Weather must be Tended.

The Carpet Shall be Sent per Soonest, I am not a little Confus'd, you'l Excuse what's amiss –

The Farmer & Tinner are Both willing to See what They can Carry & Digg the Gravel for, before they make an absolute offer, in the mean Time will Talk to Mr Lee as you direct.

I am Sir
Your Faithful
N Rowe

Sely having nothing to do, Fetch't Deals from Topsham, Last night, for the parlour Floor, Says he'l [Fi]t 'Em to be Layn when you please.

[I] don't advise These Things, neither can I oppose Them.

They have brought into your Garden 30 horse Seams of gravel, from which the Farmer Says he can't Carry it under 9s. a Hundred, and the Tinner will dig it for 1d. a Seam; I have Talk'd with Mr Lee, who Thinks They can't do it under –

The Elms are in, & the Firrs will be today – a hard Frost.

F296
Nutwell, 13 December 1754

Sir

Your Letter of the 3rd Instant has given much Concern: Bodily ailments we are all Subject to, But as to mental Obstructions, I shou'd hope your Philosophy & your Reason cou'd remove Them, and Join with you for amendment of Both.

By this Time I presume the Oxfordshire Election is Determin'd.*

The Gardiner's manner of Working is nothing Extraordinary, he is not much absent in the Day time, he's now pruning the Trees on the higher Wall; I wish he may Answer your Expectation, to me he don't Seem Solid Enough for a Chief Manager; he's about making in the Center of the Middle Walk in the Kitchen-Garden a Pit for Water, which he calls an Octogan, and he Says by your permission; when he has prun'd your Trees, and Lay'd the gravel Walk, his dexterity will more appear.

Sunday night & Monday all Day we had a Violent Storm at S.W. with very much rain, which Over Flow'd great part of the E. Meadow, the Open gutter not being Deep Enough to Carry off the Water, which had Like to have Flooded your garden. The gutter, They are now Opening, being Stop't; the Water cover'd the Bottome of the Parlour, & most of the Kitchen; when it's done, 'twill be of great Service to the house.

The Wet in the new Wall in the Garden comes from the Top, which Nicolls [sic, 'Nicholas'?] Says is for want of Coping; this late Storm has Try'd the house; in the Long Gallery next the Chappel and in the Little room over the new Window, the Water Comes in, and whenever it blows Strong, & rains it beats in Over the Windows in the new Buildings, according as the Wind is; the Leak in the Chappel shou'd likewise be Stop't, and That in the Men's room, both being in the Led, is Plumber's work.

Nothing can be Done in the Parlour for Some Time, tho' the Boards are prepar'd for the Floor; the Joiner when you See him, will acquaint you about it; had Nicholas been Earlier, all might have been Done, as you are pleas'd to observe, But now it must be Let alone 'till Spring, as the room now is.

The painter will Finish today, or tomorrow at Farthest; he has had Some white Led & Oyl, having not Sufficient; in my next I will acquaint you what he had in all, That his Master may account with you for it; the Moisture in Frosty Weather Settles so much on the insides of the Sash-Frames, That they dab up much Water, which in Time will deface the Varnish. Nicholas today will plaister the top & Sides of the Frames, thro' which the rain beats in Stormy Weather. The painter has been absent one Day only.

The Joiner's Chest, and the Carpet in a Case directed for Messrs Spinage &c, 2 Hampers & 2 Boxes directed for you were put on Board a Ship at Topsham today; as the Joiner goes with Them, he has promis't to take care of 'Em & give you notice. He has been two Days Absent only, as I know of.

The gutter which I wrote you about, is doing as Fast as possible, it reaches from the Back Door to the green; it puzzles me much, But They Say 'twas absolutely necessary to be Done –

At present I am very unfit for anything, much more an Overseer – I hope this will Find you as well as I wish you.

I am Sir
Your Faithful
N Rowe

I wish the Fruit & the preserv'd peaches may Come Safe; The Late Storm Sunday night & Monday has done much Damage.

I hear There will be an Entry Soon at the Dock; I hope you have wrote to Commander Rogers in Favour of young Thomas Wyatt.

Very hard Rain, & wind all last night & this morning at S.W. Even to a Storme & Still Continues, So the Things nor the Joiner can't go as yet.

* The result of the Oxfordshire election, famously satirised by Hogarth, was declared in April 1754. The two Tory candidates had a small majority, but the returning officer referred the decision to the House of Commons. The House of Commons had a Whig majority and declared the two Whig candidates successfully elected in April 1755 (see note to F317, and F319). One of the successful Whig candidates was Viscount Parker, son of the Earl of Macclesfield, a relative of Sir Francis on his mother's side.

F297 [attached slip]

Bought for the Painter at Exeter –

		s.	d.
13 September	6 Lb Whiting	0	3
	1 Lb Red Lead	0	3½
	1½ Fine Spruce Oker	0	7½
three quarters	White Copperas	0	4
	Lamp black	0	1
		1	7

		£	s.	d.
21 October	Oil of turpentine 4 Quarts	0	5	0
	Carriage of the above	0	0	6
7 December	Linseed Oil, 1 Gallon	0	3	8
	10 Lb of White Lead in oil 5d	0	4	2
	pot	0	0	1½
	Carriage			
11 December	Linseed oil, one gallon	0	3	8
	10 Lb of White Lead in Oil 5d.	0	4	2
	Carriage			
		1	1	3½
	paid Freight of White Lead			
	from London	0	1	
	paid Carriage from Exeter	0	1	3
	paid Painter's Horse & Turnpike	0	0	4

Had the above   William Elliott [signed, Elliott's hand]

F298

Tavistock, 17 December 1754

Sir

With great Difficulty got here today; Mr Edgcombe's Summons was very Suddain; as I had not heard from you about it, thought the matter was Respited; He shall have the Counterparts he wants, But 'tis a pity he had not access to Them upon any Occasion.

The Painter was out in his Calculation about Colours, But he Says his Master will allow it; Enclosed is what was bought for Him. He nor the Joiner were gone when I came away, But had finish't Everything last Week; He on Friday and the Other Wednesday Last.

Nicholas is plaistering the Outsides of the Sash Windows, which is highly necessary as the rain beats in, and will Finish the Rest out of hand.

Your 3 Covers of Crab-Seeds I have given to your Gardiner; I wish you may Like his pruning, I Think he Takes away too much, But I don't understand it; He Comes after Christmas to prune the Trees at Buckland; I will Let you know what he do's There.

Mr Edgcombe was oblig'd to go away as Soon as I came in; Coleman* comes to Him in the Holy Days, when we will Talk to Him; I wish you wou'd Determine with Yourself your utmost Concessions; Tho' Such Chaps are Brutal, They are necessary Evils, and I wish you cou'd keep Him, as it wou'd Save you a great deal of Trouble.

You will be so good to Excuse my Scrawl from Exeter, I hope what you cou'd pick out, you Communicated to your Mama –

I hope this will Find you in better Spirits; my Lameness is not better'd by the Journey, you will Let me know your Commands at Buckland.

I am Sir

Your Faithful

N Rowe

Betty Dyer makes Fires Frequently.
    2 Days Fair!

* Coleman, the Nutwell farmer, as in F234 and F269.

F299

Buckland, 20 December 1754

Sir

I wrote you last post from Tavistock & Enclos'd one for your Sister, which you'l
Excuse, as I don't know how to Direct.

To See this place, makes me Lower if possible than before; it rains in to all the
rooms in the house, part of the Ceiling in the room you Dine in is fallen Down, the
gardens look Wild but all your Trees Thrive –

Tho' I bragg'd of the two Days Fair in my Last, I was wet Thro' afterwards
Coming here.

I have Sent Mr William Edgcombe the 4 Counterparts.

The Hine, the Little I've Seen, Seems to manage Things very well –

They'l make between 2 & 300 Hogsheads of Cyder, this week will Finish it.

Your mare here has Slip't her Shoulder again, the Hine has not rode her for Some
Time; he is under much Concern, That the pears you Order'd to be Sav'd, rotted
away so fast, he Could not Save Them; He Says your Brother was to Sail as [sic]
the begining of the Week; He has Sent for none of his Things from hence, which I
much wonder at –

The Hine Saw Captain Frank (who is at Mr Parsons's) last Saturday; he Says he's
going apace, as he Spits up all.

I am quite off the Hinges at present, but when able, will See him, & Let you know
how he is –

[also?] Mr Porter about his Aldermanship, which I fear he'l Miss; and poor Mr
Wyatt will break his heart, if you don't Write to Commander Rogers in favour of his
Nephew Thomas, to be a Quarterman, as Some are Soon to be made.

I hope to hear your Spirits Flow.

I am Sir
Your Faithful
N Rowe

I fancy your Uncle Harry is Coming into these parts, as I saw a Letter directed for
Him from London to be Left at Mr Edgcombe's: it did not Seem from your grand
[sic].

F300

Buckland, 24 December 1754

Sir

I received yours of 17th from Nutwell yesterday, & one from your Brother of 19th
From Torbay, from the Cutter, which I understand from thence he has Taken away;
he was then well, and propos'd to be Soon at Plymouth. So I presume I shall See
Him.

I am very glad to hear you find yourself Better, as I do that you intend to use means; Exercise is a fine Medicine, I wish I cou'd use it; I hope you will find the good Effect, as I wish you Everything Agreable.*

I wrote you in a Flutter from Exeter of Mr William Edgcombe's hurrying me down for Some Yarcombe Counterparts, which were to be Executed (I mean Leases therefrom) by you by Christmas; I'm Sure nothing but your Service, cou'd have Enduc'd me to take Such a Journey Just now, as I have not recover'd it yet; For I must own to you, my Dear Sir Francis, I can't do what I did formerly.

You need not desire Mr Edgcombe to go to Nutwell, for Coleman comes down these holy Days to Talk with Him – I hear he's about Warely, But I don't Think he's Strong Enough (as they Say here) for Such a Take.

Nicholas has plaister'd Over & about the Sash-Frames in the New Buildings with Terrace, which he Says will keep the Water out There, But he Says the Water Soaks thro' the Breaches of the old Stucco, which nothing but a new Coat can prevent, Tho' I hope this for the present will do Some good.

What I wrote to yourself & Sister about the Fee-Farme-Rents requires Care, or difficultys may ensue; I hope you sent her Letter.

As I am press'd, must beg your Favour for young Thomas Wyatt, That you wou'd be so good to write to Commander Rogers in his Behalf.

My Lameness is much Better, I Thank you, and will Endeavour to go to Plymouth –

I presume you have heard the Case is Come There; when the Hine can get his Boat Trimm'd will Fetch it; I shou'd Think Captain Drake's Boat might bring it up, when he Comes in, wou'd if you wrote him –

Shall I put the Treasure in when it Comes? I wait your Commands –

With the Compliments of the Season I am Sir

Your Faithful

N Rowe

* See Introduction, section 5, p. 55.

F301

Buckland, 31 December 1754

Sir

I was in hopes when I wrote you Last, That my Lameness was better, but it is return'd again with more Violence, which much Discourages me.

Your Gardiner came here Sunday night Last, and has begun first with the pear Trees in Lady's garden; here are neither Nails, nor Scrips, Both which must be got.

He desires to know, whether you intend to plant the Meadow this year, Becaus the Farmer Scruples to plow it without your Order – Do you propose to Dress it now, and to have the ashes Sol has Contracted for at Limpston – you have never Said if you approve of the Tinner's digging the gravel at a penny per Horse-Load; Mr Lee thought (as I wrote you) it was a reasonable price, and the Farmer's price of 9s. the Hundred Load Carrying.

The Joiner was not gone last Satarday, I wish the Fruit may come well –

If you have any Directions for the Gardiner, whilst here, you will Let me know.

There is Some prospect of Led-works in Newfound Land, Mr Brice is going to Send over the Tinner in the Spring to make an Essay, & to apply to you <u>for Aid</u>.

Your Uncle Henry (as Mr Searle told me, who Saw Him) has been at Plymouth, Tavistock & Westward with his usual parade, and Talks of Settling at Falmouth to Carry on the Tinn-Trade in an Extensive manner.

You will Let me know your Commands, I hope this will Find you as well as I wish you.

I am Sir
Your Faithful
N Rowe

I have not been able to Stir out, Since I have been here, to my great Mortification.

As the new walls at Nutwell Take water at Top, wou'd not plaistering the Top with Terrace prevent it? the Gardiner Says it wou'd.

F302

Buckland, 10 January 1755

Sir

I am now to thank you for your Obliging Favour of the 30th past from Hursely – I am very Sorry to hear you have been so much out of Order, But hope this will find you well; as you intimate you were much Easier, I heartily wish you a perfect Restoration, which I wou'd not have you Despair of; you have youth of your Side, But must Relax – Dr Huxam always Says when I see Him, you must Lessen your assiduity.*

I have not yet been able to go to Plymouth, my Lameness still Continuing; when I am, will give him your Compliments, to which I am Sure he'l give his in return – do's Sir Francis read & write so much Sitting, he'l Fix a weakness in his Bowels which may be very Dangerous: I'l get him to write you a Line of Admonition, I won't Say of Advice, as you'l know their Secret.

I am not yet able to go to Tavistock, will Let Mr Edgcombe know Lady Drake's intension about prosecuting Smith [?].

As to Farmer Coleman I agree with you, That he is an Ungrateful Fellow, There is more Self in Such Creatures than any other Consideracion; when he comes down William Edgcombe & I will Trye what can be Done with Him – He Seems Jealous of me, but all I can find, having Sifted him often, That he has a hankering after the Estate, But wou'd have it on his own Terms, But always positively insists to have a House built, Before he Enters into any new agreement, But you Take no notice of <u>That</u> in your present Directions, which you will Consider of; when I know his Ultimate, will Let you know what a Scheme I have.**

As to this place, you know There has nothing been Done to the House, I mean that part which is inhabited, for a Long Time. The Hine intends to new hell it ['apply stone cladding'] this Spring; now, if your Mother & you wou'd Rough Cast it, & paint the Sash-Windows at your mutual Expence, it might Save it; But the Hall Ceiling I fear will come down too – as to the new room, how the Cieling [sic] come to fall I don't know;*** I fancy the pointing outside has in a great measure Lessen'd the Dampness, Tho indeed, 'till This winter, the room was never without Constant Fire, and the Hine will have one often; I Fancy he'l do very well.

He has, He Tells me, 50 Hogsheads of good Sweet Cyder. I will Inquire of George Edgcombe about the Blow-Skin; he promis't me to get you a Hogshead.

Poor Mr Wyatt writes me he has had a very Severe Fit of the gout, for above six Weeks, Confin'd to his Bed; He will be much oblig'd for your Kind Favour to his Kinsman.

John Reed is a very Worthy Young Fellow, & deserves your Favour, But I know nothing of his Sister's Husband.

Mr Elford is much out of Order, they Say Breaks apace – as do's Chancellor Fursman.

Your Uncle Harry came here last Sunday in his return from London, is going down to Falmouth to Settle as a Tin-agent, which is all I know.

Your Gardiner went away last Sunday Morning, he has prun'd all your Trees; Mr Stapelton's were before he Came, Tho' your Offer was Communicated; The Man has been very Flashy & Foolish, has promis't to reform, & I Think do's; in his pruning he's very Free with his Knife, but Lays the Branches well Enough; he has promis't to be very Diligent, and That you shall See a very Visible alteration in your gardens when you come Down; I don't understand much of the Matter, he Seems a Little too Forward, But you'l Soon See if he'l answer your Expectation, upon this Summer's Trial; Sol & He will never do, & when you come Down, you'l Find it best to Send him [Sol?] to his Family.

Your Brother the Captain Sent last Week for Some of his wine & a Dozen of the Claret; There is one of the Baskets Empty, one out of which he has had the Dozen, and One untouch't; you Say'd you did not much Like it, Suppose he had it, perhaps he may be able to get you Some Better: He's gone a Cruise to the Westward.

As to Captain Frank**** I fear his return to Scotland, & wonder he keeps his Equipage, But whilst there's Life, there's hope, which we all Flatter Ourselves too much with.

I can't Think what Occasion Lady Drake has for a Steward; if She's put to Difficultys in any part of Her Business, I Fancy that about the Fee Farm look'd Like it, But then One wou'd have a person of Some Credit.

There, you'l be So good to Excuse the Trouble I gave you, As I did not know how to direct to your Sister.

My Dear Sir Francis, my head & heart is so Confus'd I don't know What to Say but Thank you, I have been so Disappointed in all my undertakings, That I'm quite Discourag'd; if you Think in my poor Capacity any of your affairs may be Forwarded, what Expence may attend That, you will Consider; For myself it is Come Just to the point; I begin to Fail in Everything, so I can give you no further Trouble.

I heartily wish you health and all the Happiness this World can afford you, I now Despair of any here; But pray don't you, I Conjure you, For if I can imagine anything agreable, it is to See you, as I wish you.

    I am Dear Sir
    Your Faithful
    N Rowe

Your Brother Samuel with his Wife is coming to Plymouth there's a —

    Cou'd I wish it Shou'd be a quite Different Fate to your Lad; There, that's too Late.

I hope you won't Forget Him, when't Ly's in your power.

When I am able I must go to Plymouth to pay my Last Compliments to Miss Archer for my Late agreable Friend – and to you I will add That I miss Her much, & after That Sir I will Endeavour to attend your Commands at Nutwell, But now I have Lost my Legs, Journeys are Terrible Things, Especially Riding, as my head is grown very Tottering.

As the Key of the new Thing is not Sent Down, must respite the removing the Writings to your Own Arangement; I wish you may read this, it is what I can Scarse do myself.

The Gardiner has got Some Ever-green Oak Acorns, & is to have more.

I presume you have heard That Mr Veale has Carry'd his Cause against the Corporation of Plymouth – They want Such a Friend, as I once projected, But it was not so Decreed.

* See Introduction, section 5, p. 54.
** Rowe's scheme for settling the conditions under which the Nutwell farmer, Robert Coleman, would take a new lease (see F303).
*** See Introduction, section 3, p. 26.
**** FHD's cousin Captain Frank Drake.

F303*

To fit up the House, by making a Chimney in the room next the Kitchen,
dividing the room call'd the Camp and making of it two Lodging rooms.
Altering the Stair Case so as to go up from Within the House
To have the Eastern Meadow & the Hay of the Other.
The great Barn to be repair'd; & between the pound-House, and the Higher Barn to make a partition for a Cellar.
And what Encouragement Besides as you think proper.
These Particulars another Tenant I imagine will insist on.
This is my Confus'd Scheme.

* This is the scheme referred to in F302.

F304

Buckland, 17 January 1755

Sir

I had no Letter from you last Friday, nor I anything to trouble you.

Only That I have Seen Farmer Coleman. I find Him in the Same disposition, That if you keep the two Meadows, and Object against building a House, he can't pretend ['presume'] to take a new lease. I have often Try'd him before, and now us'd all the arguments by way of inducement, nay even offer'd Encouragements as from myself, That I believ'd you would make the House he now Lives in more Commodious, But all to no purpose – Says he has long Found a great inconvenience in two Familys living so near.

A Midling Farme House will cost near £300 and if ever you Shou'd like to take the Home-Estate into your own hand, Such a House wou'd be quite Useless, So that I don't know what to advise: For I Fear any Other Tennants will make the Same

Demand (as these Farmers don't Like to live under the Same roof as Gentle-Folks), Especially as it has been Done by Coleman; I mean to have a new house Built.

I am not able to get rid of my Lameness to my great Trouble; when I am able to go to Nutwell, if you Think I can be of any Further Service about Coleman, you will direct me, But I despair, as Mr Edgcombe cou'd not recede from your Directions, as the Farmer Told me, For I was not able to go to Tavistock.

The Tinner has been here, Tells me he has an offer to Oversee the mending of the Roads about, and is to have 10s. a Week to Employ him for 2 or 3 year, Says he shall have done the gravel, & the gutter at Combe Farme by the End of next month, and the Beginning of March He is to undertake this Jobb, unless you have anything particular to Command him, for a Forth'night or 3 Weeks, which he can be indulg'd in.

I hope this will find you well.

I am Sir

Your Faithful

N Rowe

I have Talk'd with Channon about Coleman, who I find is very Intimate, and knows the Estate. Will take him up with me, and Trye once more; cou'd not you fence in your Plantations in West Meadow, and Let him have the grass & Hay.

I only propose Channon's going up for your approbation, But I fear neither Coleman, nor any other Tenant will Take Nutwell Estate Entire without the Meadows, and to Let it in parcels is the Way to beggar it out. Besides here's another Difficulty – Coleman wou'd have all Scott's ground and give up his part of Exon grounds – Coldridge perhaps won't Exchange. Please to think of the Enclos'd and Let me know your finall Determinacion.

You must Excuse my Confusion, as I am Scarse Compos.

F305

Buckland, 31 January 1755

Sir

Though I have not heard from you Some time, I hope you are well; for my part I am Still Lame, and almost *Quasi non* ['as if not there']; the Cold Weather too presses me much, as I can't move about as I wou'd.

Mr Edgcombe sent his Kinsman Carpenter to me last Saturday with a Letter, which he had receiv'd from one Mr Musgrave, an Attorney, Making a Demand for money due on a Mortgage to the late Dr Musgrave for part of Sheffain* – and that you had directed him to apply to me for information about it: I cou'd not then give him an immediate answer, But thought it very odd, after 50 years possession, to have Such a Demand made – I found upon Looking over your Writings, a purchase made by your Grandfather of Dr Musgrave of 1/4 and 1/8 part of Sheffain dated in September 1705, and the October following a Mortgage made by your Grandfather of the Same to the Dr, which Mortgage was paid off in 1708, and that's a full answer to the Demand made by the Gentleman – But he mentioning in his Letter That he had found a Deed of one Naish relating to the premises, it puzzled me not a Little, no mention being made of it in Dr Musgrave's Conveyance to your Grandfather – So I was resolv'd to look over Everything relating Thereto, and at last Found the

Enclos'd acknowledment [*sic*] from Dr Musgrave, But that not Satisfying me, upon
further Search I found in an old Box a pedigree drawn by Lord King, viz Giles
Martin the last Heir Male deviseth Sheffain to his 4 Sisters one of which viz Sarah
marry'd Thomas Naish Clerk, who Convey'd Her part to Dr Musgrave, & he to your
Grandfather without mencioning his Title from Naish: So Naish's Conveyance is the
Dr's Title: I have been so particular to show how necessary it is to get in all Deeds
in purchases, and I wonder your Grandfather on the Discharge of the Mortgage did
not call upon the Dr for the Delivery of Them.

If you wou'd have Mr Edgcombe to Show the Mortgage, and to demand the
Deeds &c mencioned in the Dr's paper, you will Send your Directions, being determin'd not to part with any of your Writings without your immediate Order.

I am Sir
Your Faithful
N Rowe

Mr George Edgcombe has a Hogshead of very good Blois-kind Cyder for you, But
Thinks you Shou'd order it to be Bottled where it is.

* Sheffain was a Drake property in East Devon. The detailed discussion of mortgage, deeds,
and discharge demonstrates Rowe's knowledge of the Drake family's property dealings, and
his standing among Sir Francis's professional advisers.

F306

Buckland, 7 February 1755

Sir

Your Favour of 14th past Came not to my hand 'till last Friday, it had the Taunton
Stamp on it, so imagine it went There which made the Difference; the key you Sent
in it, only opens the Outward Door, and as many of the Drawers are Lock't, to which
I can't Find any key, the putting the Writings must be Deferr'd: when you come
down it may be very Easily Done; as They now are, it's Just the Same, as if put in
the new Case, as I have brought the Escrutoir [*sic*] into the new Room.

I have wrote you about Mr Musgrave's affair, and Let Mr Edgcombe know
how the affair is, it only now Waits your Order for Showing the Gentleman the
Mortgage Discharg'd, and to have up Naish's Deed &c according to Dr Musgrave's
acknowledgment.

I have wrote you Every Friday Since I have been here (Except 24th past). I
am very much oblig'd for your kind Concern, my unaccountable Lameness still
Continues, as Soon as I am able to go on my Feet, or get on my Shoes will attend
your Commands, as yet have not been outside the Walls.

I am Sir
Your Faithful
N Rowe

Your Brother is not gone.
I'm glad of his good Fortune, But may he Take better prizes.
Captain Frank Drake is on his Crisis!

F307

Dock, 17 February 1755

Sir

With Some Difficulty I got here on Saturday, I came at Mr Wyatt's immediate request, and have Seen the Commander who will answer Expectation. Mr Wyatt is very Sensible of your Favour; and with his Compliments returns you his hearty Thanks.

I saw your brother the Captain yesterday, and am now going to Plymouth to meet Him & your Brother Sam, at Mr Porter's; His Captain has got a bigger Ship, cou'd not you procure for poor Sam to go in a better Ship than a <u>Sloop</u>, now there are Such naval preparacions making, I hope you will be so good.

Admiral Mostyn came here on Saturday night, They are very Busy, Here in the Yard, Work night & Day, and Sundays too. Here are 10 Ships already in Comission but Few Men, That Sort of People have been much neglected, and now the Want of 'Em is Sensibly Felt. Yet it's to be hop'd There won't be a war –

I purpose God Willing to go for Nutwell on Thursday next; as I find by yours you are Determin'd to keep the Meadow you now have, you will let me know, whether you intend to plant it this year, for if so, it must be plow'd round by the Hedges directly – you will send me to Nutwell your Resolucion.

Your Brother the Captain has been much Troubl'd with the Piles too, I hope it will do you Both Good.

I am Sir
Your Faithful
N Rowe

Plymouth 18th

Sir

The admiral order'd your Brother the Captain to Sea immediately, he Said Yesterday Morning, so did not See Him here, but your Brother Sam I did, He is Still here, and relys entirely on your assistance.

I have seen Dr Huxam, who very Cordially Sends you his Compliments & Thanks for your kind remembrance –

Poor Captain Drake is not Fit to be Seen, and will I fear be Dead before this reaches you.

Mr & Mrs Porter desire their Compliments.

Miss Archer is in Cornwall, & poor Mrs Prowse has made a Charity Will which will be Litigated by her various Heirs.

F308

Nutwell, 20 February 1755

Sir

I got here last night, & came round,* there being much Snow in the Moor, and I think as Cold a Journey as I ever rode, it now Freezes hard, and very Likely for more Snow.

You will Excuse my being more particular now, having not been able to Look about me, the two Walls in the green Court are in part down, and the Mason has done the parlour Floor –

Mr Kingman & his Wife are Both Dead, are not you now to look for a new Tennant?

William Wills our host at Beer is dead of the Small Pox, his Wife, Daughter and her Husband too. So a new place must be Sought out to Dine in.

I sent Mr Edgcombe Dr Musgrave's conveyance & the Mortgage to Show his Grandson.

Betty Dyer presents her Duty, & desires to know if the preserv'd peeches came well, as I hope the Carpet & Fruit did – the Gardiner desires to know if you wou'd have the Meadows plow'd – Channon came up with me, I had the Farmer in with Him, but wou'd not be Explicite without your particular Order – to be a little reserv'd is not amiss, But however he shou'd put the grass Seeds in, now being the Season. I am in Queer way which I can't Describe.

But always Sir
Your faithful
N Rowe

* The way 'round' was approximately along the route of the present A38, whereas the usual route from Buckland to Nutwell was over the Moor, via Moretonhampstead.

F309

Nutwell, 25 February 1755

Sir

The Weather has been so Severe That little has been done Since I came.

Nicholas came on Wednesday last to work on the gutter in the Kitchen garden, that is to carry the Water to the House of Office – Says he can't go on with the parlour Ceiling 'till he knows your pleasure as to the Timber work which the Joiner promis't to inform you of. He desires to know if you intend to have any Helling ['re-roofing'] done this Spring.

The gardiner went a Wednesday to Mamhead and took Sol & the Tinner to Fetch Things from Thence, the Frost has been so hard, that Little has been done in the garden, only Digging the Ground and bringing in the gravel – there are about 900 Load brought in – The Tinner will Soon have done – wou'd you have Mr Edgcombe to settle his account?

As to Farmer, I can say nothing Further; Concessions seem to be flung away upon him, when you see him, you'll be the best Judge: the Gardiner desires to know if you wou'd have him to get the Meadow plow'd, I have wrote you before about it. And Sol wants to know whether you wou'd have the Ashes he has bespoke.

What with the Journey, Lameness & the Cold, I am a Meer nonentity
But Sir
Your Faithful
N Rowe

It has thaw'd these 2 Days.

You will give Orders about the grass Seeds, now is the Time, the Farmer might put 'Em in with his Corn which is the best way, if you agree, for a new Take or not.

F310

Nutwell, 7 March 1755

Sir

I have your favour of 25th past, I am much oblig'd for your Regard for my health. I am Still Lame, but hope, Tho' I can't yet walk or put on my Shoes.

I heartily wish you may Succeed for your Brother Sam.

I wrote you on my Coming here, how Things were, I have not much to add – the gardiner is filling up the Side of garden design'd for a Nursery, and next Wednesday he go's again to Mamhead for more Things to Compleat his planting and if he receiv's your Orders for Trees for the Borders in the best garden may bring 'Em at the same Time – he Says he has Acorns Enough to sow the Borders in the Meadow, So it will be plow'd – from whence the Farmer now concludes you are resolv'd to keep it, and on which, by what I can Find, he is determin'd not to take a Farther Term – I have Try'd Channon, who Thinks so Too, and that a Tenant can't well do without it. As to the Lime Kiln, I find Kingman's Representatives intend to burn up the stock of Culme they have by 'Em, and I don't Think it proper as yet to Say anything about it, as it may be a Means to let this Estate. Mrs Aggy is now ill, perhaps the Farmer waits the Event before he Determines.

As to Beer – I think the Public House the Best place to fix at, to have an Ordinary for so many as you think are your Friends, and not the Lord's Tenants in general – your Grand Father did so in Former Time as I have heard – the poor that us'd to have the Overplus at those Times, you will Think of, and order your Steward to Settle it with Mr Carpenter, or rather you & Lord Buckingham – as it is his immediate Concern.*

Mr Musgrave can have no pretence for any gratuity, as his movement was entirely for his only advantage; But the deeds he has, he ought to deliver up in honour to his Grandfather's memory, or you may oblige him.

Betty Dyer is very glad the peaches please you. She will Send the Chintz Curtains &c as you direct. She is in no Want of anything particular, unless you wou'd please to order a Copper Dripping Pan.

The Wall next the garden (as Nicholas measur'd it) is in length 43 ft 7 in: from that to the gateway 37 ft as you'll see by your paper which I inclose again.**

Your house at present is Somewhat Confus'd, I cou'd Wish you Saw the Beams and Joyces in the parlour, before it is plaister'd, how rotten they are; you have the Same room to dine in you had.

The Tinner go's away today, Dr Salmon having sent for him about the Roads as I Wrote you.***

The Mason is removing the Stones in the Green Court in Order to build the Wall – a Bomb Ketch, & a Tender lying at Star Cross Frightens away all the men in this Harbour.

I am Sir
Your Faithful
N Rowe

I presume you have heard Captain Frank Drake dy'd 24th past.

I desir'd Mr Porter to write you to procure a protection for a Barge at Buckland, which will be of Service to your Friends, as well as your Mother; your Father always did it on Such Occasions. Farmer Bowcher Complains much of the Colts at Combe Farme, how Breachy They are, don't you intend to take 'Em up this Spring?

Here has been a She Ass and her Foal, ever Since Christmas; They have been pounded and Cry'd, as a Stray; what wou'd you have done with 'Em? They are now in the Wood.

Since my writing the within, They have Try'd to plow the Meadow, but the ground is so full of roots, it can't be done by a plow, but must be Dug up by men, which is now too Late, So the Gardiner will put the acorns in a Bed in your garden.

It is now fine Spring Weather, a great alteracion within this Week!

* Lord Buckingham, lord of the manor of Bere Alston (see note to F205).
** See F313.
*** Dr Salmon of Tavistock; see F304 for the tinner being hired to work on the roads.

F311

Nutwell, 14 March 1755

Sir

I had no Letter from you last Friday, nor have I anything particular to write you.

Enclos'd is the Tinner's account. Such things shou'd not be Let to run so Long, the 1st article was before you went away, the 2nd I know he was here, but on various Jobbs, as they cou'd katch him, the 3rd whilst I was wanting, was in attending Nicholas about the House & the gutter; the Money he had of the Farmer, was advanc'd at Several Times, Tho' Charg'd in one Summ; he has Left Something to do at Combe Farme & 2 or 3 Days in the Meadow, which his Brother is Finishing.

The Pressing has Frighten'd away all the Workmen,* So Nicholas has not been here for Some Time.

As to the progress your Gardiner makes, I am no Judge, he has Dug & Lay'd the 2 Borders in the best garden for the Trees you said he shou'd be Sent to Mamhead for, but no Order from you about it; There has been much Snow, it fell on Teusday night and Wednesday and Still Lys on the ground, So that the Gardiner cou'd not go to Mamhead yesterday for the Things he wants to fill up the Nursery Ground. Enclosed is a Sketch of what is done in the Kitchen Garden.

I am Sir
Your Faithful
N Rowe

The Snow is much melted, and the gardiner & Sol are gone this morning to Mamhead for more Things.

I hope you are well, my Lameness Still Continues, to my great Grief.

* Press gangs were seeking men in preparation for war. The Seven Years' War started the following year.

F312

Nutwell, 21 March 1755

Sir

My Lameness I fear will Stick by me, as I don't find any Weather alters it.

As to the Farmer's pretences, I think them very Frivolous, Therefore imagine he don't intend to Take the Estate; his Wife is in a very Dangerous Way, whether that influences anything I can't say, perhaps he reserves himself to determine with you. For more cannot be done by any Other.

Betty Dyer has been very Careful in airing the rooms, I don't see the Weather has affected any of the Rooms. She sent the Chinz Curtains & Seats to Exeter last Monday directed for you.

Parson Lee was here a Monday and Look't on the Chimney piece in the green room, Says as it is a plain One, he do's not Doubt but a Stone Cutter at Exeter can do it, will Send one out to Look on the Slab – it is 6 ft 6 ins Long – 4 ft Broad, & 6 Inches Thick – a Stonecutter Several years ago Told me it wou'd go three Cuts; if so, one Cut will make a Chimney piece & Slab of the Bigness you mention. Mr Lee is oblig'd for the Trees you have Sent Him, but seems much uneasy, he has not heard from you Since he drew the bill, fears he has disoblig'd you in Something.

As to the parlour, I am not Architect Enough to know the real Danger, but the yew-room seems *in Statu quo*. The Joiner's Brother was out a Sunday & Measur'd Some part of the Parlour by his Brother's order.

I have given the Gardiner the paper you Sent about the Borders, his planting is a Mystery to me, So I have directed him to draw out what he has fetch'd from Mr Ball's and how he has dispos'd of Em – he has received Directions from Hewet about what you Sent for the Borders.

The Gallery looks very Lightsome with the White paint.

Mr Murgo has not Sent any Chesnuts. The Gardiner went in to Enquire after the Trees a Teusday. They were not then Come; Mr Alderman Lee Told Him the Waggon's coming in was very uncertain, But wou'd Send Word, when it did.

Mr Edgcombe I have not yet Seen. What the Lord* & you agree upon, your Friends will Like. Enclosed is your Gardiner's account of his planting; he may be good in practice, the Whole your Judgment will Distinguish; the other paper is the plan Hewet sent him; no account yet of the Trees from London.

I'm glad for Captain William's, I hope poor Samuel will be next Oars.

The fear of a War makes the People here very Melancholy, 'Twill Lower Limpston – as for this place, it Looks at present very Confus'd, I hope your Directions will put it into better Order.

The pipe at the back door is broke so no Water to Either of the Houses – Mrs Aggy is Just gone, So the Farmer is on the Brink of hope & fear, which is the Case of the World & particularly of

Sir

Your faithful

N Rowe

* Lord Buckingham, lord of the manor of Bere Alston, as above.

F313*

Sketch of the Green.

Distance along the edge of Best Garden from House to Green: 43 ft 7 in.
Distance along top of Best Garden to Gateway: 37 ft.

* This is the sketch referred to in F310.

F314

Nutwell, 22 March 1755

Sir

I received your Favour of 18th whilst Mr Edgcombe was here – He met Farmer Coleman by the Way, & I desire he may have the Merit of knowing more from him Than Ever I cou'd Find out, I mean whether he will Take your Estate or no.

I have Found out an Expedient to divert Mr Wills from fixing with Him, which is to adjourn the Court for this Time, & by Michaelmas it will Come Easily to be at the public House.

Your Trees came here last night, They were a Little Drye, otherwise well – The Gardiner has put the Lawrells next the Wall, and has ventur'd to plant the rest in the Borders according to Hewett's Plan, which I sent you yesterday, & hopes they will be plac'd according to your Liking; as to artificial naturals, I am no Judge.

I have Sent to Nicholas to hasten the Wall But fear as all Sorts of Workmen are Frighten'd away on account of the Press, it will go but Slowly on.

The Curtains Betty Dyer Sent last Monday.

As to the old Parlour, the Water Comes in at the End of the house, whether it is owing to the Pavement being Still open, or the pipe being broke, I can't Say; when I have Nicholas's opinion will Let you know, There Seems a Sort of Moldiness on the Bricks.

I am very Sorry you are so much out of Order, Pray Take Care of yourself; as for me I am not worth Enquiry.

I am Sir
Your Faithful
N Rowe

Your Mother's Steward has been at Boyle Street,* That's Enough.

Poor Mr Wyatt I hear is in Fear of Superannuation, Mr Mostyn makes the Most of his Power.

* Boyle Street was Lady Drake's London address.

F315

Nutwell, 4 April 1755

Sir

As I had no Letter from you last Friday I hope you are Well – I have nothing in particular to Write you.

The Things you Sent Seem all to growe.

The Gardiner is now Laying his Walks, & preparing for his hot beds.

There Seems much blossome, and all the Trees that were remov'd to the new Wall growe.

The Weather is so unsettl'd, That Nicholas has not begun about the Wall.

Mrs Aggy is Just gone, the Farmer is in a very Forlorne Way, I hear Says, if She dy's, won't be a Renter again: you may then have him as a Hine: if you don't Choose to Let your Estate about the House; For Certainly if he cou'd Do for himself, he may for you, and Then you may do with any of the Fields as you Please, and Take his Stock too, if you Like it; This I only Surmise, your Judgment may Determine Better.

I have not further to Trouble you with, you have more Essential Things to Employ your Thoughts.

Poor Mr Wyatt presents you his Duty, he is, he writes me, very Ill of the gout, in great Fear of a <u>Superannuacion</u>, and his Nephew not yet provided for.

I am Sir
Your Faithful
N Rowe

I am still *in Statu Quo*, & have no prospect of an alteracion.

Betty Dyer presents her Duty, Says the Saucepans & Stewpans wants Tinning, which if you Think proper Should be done, before they are wanted, <u>for your use</u>.

F316

Nutwell, 11 April 1755

Sir

I have your Favour of the 1st and wish I had anything more agreeable than my Lameness to Entertain you with; That it Still Continues is my great Trouble, but I can't interrupt you with any more about it.

Sol says 'twas later last year, when the ashes were put on the Meadow, and as there has been much rain & a Likelyhood of more he has brought in 12 Load, & intends more as the Farmer can Tend it; the grass grows much, & Meadow begins to look green, So think it too <u>late</u>.

The Gardiner has not Laid the Walks in the Kitchen garden yet, Says there is Turff Enough to be had on the Bowling Green, as they call it, which belongs to Farmer Whedon, But fears he & Sol can't do it without more help in Season, the best Garden as you mencion.

Your People planted Parson Lee's Trees, which Came very well, I Thought he might have Thank't you himself.

I am very Glad you are Like to get Something for your Brother Samuel.

The Weather is so unsettl'd, that the Wall is not yet begun, Everything looks Confus'd, But Sunshine & Time may make an Alteration.

I am Sir
Your Faithful
N Rowe

Poor Mr Wyatt is in fear of a Superannuation, and begs I wou'd come to him, Lord what Can I do! <u>was I able</u>.

Farmer Whedon says you may Cut what Turff you please.

F317

Nutwell, 18 April 1755

Sir

I have your Favour of the 8th. I still Live In hopes, But fear I shall come Lamely off, as I find Little alteration.

Shou'd your affairs permit you to Come down, you'd then be better able to Judge of Everything, Than I can inform you – as to the Farmer I can Learn nothing more, he Told Mr Edgcombe at Exeter, he Shou'd know his final Resolution, when he come here at Court – the poor Man is to be pity'd, his Wife dying, & his affairs in great Confusion, the Event will Soon Show.

I am very Sorry for poor Mr Wyatt, his long Service intitles him to Some Regard; as he can't Last Long, he might be Let to Continue, a Removal demolishes him at Once: But without a Friend I fear 'twill be his Fate.

I hope his Grace will prevail for your Brother Sam; Tho' I thought you wanted no advocate with <u>Lord A</u>: But Such Turns I find will be.

The Weather has been good for a Few Days, as to your Garden I am no Judge, your Operator promises mighty Things, There is much Blossome, But Other Things make yet but a Little Showe, Either in the Kitchen or Nursery ground; Yet the warm Weather may Effect much.

I am Sir
Your Faithful
N Rowe

Betty Dyer has the Blanketts, They are on your Bed, & more are Wanted for the Servants' Beds.

The Things She will get Tinn'd; I think She Takes particular Care of Everything.

The Fear of a War has Sunk this Neighbourhood – I hope the Oxfordshire Election will End well for the Sake of — [sic].*

* It is not possible to fill the blank, but see note on F296 for the election outcome in 'the new interest'.

F318

Nutwell, 25 April 1755

Sir

I have your Favour of 16th. I have heard Nothing about Mr Wyatt Since – I wish it may be only his Fear, But his Frequent Disorder, and his old Distemper give too much Room for Such a Dismission, which nothing but his long Service can plead for him; however he Shou'd not rouse an adversary, your goodness to him is great, But difficultys Shou'd not be rais'd without Foundation, nor his Friends Troubl'd.

The Gardiner went immediately about the Plane in the best garden, but he must use the Turff, not yet Taken up there in the Kitchen Garden: he proposes an additional Border to answer That on the Other Side, So the grass Walks on Both Sides will Take up all the Turff (with the plane) That can be got abroad.

Mr Lee will soon Send out a Man about the Marble, he do's not Seem to Like the Man he Employ'd before.

Whatever your intensions are about the Parlour, I hope you won't have much Day Work.

There is a great Quantity of Blossome on the Wall Trees, and it promises to be general.

The Fine Weather, which has been for Several days, gives a new Turne to Everything, I hope it will to my Lameness.

I am Sir
Your Faithful
N Rowe

Nicholas has promis't to do the Wall out of hand.

Mr Edgcombe has appointed to be here next Monday to hold Court, when he is to have the Farmer's Final answer: his Wife is not Dead, But they Say can't recover.

Fine rain which was much Wanted.

F319

Nutwell, 2 May 1755

Sir

I have your Favour of 22nd past, I hope you had a good Passage Over, and That you'l have the Oppertunity to take the Tour you propos'd, I wish you an agreable passage back: and at your Return shall be very glad when your affairs will permit you to come down.

Mr Edgcombe came here last Monday & went away for Yarcombe Wednesday morning; Farmer Coleman has given him his Final Resolution in writing, But as his Demands are so Exorbitant, and withall so peremptory, he must imagine, you don't know what to do with your Estate; to have the Kiln in, & half a year's Rent given him 'for Encouragement' as he calls it, must be Solely in yourself to determine; for my part it is so unreasonable, I am at a Stand – When you come down you will be best able to determine, So 'till then must refer you to his paper, which Mr Edgcombe promis'd to send you, for your Consideration.

I have had no Letter from Mr Wyatt since, But Mr Edgcombe Told me, he heard he was superannuated; if so, I am glad he'l have so good an allowance as you mention – Mr Folcher is turn'd out, & 2 more.

Betty Dyer says only one pair of the Blanketts you mention are on your Bed, the other pair she has Lay'd by carefully; She don't want any more Ordinary China – There are now 14 Collyers in the River, & in these Doubtful Times, 'twill be Best to lay in a stock, 'tis believ'd they'l come for 10s. a Quarter.

I am very glad the Oxfordshire Election turn'd on the new Interest;* I hope all political affairs will conclude as well, and that his Majesty will have the influence wish'd by his loyal Subjects.

As to your garden I am no Judge, Therefore may be mistaken, you'l distinguish presently whether I am or no – your Gardiner is about the plane in the best garden; I wish, you may find everything to your Liking; There was last week some Warm Weather, & this some rain which was much Wanted.

Mr Lee has brew'd for you both strong & small Beer, of Each Two Hogsheads Strong, Ditto small; his Father promis't to send out a Stonecutter about the Marble, But he has not yet been here.

Mr Brice is willing & ready to pay an acknowledgment for his incroachment of the Wharf, and intends to hold the Kiln another year.

There seems to be one, or two places in the Meadow not quite drye, I fancy the Springs were not up, but may be Easily remidy'd.

I am Sir
Your Faithful
N Rowe

The Horses are Stray'd and can't yet be heard of, so they must be put in the Exeter paper.

* The Whig interest.

F320

Nutwell, 9 May 1755

Sir

After my Letter was gone, I receiv'd yours of the 6th and in answer to what you desire about Mr John Wills's request in behalf of young Hunt, who is a Lad, I think him too Free with you; he may as well ask to have him made a Builder, Tho' he's only a Quarterman, and a very Young One too – The answer I shou'd give him (was such an Application made to me): That he is too young for such an Employ as Mr Wyatt's – But as I presume you not knowing him, wou'd not be so particular; you may put him off, That you can't at present Trouble the Admiralty. I will be more Explicit when I see, But I Think such Eclats shou'd be nip't in the Bud – I am very sorry for poor Mr Wyatt, I have heard nothing from him Since – I am very glad you are return'd Safe – you'l Find me a Worne out.

I am Sir
Your Faithful
N Rowe

As to Coleman when I have the pleasure to see you –

F321

Nutwell, 7 May 1755

Sir

I have your Favour of 13th Instant. I Think such unreasonable requests as Mr Wills's shou'd be Check't with a repulse, which your good sense knows best how to regulate.

I have acquainted Betty Dyer with your Directions, she will get Everything in the best Order you can Expect in the Confusion the House is; She Says if you will please to Order some Orange Flower Water, & Vermacelly, for the rest She will get as you Order; as to the Wall nut room there is a Little pull'd down about making the Chimney in the parlour, But the Gentleman if you don't Like That must Lye in the red room; Both shall be made as Clean as possible, He'l be so good to excuse it, as you are not in the order you wou'd be.

I have heard nothing more about Mr Wyatt, But Mr Porter has wrote me about your Brother Sam, That he and his Captain can't agree, which I am very Sorry for, and the more, That he is so precipitate to do anything without your approbation first had.

Mr Lee was here yesterday, he has not Taken in his Coals yet, But in these doubtful Times, it is not prudent to Slip this Oppertunity; he will inform more next Week: He's much pleas'd with the Favour of your Letter.

We had the rain you mention the Same Day – your Gardiner next week will have Lay'd the plane in the best garden; I hope you'l Like the Turff, 'tis much better than I Thought the place wou'd produce – the Wall I hope will be done by That Time too.

As to myself I won't Trouble you, But will put the best Face I can upon a Tottering Foundation.

I Depend on your informing when you intend to be here a Few Days Before, I wish you a good Journey Down.

I am Sir
Your Faithful
N Rowe

A Stone-Cutter from Exeter has been here, & Look't on the Marble Slab (which he says will Make more than One Chimney piece), and he'l Engage to do his Work well. It is Namure stone.

F322

Nutwell, 24 May 1755

Sir

I have your Favour of 24th, am very sorry for poor Captain Williams, an honest inoffensive Man, and I dare Say had a grateful Sense of your Favours – You have been very good to regard Him in his last helpless Condition; I imagine as you do his Effects will scarse answer the Demands upon Him; and for his Sister She has Lost her Support.

As to the dangerous Situacion you are Told the yew room is in, I won't pretend to Contradict, as I am no artichect [sic], all I can Say is, That it seems to me to be Just as it was, Since the Cieling [sic] was Taken down; God forbid its Falling, For I go into it daily; Betty Dyer has made it very Clean, and you are to do, as you shall see proper when you come down.

The Man Says the Slab will make 2 or 3 Chimney pieces, & hearth paces, or Slubs, but it will come to polishing Cutting &c 3s. per Foot, and you may have all Entire for 4s. or 5s. per ft.

The Frosty mornings & Easterly winds have made havock in your garden; 'tis now very hot wind N.E. – The Gardiner will have Laid the plane in the best garden tonight, the drye Weather has Try'd the Turff, But I hope 'twill Stand it.

The Bricklayers will Finish the Wall this Day – the room over the Gateway is capable of being improv'd, and may be made an improvement rather than Ey-Sore to your house.

I am very much oblig'd for your kind offer, But I have nothing particular, that I can trouble you about.

Whenever you Set out for this place, I wish you good Journey, in the mean Time & always health & happiness.

I am Sir
Your Faithful
N Rowe

The Farmer has Taken in 20 Quarter of Coals, as believing there'l be no more this Summer.

F323

Nutwell, 19 September 1755

Sir

I have your Favour of 11th as to Scaffolds, Mr Brice has no Baulks – Nicholas shou'd have got his Materials ready before he pull'd Down the Building; he do's not seem to go about it with any heart, Says is Sure was you to see it, and the Expence it will be to build up the Walls the highth & Thickness they must be to Take the Roof, you wou'd hardly be at the Expence, but I Told Him as the Timber was Come & the whole Contracted for, you wou'd undoubtedly go on with it. Mr Brice has Boards, so I propose to have Some of him for Scaffolds, Tho' you Say nothing about 'Em, as they must be had; and for Supports, Solomon has Cut down 3 dead Trees, and They'l make some Shift for the rest, as the work shan't be hinder'd, wou'd he but come about it.

Seely has had a Letter, that the Windows for the Parlour & Room over will be Sent this Week, so the Parlour can't be Finish't 'till they come; the Cornish, & Waste Boards will be put up this Week in the room over; the Joiners will have then Finish'd on your Account.

I am Glad your Brother Samuel will be out of subjection, so Irksome to Him; your Interest I hope will Extend his Command.

Parson Lee says, if John has bought a saddle for him according to his Directions, he will have it; Else Let it alone 'till you go up again; & returns his Compliments & Thanks – he's under some Concern about his Brick-affair – the Man having Deceiv'd him so the Kiln must be Burnt over-again.

I am Sir
Your Faithful
N Rowe

Two of Nicholas's Men came here this morning to hew Stones But he is not come yet, 8 a Clock, Tho' he promist to fix the Scaffolds today.

There has been so much Drye weather, that the Countrey is <u>Burnt up</u>.

But now & last night rain.

F324

Nutwell, 7 November 1755

Sir

I have your Favour from Dorchester and am glad you got so well there, hope you reach't Hursly before the bad Weather, for Wednesday was very Stormy rain & large hail –

Moor has remov'd the Tree you directed by Solomon who has put a Lock on the Lead, and I Sent in a Teusday 16 Hundredweight to Mr Arthur, & there is 20 Hundredweight now in the Cellar, which I Think had best be Sent to Him too; you may Then have it in money, or in exchange for new Lead, as you shall want it; He has Sent out Lead for the Chappel gutter, & Solder but his men are not come. Sol has put 262 pieces of the Building Timber in the Stable – the big ones may Lye out; I Think Safely.

Nicholas is not so assiduous as he shou'd be about the Hall Windows, he must be Spurr'd as it ly's so Open. The Joiner is very importunate about his Brother's Subsistance.

As the Carts can't be had 'till next Week Little has been done in the Meadow; Sol go's today to Mamhead.

I can add no more
But That I am Sir
Your Faithful
N Rowe

Sol return'd in the Evening about 7 & John went away Monday Morning.

F325

Nutwell, 21 November 1755

Sir

Sol & the Tinner have been about the Meadow ever Since you went. & have not near done yet. There was a violent storm of Rain & Wind last Monday; as the wind was South, the house Escap'd to a Miracle; some of the Helling ['roofing'] over the Chappel, the Porch & the Red-room is rip't, & shall be mended; the Weather has been indifferent since.

The Joiner return'd from Mamhead last Saturday, but has not been here at Work Since; his Brother is about the Book-Case, for which some Deals will be Wanted.

The Masons have put in two of the Window Frames in the Hall, & are about the other, but as the Mortar is all done, they were oblig'd to borrow a Hogshead & half of Lime of Mr Brice, to finish it, so I presume you don't intend to stop up the other Window yet. I mean the Back one: Sol & the Tinner have but Just Levell'd the Hill in the Meadow; it is so wet, That I think they can't do much more, 'till dryer Weather.

I am Sir
Your Faithful
N Rowe

The Newfoundland geese are confin'd to the Chappel Court, the only place, but a wretched Confinement.

I have yours of 18th which will observe, & answer per next, am Glad you got up well & are so –

We have had very Bad Weather Since you went & I never was more Sensible of it, which I don't wonder at, as I find the Difference Daily.

F326

Nutwell, 29 November 1755

Sir

Your Favour of 18th came to my hand, Just as I was Sending away my Letter, so Cou'd not be particular Then.

The Joiners have put up the 3 Windows in the Hall, they give Light Enough, but on the outside, there seems to be something wanted to fill up the Space between; wou'd not a Row of painted Windows on the Wall be Ornamentall?

The Meadow is so Wet, nothing can be done as yet; as to the sweet Heap, Sol will Turn it Over, and Spread it as you direct; The Farmer has Thought about the Soap ashes, & Enclos'd is what he will bring Them into the Meadow for, But can't have any before Candlemas – when He go's to Exeter will Enquire about the Stove.

Sol cou'd not get many Cones at Mamhead; he brought Several Mountain-Ash, Some Laurel, but the Gardiner, who was There, & is Dismist, pull'd up all the Flowring Shrubbs, & Flung 'Em away; Sol intends to go there again soon. Sol Says he do's take Care to fill up the Levels as well as he can, & believ's the ground will sink but Little.

Mr Brice has Flung the Refuse of the Blubber on his own ground.

The Weather was here that Monday, as you Mention it was with you, Violent indeed! in the afternoon about 4.

Mr Wyatt writes me the *Falkland* is put in to Comission, & a Lieutenant is come down, & has hoisted the Colours; he says nothing of the Captain – I shall be glad to hear your Brother Samuel has a Comission too.

The Masons have done for the present, unless you order 'Em about pulling down the Gate-House;* the rain must injure the Floor, which Ly's open, & That can't be Taken up, 'Till They have pull'd down the Stones below it, as They must Stand upon it: Enclosed is Nicholas's Scheme about it.

I hope you have Recover'd Both your Fategues – Shou'd the Weather prove as Bad as hitherto, you can have no Inducement to visit this place, which at present is in a Dismal Condition, tho' your presence wou'd be very agreable.

I am Sir
Your Faithful
N Rowe

The Geese are Let to go, in the best Garden for the Benefit of the Water, by Day.

The Joiners have now Little to do, only the Chimney piece in the room over the parlour, & the Book-Case, for which they must have Some Deals for the uprights; the old Cases have serv'd for the Back & Shelves.

Enquiry shall be made at Exeter & Topsham about the Stove, the Farmer on account of Tilling, did not go last Friday.

I am very much oblig'd for your kind Regard, I hold out as well as I can under all Difficultys, Tho' I daily grow Sensible of the alteracion, from many proofs, I never was so affected with the Weather as now – Scarse fair Since you went one Day!

The Tinner was Sent for, away to Lord Clifford's last Wednesday. He worked with Sol 3 Weeks in the Meadow Since you went away – they Say the Little Meadow at Scott's, design'd for an orchard, must be gutter'd, before the Trees can be planted.

The pipe over the Middle Hall window must be alter'd and the plumbers must come out to do it: wou'd you have the rest of the old Lead Sent in to Mr Arthur, There is better than a Tun weight now in the Cellar.

Mr Hull's Gardiner has sent to know if you want anything out of Sir John Coliton's garden, I suppose by his Master's Direction, Sol says he had no Orders from you about it.

There has been a frost 2 or 3 Mornings; Shou'd it Continue, wou'd the Farmer's

Sheep Eating the grass in the Meadow do it any harme, before the Seeds are Sowne? Sol Says not.

The Joiner went to Exeter yesterday to See a Room at Mount Radford, which Mr Baron has bought, to be done in Taste. This is a November Detail, which you must excuse in me _Ergo_ ['therefore'].

A man will give half a guinea for thc Organ.

Harry Warne has been with me, & offers to give 15 Guineas for a Lease of 3 Lives in the Lower Cottage. Nicholas Talk'd if you wou'd give Him a Lease of the other, He wou'd Build a new House on it.

Enclosed is what the Joiner has done by your order about the Curtains, for yours, & the opposite Chamber.

I hope the Melancholy news, That all Lisbon is swallow'd up by an Earthquake is not True!** – very shocking indeed!

* For the demolition of the gatehouse, see also F330, F332–F334; and Introduction, section 3, pp. 28–9.
** Lisbon was indeed shattered by the earthquake of 1 November 1755.

F327

Nutwell, 6 December 1755

Sir

I received your Melancholy Letter, is there no Balm in Gilead? There are Judgments pass in the World; and it is God's Mercy we are not Swallowed up too. The not hearing from the English Merchants at Lisbon carrys a very Doubtful aspect: That wc are yet Spar'd is not Our Goodness.

I wrote you this Day 7 night, which I hope by this Time is come to your hands, as I therein Enclos'd the Measure of the new room & your Windows, as I do now that of thc Parlour. As to the Chimney piece for the Chimney in the new Buildings, and that in the Parlour, as I wrote you, the Stonecutter has done nothing, nor been here, So it's impossible for Either to be done in Time – The Bed however may be put up, which I have Told Betty & the Joiner about, and you may Lye in it if you please notwithstanding, and I hope may yet Sleep There many nights _Sine periculo aut timore perd..._ – ['without danger or fear of loss'].

Nicholas was here to know your pleasure about pulling down the Gatehouse, But why should we Talk of Such Things, when the Enimy is expected so Suddenly – a Drye Tree is fit only for Burning, But the green may growe and Flourish, as I wish you Every Happiness

I am Sir
Your Faithful
N Rowe

I hope you have received Seely's Letter, he is just out of work.

F328

Nutwell, 4 January 1756

Sir

Your Letter to Betty Dyer this post gives me a geat Sense of your goodness, but at the Same Time a great Concern, That I shou'd give you so much Trouble – my not writing you was my Daily Expectation of hearing from you of your Coming down: Whatever my ailments are, They do not I Thank God require Phisical aids, & I hope will not. But poor Betty Dyer is not able, She Says, to go thro' your Business here without Somebody to help Her; She Took it when you hir'd Her, She was to have a Maid under; has done it as Long as She's able, but has not Strength to do it any Longer. This She desir'd me to acquaint you with in a very Respectful manner.

This Day the Brickmaker from Sir Thomas Heathcote came here & must return again a Wednesday. He will look on the ground tomorrow, & you shall have his opinion. Mr Lee shall See Him, and I wish you wou'd write Him, whether you will allow the young Joiner 7 days for 6. It was a difficulty the parson Started when he paid him last, as he had not your Order.

Mr Brice is in fear he Shall be intercepted by an application about his Mineing affair, hopes to hear from you Soon.*

Farmer Coleman Begs, as he's Marry'd, you'l please to Order about his House – Nicholas too has been to know your pleasure about the Gateway.

Your Tenants Butcher, Coleman, and Watts have had Several apple Trees out of the Nursery, They Say by your order, Sol says they want more than 200. He desires to know if you had those grafted in the Nursery to Table Fruit, planted in the Home Orchard.

There has been so much Rain, & is so Daily That the Meadow is so wet, Sol Thinks the Soap ashes should be Deferr'd 'till after mowing; They are now making up the gapps next the Road.

I am Sir
Your Faithful & Oblig'd
N Rowe

I hope you have received my Letters of 29th past & 2nd Instant.

* Mr Brice's project is also mentioned in several following letters. FHD was asked to speak in Council on the project, as recorded retrospectively in a note to F350.

F329

Nutwell, 9 January 1756

Sir

Your kind regard for my health in gratitude obliges me to give you more Trouble of this kind than I shou'd, or indeed have room for: as Little here Occurs now.

I wrote you by Friday's post in answer to yours of 30th past, That I had Dismis't the Joiners, and have Since given Mr Lee an account of the young one's Time, who has promis't to pay him; you'l let him know if you allow the 7 days for 6.

Here is a hot press, & they come here a days to work for Themselves as a Sort of protection, being somewhat afraid, the Elder being in hopes of a Jobb at Exeter.

William Sherley the Brick-maker went away yesterday Morning; he Likes your

Clay very well, Says the reason your Bricks Scale so, was their not working the Clay enough, so advises to have it dug Some Time before – he has promis't to write you very particularly his Thoughts when he gets home – he had, he Says, a guinea of Sir Thomas Heathcote, & 10s. of me. Says he deserves 2 guineas for such a Journey, & indeed in Such bad Weather I Think so Too. He Saw Mr Lee & his Bricks; Says your Clay is Better, & the Reason his are so Bad, is for want of a Kiln, which he much reccommends –

We have Continual Stormy Weather, am Glad for that reason you Suspend your Journey. I Heartily wish you health & happiness, whatever is my Fate; I am much oblig'd for your Kind Wishes, Tho' I can't expect Either.

I am Sir
Your Faithful
N Rowe

Mr Lee's incumbent is very Ill Just now, So probably you may See Him soon.

One Carter of Limpston is gone up to London. Mr Brice is much affraid, he's Endeavouring to get in Between Him about the Mineral affair, hopes you'l prevent it.

Seely the Elder has been Several Days absent:

in	August	3 Days
	September	1
	November	14 1/2
	December	5
		23 1/2 days to 24th December

The Geese are very Tame, But Sol Fears They'l hurt the Trees as the Spring comes on, They being frequently picking Them.

F330

Nutwell, 16 January 1756

Sir

Your last most Obliging Letter has made a Deep impression – I always had the Tenderest Sentiments for you, Fix't in the most Faithful Friendship, which will Determine ['end'] only with my Life. But my Dear Sir Francis, you are at the Summit, and I at the Bottome; you I hope will gradually Descend full of Days and Honour, and Long Continue an Ornament to your Countrey & Family whilst I Sink in the Obscurity I have Liv'd without any Further Notice – you honour me too much by your Friendship, & if anything can add to it, it will be your Remembrance, That there was Such a person – But for Godsake no Such Melancholy imaginations as to yourself, it had much Better have been, That I never was, Than it Shou'd Contribute to your uneasiness, which I pray God it never may: and the greatest Favour you can Show me, is to assure me, it will not. As to myself, I am very Thankful for your kind offer, my Wings have been Clip't so near, & my Leggs Fail me – That I don't know what to ask, or Think I am Capable of.

With a great deal of difficulty have got all belongings to the Stove, except the Shovel, which the Master can't Find; when Seely comes next, he Shall Fit a Board; Betty Thinks it a very Cumbersome Contrivance, which She must have assistance to remove from one Room to another.

Nicholas has been with me again to know your pleasure about pulling down the gatehouse, Says it is now a Leisure Time, and and that he cou'd do it much Cheaper now, than in the Spring, and will undertake it on your Own Terms.

I Fear Mr Brice's affair will be more Expensive than the Undertakers are Capable of.

I am asham'd for the Fool Alex, But there is no Sense of Gratitude in Servants.*

The Bridge in the Meadow was Taken up before the Flood, the water came in at the Porch Door, But I hope there won't be Such another (Tho' Stormy Weather is very Frequent). Opening the great gates, Discharg'd the Water presently.

If your Mama & you are agreed about a Wear ['weir'], Shou'd not timber be order'd, now in the Felling Season? It shou'd be Built by May.

I have told the Joiner about the Door Model, He Says he thinks the Door can't be manag'd to go over the Carpet, with a Common hinge, But will Try, if you'd please to have Him.

One of the Large Elms in the wall going down to the Water-side is blown down, & I wish more mayn't go too, as They Lean much – nay, I wonder part of the House don't move, the Violent Storms we have had of Late; the Wood has Escap'd, onely one of the Trees on the Hedge you pull'd Down, is mov'd from the Roots, But not down.

As to your Coming down, I hope you won't undertake the Journey 'Till the weather is Better; pray Take Care of yourself, you are of Consequence, as for me, n'importe – I can but Love & Thank you, more is not in the Power of

Sir

Your Faithful and Oblig'd

N Rowe

* The ungrateful one is Sol's son Alex, taken as servant by FHD to London on Rowe's recommendation. See also F380.

F331

Nutwell, 28 January 1756

Sir

I am to make an apology for not acquainting you before, it was thro' forgetfulness, the Ship which formerly gave you offence, the Man's Son has brought to the Same place, only have not fasten'd it to the Oak; the Farmer forbid them Coming in, But the Ship is There Still, and it's fear'd the Ratts are Come again.

Betty Dyer Says her Work is much increas't, more rooms & Irons to Clean, than She is able to do. She only Wants an Ordinary Servant of about £3 a year, not for Her, but your Service!

I have Sent to Nicholas, but he has not been here yet; I don't know what he may deserve, I will get Mr Brice to Talk with Him.

Sol has made up all the Gapps in the Meadows, that by the Canal, requires a good Deal of Labour outside – he has had the Tinner 3 weeks & Shelston as Long; He will want him more, you will order How They are to be paid.

Your Books are very well.

I am Sir

Your Faithful

N Rowe

Since my writing This Nicholas Came here & will Leave it to Mr Brice & next Week will go upon it.

F332

13 February 1756

Sir

What I wrote you about Sol was upon great Reason, But I hope he'l repent & Reform – But as he has little victuals and Less Drink, when he gets any given, he uses it to Excess, & I fear unless he has his Wife to keep him Regular, He'l break out again.

Today I have Sent in the remainder of the old Lead 48 hundredweight and 24 lbs. So that the whole amounts 4 Tun, 5 hundredweight, 1 quarter, 2 lbs. Mr Arthur desires to know, whether He is to buy it of you, or Take it in Exchange. He offer'd 15s. a Hundred, when Here.

The Farmer has Spoke to me to desire you wou'd please to take the prentice girl, for he can keep her no Longer; I Told him he ought to write you Himself.

The matter of pulling down the gate-House and Drawing away the Stones may be done, I am perswaded, by Mr Brice's interposition, without occasioning you any after Trouble; For to make an agreement now, I think is in a manner impossible – I'l Endeavour to know how many People he Employs & how Long he's about it, you may Judge from That.

There was a great Deal of rain a Monday, very windy yesterday.

As the Quantity of old Lead above 4 Tun weight is so Considerable, wou'd not you have Mr Lee to settle it with Mr Arthur, & inform yourself of the value in Town, 'tis very good of the Sort.

I am Sir

Your Faithful

N Rowe

I Thought to have Sent my 1st as Dated but was prevented; whenever you come down, you must Regulate your <u>Solomon</u>.

The Geese do much Harme to the Trees, & Digg up the Grass Walls.

Everything is in great Confusion here, & what is to be Done with the Stones & Timber Seems no Small Difficulty: part must be remov'd Somewhere, or there will be no moving.

F333

Nutwell, 20 Feb 1756

Sir

Your Last Staggers me quite – What no Fence against a Hail? There, you must know better than I. Still there is a Providence which governs the World, and on that we must rely; Nevertheless to use Humane Means; I hope that has not been Omitted.

I have aquainted Mr Brice with what you Desir'd, He is very Thankful, and is fitting out Men to Seek for the Hid Treasure, who go next Week, without waiting for the Result, which I don't understand.

Last Teusday night & Wednesday most part of the Day it Snow'd hard, yesterday and today hard Frost: the new glass has fallen & risen of Late Suddenly &

Surprizingly! The Tillage is over: it wou'd have been a Shame to have neglected so much good Weather.

Enclosed is the Plumber's account of the old Lead as he States it, it was all weigh'd here, the Difference on account of some Dirt wrap't up in the gutters was about 1 quarter. He is ready to pay the Ballance as you shall Direct.

Nicholas is got below the upper windows of the gatehouse, yet much is Stil to come down; There will be a vaste Quantity of Stones, Before They come to the Foundation: I wish you may be able to see it, you will then be Better able to Judge than I can inform you; But if matters are so precarious, what Signify Such Trifles –

Betty has sent about a Maid, & Sol is about Sowing the Cones from Mamhead, I wish the Nursery affair may Succeed Better than it did under your late Gardiner, who is married to the Wench to fix Both in Misery: I hope your present one will Take Warning.

I am Sir
Your Faithful
N Rowe

The Joiner has got the Jobb of Mr Baren.

Mr Porter writes me with pleasure That the Turn-pike is fix't according to your System.

Farmer Coleman desires to know if you will have the Soap-ashes, as the man must have an answer next week.

F334

Nutwell, 27 February 1756

Sir

I have your Favour with the Plan of the Stove for the Parlour, I have Shewn it to Mr Brice, who perfectly understands it; Nicholas has Seen it, Says when the Stove comes hopes to be able to fix it; I wish you had Sent word by what Coaster it Comes, & that it may prevent the Smoke.

As to the Gatehouse, it's pulled Down to the Gate, and I dare Say will prevent the Eddy Wind; when it is Directly West, 'twill blow against the house; So it did Before. Mr Brice has promis't to write you his Thoughts about it, Enclos'd is his Calculation; The Farmer & Nicholas will be Determin'd by him; and upon that Footing I will have Some of the Worst Stones drawn away, as there is no moving; you can't imagine what a Quantity there is already; as you give hopes of you Coming down Soon, you will be Better able to Judge than I can inform you; as you will from Sol's Behaviour in the mean Time, whether he will Deserve your Favour – he is now Taking down the old Trees in the Wood, he has put abroad all the Dressing in the Home-Meadow, the other is so Wet with the Rain & Snow, That there's no doing anything there – But he must have Men to help Him to wheel away the Rubbish as there is so much of it.

Betty Dyer has not yet heard about the Maid, She is about Twenty. She never has been at Service.

Your Brother did not Call here. To be Sure Mr Lee has wrote you, That he's got his Second Parsonage. I hear he is in hopes He need not go to Town.*

As you have heard from Channon about the Extent of the Damage to the

Wear-head ['weir-head'], & have found Martin's Estimate – 'Tis high time to set about it as the early fish will help to pay the Charge.

You don't Say where the Trees & Shrubbs are to be planted. Sol says 'tis full Early to plant the Strawberries, however they Shall be Sent by next Monday's Coach Directed for you.

Captain Compton who brought the 1st Stove never sent the Shovel belonging to it, Says he had none; he is now in London, if you think it worth while, the person you bought it of, may Tax him with It.

The Rain was the means of the Snows going off so Soon, Else as it fell fast it would have been Deep; the Frost went off very moderately, it was windy here the Day you mention – This winter has Try'd me more than I ever met with Before, & my Lameness Seems Fix't. Your Regard I have a due Sense of.

Your Neighbourhood are highly Sensible of your Favour about the Road to Horrobridge.

I am Sir
Your Faithful
N Rowe

I shall be glad to hear your Brother Samuel has a Ship.

The Snow was very Deep on the Moor, & on Haldown. 3 Horses were lost, there is Some there Still, you have a full prospect of it now.

The apple-Chamber & the Stone-wall are down Even with the ground & the rest of the Gate-House to the planching, so the House is now quite open.

* Nutwell's neighbour Parson Lee of Lympstone acquired a second benefice in London; on account of expense he hoped not to have live there.

F335

Buckland, Sunday Evening

Sir

I reach'd Moreton at 9 Last night, & got here about 2 this Day, where I found young Thomas Wyatt, who inform'd me That Captain Drake wou'd be here tonight, But as it rains hard I Doubt it. Darty moor, may now be justly called Durty, it being as rotten as I have known it – which with the High Trott of the Mare, made it more Difficult. Channon has lost a Horse so can't Spare Her now – I must therefore Desire, when Sol comes next Sunday, that he brings me Farmer Coleman's Little White Horse, as the Mare must be return'd; I wish I may be able to get Back, being Quite lost for a Rider.

I can't Find the 3rd Volume of Dr Huxum, will bring it with me, if I can Find it, the rest I've Sent, with Bishop More's Sermons.

Whilst I was writing This Captain Drake came Here.* He has been much out of Order, is now Tollerably well, will write you by Teusday's post.

Monday Morning

It has been Such a Stormy night & so much rain That the Waters are out, and withall such a Fogg, That 'tis impossible for Sol to Set out today.

Monday night

I am just return'd from Beer, where I attended Captain Drake; we were wet to the Skin going There, But for want of a Jury the Court was adjourn'd, a wonder so many, 11 in wet coats.

Sol I hope will be able to go tomorrow, a great Flood – He brings 2 Bottles of Cherry Brandy, I hope you'l Like it, the rest is reserv'd – poor Mr Porter's *Teal* brought Him in all the rain – He's now Here, the Captain's & His Compliments wait upon you.

The Captain Sends his to Mr Lee, He Expects double Tith[e]s, as to Beer – Phillis, & Turkeys –

I am Sir
Your Faithful
N Rowe

My Compliments to Mrs Elliot.

* FHD's brother William, also a freeholder of Bere Alston.

F336

Nutwell, 14 May 1756

Sir

I was very agreably Surpriz'd with your Favour of the 8th and the more so, as you got well; I hope this will Find you so – It rain'd here most of the Day you went – the Parson no Doubt dislik't a wet Coat, But wou'd more your Abstemiousness! Tho' I wish He may get over the Rest as Easily.

I have given Sol the Powders you Sent, who Takes 'Em as you direct. He has no Fit since you went, He has put in the Trefoils, will get Mr Lee's Cart for the Turff, is preparing the ground for it.

I have given Betty Dyer your Caution about the Coals who will observe it – the Peaches cou'd not be Sent as you directed, But they were Carried in a Wednesday to go by next Monday's Waggon, they are in a Keg directed for you –

It is the Outside of the Barn the Farmer wants to be repair'd, Says it must be Done before Harvest, or he can't put in his Corn: Hopes you'l Take the Prentice Girl, as he is not able to keep Her any longer.

The Melon Seed, which was Sown before you went, did not Come up. So Sol sow'd some of the Cantalupe he had by Him, and I gave Him a paper with 4 Seeds, wrote on the outside <u>Cantalupe from Mr Miller</u>, I hope the right.

Sam Tricky brought the agreable account of your all getting Well to Dorchester – no Doubt 'twill be vastly so at the Parsonage, That Master got well to London; But the great Satisfaction at Exeter will be to hear a good account from Lambeth – more than to Somebody else, of the Choicest of Diana's Train, or a Ridotto – you will give my Compliments, as you See proper, to your Fellow Travellers – you won't Forget to Let your Sister know of Miss Archer's approach to Town, and the Seraphics are to be Expected, which I hope will prove to Her & Their Female acquaintances' Edification.*

It rain'd till Sunday after you went, Wednesday and yesterday Foggy & rain (tho' the glass at Set Fair), today the Same.

I have nothing further to Trouble you, I am glad you have wrote to Channon, I wish the rains mayn't impede Them.

The Model of your 3 Wheel Cart was Lent to Mr Duke of Otterton, but not return'd; it shall be Enquir'd after.**

I am Sir
Your Faithful
N Rowe

* Miss Archer of Whiteford, greatly admired by Rowe. See F234, F240, F258. The Seraphics may perhaps refer to members of a female religious community such as that founded in Bristol by the Calvinist Countess of Huntingdon, satirised by the poet Evan Lloyd in *The Methodist* (1766). See Emma Major, *Madam Britannia: Women, Church, and Nation 1712–1812* (Oxford: Oxford University Press, 2012), pp. 148–149.
** The loan of the model cart to Mr Duke of Otterton continued to cause trouble. See F339; and F350 for its eventual return.

F337

Nutwell, 21 May 1756

Sir

I have your Favour 11th with the Seeds, which I have given to Sol – we have had a Drye E. wind for Some Time, the garden has been Water'd and the Things cover'd in the Meadow and Warren Hill, I don't See much Harm to 'Em yet; The Blaste affected your wall-Trees, But their Leaves Seem to be recovering – the Trees & Shrubbs look Tollerably.

The Butter is bespoke, & as Soon as ready, shall be Sent as you Direct, and you shall know the price.

The Things are put into the Chapel, Seely Senior has been here, Says he will Send a Man to fix the Scaffolding in the Hall, which must be done before Nicholas can pull down the Cieling [*sic*], which he promis't shou'd be done directly – I Expect 'Em every Day – pray what must be done with the Clock? and where is Sol to Lye?

Sol has laid the Turff in the Best garden, & is going about the Walks –

Since my writing This Nicholas has been here, Says he will go about the Hall the week after next without Fail, hopes you'l be so good to Excuse him 'till then, being ingag'd in work, which he's oblig'd to go thro' with.

A Clockmaker at Exeter offer'd to put the Clock in order for a guinea; wou'd you have it sent in to him, and put up in the Little room on the great Stairs, it wou'd be very useful to your House & out of the way – and if you approve of it, a Bed may be put up in the Little room by the Library for Sol for the present, 'Till you otherwise order it.

Betty Dyer's Girl, her mother being Sick, has Sent for her home, where She go's at Whitsuntide; Betty desires to know your Pleasure, whether you wou'd have Her Take a Servant, or Such a Girl as She may get in this Neighbourhood –

I have nothing further to Trouble you with, the return of my lameness is enough for me – The Days are come in which I can Say I have no pleasure in Them; whilst They Last I shall Be

Sir
Your Faithful
N Rowe

No news of the Horse yet!

Harry Warne desires to know your pleasure about the Cottage, if you approve of Him as a Tenant he wou'd repair it this Summer: as Carpenter Ridge wou'd rebuild the other part, if you wou'd Let it to Him on that Consideracion, & a Small reserv'd Rent.

A Shower this Morning, wind at S. & Calm.

F338

The Geese do much Damage to the Garden, & dig holes in the Sides of the Canal; might They not be put in the green by Day (their wings being Clip't) & brought in by night.

The Ratts are got under the Frames & about the Garden, and Both Houses & Barns more than Usual, which they impute to the Ship's Coming so near. She is now put off in the Channel.

Very Fine Weather for Some Time, and little rain. A Black E. wind, & Some rain Now.

Seely is fix't in a Jobb to repair Mount Radford near Exeter for young Mr Baren, who has Bought & is about Decorating it in Taste.

F339

Nutwell, 24 May 1756

Sir

I have your Favour of 18th; as the Ball is up, God only knows where 'twill Fall. I fear not Favourable. I'm sure 'tis not so Hereabout.

I Think as you do about the Girl, She is 14 year old, very Strong, and may be Brought to be Soon useful – as the Wench got away at Whitsundtide, Betty Dyer can have no Objection, if you allow Her, as you intend, when here, a woman to help her – I will mention it to her, if you think proper. Sol has mark't the pots with the Melon-Seed, as you Mention – The Raspbery Tree he fears is Dead, the Emony is budding. But the Blight has made a great Havock in your garden, Everything almost Touch't; all the Cypress I fear are Dead, the Strawberry Trees look Bad, they shan't want Watering: But the continuance of the Drye E. wind cheques Everything, Especially your late Planting.

Can't Parson Lee get the Ordinary's *legit ut Clericus* ['reads as a clerk'], Then let him be Branded; But a Smooth Chaplain can like Charity hide a multitude of Faults, such as this pass frequently with Plurality's without Criticisms in Greek or Hebrew.

The Cart, the Farmer has ingag'd to produce your Cart – your Caution shall be observ'd in *Futuro*. It ought to have been return'd long ago.*

Sol takes care in gently Watering the young Pines & Cedars, which don't yet appear – as to the Beans Pease &c you intend to Send, he says he has ground Sufficient for 'Em.

Captain Pike call'd here a Sunday, put into Dartmouth by this E. Wind, Says he has got Some Vines for you, which he will leave There, if he can't Send from Thence, But how to get Them Here? He came from Gallipoli bound to Holland, he's

Thunder Struck with the War, in fear of a 3rd Capture – Says he Saw Admiral Byng in the Streight, but Fears too Late for Mahone.**

The Clover do's come up in the Meadow & the 2 pieces are Sown but this drye Weather stops it.

The Horse is found & was brought Home a Sunday, he was Taken up at Alphington the 10th past, where he has been Ever Since. He was advertis'd in Brice's Paper by the Farmer, & the Same Day by the Person who took Him, So that what with one Expence & t'other it runs high.

I received a Letter from your Brother Samuel from Plymouth, in great Anxiety least he shou'd be oblig'd to go to Sea again in the *Windsor*; I don't Doubt but he has wrote to you, I hope he'l be remov'd to his Satisfaction.

I am very Glad the Colt got so well up, hope he'l prove to your Sister's Liking.

The geese have rinded the Weeping Willows in the green, the plane Trees do very well – But I fear neither the geese nor Horse will remain long There, as They are so often getting out.

I am Sir
Your Faithful
Rowe

I hope the Lambeth Wand Did not prove a Rod to the Parson, nor Dr Foster a Dr Faustus.***

* See F336 and F350.
** Port Mahon on Minorca, awaiting relief. See F349.
*** Rowe hopes that Parson Lee, with his new benefice in Lambeth, has not come to grief, e.g. by falling metaphorically into the water, like Dr Foster. The Lambeth Wand is perhaps the River Wandle at Lambeth/Wandsworth.

F340

28 May 1756

Sir

I intended to have Sent my Letter as dated But was prevented – I have Since received yours of 22nd with the Seeds, which Sol will Take care to manage as you Direct – as what you send by the Coach shall be when They come – and Millar's Dictionary shall be Consulted* –

The Cedars are not yet come up – Sol waters your new Planted Shrubbs & Trees often, But I fear several will miscarry thro' the drye weather & late planting; it has been Such here as you mention with you.

I am glad your Brother Samuel is order'd up, to his Command – His assiduosity I hope portends a brisk alacrity Elsewhere, and That He will show it to his own advantage, as well as his Friends' Satisfaction; & That he will acknowledge your Care for his Interest – may Both your Brothers answer your Expectation – There seems an Oppertunity for it.

There is a good Quantity of Fruit on your Trees, and they Seem to recover Daily.

I have acquainted Mr Brice with the progress you have made in his affair, is very much oblig'd & hopes you'l soon get the Board of Trade's report, That he'l readily answer the Expence, as you will please to direct – Says he has & shall be out £500 before he can have any grant, Wishes, as Things have Fallen out, he had not sent the

People the 2nd Time, yet is willing now to proceed – He's fitting out his new Ship for a Privateer.

A report is Current That Admiral Byng has Fought the French Fleet, lost 2 Ships and Taken & Sunk 5 of theirs – I am Confus'd & so is this account.**

I am Sir
Your Faithful
N Rowe

* Philip Miller's *The Gardeners Dictionary* appeared in 1731, and in a total of eight editions during his lifetime (see Introduction, section 4).
** Rowe was not alone in his confusion regarding Admiral Byng's engagement with the French at the Battle of Minorca, his withdrawal to Gibraltar, and his subsequent court-martial. See also F342, F344–F346, and F357. There is no Rowe letter referring to the admiral's execution (14 March 1757). Lady Fuller-Eliott-Drake prints a compassionate eye-witness account by Samuel Drake, from a letter to his sister Sophia (*Family & Heirs*, vol. 2, pp. 286–287).

F341

Nutwell, 8 June 1756

Sir

I have your Favour of 1st, hope your Brother Sam will always be Truly Sensible of your Regard for Him; if he don't Express it as he ought, I hope you'l impute to his head, not his heart, any Deficiency.

Betty Dyer continuing still Bad, you'l be so good to indulge Her with the help of her Kinswoman; when well, She can have no objection to the Girl – the Farmer still perseveres in His Desire to part with Her. I have sounded Him about the 3 Culverys, he don't seem inclinable to part with 'Em, they will come in next year with Clover, perhaps that may be the reason. Says he once offer'd 'Em and you refus'd 'Em; he's a Silly Chap.

As to the Pales, Sol Says he had no Direction from you about 'Em – wou'd you have any stuff taken down now for 'Em? The grass Seems at a Stand in Both Meadows – as to the Fallows, Sol Says to plow 'Em again wou'd Do much Damage to the grass; Shou'd the weather alter, that meadow wou'd be fit to cut in about 14 night – pray who is to plow it, and where are they to have Horses to Save the Hay?

As to your Plantations in the Garden, Meadow and Warren Hill, they are frequently Water'd; Sol thinks better of 'Em, than I do. Shou'd there come a good Deal of Rain well, else they must be Sav'd so as by Water – the blasts have Touch't Everything, the Trees in the Middle of the higher Wall Look very indifferent, the Tree next the Door in the Lower Wall I fear is Dead: Sol will Thin the Fruit as you Direct. When the plantations mend will Let you know – Mr Lee thinks Considering how it is with Him, your Garden is very Well – He Looks as most Succesful do, Elate, and no Doubt his Father is Easy, now he's in possession.

I am very Glad Colonel Eliot has got this Step higher.*

When the people come to work, will consult about the Clock's being put up in the little Room, which I shou'd think may be done.

The Raspberry tree is certainly Dead, the Tuberose roots are put in a moderate hot bed as Mr Miller directs, & shall be manag'd so in their progress.

Mr Brice has measur'd the Distance very exactly Between the new Wall, and the edge of the new Buildings, which is one hundred & two feet, and Six Inches – the old wall was 2 ft within the new building.

The highth of the red Bed from the Bottome of the Cornish is 7 ft 6 In, the Bredth 5 ft 6 In, the Length 6 ft 6 In; the valance, & Bases are very much Faded, the Latter much worne, I fear new Curtains won't Set it off, as Even the inside looks Faded; I presume you know it is Serge.

Channon sent here 12 Calves & desir'd they might go a little while in the green, till he cou'd Send for 'Em, and will pay you for their keeping; I thought as there is only the Horse, & the grass decaying, the Difference cou'd not be much.

Harry Warne offer'd 15 guineas, will give no more, for the Lower Cottage, won't be Concern'd with the Other, which is a ruine; Ridge the Carpenter will build up the other, if you'l grant him a Lease of 3 Lives without Fine, on a small rent.

Mr Creed has wrote that Moor** will be at Newton Bushel next Sunday, Sol shall go for Him as you Direct: is He to go afterwards to Buckland?

Farmer Watts is very willing to let you have the Withy Plot, provided you make Him a Watering place, having none Else but There on the Estate, Says 'tis worth to Him more, But as you intend it for the improvement of the Estate, you shall have for £3 a year during his Term, the whole, which is more than 3 acres.

* FHD's brother-in-law George Augustus Eliot was promoted Colonel.
** Hercules More, the pruner, as in the following letter.

F342

Nutwell, 18 June 1756

Sir

I have your Favours of 8th & 10th. Betty Dyer Seems to be Better, She is very Sensible of your Goodness, and returns you her humble Thanks in the most Dutyful manner, But Says as Mr Gely has her under Cure, & She has good hopes of his Success, She is willing to abide by his management: I agree with you, Such old Sores, with the ancient are not Easily Cur'd.

Moor & his Son came here a Sunday night, he Says you have more Fruit than all the Countrey, he Thinns 'Em as you direct; he Says the vines must not be remov'd as yet out of the Barel – he will Tye up the Espaliers by the Canal, one of 'Em is Dead.

Seely call'd here a Sunday & Compleated the plan, which I now return you, Says you had the Section of the room, where the Prints are, But when he comes here next Week will do another; he makes a Difference in the measure of the Red Bed.

I am glad the Butter came well, & as a rarity it may be Lik'd; But you never Said anything, whether you received the preserv'd peaches. There are no Brass handles wanting but for the window Shutters in the room you Lay & the next room, all the Rest have 'Em.

Mr Brice I presume got to Town a Sunday.

As to the Letter you sent me, Such Things often Come to Light in such a manner, But whether true all, it's worth your own Looking into: if you remember when I was with you at Yarcombe, old Mrs Newberry's Man gave you an Intimacion about Timber – I must own I have not an implicit Faith in Mr Bond's Morals, or Management, Tho' I believe the late honest Man* trusted too much to Him; What his Brother do's, I know not: But wou'd Take no notice of the Letter.

I hope the news about Mr Bing is not True, the Country are Free in their Invectives: Sure He wou'd not refuse to Fight, on the Odds too.

Nicholas begun on the Hall a Monday, and the Joiners come next Monday, the Cieling [*sic*] is down, & the partition over.

Sol is about the walk next the Canal; he is but Slow in Levelling ground, Seems to do it Tollerably well, most part of his Time has been taken up in Watering – He has had Thomas Parsons & the Woman almost Ever Since you went. There has been much more rain Westward & all about, than here; Channon Said the Moor was as Bad As for the Year; But 'till Sunday not much here, and Since very Windy at S. & S.W. with some Misty rain, Just Enough to Save Water:

Parker, Savage, Christophers, Rowe, & Wolcomb the Sail-maker have been about their Bills – the Lime-Kilne is Lighted, wou'd you have the Parlour & room over their Cielings [*sic*] now Finish'd?

The Timbers over the Hall Seem to be Bad, but that Seely will report.

The Corn is much refresh'd by the Showers, Mr Lee says this Countrey is far beyond where He came from – He's now instated, and His, & His Father's Fears all over; I wish my Lameness was. I'm oblig'd for your Care

& am Sir
Your Faithful
N Rowe

I Thank you for the Spectacles. 'Tis an odd Thing to Tell you, I see better than I Ever did.

You are mending the inside of your House, But the outside is very Bad; Shou'd it be as windy a winter, as it has been a Spring & Summer, great part of the Helling ['roofing'] will come down – There, the South must help the E. but what will come in of the W. God only knows – I Congratulate you on Mr Creed's account. The geese I fear will be Lost Here. Channon will Take care of Them at Buckland. There are many Figgs, and much Blossome on the great Strawberries. The Melons are prosperous.

Fine Shower this Morning, hope more.

* John Edgcombe.

F343

Channon came Here a Monday about his Calves, Says the Barton is in a very Flourishing Condition. The Corn looks well, plenty of grass, and a good Stock – a great prospect in the orchards, Tho' very Little in the gardens of Fruit.

As to the Wear ['weir'], it is so Forward, That he hopes to open it next week, and That it is so Firmely Done, it won't want repair in haste –

I choose to write this in this manner, That I may insert the Success of One Draught with the Net viz One Hundred & Thirty Salmon, which were Taken in the Wear-pool and Sold at this Cheap rate for £18 – So there is a great probability this year's Fish will pay the Expence of the Wear.

Channon will write Lady Drake and you very Soon; and Send an account of the Expence.

Salmon Sold at Limpston by the pound at 3 pence
        Honiton   Ditto @ 4
        Tavistock & Plymouth   2 & 2 ½

F344

Sir

I acknowledg'd receipt of yours of 15th last Friday and aquainted you, That Stancomb Writings were not in the Box.

Mr Brice came here last Saturday Evening, a quick return!

The Farmer is very Penitent, Says whatever he has done or may do for you, will be determin'd as to the reasonableness of his Demands, by any that are Judges, is very Sorry he has disoblig'd you: I am no advocate, But am sure he is the most Convenient to be Employ'd in your affairs. I own these Sort of people are Selfish, and Strangers to Gratitude; yet necessary Evils.

Betty Dyer is in hopes of being Cur'd Soon of her Disorder, and will Take Care to keep the House as Clean as she can, But at present 'tis in great Disorder, all open and in Rubbish.

Seely has been here & I got Mr Brice to be here too; They both viewed the Timbers in the Hall, the Beams are all Bad, not fit to be put up again & many of the Joices, the principals in the rooms over rotten at Bottom, & Some of the roof Bad, the partitions and the Cielings [sic] are down, the 2 Joiners are Securing the Timbers as well as They can; as Seely has Sent you a State of the whole, I referr you to it, it Looks to be a very Bad Jobb!

Mr Brice is so busy about his Privateer, That he can't Spare anybody about the pales yet But when the grass is cut, will get 'Em put up.

Sol went yesterday Morning with More to Buckland; he finished your Trees a Teusday night, he Says They are much Better than any in this Countrey, he do's not Seem pleas'd to be in the manner you order'd Him, Says things are very Dear here, & 'tis very inconvenient for him to provide for Himself &c. He was one day at Mr Lee's – Sol has done the Walk by the Canal, & at his return which will be Saturday, he will finish That by the Garden House – and on Teusday next intends to Cut the Higher Meadow.

The Calves are gone, they did no harm to the Trees; But someone has broke off the Top of one of the plane Trees.

As to the Cottage, I can't Think it is worth more than Harry Warne has offer'd for it, and if Ridge builds a new House on the other part without any Fine, it will be no Detriment – But a survey for it, when Mr Edgcombe is here at Michaelmas, will be putting it to a Certainty.

As to Watts, he's a Silly old Fellow, and not worth your Trouble. I wrote you That More thinks removing the Vines will kill 'Em.

I sent you the Measure of the pier in the Bed chamber, in the new Buildings, and Seely has sent you the Section of the room with the prints.

They will have it here that there has been Some better Turn, where Mr Bing was Concern'd, pray God it be so.

I am very Sorry your Spirits Flagg, mine must Fail, But yours I hope will Freshen.

Your Trees were revived by the late Showers, But They have been oblig'd to Water again; Yesterday whilst I was writing this there was a Fine shower from 10 to 12 & rain to 7, which has done much Good.

I am Sir
Your Faithful
N Rowe

My Speculative Glare was only a Flash in the Socket, Thus it was; and Thus 'twill be.

F345

Nutwell, 2 July 1756

Sir

I have your Favour of 22nd past, and am glad if I can be of any Service to you, But in my present Situation it can be very Little.

I am Glad you have Finish'd with Moore: Wat Pike has introduc'd his adopted very well.

As soon as any Lime was Burnt, Nicholas Layd in Ten Hogsheads, and the Mortar will be fit for plaistering next week, when he will do the Cielings [*sic*] of the Parlour and Room over; He has noggin'd ['set brickwork in the timber frame of'] the Stair Case as you direct, and wil Plaister it with the Rest.

I am Glad Channon has wrote you about the Wear ['weir'] –

Sol Says they are very Succesful in Fishing, very Little Fruit at Buckland – Mr Stapleton is to write you as to the Trees.

As Channon intends to new Hele ['roof'] the Tower and Some more of the House this Summer, the Sprys can't be Spar'd; and I shou'd Think Nicholas, as he is upon all Calls, may do what you want in new Work as well as the Other; But as to Cheapness I can't Say, But will Enquire if you Think proper – that part of the Hall next the Back Court, which he new Covered a few years ago, Seems to be good Work; the other part is very Bad, as it now appears open; in short, Sir, your House is now gutted, your Hall is a Barn, all the Timber & Floors over Taken down – The Beams all rotten, Cramp't with Iron in a Shocking manner, your Orders are Wanted how they are to proceed; Mr Brice has Firr Timber fit for the purpose, and the two Joiners have now nothing to Do – to be sure, Seely will have your Speedy Orders.

We had last Sunday Evening much Thunder & Lightning, and very Dark for the time, with Smart rain; & Since Several Showers, which give a new face to your Gardens; But is uncertain Weather for cutting your grass – you will order money to pay the People for making the Hay &c.

Mr Lee is in high Business at his new Parsonage making gardens &c – Thinks of Lambeth only, as to the Expence; his Things from London are Come.

May there be a good account from Mr Byng, Various are the Reports Here.

Your house at present is in great Disorder, I wish the roof may prove better than it Seems.

Mr Vaughan came to Mamhead last Monday.

If no Directions come from you to Seely this post I don't know what to do with the Joiners. The Masons are Finishing the Wall at the End of the Canal. Sol is doing the Cross walk to the Garden-House.

It rain'd most part of yesterday.

In all weathers I am Lame.

I am Sir
Your Faithful
N Rowe

F346

Nutwell, 9 July 1756

Sir

I have yours of 29th past – as to the Farmer, He won't I Dare Say part with the Culverys 'Till he has had the Clover out, whatever he Do's afterwards, the penitence of such people, never go's beyond their profit.

The Joiners are now at Work on the Girders, which They have had from Mr Brice; what of the old Stuff will do again for Joices, will be made use of, but they Say they must have Several new, which Seely will acquaint you of; and I hope will Dispatch it, for the House is at present in an odd position.

As to the Sprys helling ['re-roofing'] the House, if Nicholas can Do it as well, it wou'd be a Discouragement, to have another Do the new Work, and He call'd in on all Occasions for mending; But if for Dispatch you think proper you may Employ Both: as it is high Time; if this Summer.

Some of the Cedars are come up, & Some of the others, but Sparingly; There will no Doubt come much good Earth from the Grass walks, But it will be some Time before the Earth will be Dugg, as other Things interfere – Teusday they began to Cut the E. Meadow, the Grass is very rank near the Hedges, and as the Weather has been good Ever Since, hope 'twill be well Sav'd; as to the Clover it is but Small yet.

The Strawberry Trees are red-Headed, but none Dead; the Shrubbs in general are Tollerably well in the Warren Hill and the Meadow, and the Garden; Some you'l Find are gone: the Laurels on the Meadow Hedge & Water house do well, and those in the garden Seem to recover, But the Newfoundland Firrs & Larch Trees are most of 'Em gone; the Wall Trees look very well, the rain we had last Week has refresh'd your garden much.

The account from Mr Byng is melancholy, don't it Look as if he did not care for Fighting? The people Curse Him Here, & fear St Philip is gone.*

The E. Meadow is down, the grass in the middle very Bad; as Soon as it is Sav'd, will get the Farmer to plow the Fallows, For you must imagine 'tis very inconvenient to go farther; Especially Just now. The plane Trees at the Bottome are very Thriving: there's a prospect of Clover.

The Man has been with me for the Freight of the Timber, Says as the Master has quitted the Ship, can't make up his accounts, 'till 'tis paid; no-one has been at Cotton's Wharf about it: the Enclos'd is the State of it.

Seely has not been here this week, I hope he will at the putting in the Girders.

Betty Dyer mends Daily, But 'twill be a matter of Time as you observe – I am Sorry the hot weather affects you so: all Weathers are to me alike Lame &c.

But always I am Sir
Your Faithful
...

The Cistus Ledon's in Flower and the Tuberoses are all above Ground, a Farmer & a Florist, what more, why at 11 Hour in the Vineyard – *nil Desperandum* ['no cause to despair']!

The Clock may be put up in the Little room on the great Stairs; But the Man will have two guineas to repair it, & Fix it There.

We had rain the Thursday & hard rain & Thunder the Sunday night as you had. – and Showers most of Last week. Fair this Hitherto.

They will Cut the Other Meadow, as Soon as this out of hand.

* St Philip was the fort on Minorca with a British garrison that Admiral Byng failed to relieve.

F347

Nutwell, 16 July 1756

Sir

I have your Favour of the 6th. I think it was very Providential, the Defects of your Hall, were seen before you made any alterations, the Girders are so Bad, as you'l See, That they might have Sunk on a Sudden. The Joiners are Framing the Floor, I don't See they can Employ more hands at present, They intend to put it up next Week being in a good Forwardness – the roof is much better than was at first Thought, and will be very well again with very little mending: I have Talk'd with Nicholas about the new Helling ['roofing'], he computes 'twill be about 25 Square; the Common price is 8s. per Square, to Take down the old, & put up the new, & Find pins; Says 'tis a very good Time to do it, and will go about it, if you Think proper, directly, it is very Bad, and hopes to complete it in Time; it is the whole Front which must be Done, & that part of the new Buildings, which Joins to it; the Expence of his Labour can't exceed £10.

As to the Wear's ['weir's'] being robb'd, I wonder Lady Drake should be against prosecuting the Rogues, you certainly do right to pursue it, For if you don't, They'l be Continually plundering, and 'tis so valuable a part of the Estate, that it deserves the utmost Attension – Surely Lady Drake won't be influenc'd by anyone to make Channon uneasy, if she do's, She'l be in a Mill indeed! I don't apprehend he'l quit the Service if the pradmatical Steward don't interrupt his Management, and your Mother must ruine her affaires, if She harkens to his weak Suggestions: I don't apprehend the reason of Forbidding Channon to pay the Workmen, I Thought you was to have the Direction, you should therefore Exert to Support the Man, & Mr Edgcombe's making up yearly the Fish account wou'd prevent Mr Mills' improper application – it will be Time Enough to Sound Channon when you go down.

Next week Nicholas will go about plaistering the Parlour, the Mortar he says won't be fit before; as it will be Soon done, the Parlour Shall then be painted the Colour you mention, the only new work which is to be Measur'd apart, I apprehend, is the Chimney piece, about the Windows, & between where the glass is, which Shall be done, and the whole as soon as possible.

I apprehend Arthur was to have the old Lead at 15s. per Hundred, you will direct how the money is to be apply'd, & it shall be accordingly.

The woman & Thomas Parsons will want their money for helping Sol in the garden, as they are going off for the present, so must apply to Mr Lee for that as well as the Haymakers – Sol made an End of the Reek in E. Mead, and the Home Mead Down a Teusday night, But on Wednesday Morning we had a hard Shower, & misty rain all Day: However as it is Fair again, hope this week will Finish it.

I am Sir
Your Faithful
N Rowe

I'm oblig'd to Mrs Eliot for her kind remembrance, pray my best Compliment to Her – I heartily wish Her Well.

You must Excuse what's amiss, For added to my Lameness, I have been so Severely attack't with the Cholick, That I scarse know what I write.

F348

Nutwell, 23 July 1756

Sir

I have your Favour of the 13th, the Sad Description you give of affairs is very Melancholy, yet I hope in God, They won't prove so Bad as is fear'd, Tho' we have too much reason to fear it: yet Providence has wonderfully Deliver'd us, when Our own prudence has fail'd.

Your House has been worse than a Barn, But it is returning into its Forme again, the Floor will be Soon in, and then the rooms over the Hall will be gone about: Seely was here a Saturday Last, he promis't to write you by Monday's post a State of Everything.

They are filling up the Window in the Hall and plaistering the Parlour, and shall go upon the Helling ['roofing'], that is fitting the Stones, But Seely Says they must not uncover 'till they have Open'd for the Windows in the Chambers – for my part Such Things are new to me, I can only press 'Em to Expedition.

Your people made an End of Hay, last Teusday night, & Finish'd Both Ricks, it was Sav'd in good Order, Tho' hinder'd by Showers 2, or 3 Times, and as often hard rain. Mr Lee Says you Shou'd Eat your aftergrass soon, the Hay in the Home is very Good.

The making the Hay has put Everything Back in the Garden. They are now Thatching the Ricks, the Several Parts of your Business shall be Expedited all I can, I wish whenever your affairs will permit you to come down, you might Find Everything agreable; you must imagine it will require Some Time to alter the Confusion – I heartily wish Things may Take a Better Turne, and That you may be able soon to come down, which wou'd give the greatest pleasure to
Sir
Your Faithful
N Rowe

F349

Nutwell, 30 July 1756

Sir

I have your Favour of 20th, am very Sorry the Hot Weather so affects you, we have had none so Violent, nor any Thunder or Lightnings as you mention, or rains: last Monday There was a Smart Shower, a Wednesday Some, Fair yesterday.

Nicholas is Lame which retards much, But he promises to go about the Helling ['re-roofing'], and to Expedite matters, as Fast as possible: no Doubt your presence wou'd Forward 'Em: but as more momentous affairs detain you, will hasten Them all I can. His Majesty's visiting the Countrey will undoubtedly put Spirits into the people, which is much wanted – Mahone it's fear'd is gone –*

The Boxes are Come, & put as you direct and none open'd; that with the China, unless you would have it unpack't, may remain more safe so, 'till you come down.

As you are so kind to offer it, if you wou'd Send Down a remnant of black plush for a pair of Breeches I shou'd be Oblig'd –

I am glad you have order'd Channon to pay the Expence of the Wear ['weir'], he shou'd be Encourag'd.

No Coals in the Harbour, your Stock holds out well, as Betty Dyer is very Saving of Them. I heartily wish you Health, mine is no import, nor to be Expected now; your Concern is very Obliging, & for which I thank you, but pray Take Care of yourself.

I am Sir
Your Faithful
N Rowe

* Port Mahon, as in F339, was the location of St Philip fort on Minorca.

F350* [beginning and end of this letter missing]

As the Hay is Finish'd, & the Ricks cover'd Sol is putting the garden in order, which was gone back by that Means – Mr Lee has paid the People which amounts to above £8.

The progress the Joiners make Seely will acquaint you, They have Finish'd the Flooring, that is the girders & Joices are in. The Masons have broke a hole for the Door to the gallery, the Wall was 4 ft Thick: They are now breaking out the Windows for the Chambers, I hope so many Breaches won't Weaken your House: They were very Careful of the Boards, which They took up in the Hall-Chamber & red room, and none Seem'd Damag'd, They will Soon go about Those rooms, to fix the Timbers for the Cielings [sic], & window Frames; where are They to be had?

Sol must Soon mowe the Wood, but as Thomas Parsons is gone he must have Some-one to help Him; wou'd you have the Brambles burnt?

You have now a great Stock of Hay, that and the Grass, They Say shou'd be Eat.

I wrote you That the Farmer advis'd to Sowe the Fallows in the East Meadow with Turnips, which he Says will Level the ground & Kill the Weed, as they are now Plow'd, Desire your answer by return of the Post, if you wou'd, Else 'twill be too Late.

Mr Duke, after many Times Sending after and Keeping the Model of the Cart near 2 year, he has return'd it, not very Civil – you may Depend nothing for the Future shall be Lent out of your House but by your Special order.**

Seely came here a Wednesday afternoon, there Seems to be a Difficulty as to the uniformity of the Chimneys in the rooms over the Hall, whether they won't interfere with the principals of the roof, but as Nicholas was here at the Same Time, They Consulted together; I hope They won't bring an old House about their Ears.

Nicholas is now about Plaistering the Parlour, and will Finish it this Week, so the Painter may come The next, and then the Room over will be done; wou'd not you have it painted at the same Time?

The Earth in the Fallows Seems to have Chang'd its Colour a little, the air & Sun will do much as it is now very Drye.

You must Excuse my Confus'd Detail; as to your Building Seely will Explain my improprietys.

You will Send your Directions, whether you will have Turnips Sowne in the Fallowes or no –

Nicholas will put about the Helling ['re-roofing'] out of hand –

I wrote you That the Man won't repair the Clock under two guineas, I wait for your approbation, Before I send it to Exeter.

The Corn promises very Well, and the Harvest will be Soon.

Like Chancellor Fursman I can go no Farther.

* The beginning and end of this letter are missing. FHD seems to have made notes on the left side of the sheet, which do not have anything to do with this letter, but do contain important information about a letter written by Mr Brice seven months earlier, and, most importantly, confirm FHD's own agency in assembling the letters: 'Mr Rowe's Letters, 1756. In this Bundle Mr Brice's Letter Jan. 19 about my [editorial underlining] presenting his Petition to the Council.' Mr Brice's letter has not survived.
** For the cart model loaned to Mr Duke see F336 and F339.

F351

Nutwell, 20 August 1756

Sir

I am very Sorry to hear by yours of 10th That Things carry such a Bad aspect, pray God Defend the nation, from the fear'd Calamitys.

I am much oblig'd for your kind regard, But as my Lameness Still sticks by me, I have little need of Shoes, so I can't Trouble you.

A very melancholy accident happen'd here last Saturday Evening – young Seely as he was fixing one of of the cieling [sic] Joyces, it broke under him, & he fell to the Bottome of the Hall; he was Taken up as Dead, and had not his Fall been providentially broke twice, he must have been kill'd on the Spot; his head is much cut, but his Skull not Touch't nor any Bone broke, He is yet so Bad, that he can't be remov'd, but Dr Gelly is in hopes he'l soon do well again, a Wonderful Escape!

Seely the Elder was here Wednesday, he and Nicholas agree in Taking down the gabel-Ends, the only Expence extraordinary will be the gutter; the Timbers, which come out of the gabel Ends will make good the roof, both which are good; it will Save in the article of Copeing Stones, your Front will look better and only waits your order to go about it, & to know what hights you wou'd like the parapet Wall, they say about 3 Feet, good part of which, in filling up the windows, will Stand.

I hope you are well, pray God keep you so – Everything is going on as you order'd – I am so Shock't I can say no more.

I am Sir

Your Faithful

N Rowe

Fine harvest Weather, though Showry.

What Copeing Stones will be Wanted for the porch & the other gabel-End Shall be got in the best manner – pray where is your Brother Sam?

Nicholas desires some money to pay his people.

F352

Nutwell, 10 December 1756

Sir

I have your Favour of 4th; you Say nothing of putting the Bullocks into the Turnips, But in They must go, as the Farmer has Taken away his Hurdles.

Stephen Says he shall Finish his Jobb, by this Day 7 night, there are no Stones Deep in the ground; you'l order how he is to be paid.

Sol says two Men wou'd make the Frith ['fencing'] you mention in about a Week's Time, But the Hedge will Take up a good Deal of Time making: which must be Cut down first: he's Covering the Linney.

I am very Sorry your Brother Sam Behaves so indiscretely – your good Sense will pardon Him I hope, as I do that his preferment will make Him Wiser.

Captain Pike has been here with his Compliments, hopes for your Favourable reccommendation to Your Brother.

Mr Brice has had no Other account from the Tinners than what he wrote you – yet he Seems Fearful, least any shou'd Step in Between, So he Seems to have Some Prospect in View.

There has been an Easterly wind for Some Days, the Glass at Set Fair But very Cold, & I have added to the rest a Violent pain in my Back which is Scarse Tollerable! Yesterday very Fine weather.

I have not to add
I am Sir
Your Faithful
N Rowe

If you wou'd have the inside of the Meadow-Hedge made first, the Frith ['fencing'] wou'd be much Sooner <u>Done</u>.

F353

Nutwell, 7 January 1757

Sir

I have your Favour of 28th past, am very much oblig'd for your kind Regard – the pain in my Back Continues & is very Troublesome – the very Cold Weather pinches me much, I was never so sensible of Winter Before. But as to setting in the Parlour it wou'd Stupify me, and I am Just on the Verge of Stupidity already: your great Care I have a due Sense of & am very Thankful for it; and for that reason will regard myself more than I otherwise shou'd.

You see by the 1st sketch of the Hay-ricks you sent, how Dull of apprehension I am; the last I plainly Take, But can't imagine there was so much Hay in the rick – pray according to the London price how do you value it? in the Countrey hay is Cheap.

Sol return'd last Saturday night, he & John Coleman are Digging the Foundation for the Wall in the Orchard: He will finish the Border for the Filberts this week, & next week will go about the Meadow Hedge.

I have acquainted Mr Brice with your advice about Lord Halifax, he is very Thankful for your intension & relys on your Kind Favour.

I hope shall soon have the Pattern for the Iron Gate, That the rails may be fix't whilst the weather holds Drye, & Painted before Eliot go's to Exeter – He has not got his Freedome yet, But the Alderman gives him great hopes of it.

There has been no Snow here, But a hard Frost with a Sharp E. wind for a Few Days, else Such Weather as you mention which was very Cold (particularly Christmas Day uncommonly so) and Seems very Likely to Continue, very healthy Weather for Those who are able to Stirr about, which is not my Case, to my great Mortification.

    I am Sir
    Your Faithful
    N Rowe

The inclosed I received from Dame Mildron the Tenant at Lophill, which I wonder She Shou'd write to me: when She ought to have made her application to yourself.

F354

21 January 1757

Sir

    You must Excuse my not answering your Letter – an Unfortunate accident has Disabl'd me for the present, But I hope next Week to be able – Last Saturday forenoon I unaccountably Fell into the Tank at the End of the Orchard, which brings in the Water to the Garden; had the Tonkin been in, I must inevitably have been Drown'd, and tho' there was no Water, I sunk so Deep in the Mudd, That I cou'd neither move hand nor Foot, & shou'd have been Suffocated, But providentially John Coleman was within Call, who with Difficulty Hawl'd me out in a Fine pickle indeed!

    Sol was gone to Prehembry for Parson Lee, & it was a Meer Chance John happen'd to be here & where he was too: Else I might have Layn God knows how Long as I cou'd not help myself. I am much Bruis'd & my head hurt, But God be Thanked no Dislocation nor Broken bone, a Mercy I hope I shall always remember with Thankfulness, I am able to Say no more But That

    I am Sir
    Your Faithful
    N Rowe

Very uncertain Weather – Frost, wind & Rain.

F355* [Betty Dyer to FHD]

Janaray the 12 1757

Honnered Sir

    Mr Rowe tells me that John Collman's wife ore the young woman that works at Mr Collman's is to help me by your honner's order, if your honner is plesed to let me have either of them for 2 days to help with the rooms and scouer the pueter and when your honner is provided with a servant in my place I hope your honner will be plesed to discharge me. From your honners dutiful servant
    Elizabeth Dyer

* This and the following letter from the housekeeper Betty Dyer, asking for her discharge and for help in paying her doctor's bills, are the only letters from servants to FHD in 346M. Perhaps he kept them because he found them entertaining.

F356 [Betty Dyer to FHD]

28 Janary 1757

Honnered Sir

I have been under the surgenes hand allmost this 9 munths who says if I stand and walk on my leg as I now am oblidged to do I shall never be well.* I have a long bill to pay and he very well deserves more then I am capable of paying him. I have wrought harder in your honner's service then I have for several years past in any famaly I have living in with a great deall of plesure to the great danger of making my self uncapable of service any more and then I must be very unhappy having no other way of getting my living so I hope your honner's goodness will pardon my freedome in writing and I will do my utmost to serve your honner to the last moment as I did at the first and as I am in duty bound from youre honner's dutyfull servant
    Elizabeth Dyer

* For Betty Dyer's health problems, see Introduction, section 5, p. 50.

F357

28 January 1757

Sir

My Fall has so Disorder'd me, That I am uncapable of anything, my head is so Jarr'd, which disables me from Writing my Back still Bad, and I have Scarse a whole part about me, which must be an apology for Sending you Such Scraps as the Enclos'd, that I write as I am able.

Betty Dyer says she has nothing in View bu[t yo]ur service, which she is not able to do alone, the Truth is, the [Ba]dness of her Leg – Enclosed is H[e]r acknowledgment.

I am very Sorry your Brother Samuel behaves so – your goodness I hope will Convince Him of his Er[r]or.

Mrs Porter wrote me Some [time] ago, That your Brother W[illi]am came as far as Exeter to meet Him, but return'd next day without Seing Him.

The affair of the French King & Mr Bing I hear are the Topic with Everyone.

Nicholas Says he will go about the Wall out of hand. There is a Bill for Lime about £10 which must be paid 3rd February next, hopes you'l please to order it & his Too.

Here has been very Stormy Weather for some days past with rain, yesterday a Frost, very White on Hall Down, can say no more But That –
    I am Sir
    Your Faithful
    N Rowe

Channon's Bullocks have Eat all the Hayrick, & Sol has cut another he says by your Order, the Linney is too Little for 'Em, so they are remov'd into the Farmer's Court.

Channon is expected here – when will Enquire about the Time for the Heifers, it can't be yet.

Sol will Enquire about Sope Ashes.

A Frost today again –

Seaward the Carpenter came here Just as I was Sealing this – as he Hew'd the Hurdles says He will put 'Em together for 4d. per Hurdle which is the lowest he can do it for.

The gate Model I presume is not made on purpose, But only to Show how to hang the gate?

F358

Nutwell, 4 February 1757

Sir

I have your Favours of 25th, 27th & 29th past, am very much oblig'd for your kind regard. But a Tottering Wall, when Shaken in the Foundation, a Fall the Sooner Ensues; it has been a Severe Shock to me, and I can't get the Better of it – a Chil, which I never Felt before, added to a dead pain in my head gives me more uneasiness than the general pain in & Thro'out – There, warm Weather may do, what I am Sure the Cold do's not.

Enclosed is all I can Find relating to Selley; when he Comes out, will let Him know your Directions about measuring the rooms – the Drawer of the Breakfast Table is not made, But the younger Selley will now Soon be able to Work, when that & putting up the Bed in the red room shall be Done.

The Frith ['fencing'] is done in the Meadow, & the Hedge outside will be gone about.

Wou'd you have me acquaint Captain Pike with your Endeavour?

The Hurdles will do for Small Cattle, Channon can't put off his, So he keeps 'Em here 'till Shrovetide; Sol has begun on another Hay-rick, he Says by your Order.

Mr Brice's measurement can't be right, to have but 4 Seams on an Acre – I don't understand it I own.

I am Sorry to hear of your Brother William's ilness; I hope Both of 'Em will have a due Sense of your Kindness, how necessary it is for their future Welfare.

The Model of the gate the Smith understands, and will Soon Do it, I hope to your Likeing.

Nicholas will go about the Wall Soon, Desires to have your particular Directions about the Higth of Both Walls, & whether you wou'd have that next the Meadow with a Hanging Level; and in what Time you Expect it to be Done.

As to Thomson he's a very impertinent Fellow, I believe his Poverty makes him impudent, he was Carpenter of a Man of War and Turn'd out for Embezelment of Stores – He applyd to me Some years ago in the Same manner & I told Him he had no pretensions – The Case you desire to know is This. Your Ancestor many years ago purchas'd the Lands of one Luce call'd in the rental Sir Francis Drake's ancient Lands – a Descendant of said Luce. Your Grand Father made a Vote (without any Deeds as I ever Saw), on his Death he allow'd John Stephens who marryd his only Daughter to be a vote in her Right, by whom he had 3 Daughters (one of which this Thomson marryd). Stephens dy'd before your Father, who then got his Widow by Dr Creed's means to declare by a Deed, that her Father & Husband held the Lands only in Trust; upon this your Father Convey'd the Lands to Nicholas Doidge, upon whose Death, his Brother John Convey'd 'Em to John Reed Senior Whose Son now holds 'Em – you'l Excuse my prolixity, it's a wonder I do so well. What Dr Creed got the Widow to Sign is the writings the <u>Fellow meant</u>.

I am Sir
Your Faithful
N Rowe

F359

Nutwell, 18 February 1757

Sir

I have your Favour of 8th, am Extremely oblig'd for your kind regard so often repeated – When the Glass runs Lower, any Shake makes an alteration: it has been a Shock to me! But I hope in God I Shall get over it, as the Weather grows Warmer without the Help of any Physitian, who can give <u>no</u> Relief to me – I am my Own Doctor – Pray God give you health, & keep you from accidents.

Here has been very Fine Weather this Week.

I have acquainted Nicholas with your Orders, Says he will go on With the Wall out of hand, the upper Foundation is Dugg: for the Other it is Time Enough for your particular Directions.

Enclosed I send you Channon's Letter, he has been very unlucky in feeding Cattle this year, the Contract being Stop't at Plymouth; that at London being 3s. a Hundred Cheaper – So he Sent for 4 of the Bullocks a Monday, & Desir'd Sol might help the Boy over the Wear ['weir'] a Teusday, when he got Drunk, Sold (as he pretended) Two of Them at Exeter, brought 'Em back here at night, and on Wednesday Morning Set out with 'Em on Foot for Buckland, without my being acquainted with it – the Fellow is too often Drunk, but now must be Mad – if your Notice of his Conduct Don't restrain Him, I am Sure I can't.

I have Told Seley of your anger about putting up the Windows, Says 'twas impossible for the Plaisterers to work without Shelter, is Sorry he has offended, & has nail'd up Boards inside & out, which I hope will prevent their being Broke for the Future.

I hope there is no Matrimony in the Case,* and that the Captain's Ilness is not incurable – I see by the Countrey newspaper your Brother Samuel has got the *Achilles*, I hope it will make a proper impression.

I am Sir
Your Faithful
N Rowe

Poor Mr Wyatt has been very Ill – presents his Duty.

* 'Matrimony in the case' refers to William Drake's liaison with the mother of his son. See also F367.

F360

Nutwell, 25 February 1757

Sir

I have your Favour of 15th and hope I shall in Time get over, what yet affects me much.

I believe Channon wishes he had never Sent any Bullocks, it has happen'd unluckily of all Sides – which I imagine was the Reason of his letting the Farmer put his Stuff in, which were only his Sheep & young Cattle, but had he known you wou'd objected [*sic*] to it – To be Sure he wou'd not.

The Plaisterers will have done the Ornamental Part this week, and the rest in about 3 weeks more – it is a very Dirty affair.

Nicholas began a Monday about the Wall. The Copeing Stones (which came out of the Hall) on the Top of the House, molder away with the Frost.

The Trees are headed for Grafting as you Direct, in the Meadow &c.

Betty Dyer has not hired the Maid, She Seems at a Stand to know your pleasure about Paying her Doctor, Says in all the places She has ever been, all things of that kind have ever been allow'd her – hopes you will be so pleas'd.

Mr B[ing]'s affair I don't understand, it makes a noise in the Countrey I hear, how Civil Magistrates can Judge of Martial Law.

I hope the Loss in your Brother's Family don't Prevent his going to Sea.

Farmer Coleman Says Mr Bass has been with Him again for the Elm Tree he Spar'd for the Cyder press, he desires to have it now being in great Want of it, and the Farmer hopes you'l order one to be Cut down for Him too, to lye in Store That he mayn't be So Distress'd again in Cyder-making: Says there are two fit Trees for the purpose on Exton Grounds.

I can't yet get the Smith to make the Iron-gate for the garden, being now so Busy about the Green-Land Ship, Says he'l do it as Soon as Ever he can – a Tedious Operator!

I presume as you Say nothing about the Hurdles, you don't approve of Seaward's making them at his price.

Sol return'd last Friday Evening from his mad Expedition to Buckland; the Butcher to whom he Sold the Bullocks, came here a Monday to Enquire after Him, and threatens to Trouble Him about the Bargain, 'tis well your Service protects Him, or he'd be in a Scrape, But if your Reprimand don't restrain him from Drinking, he'l be fit for nothing.

I am Sir
Your Faithful
N Rowe

Don't you intend to have Blowskind Grafts from Mr George Edgcombe – for the young Trees in the Orchard.

The Newfoundlander is now quite gone.

F361

Nutwell, 27 February 1757

Sir

Your Letter of 22nd gave me infinite Concern, & the more as I had hopes of hearing from you to Do as you intimated, if you was Better I shou'd, But as no Letter came my Fears are greatly Encreas't, and Shall be in Continual uneasiness 'till I hear you are Better: For Godsake take care of yourself; your Friend I hope will assist you:* my Spirits are very Lowe, and This almost Sinks 'Em – But what are They or I to your Welfare!

Your Relations I don't Think Treat you well, as you Engag'd in the Sales by their appointment and in honour they Ought to Support: these Contrarietys in Brothers are Shocking!

I Dare Believe the Lady will take no advantage of your Warning; but Shou'd not your Disappointment be intimated to Her?

I Long with impatience to hear how you Do, I hope I shall Soon, That you are Better, which I pray God I may.

I am Sir
Your Faithful
N Rowe

I Can Trouble you with Nothing now.

* Probably Dr Mark Akenside. See Introduction, section 5, p. 48.

F362

Nutwell, 6 March 1757

Dear Sir

Your Letter of 1st Damp't my Spirits so much, That yours of 2nd, for which I very much Thank you, has Scarse recover'd 'Em – What with Both Extremes I am in Such a Flutter I can Scarse regulate 'Em to any Consistency.

My Dear Sir Francis, my Love, & Esteem for you is attended with Such a Delicate Tenderness, That I can't Express how my Fears were, or my hopes are affected. Your relyance on your Phisitian, & his ability gives me great hopes, and I shall always honour Him for it, and what a happiness it is, That you are, where you can have the assistance you so much approve of – I Flatter myself you will make use of Every means to preserve a valuable Life so necessary to the Welfare of your Family & Friends.

For Godsake Take Care of yourself, Don't Trouble yourself, now you are so weak, to Write, only once a Week as usual but 2 Lines how you Mend, Which I heartily pray to God you may: & That you may Live & be as Happy as I wish you many Years.

The Flutter I have been & am in has pull'd me Backward, & push'd me forward so much, That in my present fluctuating Condition I am only able to Say

That I am Dear Sir
Your Faithful & most Affectionate
N Rowe

I can't Trouble you with anything now – will mind Everything you Say.

F363

Nutwell, 11 March 1757

Dear Sir

I am still in great Anxiety, tho' your Last Letter gave me hopes, neither can I be Easy, Till I know You are Quite recover'd, which I pray God you Soon may.

The Parson is a True Priest – no Pence no Pater noster. He might have let Poor Nicholas have a little more money, as he knew he was Working for you, But he Told me he wou'd not <u>positively</u> – I Fear his Respect Extends no further than Selfish Views!

You Sure shou'd not Trouble yourself about Writing 'till you are Better – Therefore I shall Trouble you with Little – I have wrote Mr George Edgcombe for the Bloiskind Graffs; Sol Says as there are 100 Trees in the Nursery, they will Take 600 Graffs, I have wrote for so many: you Say nothing of the Worcestershire Pear graffs, the Trees are headed for Them, and it is now Time; nor of the Farmer's in the new Orchard.

I wrote you 25 lbs of Clover wou'd be wanted for Both Meadows; if you propose to Eat the home One this year. He (Sol) don't intend to Close up the Gate now, Becaus they must then go thro' the Other with Cattle, which must Spoil the grass, when heam'd ['ploughed'] up; your Directions will be necessary, as they are about Stoning the Hedges.

I Thought the Lady woud not make Two Lapses; tho' I believe she'd gladly make a Third. [?]

Mr Porter writes me your Brothers have made an Exchange; happy Mortals that have Such a Brother!

I sent Mr Creed the Counterparts, that he might Describe the particular Estates according to the Leases, which wou'd be more acceptable to the purchasers.

Nicholas is about the Wall; two Joiners are at Work; and the plaisterers promise to go on – the Smith has not Done the Gate yet, he do's nothing but make Excuses.

Here has been Various Weather of Late, Frost, Hail, & Rain – I Buoy myself up with Hopes, which

I heartily Pray for, your Recovery, Pray God send it, is the hearty Wish of
Dear Sir
Your Faithful
N Rowe

Sol Desires to know What Melon-Seed you wou'd have this year.

F364

18 March 1757

Dear Sir

I am very Sorry to find your Journey did not answer your Expectation, yours of 7th gave me such Hopes – But your want of Spirits blasted Them – I don't Think there is a more shocking Thing in nature, as I Feelingly Sympathise with you: the greater is my Concern! It wou'd be preposterous in me to advise you, who no Doubt have the Best, which I hope God will give Success to, and therein I Trust.

I am glad you found your Brother William Better, I fear he owes too much to himself; your Brother Samuel I am glad you Saw, his preferment I hope won't be a prejudice to the other when able:

As to Parson Lee he has been here but once Since you went, & That I imagine was to See if Nicholas was at Work for you – the Beer is brought home, But what Occasions his not writing I don't know, good Manners &c I shou'd Think might Dictate better Behaviour.

You'l Excuse my inlarging, I can't Trouble you with particulars, not Even about myself, my Concern is wholy about you, I pray God restore your Health is the Constant Wish of

Dear Sir
Your Faithful
N Rowe

Mr Creed has never Wrote me of the receipt of the writings, Quite <u>wrong</u>.

Mr Lee has let Sol have his Cart & Bullocks to draw Stones.

F365

Nutwell, 17 June 1757

Dear Sir

I have your Favour of 7th. We have had no rain, Since you went, only a Shower Teusday Morning, which made a Small Show. Pray God Send Some more as it's much wanted: your new Heifers thrive, but a Small Difference can be Seen yet, they promise well.

I perceive you can Frame Likenesses from Bad Dawbing, my Sketches in all Shapes are so, But your imaginations are Strong; however you only Say Madam Sophy is Charm'd with the Brunette,* not a word of Mama, or your own Opinion – I hope this will introduce a more momentous reconciliation, I mean your Sister Eliot! I am very glad you have Settl'd your own affair, I hope the General One will Soon be <u>too</u>.

Your Trees & Shrubs are duely Water'd, your Flowers Some are Come up, others not yet, & Few of the Cypress, But <u>1</u> of the Cedars, the Rest may, nothing Worse than you Left 'Em, the Firrs in the Meadow look redish, They have been Soundly Water'd – But rain is Wanted. The Weather has been much as you mention, mostly N. & E. yet at Times very hot.

Selley was here yesterday, wants to have the Hall passage Brick'd up, that he may fix the Door place – so Nicholas is to do it with the old Soft Bricks – He go's on with the Wall, the Higher one is not brought to the Highth yet, of the End next the Door.

There will be more Lime Wanting for the Plaisterers, as there will Hair &c. Selley Says he can't go on, 'Till They have Done the Sides & Cieling [sic] – and Nicholas the passage Wall: you will Send your Orders.

The Parish of Woodberry want to know, how you will please to have the Indentures for the Boy put on Broad-Meadow, made, to yourself or Whom? Farmer Coleman Says he will Take Him for £4. But hopes you will Take off the Girl, & allow Him for keeping her 5 years. As to the Garden is willing to keep it, provided you will please to lessen the proportion from the Orchard, which is much more valuable: he Left it he Says, as he Thought you intended to take <u>Both</u>. It is a pity it should Lye as it do's, & you've no Use for it.

I have not yet the Rest of the Bills, Tho' I have Spoke for 'Em, neither have I heard from Mr Lee about Arthur's Money, Since what I wrote you.

Miss Martyn may be Said to have Marry'd a Gentleman; But the Horse will badly keep the House – a Melancholy Castastrophe [*sic*]!

I hope you are Well, I heartily Wish you so: I am as I fear I always shall be.

The Painter came here a Monday, is painting the rooms over the Hall; he go's next Week to give the Finishing Stroke to Mr Alderman Porter's House, which is he Says Decorated indeed, as intended for your reception.

I am Dear Sir
Your Faithful
N Rowe

Since my writing this I have received of Mr Arthur £30. There remains in his hands to ballance his account 14 odd Money which He is willing to pay, or to Work out as you think proper, and you are to Order, whether he's to pay the Money remaining, or not.

* Relations were evidently strained between Lady Drake and her elder daughter, Anne Eliott. The 'Brunette' and the 'Deal Lady' refer to Samuel Drake's wife, in the meantime favoured by Lady Drake, if not by FHD or Rowe. See also the following letter.

F366
Nutwell, 1 July 1757

Dear Sir

I have your Favours of 21st and 23rd past. I hope the Attack on the D[uke] of [Cumberland] is not so bad as Thought* – as I do that the Situation of Affairs will alter at Home.

I am Sorry That Mrs Eliot don't Come in for a Share of Favour – the Deal Lady has better Fortune – But I perceive you don't Think Her Descended from the Bishop of Winton: your Sister Sophy has not read so much History, is plain; your <u>Mama</u>!

Nicholas complains He's in very great Distress, They don't Care to give Him any More Credit, for Lime, That without your assistance he is not able to go on with the Work: Curtis & Braddock the Lime-burners have been with me, to know if you wou'd See Them paid, as They have no Confidence in Nicholas.

The Masters have been with me for Freight as by the Enclos'd – He who brought the last Chairs, has not Sent the other parcel, I wrote to you to be inform'd, as I know nothing of the particulars.

Sol made an End of mowing the E. Meadow yesterday, Hope 'twill be well Sav'd as no rain as yet, neither has there been any as you mention – you'l be so good to Excuse the blotted Scrawl, I Flagg Daily, That can't Do as I wou'd.

The Enclosed from Mr Porter came last post. Pray God preserve your Health, mine is of no Consequence: your kind regard I have a Due Sence of.

I am Dear Sir
Your Faithful
N Rowe

* William, Duke of Cumberland, son of George II, was at this time unsuccessfully leading the defence of George II's Hanoverian electorate against the French, in a key engagement of the Seven Years' War.

F367

Nutwell, 8 July 1757

Dear Sir

Yours of Sunday's post, for it has no Date, gave me great uneasiness; That my Spirits Sink is a natural Tendency to an End, But that yours shou'd so frequently Flag at this Time of Life is very Disagreable: I hope you will Take Every Method to raise 'Em, Exercise & agreable Conversation, Both which you have in your power & I hope you will make use of 'Em, I beg you will, as your Welfare is the Chief of my Wishes.

Six of the Leather Chairs & the Other Things you mention are Brought, the other Two, the Master cou'd not get out at Topsham but wou'd Leave 'Em There at his return from Exeter, & 'till then Take Care of 'Em, They Shall be Enquir'd after.

Enclos'd is the abstract of Betty Dyer's Bills, She was She Sayd in great Want of Money, so I paid Her the Whole Summ: But if you disaprove any of it, She must rectifye it. I send you the Farmer's bill itself, which you will please to return with your Directions, I will pay as far as the £30 will go.

When you Send any Money you will Order how much I am to pay Nicholas, he Says the Walls shall be all Done by Lammas, I have Told Him how high you intend 'Em and as to the Bricks you won't Spare: The Man of the Kiln has promis't me an account of what Lime he has had. Last year 43½ Hogsheads at 3s. 6d., £7.12.3.

I believe as the Sand is your Own, and what Mortar is Left will be on the place, you may Let the plaisterer have those 2 articles. But for the rest I think it is for your Interest not to find 'Em, unless you will add Hair. He Sent in a parcel of Laths, which are here, But how many, I don't know, only That none Have been us'd, but by <u>Them</u>.

As to the Prentice Boy the Justices have fix't Him on Broad Meadow, and Since that Time he is at your Expence So I Think it is best to let the Farmer have Him – He Says no-one will Take Him under £4 as he is not 9 year old. The Boy Farmer Colridge had was 13. He Says if you please to have Him yourself, or anyone Else, But he'l never Take another Girl: and hopes you'l Take off This, and allow Him for the Keeping of Her 5 year.

Your Hay was put into the Rick Saturday night, there was a Shower in the Morning but so little, that it did not hinder above an Hour or Two: it's well Sav'd & Sol has Thatch't it.

There was a Smart Shower a Monday about 3 in the Morning, whether the rain or heat but Several of your Trees on the Wall are Touch't, Several of the Trees in the Meadow are Dead tho' Water'd, the grazing Meadow is much Burnt, yet must be skim'd over, as the Cattle won't Eat the Drye Top.

I am Glad Things are Settl'd at Last, I hope They'l Continue So – But the news from Abroad if True, is very Bad, Pray God send Better.

I hope your Brother, now his Friend is restor'd, won't be Kept from Sea by no remora ['hindrance'] whatsoever.* I heartily wish Colonel Eliot Success; But I pray for your health above all Things, Pray Let me hear from you, & For Godsake Take Care of yourself, as for me it is of no import.

I think all your Trees & Shrubs Fare much Better than this Hot Drye Weather cou'd be Expected – your Melons are very Flourishing, But as More don't Come, Sol shall do what you direct, as I dare Say he wou'd under your Ey become Soon Capable to Cut as well as nail.

I am in great Anxiety Dear Sir
Your Faithful
N Rowe

The Plaister on the Walls in the Library & Chamber are Both quite Drye.

Mr Brice Says he has Sold Some Tun Weight of old Iron to the Smith at 1½ d. per pound, and don't Think he gets anything by yours.

I wish the affair at D– may answer your Expectation.

Wheat don't Fall here, no foreign arriv'd here, 'tis up at 9s. & 8s. 6d.

No alteration of the weather yet! Justice Tanner has Sent the Boy for Broad-Meadow.

* The 'remora' is the mother of William Drake's sons.

F368

Nutwell, 22 July 1757

Dear Sir

I have your kind Favours of 12th & 14th. My Time is come to expect an Alteration – But That you so Soon in Life shou'd have Such Frequent uneasinesses is very Melancholy indeed – the Weather has been Extreme Hot, as you mention last Week, But Since Saturday more Moderate – last Teusday there was a Fine Shower, and by the Glass Falling it Looks as if there wou'd be a Change, as there has been much Thunder of Late: my Concern for you is very great, I pray God send you health. I wish your affairs wou'd permit you to be here at this Time of the year, That you might have the Benefit of Bathing, which if ever, must be good now: Tho' the Countrey looks very Rusty – the Harvest is begun, Pray God send good Weather, as the Corn is generally well-Kern'd.

Selley was here a Wednesday Evening, as he acquaints you with his progress, I need not.

The Lime-Kiln is Stop't for want of Stones, so the Plaisterers can't go on, till they have Lime, nor Nicholas Lay the Floor of the Hall.

As there is nothing I wish more than your Welfare, I hope I shall soon hear you are Restor'd to the health I pray you may have a Long Continuance of; I can't Expect it, your Care for me is very engageing: you must Excuse the Enclos'd Scrawl – my head is so Confus'd with my old Disorder, That I can't Do as I wou'd But in all Conditions whilst I remain

I shall be Dear Sir
Your Truely Faithful
N Rowe

The People are very Pressing for the Freight of the Things I wrote you – the Farmer says Mr Edgcombe order'd Him not to pay anything – Fine Showers yesterday & today – much Lightning & Thunder, thermometer about 60. No Want of Water 'till now.

F369

Nutwell, 12 August 1757

Dear Sir

I have your Favours of 3rd & 5th; the Black wax alarm'd me not a little, But it was soon Dissipated, as you were well &c. I am very Glad to hear your Journey has been so agreable, & I very heartily wish it may Confirm your health.

I was forc'd to pay the Smith, who was so pressing, That I am now able to advance Nicholas but £40. Becaus of the Other particulars I wrote you, He thinks as you will want the pieces of Bricks to build your Garden-House &c it will be Cheaper for you to buy Samel Bricks, which I suppose Mr Lee will not sell under 20s. per 1000, unless he may make you a Compliment.

Sol will order the ground as you Direct, as soon as the Masons have done, and he can have help, But 'till the Harvest is over, he fears he can't have John Coleman.

As there is good grass in the E. Meadow, where the Cattle now are, it will very well keep 2 more, so I have wrote to Channon about it.

I will Endeavour to get the rooms paper'd, and Painted as Soon as possible, and order'd as you direct: I hope your sister & the Colonel will come with you, whom I shall be very Glad to See. Mr Porter writes me he hears your Brother William has got a new 36 Gun ship, I hope it's True – then Both are provided for.

The Weather was here as you mention, & last Saturday hard rain 'till noon, afterward very Fair, 'till now.

Here is very Little Corn left, none sold under 8s. Friday Last, Oats were never higher than 2s. 6d. per Bushel, now 2s., if this weather Continues Harvest will be over next week – the Badgers must then Borough.

I hope Things abroad are not so Bad as reported, Either as to the King of Prussia or the Duke.

Whilst you are well, I will never Complain, as
I am Dear Sir
Your Faithful
N Rowe

They won't believe Corn is so Cheap Eastward.

Selley was here a Wednesday, the Plaisterers are about the Hall, & the two Joiners putting up the Paper &c.

I have paid Nicholas £40. He says the Laying the Hall with new Salmon Bricks will be Cheapest, it will Take about 3000, Else you must buy new Hard ones for your Garden House &c.

F370

Nutwell, 16 December 1757

Dear Sir

I have your obliging Favour of 6th; the first of my Wishes is your Welfare, if you have one agreable, I wish you a Million, I only meant your absence was Disagreable, I am sensible I am not to hope for much of your Company, I have had more than I cou'd have Expected; I am very much oblig'd for your kind offer, But I have nothing I can Trouble you with, I am sorry my Soliloquys should Start out, my Spirits were Low, and your absence occasion'd the Melancholy; But I beg it may give you no Trouble.

As to Betty Dyer I am Sorry she continues in her obstinacy, She was very inquisitive to know your Determinacion about Her; I Told Her as you hinted, That you wou'd rectify the Mistake about 10s. and the 15s. if it appear'd so, But she reply'd if I had not, That she desir'd I wou'd repeat to you, That she desir'd to Leave your service, when her year was up. I Think she do's not duely Consider her Interest: But She Seems Determin'd. You don't mention the 10s. in the paper you Left with me, & state the Board Wages £7 1s. 0d., & it is 7.16.0, with the Two weeks to Joyce – In Short She's a Silly Wench, Considering how she's involv'd with her Dr and her Newfoundland Adventure, which is Come to Nothing, & a call notwithstanding.

Stephen Philips is return'd and Desires to know what imployment you have for Him & his Boy, as you Said you wou'd Employ Him when he came Back, & being out of Work, I have put Him upon making the Gutter at the End of the Garden, 'till your pleasure is known, what you wou'd have Him Do. His Brother & 2 or 3 more are come with Him: which I presume you may have if you please; he Says he is not involv'd as is given out, & is gone to Tavistock; He has brought you Several Sponce ['spoons'].

Sol will Endeavour to get in the Trees before Christmas, he went yesterday about Those from Exeter; Falkner will undertake the Hedge, But he will Trye a Day with Him by way of Computing the Value – he & John Coleman shall go on to do what They can, & after Christmas you shall be inform'd what is Absolutely necessary – John Coleman has been but 1 Day this Week, & Sol has been making the guttering next the Horse pond, & Faggotting to make room for Nicholas, who has got in Lyme for the Wall, & 10 Hogsheads for you at Last.

I am sorry the Captain has any remora ['hindrance']* to impede Him, & has a son too: a ship is fit for a Family.

Enclosed is Captain Scott's Sketch, which He Took from the Place, and your Directions.

The Ship Timber is brought into the Meadows, & will be only us'd for the purpose you intend it.

I am very Thankful about the *Chronicle*, But I see the Exeter Paper now & Then, which answers my Curiosity –

As to your kind offer of Shoes, my Feet are So Swell'd, That I have no-one will Fit me, nor I fear shall in haste, so with my Thanks I can't Trouble you.

I fear'd we shoud have had a Flood, so I got Sol to raise the gutter next the Horse pond, which He has done effectually now I hope, & will Do that in the Meadows with the plank as Soon as possible.

I am not a Little Confus'd, I am Sensible, so that I fear I am not so Explicit as I shou'd about Betty Dyer – She wanted much to know what you had wrote about Her; my acting as you directed, by not being particular, made Her say she believ'd you had; But if you had not She desir'd I wou'd repeat to you her Request, That she desir'd she might be Discharg'd when her year was up, But if her Staying a Month Longer might be of any Service, She was very Willing, and profes't a great Deal of respect.

It is very Fine Weather & has been so for Some Days, There are but 4 Lambs yet. Tho' 3 of the Cows were sold at Exeter Fayr, 2 of 'Em were brought Back, & are to remain 'till Christmas, Sol & John Coleman Spent the whole Day Driving 'Em in & Bringing 'Em back.

Your Puppy grows much & knows the name of Ponto.

I am with Respect, Dear Sir
Your very Faithful
N Rowe

Stephen** when he returns next week, Sol thinks it best to help him in Clearing the gutter & Fixing the plank in the Meadow; you'l send your Directions What Farther you'd have him Do.

* Again, the 'remora' is the mother of William Drake's sons.
** Stephen Philips, the tinner.

F371

Nutwell, 3 January 1758

Dear Sir

My Letter was gone to Exeter, Before I received yours, which was the Occasion of my Troubling you with Two by the same post: By the Enclosed account you Saw I cou'd not pay Betty Dyer the year's Wages, which you was Sensible of, when you gave me the Money (Tho' you forgot it) when I ask't you if I shou'd pay her any in part, and you Said no, But That you wou'd Order money for it, & Some you was to pay at Exeter: I can say nothing for her Behaviour, only imagine, what She is to pay to her Dr & her Newfoundland project Embarrasses Her beyond what she Expected.

Stephen is gone to the late Mr Sydenham's to trye a Lead Mine for Mr Brice, & Mr Rowe the Iron-monger, who are not yet weary of their projects! I kept an account of the Days he was about the Gutters, & he made but barely wages.

The Men have very near pull'd Down the Hedge between the Meadows, which according to their reckoning will Come to near £3, which Sol shall measure when Done, & then They will Expect to have their money. Where must the Trees be remov'd?

Sol is planting in the green, finds much Difficulty in getting plants, don't know how to get Black Poplars, as he's unacquainted with Budley, or any There. Will go next Week to Mamhead about white Elder.

The Frost is going off with a Moderate drye Thaw, People are very Busy finishing the wheat Tillage after Turnips, it has been very Dull weather for several Days with an E. Wind which is now chang'd to N. & promises Better.

I hope you are well, I wish you so & am
Dear Sir
Your Faithful
N Rowe

But 18 Lambs yet.

Seaward says the But Ends will serve for naves.

F372

Nutwell, 27 January 1758

Dear Sir

I have your Favour of 17th, am very Glad you are so much mended; I rub on tho' Lamely: this Cold weather Trys me.

Mr Brice says 'twill be Cheaper for you to Build up the Barn with Brick, as Boards are so risen in their price; and was it his he wou'd Do it: They are putting fresh props by his advice at the hither End, as the old Ones are Decay'd, so hope 'twill Stand 'till you See it & Order as you See proper: the roof was Secur'd some Time before: or it wou'd have Fallen.

Seely will Send you the Size of the glass &c. His Brother went last Monday to Mamhead, But did the passage: Neither Mason, Plaisterer, or Stone cutter can Work now.

Sol is recover'd to Work again, But not quite Sound.

The remains of the Hay-rick at Exon fell down, so They were oblig'd to fetch it home.

Sol is planting 2 Trees as you Directed, from the Meadow hedge: the Men are forward in pulling it down.

All that you planted in the Meadow grow, and Look Green.

Sol has got home the plank, which he Says will Finish <u>all</u>.

Stephen in the Guttering did but Just get his Wages, Himself, Boy, & a Man to help: I have Let Him have Some money in part; he is Still at Limpston out of Work, I imagine waiting to know if you will Employ Him.

I am Sorry your Mother & Sister are so out of Order, I cou'd wish They were reconsiled, as we are in so uncertain a State. Your Brother Surprizes me! See the Difference, Some flye; & Some Follow Fortune & can't overtake Her   I wish he may be able to be his own Carver. I am oblig'd for your kind Care; I heartily wish you Health & Happiness.

I am Dear Sir
Your Faithful
N Rowe

But 13 Lambs yet.

We have had Frost for several Days, the Cold affects me more than I remember, I hope you guard against it: it now Seems to Thaw a Little.

F373

Nutwell, 10 February 1758

Dear Sir

I have your Favour of 31st past, I am very much oblig'd for your kind regard; the weather is alter'd, & I hope in Time I shall, But at present I don't expect it.

I am very Sorry for the Captain's refusal! Surely your Mama won't always Continue so! I hope not. God has given you, my Dear Sir Francis, a wise heart, and will no Doubt direct it right, which is beyond all Humane aid, to that I humbly recommend it.

As to the Barn, when you come to See it you will Consider of the best Way. Brick seems the Strongest.

Sol will prepare the ground for the Pines as you direct, and Sowe the Seeds; what must be done with the Weakest that come up?

The Hall is not Damp as I can perceive, But that part next the passage, is Longest Drying.

Sol is recover'd, no Sign of any remaining Hurt. Much Time is Taken Looking for plants to put in the Green, which is now fill'd out near.

Richard Blanchard came here Wednesday Last at night, under a frivolous pretence to ask your Favour about the annuity your Grandfather Left Him; He has been Sick, or pretends to be so, Ever Since; I fear he is under Some Difficulty; what to do with Him I know not, can't well Turn Him out as He is, Tho' he don't Deserve any Favour from the Family, having been a very Indifferent Hind.

I hope you are Well, pray God keep you so.

You have now 15 Lambs.

I am Dear Sir

Your Faithful

N Rowe

Some rain & wind, But Fine weather for the Season – Paid Langman 27 Shillings for Bringing the Hurdle Stuff &c. Blanchard go's away a Sunday, Fears to go before.

F374

Nutwell, 24 March 1758

Dear Sir

I have your Favour of 14th; the garden Door you propose won't be 4 ft wide, so you can't get the Trees thro', nor anything but a wheel-Barrow. The Wall being Left open for the Rubbish is a Hinderance to your work, which must Stop too for want of more Bricks – 4, or 5000. The Walks must be Lay'd out and Dug to receive the Rubbish, & those Trees which are in the way remov'd.

There were but 4 Bundles of grafts

    1. White Styre
    1. Red "
    1. Fox whelp
    1. Red Strake

All grows in the Meadow, but the Trefoils.

On Teusday night Last there was a violent Storm at E., rain & much Snow – 5 of your Trees in the Meadow are blown down where the Hedge was, 2 of the great Elms by the necessary House are mov'd, Shou'd they not be pav'd up to favour Them least they Fall & demolish your new Wall – it was the greatest Flood has been yet, it did not break into Either Meadow, but cover'd your Border in the Farmer's Court; and the Water broke thro' the Wall from the Orchard into the pound House & Stable to Some Feet high – that the Farmer can put nothing in Either, which in Time will bring down the Buildings – a Cover'd gutter, they say, wou'd prevent it; if you will find Labour, the Farmer will bring Stones – He hopes you will order the Chesnut Close to be gutter'd, it is now so wet he has no Benefit of it.

The N. Side of the Chapel is rip't in several places by the Storm.

I am in great pain for poor Mrs Eliot, pray God she may Do well – we have

Melancholy Weather indeed! Snow on Hal-down like Christmas, the Most Wet with an East wind I ever knew.

Pray God keep you in Health, mine is as uncertain as the Weather, But in all Conditions

I am Dear Sir

Your Faithful

N Rowe

Today a Frost in the Morning, the rest Fair & moderately Warm. N.W. So with the Change of the Moon may the Weather alter for the Better.

F375

Nutwell, 27 March 1758

Sir

I am Sorry to find by your Letter of 21st That you have not mention'd any Time of your Coming into the Countrey; as your presence in Devonshire on or about the 20th of next Month is of Absolute necessity for your affairs.

I hope Mr Creed will Expedite the Deeds, was you on the Spot, He cou'd make no pretence for Delay.

Nicholas has got up 3 ft of the Brick-work so what you propose is too Late, But there is good Highth of Stone work at the Bottome, almost as much as in the opposite wall: I wrote you about 5000 Bricks will be wanted to Complete it, So They Stop from today, 'till you order where to have Them – They are got as far as the gap, which is left open for the Rubbish, what the Detriment is, they can't Bind the work to the End: He says the Door you propose will be too heavy for the <u>Wall</u>; and Sol says too narrow to get the Trees out.

Sol says the Best way is to bring in the Rubbish by 3 Horses, which are as many as a Boy & Man can Load & Drive, and that Day work is the Best, a Horse will carry 30 Seam a Day, which will soon Clear it, and he must Lay it as they Bring it in, about ½ pence per Seam.

The Weather is now good, I hope you'l Find the good Effect of it in your intended Tour; your Health I heartily wish, your presence is vastly Desireable to me, But I can't Expect it, & wish you Every agreable Entertainment.

The *Union* is not arriv'd, neither will they break Bulk Till They have Enter'd at Topsham (as They Tell me).

The Mezerions ['species of Daphne'] have been Blown this 14 night:

I wish you Everything as you Desire.

I am Dear Sir

Your Faithful

N Rowe

I wish it well over with Mrs Eliot & her Children.

Betty Dyer is about again & much Better.

Stephen Philips is at Dulverton on the late Mr Sydenham's Estate, on a Mine project.

F376

29 March

I hope the Sprys won't come 'till the Weather is Settl'd.

Nicholas Says the new Building Heling ['roofing'] may be mended to last many years: But the N. Side of the Chapel must be new Done, it is much Tore by the late Storm.

Channon came here Sunday night, he has agreed with Spry for 6s. a Square, and They will Come next Week, if the Weather is Settl'd then.

Wou'd you have the Chapel done first, and with the Stones which came from the Gate-house; the Laths from Mr Brice, & the nails from Limpston as usual; the new Buildings to be Look'd into after.

Channon will write you Himself of your Farm-Transactions. Channon proposes (as you have so much Hay) to Eat Both Meadows this year – and as Sol has fenc'd out your Plantations in the E. Meadow with the Hurdles, the rest must be made to part the two Meadows for a Change for the Stuff, as the Spring advances.

He has Sold all your Stock and Bought in 3 more Cows.

30 March

I did not Send the Letter as first Dated, Becaus I wou'd not give you any Trouble in your Tour.

The Plaisterers came here Teusday last to finish the passage (4 Men) but becaus it was not drye were oblig'd to go back again, without doing anything, & I Believe it won't be fit this 14 night.

You will order about Bricks, you may have Them of Parson Lee. The Weather is now Fair.

F377 [Marginal note, cut off left-hand edge of a note or letter]*

[April 1758]

Here is a report your Mother is very Ill, pray how is She:

* See Introduction, section 1, p.5.

F378

Nutwell, 14 April 1758

Dear Sir

The surprize Thomas Wyatt's Letter put me into having heard nothing of his Uncle's Ilness, must be an apology for my Last. I believe he's Dead by this Time; poor Man, it was his Last Request to me, That I wou'd give you the Certificate I sent you: which you are to do as you think proper with.

Mrs Elliot runs much in my Mind, I shall be very glad to hear she has got well over, a young Woman dreads Disfigurement almost as much as Death.*

As Parson Lee is all for Selling, you have only to buy Bricks, or wait for your Own, you will determine about the Door when you come down.

Sol went yesterday Morning with the Mare; She is very gentle, & he will Take great Care of Her; at his Return He will get the Orchard Plow'd, and prepare the Walks for the Rubbish: the Trefoil Seed is Dead.

John Coleman is gone today to Moreton for Sprye, will Consult with Him what is best to be Done.

All your Wall-Trees are full of Blossome, and the old Apricot Trees had some too.

The Herefordshire grafs are put on the 3 great Trees in the Orchard, as he says you directed; had He not, They were too big for the Trees you mention.

Have Desir'd Mr Brice to enquire about the price about Salt-Water.

The passage Floor is Lay'd, were the Walls drye (which they are not yet) the whole might be Finish't, But a Lock is wanted for the Door.

No News of Compton yet.

Since the rain a Monday spring Weather but Windy S.E.

I hope this will find you well.

I am Dear Sir

Your Faithful

N Rowe

* The Eliott family household was afflicted by smallpox. See also the following letter; and Introduction, section 5, p. 57.

F379

Nutwell, 21 April 1758

Dear Sir

I have your Favours, am Extremely Glad Mrs Elliot is out of Danger, having been under great Concern about Her: I am vastly surpriz'd at the Disregard you mention, when Death is Daily at the Door, 'tis shocking indeed! the poor Maid's Death, I hope was Kept from your sister; your Kindness is very indearing, God will bless you for it: pray my respects to Her.

The Dampness of the Passage is owing to the Thickness of the Walls & the Wet Weather, the Nitch ['niche'] is as Drye as the rest, and it is Lin'd with Bricks; I don't Think 'twill be fit for the stucco, 'till Midsummer: the porch Cieling [*sic*] shall be new Done, you'l Think it proper.

Considering how Friendly you have been to Parson Lee, I thought he wou'd have been more Complaisant, But he's a low Chap.

The Things by Compton are all brought here but the Hamper, which cou'd not be Come at, when I sent the Farmer to Topsham for 'Em, But hope to have it this Week; the Trees in 4 great Baskets cou'd not be Brought in a Boat, & as Sol was not here, wou'd not Trust Them so; he has put them in the pots as they are into the ground, wou'd know if you'd have Them taken out, He's in doubt for the pynes, as the Taproots are cut off. Everything came well.

There is a great ope in the Meadow Hedge now the Trees are Down, there are but 3 standing.

Poor Mr Wyat dy'd last Friday, Thomas is sick, so you may have no Trouble about Him – I wonder at Mr Wills!

Nicholas will Enquire about Bricks, But fears there's a scarcity of 'Em in the Nighbourhood.

The Orchard shall be plow'd as Soon as possible, We have had Terrible Weather, Snow a Saturday, hard Frost a Sunday, & rain almost Ever Since and wind, very Cold. The Blossome has been Touch'd, yet you have much.

Sprye will begin to Cover the Chapel, as soon as the Weather permits – he has got Everything ready.

The House Door will be up this Week, But the lock is wanting.

I hope you are well, pray God Keep you so: this weather has Try'd me.

I am Dear Sir

Your Faithful

N Rowe

Sol got the Mare well to Dorchester, Hope the Man got Her so to Will.

Mr Edgcombe came here a Monday noon & went away Teusday afternoon for Yarcombe. Since I wrote my Letter, the Plaisterers came here and will Stucco what is Drye of the Passage, & will finish the rest with the Porch.

F380

Nutwell, 21 July 1758

Dear Sir

I have your Favour of 11th; am glad you got so well up with so much Expedition & so Little Fategue – a Courier's Dispatch!

Here was a storm in the night between 14th & 15th, hard rain & wind at N.W., had it been more W. wou'd have Done more hurt: as it was, it blew Down One more of the Trees in the Meadow, Disorder'd Several of the Espaliers, & made a havock among your Flowers in the Border by the gravel Walk – I was in pain for the great Elms, had the wind been more West, it wou'd have Try'd 'Em; the Trees by the Iron Rails far'd better than I Expected. Hard showers Saturday, Sunday & Wednesday.

As to Fawkner Sol says, He with John Coleman will Do, what you Order'd Thomas Philips – as to the Rubbish I fear there'l be none Carryd 'till next week, when if the Weather settles Fair the Meadow must be Cut: They have been 2 Days, Sol, Seaward, John Coleman and Fawkner, Taking Down the Trees for the Turn-pike & han't Finish'd. The Overseer was here today to have'Em Drawn away, Sol Thinks to put 'Em in the Hop-yard against Horrils'.

Nicholas is about the Wall, has brought 3850 Bricks from the Kiln, They are the Refuse from the Eys, but they Look well enough in work. He proposes to burn over again a Small Ey of the soft ones, for which he will rely on your generosity; in my next you will have an account of the number of hard ones.

I am very Sorry Alexander is such an ungrateful Fellow,* But servants are all so; his Relation here wou'd be I fear the same, had he any Pretence –

Betty Dyer is as She was, has Taken Phisick again, wants your Leave to go down to See Her Relations once more, will be wanting but a week.

I hope Buxton will made [*sic*] an agreable alteration in your Mama; my Compliments to your sister Eliot, I hope you are Both Well.

I am Dear Sir

Your Faithful

N Rowe

The Box with the Frame of the Flead ['pigskin membrane'] was Sent Wednesday.

Hard Wind at E., like to rain.

---

* Alexander's ingratitude was already noted in F330. His 'Relation here' is his father, Sol.

F381

Plymouth, 17 December 1758

Dear Sir

I hope you got up Safe & Well, and That This will Find you so.

I reach't Tavistock Teusday a.noon with a Flead Posteriors,* and am Still in a miserable Condition (Tho' under the Care not <u>Cure</u> of two Honest Chirurgeons,** One from Oakhampton & One here) – another such Excursion Demolishes your humble Servant.

Upon Channon's information (who I met at Tavistock) I went with him Teusday Evening to Buckland, where I Found your Brother Samuel, his Lady & Sister, of whom if Ever we Meet again, I have an Eclat. I came away Thursday Evening with the Ladys & Lay on Board the *Faulkland*, came here Friday Evening, But God knows when I shall be able to go away, Being unable to Set or Lye but in great pain: as Soon as I am, propose to return to Buckland, where I shall be glad to receive your Commands.

Your Brother is not Sail'd having receiv'd Some Damage from the *Warspight*, who carry'd away his Bowspright &c; he hopes to Sail tomorrow if the wind permits: as he Told me, when on Board, For I have not seen or heard from Him Since.

Mr & Mrs Porter present Their best Compliments. He is as well as I ever knew Him.

I am with the Truest Respect Dear Sir
Your Faithful
N Rowe

* Backside worn to a thin membrane ('flead' as in previous letter).
** See Introduction, section 5, p. 65.

F382

Tavistock, 6 January 1758/1759

Dear Sir

Though I have Not had the pleasure immediately from yourself, yet I am glad to hear by Mr Carpenter That you are well, may you long Continue so, I have been Oblig'd to Take of Him Five Guineas, I hope never to have the like Occasion. I am in a Queer Way, yet hope Soon to be able to go to Buckland. – The Odd Behaviour to the Man & Woman was Such, That if They are Treated so again, He'l Quit the Service.*

I have Seen Mr Burnaford, who sends you his best Compliments, Mr Toll & Mr Windyat do the Same, all very hearty: if a Late dismission shou'd Occasion any Coolness in a certain Family, I know how to fill up the Casm with Such persons, as I am Sure you will approve of.

With the Compliments of the Season
I am Dear Sir
Your Faithful
N Rowe

I have a Design to Trye Mr Tremain by J Herring, who is in Hopes for his Nephew, Knab for Knab ['bite for bite'].

Since my writing This I received your Favour, I am Sorry you are so Fategu'd with your Journey, I am so in more Senses Than One, yet will persevere to the Last in my Zeal for <u>your Service</u>.

[Notes on reverse]**
    to pack up what 4 Counterparts may be useful.
    Respecting Kelly's Land.
    Respecting the River at Yarcombe.
    Sending up Survey Book.

* In Rowe's view, John Channon and his wife were poorly treated by Samuel Drake, and especially by his wife and sister-in-law.
** Rowe had repeatedly needed to look out counterparts on FHD's behalf, and travelled from Nutwell to Buckland for that purpose (see F288, F289, F298, F300, F363). The notes on the reverse of this letter are perhaps in FHD's hand.

F383

January 1759*

Dear Sir

I have your obliging Favour & am very Thankful for the kind regard you Show for me, am very Sorry my Soliloquy gave you any uneasiness, I beg it may not – But my reflecting on past and present Things, and what very probably may Succeed, it flung me into a reverie that Shock't me very much – I have had an uncomon Flow of Spirits, they have Flagg'd greatly of Late, and when they do at my Time of Life, They sink precipitately. That has been and is at present my Case – it is no Small Concern to me that it broke out, I will Endeavour to conceal it for the Future – in my present Circumstances I am not able to go to Plymouth – nor anywhere Else – Tho' I am much oblig'd for your kind proposal. 'Tis not that this place is more Disagreable than it has been, But its Decay happen'd, Just Then to Strike me more Feelingly – I wish that and Several other Things were in my power, it wou'd greatly add to my Future Felicity: But That I Trust is reserv'd for One more proper – my being here is of Some Service; Tho' the House is Drye outwardly, it is very Damp inwardly, & I cou'd Scarse open your new Chest of Drawers, which Fires have alter'd.

John Carpenter has Occasion to come here on your affairs, the provision the Hine makes for Him, you will in a proper Time take notice of, as There is nothing here – For my part I only Share with your Mother's Servants (Fire Excepted & That only at nights); the weather is various, Sometimes fair & Frosty, & frequently wet, Tho' uncommonly mild, But the Effects don't affect me, they Lye Deeper.

Inclosed I send you Copys of what your Mama's Steward Sent me from Mr Carpenter – Kill Meadow was about an acre of ground, opposite that part of Causeys Meadow, where the principal Bents were put on Beer-Side, and yet it's almost wash't away; it fell into the Lord's hand 25 years ago at Least – Gnattam Mills have been down ever Since I was in this Countrey, probably your Grandfather let 'Em go to Decay on his purchasing new Mills; the Lease Expir'd on your Father's Death, who was the last Life: the Time is so long Elaps't, They can't oblige to rebuild, it Seems odd They never made any Demand so Long – As to the Chief rents, I never Saw any account that they were ever paid, nor know anything about it – if any Further application is made you may respite it, 'till you come into the Countrey, & in the mean Time give your Mama one of the Copys, if she han't one from Her Steward already; I shall write him to the Same Effect.

Mr Heywood, it's Said, is Expected Down in the Spring with his Family, his Conduct has been too freely Censur'd.

I hope this will find you as well as I wish you, may you long Continue so, Shou'd be glad to hear your Sister Elliot received Benefit from the Bath.

I am as always Dear Sir
Your Faithful
N Rowe

I wish your Brother Samuel a good voyage – his Mate affects an artful woman, her sister is a Bollolla ['shrew'?] – I hope your Brother William is Established in the *Edgar*. I heartily wish you all well.

* Dated on the reverse, perhaps in FHD's hand.

F384

Nutwell, 23 March 1759

Dear Sir

Your Favour by Sunday's post gave me great pleasure as I had none by Friday, Every Interruption adds a Damp to my Lowness; I am very much oblig'd for your kind Regard, But beg it may give you no Trouble, That gives an addition to what I am Forc't to bear besides – I return you many Thanks for your kind offer, But I can't Trouble you for any Thing now.

The grafts shall be manag'd as you direct, when they come, as also the Tuberoses.

Selley & Eliot were here a Sunday, will write you about painting.

Mr Lee for more reasons than One wou'd very readily Let you have Phillis, if you ask't it of Him, to assist about your Dinners, for which Joyce wou'd prepare Everything, so she need not be Here but from 10 to 4.

I am very Glad for Colonel Eliot's promotion,* may Everything that's good attend Him & your Sister. Mr G Porter I'm sure heartily joins, I hope it's worth more than £1000 per annum.

I am very glad your Brother Samuel was then well, & That He do's show the Respect to you He ought: I hope the other do's the Same.

The Cedar Drawers are come, but the Windows are at Topsham still, I had no Notion about 'Em 'till your Letter brought it to my remembrance, That you Talk'd about sending for 'Em before you went away: I have made Enquiry about it – The Farmer Says he brought word about it and offer'd to Bring them from Topsham, But That you Told Him Mr Brice wou'd, who call'd for 'Em, But they wou'd not Deliver 'Em without payment – of the Freight & Cellaredge formerly & now Due, the Farmer wou'd have paid it, But had no Orders – I have Sent to know how the Matter is. Wou'd you have Mr Brice & Farmer fetch 'Em.

I always Thought your Stewards very Indolent, your Looking into your Estates yourself, will I hope make your present One more Diligent; as he is under so great obligations, your own Ey will give a Life to Matters.

Sol don't want any seeds but the green Savoy Cabbage which I wrote to you for; they are now about the orchard Hedge, He Thinks when they fann up those Elms by the Necessary House, if you wou'd have some of the Top Limbs Taken off, it wou'd Ease the Trees much in windy Weather.

Joyce shall Clean the House in the Manner you direct, but I Think the Library shou'd not be wash'd; it is so Damp tho' I have had, & there were in my absence frequent Fires, yet I have been oblig'd to take down all the Books & wipe 'Em, or they wou'd have been <u>Moldy</u>.

The removal of the pidgeon House gives great Light to the places you mention, & the Chapel Window shows itself to great advantage.

You'l See by the Enclos'd the Storm extended itself; Sol brought 3 insted of 2 <u>Cows</u>.

Poor Mrs S– is Left with 4 Children, I fear very Bad – a short Taste of Grandeur! I hope you are well, pray God keep you so.
I am as always Dear Sir
Your Faithful
N Rowe

The Tinners not here this week, nor Stephen since I came.**
No account of the Malt, or Grafts yet.

* Eliott was promoted major-general at this time.
** The tinner Stephen Philips was sometimes assisted by his brother and others. See, for instance, F396, F397.

F385

Nutwell, 29 June 1759

Dear Sir

I am very Glad you got up so well, & that your Sister Eliot is so.

Your kind regard I have a due Sense of, But I can't Trouble you any more, I have run the Rig, & the Wheel has overturn'd!

I have acquainted the Farmer about Mr Hall, he will Supply the Men as you direct: and as to the Wheelbarrows, you will Fix it with Stephen; without Such the Men can't remove the Stones.

By the advise of Mr Brice a sawpit by the old Oak, at the Water Side, which was formerly Us'd, has been righted, & the Men began about Sawing the Plank Wednesday –

Seaward has fix't the rails in the Meadow as far as the Water where you intend a Nursery, & next Week will finish the other Side; he has Taken up the Stuff very well – Sol Says he can't Find anyone to hand beat the ground by the Jet.

I fear Betty Dyer will rue her Changing.

I wish Malvern may Mend your Mother, & that Whiteford may alter Miss Archer, Both for the Better.

The Masons go on with the Stable, & Harry moves away the Stones, But not so much, as to give you any Particular account; in my next hope I shall – will keep such an account as you mention.

The Bullocks are chang'd, & the garden Secur'd as Far as the Hurdles will go –

Sol & the Woman have been all this week Digging & putting Things in the new garden. Something continues to pull off the Strawberrys, as They ripen, Sol thinks 'tis the Water-Rats; whatever it is, Spoils the Fruit.

The Ale shall be Bottled, I am oblig'd for your kind offer But it shall be kept for you.

My Dear Sir Francis, I wish you Every Happiness, my head is Turnd & my heart is – the Little Time I shall Continue I will always prove myself

Dear Sir
Your Faithful
N Rowe

The heat has been very Violent here for several Days, But Wednesday it rain'd Most of the Day, yesterday very Fair.

The Door Case of the Stable now it is Taken down, Mr Brice Thinks it won't do again, it being an old Lin'd Thing, & too heavy for your Slight Brick work – So I have wrote to Selley to Come & Look to it directly, as the Masons will Stand Still.

Sir William Courtnay came home Wednesday Evening.*

Sir Richard Bampfield had out his Regiment on Teusday, gave the Officers notice they were to March next Week.

All the Officers of the French Prisoners are Sent up the Countrey.

Commander Rogers is order'd to Correspond with the Admiralty Every Day by Express – He has Sent one to Mr Brice to hire his Ship for a Privateer, & orders are Sent, he hears, to all the Ports to the same Purpose – so the alarm is great in the Countrey. Pray God Defend us!

* Sir William Courtenay came home to Powderham, across the River Exe.

F386

Nutwell, 10 August 1759

Dear Sir

I Thought Nothing cou'd have made me Lower – but your Letter has quite Sunk me, & Render'd me unfit for anything – I don't know what to Think & Write – as I can be no Judge of the Cause of your uneasiness, I can Say Nothing but pray to God to Support you! – Surely nothing can happen to you But what your Age, Character, & every Other Circumstance will under God be a Sufficient and – if God give you health – as you Say your Feaver has Left you, what can you Fear! Was I able I wou'd go or Do anything to give you Ease as your welfare is my Chief happiness. Therefore I beg you will qualify Every Disagreable Thought by a Better Dependance – I can have no Ease nor Satisfaction 'Till I hear from you, That you are more Comforted.

Mr Carpenter has wrote me for the Stancomb Deeds which I have sent Him; I Kept 'Em as Sol did not go, Expecting with more Certainty to know how to dispose of them. I hope you'l have a good issue at Last.

Poor Mr Brice is under such great Trouble for the Loss of his Ships, That I Fear he won't be able to do much – he has received your Letter.

Mr John Pit is come to Sir John Coliton's House at Exmouth, he is but a Captain in the Militia – Sol Carryd him Some Fruit a Sunday, which he was much oblig'd for, & wou'd write you his Thanks – He Sent yesterday for Some more Fruit; as it begins to Drop, it is better than Spoil to Oblige your Friends, as you Don't use 'Em yourself.

I am in such Confusion I can't Trouble you with anything Here, not knowing how to behave – for Godsake Support yourself: in the greatest anxiety

I am Dear Sir
Your Affectionate & Faithful
N Rowe

I Live in hopes of hearing Better from you.
  Extreme Hot, Fine Harvest.

F387

Nutwell, August 1759

Dear Sir

Your Two Letters came both Together a Sunday so I had 48 Hours inexpressible anxiety more than I shou'd, had the first come in Time; I am Extreme Glad you are more Easy; pray God Confirm Everything & restore you to your Health – which I heartily wish.

Mr Brice insur'd; but the loss of the Cargoe (having Caught 2 Fish)* & Everything Else is a very great Disappointment. However he's going on again, having order'd Mr Shepherd, who is got to London, to buy another ship – the people of Both were all Sav'd but Dispers't. He is indeed a Man very useful & Deserves Regard – He bears it wonderfully.

Joyce & her Daughter are poor needlers; if Coarse sheets, will do her Best: your goodness to Her I hope She'l be grateful for.

I am glad your Brother Sam came off so well, I hope he will the Same with the Admiralty, as he Sav'd his Ship: I don't See he cou'd Do more.

Your not writing to Selley about the Beams in answer to his Letter & poor Mr Brice's Loss has occasion'd a Stop to your Building, But I hope it will now go on. Pray Take Care of your health – the Harvest almost Done here, hope so with you – hard showers, Saturday & Sunday, Monday.

I am Dear Sir
Your Faithful
N Rowe

I have had no answer from John Carpenter of the receipt of the Stancomb writings, which I <u>wonder at</u>!

* The 'Fish' Mr Brice has lost are presumably booty from two captured vessels, his ship having been fitted out as a privateer (see F340, F344, F385).

F388

Nutwell, 31 August 1759

Dear Sir

The Several Melancholy Letters I have of late received from you, have given me great Concern, But your Last is very affecting – the Tender Regard you shew for the Valuable person you have Such a Respect for in such a Melancholy Condition is very Commendable and from your Character Justly Deserves it, & the more as Such is very Rare!* I therefore hope for Both your Sakes to hear a more Favourable account from your Care & Means – But my Dear Sir Francis, as such accidents are the Consequences of humane Nature, what we can't prevent, we must Submit to, &

I dare Say your Friend, if Capable, wou'd Desire it of You: to arm against the Worst is the prudent part of Everyone, But who is Sufficient for these Things!

You know the value I have for you, you are Sure Everything with me is with yourself. But you can't Conceive the Trouble I have for you – God will give an end to Everything, and I hope to your present Grief such as I wish you,

Being Dear Sir
Your Faithful
N Rowe

I wrote you by Last, imagining all was well, an improper Letter, which I ask pardon for.

* See Introduction, section I, p. 7, drawing on *Family and Heirs*, vol. 2, pp. 294–295, for the likelihood that 'the Valuable person' is Miss Knight of Plymouth.

F389

4 September 59

Dear Sir

Yours of 29th past quite Confounded me; to hear you are under Such uneasiness, & not to be able to give you any assistance is an inexpressible Trouble – God & your own Prudence I hope will Enable You to Submit to what there is no remedy – I hope the Dr your good Friend as well as Phisitian* will advise as well as prescribe, and what the one can't Effect, I trust the other in some Measure will, at least to bear Everything prudently – I won't pretend to propose – But I cou'd wish your own Inclinations prompted you to Come here – Certainly the properest place at this Juncture – But if you don't Think so, Let me know what you wou'd have me Do, & to my utmost you may Command me – What I Feel for you I can't Express nor Can I say any more But to pray God to give you Proper Sentiments.

I am Dear Sir
Your Faithful
N Rowe

Job was better reconsil'd in the Conclusion, I hope you will too.

* Dr Mark Akenside.

F390

Nutwell, 10 September 59

My Dear Sir Francis

The Letter from your Servant geatly Surpriz'd me, But it pav'd the way to what I fear'd from your own – For God sake Compose yourself as well as you Can – Tho' I must own the Tenderness I have for you, this Our melancholy Correspondence has made such an impression on me That I am like a Batter'd Wall so full of Shot that one Strikes against another – in my Concern for you I have had many Conflicts, But none like this, as I did not know 'till very lately the real Cause, which occasion'd very many Suggestions – now We know the worste!

Lord Bacon Says *dolor decrescit, ubi quo crescat non habet* ['sorrow decreases when it has nothing to make it grow'] – I am too low in Spirits to advise, your own prudence will Tell you where there's no Remedy, we must make Our Submission to Almighty God, who is only able to help us, to whose good pleasure we must all resign; as I trust you do in a manner Sutable to the present Occasion – my Friendship for you is great tho' insignificant, such as it is you have the Command of it, and the only proof I can now give is that I truly Sympathize with you – pray Comfort yourself and Believe me to be with respect

Dear Sir

Your Faithful

N Rowe

I long to See you.

I can't Trouble with anything.

F391

Nutwell, 14 September 1759

My Dear Sir Francis

Your melancholy Letter quite Turns me! For Godsake Endeavour to Support yourself – I am very unfit to advise – But I hope God will Give you ability –

You must not think on me; whilst I Last you know I Love you, But you never can how much: I Trust you'l Find much Better, when I am no more – 'till then you are Sure of my Every Endeavour to Serve you.

The grate is come and a Small Box & Mr Brice has got you Some Coals, which have prov'd a <u>Dear Cost</u>!

Your orders about Beer & the Beds are Comply'd with But the Curtains of your Field Bed are not come yet.

I can't Trouble you with what is Doing here, That you'l See when you come, which I wish you well to Do, being

Dear Sir

Your most Affetionate & Faithful

N Rowe

Mr Collector has Sent the mats & wants your Company to choose the Mayor 17 Instant.

F392

Nutwell, 26 October 1759

Dear Sir

I am glad you got up safe, hope you won't Fategue yourself with such quick Journeys – your great Uneasiness I trust Time will aleviate, & give a Turn to your Spirits: the pain of the Mind is the Worste of Maladys – pray God Send you Relief.

Mr Carpenter & his wife returned here on Saturday Evening & went away Sunday Evening – I Suppose he'l write you about the Slats, That he had agreed for the Carriage & Some were Brought to Maristow.

Channon came here a Teusday Evening & the next Day had away two of the cows, which he Sold at Newton Poppleford Fayr, he had Sol to drive 'Em There.

Tho' the Magnolias were Covered with Matts, as you directed, yet the Frost we had Friday & Saturday has Touch't the Tops of 'Em. Sol has Ever Since you went been Digging Ground & Setting Currance & Goosberries in the new garden –

The Thatcher has near Done, has gone as far as he had reed.

The Joiners han't been here Since the 17th.

The Masons have Taken Down most of the Garden-Wall –

This new Disorder has weaken'd me much. I am under the greatest Concern for you – pray reconsile yourself to what you Can't remedy – I am very Sorry for your Sister Eliot, pray my best wishes to Her – we are born to Trouble *variis modis* ['in various ways'].

I am Dear Sir
Your Faithful
N Rowe

Quebec is a great Eclat!*

* Quebec was captured by the British from the French in September 1759.

F393

1 December 1759

Dear Sir

Your Melancholy Soliloquys deeply affect me – may God give you that relief, which Humane reason is uncapable of.

The weather has been & is uncommonly Mild – no Snow, nor any Frost Since 22nd past, only some rain 2 or 3 Times.

More is pruning the Trees, you will Send your Directions about Him.

Sol is Clearing the Kitchen garden with the Woman; next week hope to get one Side plow'd; you will be particular in your orders about Trench-plowing which is not understood here. The Trees from London are Come & Planted, 3 Barberries.

None of Your Work-men here – I wish you may Like the <u>Thatch</u>, of your new Stable; it Looks Dirty already.

To be Sure if you Think it worth your while to Come down this dull Time of the year I shall be very glad to See you; But I can't promise anything! My Spirits Sinking Daily – I hope you'l have better Resources.

I am Dear Sir
Your Faithful
N Rowe

You will Let your Servant carry the Enclos'd.

As the Mason is going about the Wall in the Chappel Court, you will Send word whether you will have the Double Doors in the garden put There, That he may leave the Space accordingly.

F394

6 December 1759

Dear Sir

Your melancholy Letters give me the greatest Concern, for Godsake Take care of yourself, or you'l Destroy your Health – the only pleasure of my Life is your Welfare, & these Turns determine the whole: I hope your Sister will give Some aleviation, I dare Say she do's what She can – I hope for your own Sake, & Those who are interested in your Welfare, you will Endeavour your part – for mine it is upon its Crisis.

I dont know what I write, Scarse what to Think – the Trifles here are not to interfere when the Main's indifferent.

Channon came here yesterday & with Sol Drove today to Exeter Fayr your 5 Cows; being fat, was in no Doubt of Selling Them.

The Stable as I wrote you is finish'd. The Masons have begun the Wall.

More will have gone thro' with the Trees this Week, he Says the Pear Trees in the Farmer's Court will be Spoil'd unless they are prun'd; I wrote you about 'Em, but having no answer, I Let Him do 'Em, you don't Say what a Day you give Him, & I don't know, So must rely on Him – if you wou'd have Him go to Buckland you will Send Word – his Walking he can't perform.

There was Snow on Haldown this Morning, but gone, a Cold S.E. wind, & last night very Violent – in the Confusion I am in for you I am only Capable of wishing you Better, & praying to God to Send you Relief

as I am Dear Sir
Your Faithful
N Rowe

All the Bullocks are Sold But not Fetch't away 'till next week.
If you resolve to Come down I hope 'twill be by moderate Journeys.

F395

21 December 1759

Dear Sir

I wrote you by Monday's post, That the Frost had put a Stop to plowing & planting – Wednesday Evening it rain'd & the Thaw began.

I have heard nothing of Harry, if he do's not come Soon, 'twill be impossible to do what you order in the Time you propose to be here, neither can the Trees in the old Kitchen garden be remov'd & Both Sides plow'd, as the Frost has hinder'd a Week, neither is the Weather Quite Settl'd – I wrote you they understand the Trench-Plowing.

The Farmer has at last got the rest of the Kitchen grate, all but one of the hold-fasts which can't be found; He has also brought the 3 window-Frames, & the Case of glass which has Layn so long in the Ware-House at Topsham, that They press't to have remov'd.

Channon has wrote me a very melancholy Letter about the hard weather & high East wind to a Storm for Several Days, has lost several Lambs, no grass for his Sheep, Several of the apple Trees in the Home Orchards blown Down, the Corn-Ricks uncover'd, But little or no Damage to the House – They are in great

Concern at Plymouth for Sir Edward Hawke's Fleet, your Both Brothers are with Him, pray God They be all Safe.

No account of your Wine, neither is There any Certainty yet, whether the weather will quite Change the wind blowing hard at S.E. & very Dark Foggy & inclin'd to Rain, or Snow – I hope your Boils are gone, pray God give you Ease & Health.

I am Dear Sir
Your Faithful
N Rowe

My Compliments to your Sister Eliot.

F396

4 January 1760

Dear Sir

Not having received any letter from you Since that of the 20th past I Conclude you have been your Journey.

I hope this will find you well, and That you have wrote to Stephen Philips your Determination of his Coming with the Men – at present They can do nothing – we have had so much rain this week & are like to have more, That the old Kitchen Garden all Mire; the South side was covered with water last Teusday, as was a great Part of the East Meadow, There being a great Rain & Flood upon the Spring Tide – Your man Solomon has been Sick too – Nothing can be Done as to Plowing or Planting – Neither have the Masons been able to do anything about the Walls – They are come to work today, But I fear the Weather will hinder them, it being very Lowering at South East, and likely to rain.

I Long to hear from you, and to know what you wou'd order – There are all the large Trees in the South Side of the old Kitchen Garden to be remov'd, & a Man is not to be got – Sol and the Woman only to do anything.

I have nothing more to Trouble you – only to wish you many happy new years,
Being Dear Sir
Your Faithful
N Rowe

The Compliments of the Season to your Sister Eliot, & all Hers.

F397

9 January 1760

Dear Sir

Your Letter of 31 past I received by Sunday's post with great pleasure – your kind assistance to the Young Lady is very good of you, & of Great Benefit to Her.

I have wrote you several Letters how we have been hinder'd by the Weather, I wrote you the 21st that Stephen came here & that he had agreed with 6 men to come to work as last Monday, But as I hear nothing of Them, I hope your Letter has Stop't 'Em, For they can do Nothing now – Sunday was hard rain most of the Day and a Flood, Monday a hard Frost, & Still continues – So Everything is at a Stop. The N. Side of the old Kitchen garden has been plow'd but once, & the other Side all the large Ever-greens are there Still; this I acquaint you with, That you may know how Things are – Friday Evening a Man came in Harry's room ['place'] who is Clearing the Rubbish of the Wall, & when the weather alters the Masons if you don't Forbid it shall Clean away the Bricks.

I hope you are well, I can Scarse hold the pen for the Cold.

I am Dear Sir

Your Faithful

N Rowe

Both your Brothers are at Plymouth by the _News_.

F398

12 January 1760

Dear Sir

I wrote you last post and Enclos'd a Letter, which Came by the Post. I hope this will find you well in London – I have nothing to Trouble you with, But that the Frost Continues very Hard, and Like to be so; it is Cloudy & looks as if it wou'd be Snow. Sol Says if the Weather was to alter, it wou'd be above a Fourteenth-night before the ground can be all ready, There is so much yet to do: He is at Work again, making up the wood, that Ly's about, He can do nothing Else.

The Man Stephen Philips Sent in Harry's room ['place'] is Clearing away the rubbish of the Wall, of which much appears now to be Standing; when this Jobb is Done, and the Frost Continues, I don't know what he can be Employ'd about, unless helping Sol about Faggotting; There, I shall know from you what must be Done.

I had a Letter from Mr Channon last post That the Two Captains,* & the Ladys had been at Buckland: Mr Porter wrote me with some Concern about you, fearing you was not well, as he had not heard from you so Long; he says the _Edgar_ is order'd out again, But that the _Faulkland_ will be some time Docking. I hope you are well, pray God keep you so – this weather pinches me.

I am Dear Sir

Your Faithful

N Rowe

* FHD's two brothers, captains of the _Edgar_ (William Drake) and the _Falkland_ (Samuel Drake).

F399

16 January 1760

Dear Sir

I am very glad for your own Sake, you did not Come down as you intended, what a Difficulty as well as Expence wou'd it have been to you, to have Mr North & 8, or 10 Labourers Stop't by the Weather, Such Severe Weather! as I have not Felt a long Time – a piercing East Wind, and very hard Frost with Snow for these two Days past.

The Man which Stephen sent, instead of Harry, is a Countrey Labourer can do all sorts of Husbandry work & Seems very handy; he has brought his wife with Him on promise of a Month's Employment at Least; he has wheel'd away most of the Rubbish from the Wall, but it is now so frozen, he is helping Sol to make up the

Wood – shou'd the Frost Continue, Sol & he might make the Meadow hedge next the Road, which is so bad that any Stuff may go in & out, & how to send away the Man I don't know, as you may want him in your planting.

You don't say Say whether, when the weather alters, They must go on with the old Kitchen garden according to your Former Directions, to plow the North side again, and then Trench plow it – Sol says the South Side may be Spitted over and cleans'd of the Weeds; & the Trees left Standing, 'till you remove them for good; For the plowing cuts the roots of the Weeds & burys them, which will increase them to Excess; This I acquaint you with for your Direction.

I hope you will spend some Time with your Sister & Divert each other, I wish you Both Health; the weather has almost Subdu'd me.

I am Dear Sir
Your Faithful
N Rowe

Do's the Marriage make any Kindred? There, you know What is Nearest.*

* This is perhaps a reference to a possible marriage between FHD's brother William and the mother of his two sons, which, however, did not take place; and to the possible kinship, with claims to inheritance, if these two sons were legitimised (see Introduction, section 1, p. 7).

F400

25 January 1760

Dear Sir

I have your Favour of 15 & 22nd; I was under much Concern about your Disorder, but as you Say Nothing of it in your Last, I hope you are well again and hope God will give you health – your Not having begun your Planting was very Lucky. If you Take your Journey Shall not Trouble you with any Letter 'Till I hear Further from you; in the mean Time Everything shall be Forwarded as you Direct. Stephen's Man Shall be Employ'd by Sol, But there is much to do about the Wall yet, as he has been absent, & the Frost Together – the Thaw is Settl'd I believe, But we have had much rain – the Springs never more up & the ground very Wet – Nothing wanting of the grate but a Hold-Fast. The Magnolia is as usual, But not Cover'd now, Sir William Courtnay's & Mr Hall's Gardiners never have Cover'd Theirs.

The Kitchen garden Walls are as Usual, no alteration by the Weather, which has been Severe indeed! There, I have rubb'd Thro', tho' with Difficulty, am oblig'd for your Regard – Know nothing of Mr Brice's Ship.

The inclosed Letter I Take to be from your Brother Sam, three Large Packets besides, which I suppose are of no great Consequence, as he has wrote me nothing about Them, So I shan't send them, unless you order it; Shall be very glad to See you, hope you'l Find your Sister Better.

With my best Wishes to you Both
I am Dear Sir
Your Faithful
N Rowe

F401

8 February 1760

Dear Sir

I am very Glad you Think yourself Somewhat Better, for Godsake be your own Physician and use those Lenitives, you wou'd prescribe to another; your uneasiness is my greatest Trouble.

We have had the most uncertain Weather – Last Sunday & Monday hard Frost, Teusday night hard rain, Wednesday a Flood, yesterday & today hard Frost again; it Thaws in the afternoon, But the ground is so Slabby, that it's bad Turning – the N. Side has not been fit to Plow again; and the S. Side not half Dug over, & I don't See how it can be Done over this 14 night if the Weather Should prove good with only Sol; the man has been sick, but don't understand such sort of Work.

The Farmer is very Thankful for your Receipt; none of his Horses, nor yours, nor any as he hears in the Countrey have the Disorder you mention: am Sorry for yours.

Pray my kind respects to your Sister, I hope you'l Both receive Benefit where you are & Contribute to Each Satisfaction – the Major General's people Beat up for drumrolls [?] at Exeter.*

My Dear Sir Francis, pray be kind to yourself, the Greatest Favour you can Show your Friends.

I am
Your Faithful
N Rowe

Sir William Courtnay left the Countrey 6th.

* This reading is an interpretation of an abbreviation (the major-general being FHD's brother-in-law, George Augustus Eliott). See F264 for the possibility of recruiting volunteers 'without beat of drum'.

F402

11 February 1760

Dear Sir

I have your Favour from Bath, I hope your Sister's Company & your own Endeavours will Divert if you can, aleviate your Disagreable –

Mr Thomas Wyatt has wrote me That Mr Andrews their Mast-Maker is very near Death and begs your Favour That He may Succeed Him if you Think proper to apply for Him – I have wrote him That I wou'd acquaint you with it, which you may Think of as you please.

You don't Say where you wou'd have the Elms &c removed to; the best place Sol says is on the South Side where he has Clean'd the ground in the old Kitchen garden, they will be near to be remov'd; the rest Shall be put into the New garden as you direct.

I am in great Distress about you, For Godsake my Dear Sir Francis don't indulge This – My Compliments to your Sister, pray God keep you Both.

I am Dear Sir
Your Faithful
N Rowe

Parson Lee has been at Limpston Since Christmas.

F403

20 February 60

Dear Sir

Like Job's messengers I send you nothing but Melancholy Tydeings – Monday night and this morning we had a violent Storm of wind at South & much rain, & it happening on the Spring a very high Tide it overflow'd the green, and ponded back the Water into the Cellar – But God be Thanked no Further Damage to your House.

There was a Ship cast away a Monday night at the Bar – & all the people Lost, much of the wreck is wash'd up by the Tide under Sowden – Farmer Watts has been here & Says it belongs to you, as yours is a Different Estate from the Rest of the Parish – But I know nothing of any such peculiar Right – Mr Hill has Seiz'd the Stuff, being mostly Timber; Mr Put as Lord of the Manour of Limpston – if you have any Pretence to Such Right; you will write about it.*

The two Trees by the Stable were taken down a Monday, it is as well they were, or they might have come down, the ground is so Loose & Wet; I am in fear for Some more of Them, shou'd they Fall, wou'd Demolish the Wall, which the frequent Floods wet & Weaken – those high Ones by the Necessary House Seem Doubtful.

The Weather is so Various, Everything so Wet, That it is Difficult what to do – I hope you & your Sister are well; Pray God keep you so.

I am Dear Sir
Your Faithful
N Rowe

Rain & wind all yesterday.
    Fair this morning, God knows how Long.
    Much Damage is fear'd at Plymouth.

* FHD's entitlement, and historic rights in the manor of Sowdon, are recurrent topics in the following letters.

F404   [a note rather than a letter]

Sowden were 3 Copyhold Tenements which by a Court Roll appear to have done Suit & Service to the Manor Court of Nutwell –

By your Title Deeds the Manor of Nutwell in Woodberry and Elsewhere is granted to Lord Chief Justice Pollexfen & his Heirs.

I have told Mr Hill who acts for Mr Put to let Mr Put know, That you will Satisfy Mr Put of your Title to Sowdon as part of your Manor of Nutwell & that you expect Salvage for what was cast on your said Manor and will acquaint Farmer Watts the Same – & to Demand Salvage.

Your holding your Manor Court now becomes more Necessary.

Farmer Watts has been here & I have Told Him to demand Salvage, and to Take care of your Right, which you will Empower Him to Do.

Farmer Watts's Horse was Seiz'd by Mr Put out of your precincts.

F405

29 February 60

Dear Sir

I have your Favour of 25. I hope you will Stay Some Time where you are, and That you will find the Benefit I wish, a resignation to irresistable Determinations: I am very unfit to advise, your own Judgment must Tell you so.

I can't Think But Lord Chief Justice Pollexfen (so good a Lawyer), had such a reservacion been in his purchase, wou'd have Left his opinion upon it for the Benefit of his posterity – when Farmer Watts's Boy was kill'd by the Fall from a Horse, Mr Put Seiz'd the Horse, and it seems very odd a Single Tenement shou'd have a peculiar Jurisdiction as a Manor – in the dispute with Sir William Courtenay & Mr Rolls, Mr Put show'd his right to the Manor of Limpston – however I will Look if I can Find anything in your Favour – as the wreck was only a Few Sticks from a Store Boat cast away, which is own'd, & only Salvage, I wou'd not stir in it without a Sure Foundation.

I Think when a Spring Tide & a Freshet meet, There can be no preventing the water ponding Back.

There is nothing further of Damage than what I wrote you – it is now Fine weather & not so windy, But Wednesday was a very cold Day.

They are now removing the Elms into the Pear garden, which is very Tedious as so much Earth is Taken up with the roots – what wou'd you have done with the Cassia Thorns, and the Weeping Willows, are they worth removing?

My Dear Sir Francis, I am sorry you Think of so poor a Consideracion as your humble Servant Just on the Verge of – Philosophy is the best Phisick – I Trust God will give you true Consolation.

I am Dear Sir
Your Faithful
N Rowe

My Compliments to Mrs Eliot. I hope she is well, & will Contribute her <u>Kind Endeavours</u>.

You See how absent I am grown, That I could not Recollect This, before I had wrote the Letter. There, we can't help Defects of nature.

F406

5 March 60

Dear Sir

You See by my last how Absent I am Grown, That I cou'd not Better inform you about Sowdon – But when you hold a Court, your Rights will be reviv'd.*

They are removing the Trees – Sol Says if he don't begin to remove the Ever-greens the middle of this month, with the help of the Man and Woman <u>Only</u>, he Shan't be able to get all Done by April.

Mr Channon has wrote me, That he Shall buy Some Bullocks for you tomorrow at a Fayr at Ashburton, and for Sol to come on Friday morning to Fetch 'Em from Exeter.

Here was Frost a Saturday, Since very moderate Weather.

The Masons are mending the Heling ['roofing'], They have Done the Wall – the

Damage done by the wind here has been very Favourable, at Exeter much among the Houses –

The French visit in Ireland was want of Provisions it's Said – I hope they will be met with.

You & your Sister I hope are well, with my Compliments

I am Dear Sir

Your Faithful

N Rowe

* FHD may indeed have held a manorial court at Nutwell, on this and on other occasions not recorded in Rowe's letters since FHD's presence obviated the need for letter-writing.

F407

12 March 60

Dear Sir

Having had no Letter from you, Since That of 25th past, makes me imagine you have Left Bath – I hope you are well, where-ever you are: However, I will venture This as usual.

They have remov'd all the Trees from before the House, which Cast their Leaf, and wait to know if they may remove the Ever-greens, before the End of this month, Sol Says they may very Safely – Tho' there has been some Drye Weather yet the ground is hardly Drye Enough to Plow – They are now Digging the Borders about the Wall-Trees, which Promise much Fruit by the Blossome.

Monsieur Thorat [?] has Finish't his Eclat. John Channon was here last Thursday night, & Sol went in to Exeter a Friday for 2 Cows & a Heifer which He bought.

I have not Further to Trouble you, but hope Soon to hear from you, That you are well.

My Compliments to your Sister Eliot, if Still Together.

I am Dear Sir

Your Faithful

N Rowe

F408

21 March 60

Dear Sir

I received yours of 18th with the utmost Pleasure, fearing Something uncommon had happen'd, For to know you are well is my Chiefest Satisfaction – I hope your Sister Eliot has quitted Bath too, That you may have her Company – shall be glad to hear She has received a Benefit from the Waters – That an agreeable Dissipation may at least attend you; for the rest I wish, what I can't Express.

The Ever-greens shall be remov'd next Week – all the other Trees are remov'd into the Pear Garden – Sol is now Cleaning the Walks & Borders, he has Finish'd the part of the long Grass walk, that was unlaid, and is planting the Filberts against the wood Hedge in the Orchard: have not been able to get the N. Side of the old Kitchen Garden Plow'd yet, hope 'twill be Done next Week – Sol is still Sure Plowing won't Clean the ground – when the Ever-greens are remov'd – the S. Side shall be Dug Through.

Your Brother Samuel Sail'd for Halifax last Saturday –

The Joiner is boarding the Stable over the Manger, Selley wants to know, where he must have Timber for the Posts & Bales –

There, I hope when you come down, you will order Everything as you Think proper, in the mean Time I wish you Health, and hope God in his good Time will give you the Ease I wish you.

I am Dear Sir
Your Faithful
N Rowe

My Compliments to your Sister.

I Forbore writing to you so often, That I might not interrupt more agreable.

F409

28 March 1760

Dear Sir

I hope you are well, I have got a Sad Cold which affects me much, the Mornings cold, N. wind & Wednesday Last in the Morning a hard Shower of Hail & Some in the afternoon, Else Fine Weather: Frosty today.

You have abundance of Blossome on all your Trees, which promise well –

They are removing the Ever-greens, which is very Troublesome, you don't Say whether you wou'd have the Laurels without the Wall, that was Taken down, remov'd.

The Joiner has done the Boards over the Manger in the new Stable & is gone; The Masons have put in the Brick-Nogging ['brickwork set in a timber frame'] in the particion.

The North-Side of the old Kitchen Garden has been Plow'd, Dragg'd, & Harrow'd a Second Time. As Sol Still is positive Plowing won't Clean the ground from the Weed: wou'd you have it Trench-plow'd Notwithstanding? They Say the ground is not Deep Enough.

The Deel Ladies are at Buckland to Spend the Summer – There, what Turns are in Life!*

Some in, Some out, Nothing is to be wonder'd at, amidst Such a Medly.

I can Trouble you no more, But to wish you Happy.

I am Dear Sir
Your Faithful
N Rowe

I don't know whether I wrote you, But part of the Brick gutter in the old Kitchen garden next the Tonkin by the Meadow is broke in, & has overflow'd the part They are now Plowing, so it must be new Done & well Clay'd.

Selley came here yesterday to know if you Sent any orders about Posts & Bails – There are Trees down, which He Says will Do.

* 'The Deel Ladies' are Mrs Samuel Drake and her sister, now in favour with Lady Drake.

F410

Nutwell, 16 May 1760

Dear Sir

I have your Favours of 6th and 8th, here was only Rain that night, not Since.

Mr Lee Enjoys *Otium cum Dignitate* ['leisure with dignity'], he has a Curate whose name is Drake, & Phillis has marry'd one of the Same name.

Your Trees Sol has Thinn'd, Taken off a very great Quantity, & yet Thick – He desires to know if you wou'd have a hot Bed for Melons, he has no Old Seed. Hear nothing of the Basket: as there come Several Waggons from London to Exeter to different Inns (as Alderman Lee is no more) if you Order'd your Servant, when you Send anything, to Enquire where the Waggon Inns at Exeter, it wou'd be of Service to Save Trouble: Betty Shelston Enquires today.

What you mention of Dartmoor, Such a Reason wou'd make me Exert, But indeed my Every Faculty Fails me – There, an appointed Time is for all – how wonderful God's Providence is! Counsellor Pyne wou'd never See the Young Woman, & yet to be his Sole Heir, for I never heard of any Else of the name – But Mrs Neel & Parson Ryder have a Collateral Claim as to assets: However Miss Pyne is undoubted Heir to his Lands; She is a very good Sort of a young Woman, & I am very glad of it: more Natural than the Quicks.

Your Letter to Parson Lee must be very agreable, as he has Shown much uneasiness he had never heard from you: Such an Instance may be There too.

That nasty great Earth Worm abounds in your new Garden, I wish they mayn't hurt your Trees; one of the Espalier apple Trees Sol Took Several from about the root, the Tree shows it, in a Decay. Pray God give you health.

I am Dear Sir
Your Faithful
N Rowe

Lord F—s [?] is a very Shocking Example; a Watchmaker's Daughter of Plymouth is now the Countess.

F411

Nutwell, 6 June 1760

Dear Sir

I am very Sorry for the Loss of your Two new Men, your Veterans must Soon Follow, Recruits will be Necessary – I wish you may always have a Sufficient Number of Independents of the Middle Sort – where will be the Least Trouble &c.

Your Neighbour thought himself more happy when a Curate of £30 a year; if so, to what End is the addition, But an imagination, not to be Satisfy'd!

There has been fine rain Satarday & Sunday and Several Thunder Showers this week, Everything grows, the Weeds do so too, & I Tell Sol to keep 'Em down – He nor the Woman did anything last Week, He was Sick, & She han't been here but one Day this. As he had made the Hot Bed & Fix't the Frame (as he us'd to Do) Before he had your Orders, Hopes you won't be angry, That he has rais'd a plant or Two.

All The Flower Roots you sent from London grow, there is Fruit on most of your Espailiers, But the apple Trees are Toutch't. Everything Looks Thriving however, particularly your Wall-Trees, which Shoot out amain.

The artichokes are Slip't, But they were hardly above ground in April, & Several Dead.

It has been very Hot this week, I hope you are well, pray God keep you so – your Brother William (Mr Channon Says) the Ladys at Buckland have heard is very much out of Order in the Bay – He [Channon] came here last Monday Evening on purpose to buy you Some Bullocks at Ottery Fayr on Teusday, But I suppose he did not, as I have heard nothing from him Since.

I am Dear Sir
Your Faithful
N Rowe

F412

13 June

Sir

The Letter did not go by a Mistake – I hope you are well –

I have nothing particular to Trouble you with.

Channon has Sent two More Cows, there are now 7 which I Suppose he Thinks Sufficient.

I wish the Major General a good Campaign, as I see his Regiment is going Abroad: Comfort to your Sister.

The Weather has been very hot for Some Days, a Few Comfortable Showers, the ground begins to be Drye, & the Weeds increase vastly, which Sol & the Woman can't keep Down.

Your Wall-Trees Shoot out very Much, they begin to want pruning.

F413

Nutwell, 20 June 1760

Dear Sir

I have the pleasure of your kind Favour the 10th. I wonderfully hold out for Which I Thank God, But must Expect Soon the Event of Humane Nature – I am very Glad you are well, Pray God keep you So – your regard for me I am very Thankful for, But beg you won't Lay any Stress upon so Declining an Object – your Company must be very acceptable to your Sister under her present Tryal. I hope the General will have a Successful Campaign, & that God will be a Support to Her, Soldiers' Wives have great need of it.

I wrote you that Stephen's Man went off at Whitsuntide – nothing has been done in Digging the ground Since, Sol & the Woman are Taken up entirely in clearing the weed in the new garden, Nursery plantacions & Pear garden – and as but half of the ground is clear'd, I don't Think it can be done this Summer, unless there is more help.

The Kitchen Stuff Thrives very well in the New Kitchen Garden, But the Magpies & Jays devour Everything, Even the Fruit from the Trees – besides the other Birds which abound – there's much Fruit in the Pear garden.

Sol is willing to allow the week he was absent, But unless he is Settl'd with his Family, it will never be well.

When the Borders are clear from the Flowers, they Shou'd be Dug up, & then Salt may be Try'd, But Salt water has no Effect on the Worms.

I have Shown Seaward the Field Bed & the Plan, but he can't undertake it. Selley han't been here these 2 Months.

The weather was very hot last week & as Cold This, Some Showers Every Day.

Mr Lee had your Letters as Soon as I received 'Em.

I am very Sensibly oblig'd for your kind offer, But I can't Trouble you for anything now –

I have not further to Trouble you – I heartily wish you Every happiness.

& am Dear Sir

Your Faithful

N Rowe

My Compliments to Mrs Elliot, I truly Sympathise with Her.

Pray Sir don't Trouble yourself about writing punctually, any Time when it Sutes your Conveniency is a Favour to me.

As the weather is Frequently <u>very windy</u> your Wall Trees are so very rank they want to be prun'd to prevent Breaking the Branches.

The grass is prodigiously grown in the wood, if it was Cut wou'd Serve for Bedding for the Cattle in the winter.

F414

Nutwell, 23 June 1760

Dear Sir

I send you the Enclosed, Least you Should not hear of it any other Way – the poor Little Honest Man I fear is by this Time no more* – a True Friend to your Family & Grateful to the highest Degree – it has given me so great Concern, That I am able to Say no more – Pray God Enable me to Prepare for the Summons when & however it may be – But who is Sufficient for these Things?

I will observe the Directions of your Last, But can't be particular now – only nothing is done as to plaistering your Stable – Clark had no Order from you about it, you will send your Directions, & as to paving & removing the pebbles from the old Stable.

Pray God preserve you & properly instruct me in this Lesson of Mortality.

I am Dear Sir

Your Faithful

N Rowe

A Line from you to poor Mrs Porter would be of great Comfort to Her. I am not able to be of any Service to Her, which is my great Concern: But you can about your <u>Security &c</u>.

* Mr Porter of Plymouth, freeholder of Bere Alston, frequently referred to as a good friend and supporter. See the following letter for his recovery, and the need for FHD to alter his deed in order to avoid a split of votes in Bere Alston.

F415

Nutwell, 10 July 1760

Dear Sir

I have your Favour of 1st, hope poor Mr Porter may get over This; But you must alter his present Deed to one for Life, which will prevent the Split.

As to Digging the ground it will be a very Tedious affair, so much wet has Encreas't the Weeds to that Degree, that they can't keep 'Em down; Sol & the Woman are Entirely Taken up in that only. The Man can't come yet. Sol do's make a Trench in Digging, which he Says answers what you Direct: I hope you will approve what has been Done; I have Told Him your Orders, but Fear the ground won't be Dug in Time.

Clark has plaister'd the Stable Cieling [sic] once over Throughout, and has Mortar Enough to finish the Inner One but more Lime will be wanting for the Outer one. I have Sent in to Selley to Let Him know you wou'd have the Inner Stable Finish'd out of hand; you wou'd have the Same Windows put up again, I imagine, So have Sent for the glazier to do it; & Clark is to do the Paving as Soon as Selley has fixt the Posts &c.

Having heard nothing from Moore, have wrote to him again; the Trees much want Pruning: I am very Glad you will have the Disposing of your Fruit yourself, It's a pity it shou'd ever be otherwise.

Wednesday Se'nnight rain'd here, as I wrote you, all Day & did by Floods much Damage at Alfington, Chidley, Crediton, run into the Houses at Exeter: There has [been] no Hay weather hereabouts for this 14 night past, what has been Sav'd was they Say but so so.

I am Sorry for your Sister's Loss, which is a Common Calamity!

I hope your Sister has heard of the General's Safe arrival; I wish Him a good Campaign, pray my Compliments to Her; your Company must be a great Comfort to Her, I wish you Both Health & Happiness.

I am Dear Sir
Your Faithful
N Rowe

Scarse a Day without Some rain. Very hard last night & this Morning, now Fair.

Clark says you can't have Less than 20 Hogsheads of Lime for what may be wanted. You will have 2 Coats on the Stable Cieling [sic].

The Glazier has been here, Says if you have Square Glass Enough 'twill be Better, as the Lights from the old Stable must be new Leaded: you'l send your Orders.

F416

Nutwell, 14 July 1760

Dear Sir

I have had no Letter from you Since that of the 1st. I hope you are well, it is now very Hot & Fair.

Moor came here last night, has been very Sick, which was the reason he cou'd not go to Buckland, will now go, if you approve of it, in a Fortnight's Time; more nails & Scrips will be wanting against the next pruning. The Farmer must pay Him.

I have wrote Selley, That Clark has plaister'd the Stable Cieling [*sic*] once; hear not as yet from Him, you will please to hasten Him.

I wrote you about the windows, how you wou'd have them Glaz'd, whether with Diamond or Square glass, if enough of the Latter can be pick'd up, and about Paving the Inner Stable.

The Man to help Sol is not come yet, he hopes to have him 4 Days in a Week, after This – Tho' everyone is very Busy about the Hay, now the weather is so good.

You will send your Directions.

Channon was here last week, he Told me your Brother & Mrs Drake were coming here with Him, I am glad they did not.

I am Dear Sir
Your Faithful
N Rowe

I presume you will have the Stable plaister'd once more – 20 Hogsheads more of Lime will be wanted –

I wish you cou'd send me a few Franks to write Channon if Occasion, having None.

F417

Nutwell, 31 July 1760

Dear Sir

I have your Favour of 22nd. I always Send my Letters as Dated Either by Farmer Coleman; the Post, or Betty Shelston; it Sometimes falls out, I suppose, That Some of 'Em are too Late at Exeter for that post, which I am Sorry for, as it is a Disappointment.

The Harvest is begun about the Countrey, Tho' the Hay Is not Over, they are making now in Powderham Marshes, But as the weather Is So hot & Drye, it will soon be General.

Clark has been here & Look't on the Walls, he Says what you mention may be Done, & as there is no Stress, will be Strong Enough, But it can't be Done with leaning over, but must be done in the garden, will Take great care about the Trees, But 'twill be Best when the Fruit is gone: as to the Coping over the Stone Work, he Thinks it best to take the Bricks off & new Lay 'Em in a good Bed of Mortar. That you will Judge of, when you come Down.

There are many Windsor Pears on the great Tree, wou'd it not be worth while to Sell 'Em, when ripe, which must be by Sol or the Woman. I hope you'l have the Disposal of your other Fruit, 'tis a great Pity it Should Fall into Such Hands.

As to the Stable, nothing is yet done in it, Selley writes to me to get 2 posts Saw'd for the inner one, I will if I can Find any Fit for 'Em.

As to Wheelbarrows, Seaward will make 'Em next week, & Saw the Posts for the inner Stable.

The Glazier has overlook't all the old Windows, & has pick't out 3 Casements, which with a little alteration will Do, But there is not Square Glass by near Enough, so the best of the Lights must Do again, which came from the old Stable.

I am Dear Sir
Your Faithful
N Rowe

It begun to rain this Morning, rain'd hard at noon & Like to be more.

Mr Porter mends Daily.

Your Brother & the Lady are Still at Buckland.

Stephen Philips has Found a prosperous Work, so Fear He won't be able to Come.

Captain Shepherd has Lost his Ship again, But insur'd – and it's Fear'd the other is Lost Too, But They Say Mr Brice is no Looser.

F418 [notes for a letter]

Channon Lay here last Friday night – He is much Distress'd with the Company – Lady Drake shou'd make Him Easy, by Sending Him Her Orders how he is to behave: the Captain who increases it Shou'd have his Mother's Sanction. The Ladies I imagine are There 'till the *Falkland* returns.

I am very much oblig'd for your Kindness but can Trouble you for nothing but the Horseman's Coat of the ordinary Cloth as advertiz'd.

Hard rain Monday & in the night and Teusday morning, windy & Showry Wednesday & Thursday, 2 violent Showers this morning & windy at S.W. & more Likely – Melancholy Harvest-Weather!

How wou'd you have the Fruit, that ripens before you Come down, Dispos'd of? It's a great Pity Sol shou'd, who do's not behave well, He went away a Teusday Morning on the pretence of going about Business to Exeter Fayr, & never came here 'till last night.

Sol begs pardon & will allow his absent Time.

F419

Nutwell, 15 August 1760

Dear Sir

If Channon shou'd Quit Lady Drake's Service, I don't know where She'd get Such another; Sure the Ladies will make room for you,* knowing your Stay is but Short, & not put you on the necessity of going Elsewhere: your Brother Shou'd write to Lady Drake to make Channon Easy, he having Desir'd Him.

The Corn is all Ripe & very Good, they Say; no rain Since Sunday, the Early sown wheat the worse kern'd.

Selley is not come out yet, Fear the Stable won't be Done in the Time you Expect. No plank to be had, must it then be pitch't with Stones?

The peaches drop from Several Trees, I wrote you to know what you wou'd have Done with 'Em; the Wasps Eat the plumbs before they are ripe & the Figgs too.

Last week it was too wet to plow the Ground, & this they are so Busy they can't, hope the next it will, But it is so full of Stroyl ['weeds'] fear Plowing won't clean it, & besides a piece among the Quinces still to be Dug, what to do I know not – the Woman has been Sick above a Week with an ague; & Sol last week 2 Days Bad with a Fall – the Walk & Slope shall be Taken up & plow'd as you Direct, the Man has not been here.

Stephen had your Letter & Told Mr Brice he has wrote you, however I have wrote Him.

Mrs Coleman Says no care was wanting about the Beer, but its weakness spoil'd it, none of it is fit for your Drinking, neither will any, that may be Brew'd, in the Time you may want it, a great pity.

I am Dear Sir
Your Faithful
N Rowe

Joyce will order Some Fowls as you Direct.

Believe there is not room for the Sashes on Each Side of the Chimney in the Walnut-room. But there are 3 Frames.

Seaward Drew the Enclos'd for the Brew House, I wish it may answer.

I have Told the Farmer he is not to bring out anything for Selley without your particular order, I presume you mean, unless he pays the Farmer Himself.

* Lady Drake would need to require Mrs Samuel Drake and her sister to make room for Sir Francis to stay at Buckland. See also F409, F448.

F420

Nutwell, 26 August 1760

Dear Sir

I have your Favour of 23rd Instant. As to the Enclos'd paper* I know nothing of it, only Think it was a great Omission in the Late Mr Edgcombe not to take notice of it, when you made up accounts with your Mother – as to the Counsellor, He, tho' a Lover of Money, was long absent to Himself: I think it a great hardship on you, to have Such a Thing Lye so Long <u>Dormant</u>!

I presume you have heard from Selley he was here a Saturday, I find he is so Engag'd, That he can't at present do either the Stable or Windows: you may have the Parson's Stable –

The Late Alderman Lee's Man's name is John Brutton, you may direct anything to Him at Mr Jonas Dennis's Salter in Exeter; he has promis't to Take care of what you Send, & give notice of it – I presume you may make use of Him, as well as Phillis, who is now Brewing, tho' under the Parson's Displeasure.

The Copper you mencion They Say holds 4 Hogsheads.

In my next will be more Particular.

I am Dear Sir
Your Faithful
N Rowe

I shou'd imagine Dr Pyne never intended to Take any Interest, He, nor his Son not having Demanded any so Long.

Don't the account you made up with your Mother mention this £100 as paid by John Edgcombe?

Mr Sparks of Dartmouth has sent you 2 orange Trees.

I suppose you have Seen Mr Brice, he is not yet return'd.

* The enclosed paper is the bill penal, F421.

F421

[Bill penal of 22 June 1717; receipt of 12 January 1735, in Thomas Pyne's hand]

F422

Nutwell, 29 August 1760

Dear Sir

Your Last Letter gave me great Concern! For Mr Edgcombe, an Agent for you &
Mr Pyne <u>too</u>, who was privy to the affair, by the Payment made by Himself, to Let
it run on so many years without acquainting you with it, is Shockingly Surprizing!

I wonder you don't hear from Stephen, I am affraid he may Disappoint you; &
That you won't Find things here to your Expectation – the harvest Takes up Every
One; But this Fine weather will soon put an End to That; yet they Say there is Such
a Scarcity of Men, That with Difficulty the Farmers get any to do their Common
Work – However what can be Done Shall – tho' 'tis with great Difficulty, & at best
will be Far Short.

Mr Jeffery has had some Fruit & next Sunday he'l go again –

The Fruit falls off unaccountably, & the Wasps & Flys devour prodigiously.

Mr Brice is not return'd, presume you have Seen Him.

To be Sure I shall be very Glad to See you, But am Sorry it is Like to be in so
melancholy a manner; there, God's holy will be Done – a perpetual Dropping wastes
Even Stones: pray God Support us All.

I am Dear Sir
Your Faithful
N Rowe

I wish Mrs Drake* may please you with the Drink which was Barrel'd up Wednesday.

I imagine nothing will be done more to your Stable till you come Down. Mr Lee
Says you may make use of his – He Sent Severall Things for Brewing – Thursday
had Company & Sent for Some Fruit which rots on your Trees & Falls <u>moldy</u>!

Channon has Sent for Two of the Cowes, & Sol go's with 'Em to Moreton next
Monday. Says they'l Sell much Better at their Fayr at Tavistock. Hard rain this
Morning.

* Parson Lee's servant Phillis, married to a Mr Drake (not related to FHD).

F423

7 November 60

Dear Sir

I am under Such Concern for you, Least the Fategue of the Journey in such Bad
roads & Weather on this Melancholy Occasion, & the uneasiness Thereon shou'd
have any bad Effect; That I can't Express it – I hope the Contrary – pray Let me hear
from you: I am much affected with the news, that General Eliot is wounded, I hope
not Dangerously for your Sister's Sake – to a Brave Man Death in his Vocation is
Desirable on a Good Occasion – all Trials are for our improvement – whatever Turn
Things take I hope you'l think on the Horse – knab me, I'l knab you ['Bite me, I'll
bite you'] &c.

There has been a great Deal of Trouble getting your Things out of Stiles – Mr Hill went Twice on Board Friday & Saturday but cou'd get nothing out of Him, Tho' shew'd the Collector's Letter – Sunday the Ship got up above Topsham, & Monday had it not blown a Storm all Day at N.W. wou'd have gone up the Works directly, & the Things must have been Fetch't from Exeter; Monday Morning the Farmer went to Topsham, & the Master being Gone to Exeter waited 'till he came (which was then noon) who Told Him, he, the Farmer, must Take out His Things immediately, for he wou'd push up the Works directly, so was oblig'd to go with his Wagon, For no Boat cou'd, and did not reach Home 'till past 9 at night, with all, but one of the Hampers of Wine & one of the Cases with Glassware &c which cou'd not be then come at; what is brought is Come Safe & unpack't, except the Desk & Tool Chest of which there is no Keys – the Master cou'd not come at the Hamper & Case whilst at Topsham, & Wednesday the Farmer call'd on Him at Exeter but cou'd not as yet come at 'Em; today he'l call on him again, I wish There may be no Difficulty about the Hamper of Wine, if there is, you must use your Interest with the Collector.

Very hard rain & wind at S.W. all yesterday afternoon & Evening – Sol is Laying what Turff he can & Harry is helping Him, the woman Cleaning the new garden, He Says There is Business Enough for 'Em; But not, if Such weather Continues.

I am Dear Sir
Your Faithful
N Rowe

Enclosed are what Bills I can get, the Farmer can't make out his now, still <u>being Busy</u>.

F424

28 November 1760

Dear Sir

I acknowledg'd the receipt of 4 Bills for £40 By Sunday's post.

Sol is now with Harry cleaning a Border for the Thorns in the old Nursery, it is so Bad to Clean, That they have been most of the week about it – if Couch can come, Says 'twill take up a Month at Least for all of 'Em to do the whole, & if you make the Hedge as you mention, a good Quantity of Stones next the Lane will be Wanted.

Phillis is very ready to Serve you at any Time; the Beer is brew'd, & Cask'd.

Joyce desires to know if you have Dismis't her Daughter, She Says She owes Mrs Coleman £5 which She was oblig'd to borrow to buy provisions for the girl, having less allow'd by you for Housekeeping than Betty Dyer had, tho' everything has been Dearer since, & the girl out of the number.

Mr Brice & Mr Lee are Both from Home, at their return will acquaint you about the Plank.

Mr Lee thinks Joe White will shift off about the Coals, thinks if he do's – if you got elsewhere 5, or 6 Quarters, which would Serve 'till Spring, when they might be Cheaper.

I am very glad the Pears came so well, & that Harry Mathews is so respectful.

Captain Shepherd is in a fair Way, I sent to him at Exmouth where he Ly's, to know what Things he had of yours besides the Chairs, he return'd there were 2 parcels more, which shou'd be sent up very soon; <u>not yet Come</u>.

Sol will go a Sunday & See if there are any Larger <u>Elms</u> than yours among the Nursery Men, if so, they must be Brought in the Farmer's Wagon; your pleasure shou'd be known – as to stuff to fence Them, where is it to be had? Sol don't know what Earth you mean at the End of the Stable, Says there's some good in the Stable –

Any Time is proper to go about the Stone hedge in the gutters, But if you Take Them off, about The Nursery, They can't Follow it as it is Dug. Next week he will root up the old apple Trees – and afterwards, if you don't Forbid it, will get the good Earth out of the Walks, & Lay what Turff remains.

I have by Mr Lee's assistance received money for the Bills, and paid Those you return'd to me.

I can't express my anxiety at your Uneasiness – But I hope you'l Soon be out of your Pain.

I am Dear Sir
Your Faithful
N Rowe

When proper, you'l Send a Few Franks – we have had fine weather for Several Days.

Sol Supposes you'd have the Thorns planted home to the Lane-hedge.

Since my writing This Thomas Moore is Come,* if you have any particular orders for him you will Let me know; the Farmer must Dyet & Pay him.

* Son of the pruner Hercules More?

F425

Nutwell, 7 December 1760

Dear Sir

I have your Favour of 2nd with the Key, and have Taken out of the Bureau the Linnen, which I found as by the Enclos'd – the 12 Pillow-Cases were brought when you came Down – I have Taken the Nails out of the Tool-Chest, But won't meddle with anything else in it, unless you Order it – the Hinges of the Lid are Started, & the Bottome Drawer so Swol'n it can't be open'd.

The measure of the Chairs I have put on your Paper, which I enclose.

The Reason Harry & Sol were so Long cleaning the ground in the old Nursery was owing to the Earth, which was Flung on the Top of the Bank being so Foul; as to the Time of Cleaning the Whole he can't be positive, will Loose no Time when he go's about it; But Couch can't come as I wrote you, 'till next month. If Frosty Weather shou'd come in, as we had a Sample last night, will go on the Hedge next Week.

I wrote you the Size of the Elms 10 Ins Girt, between 20 & 30 ft high, price 2s. Each; I suppose you don't intend the Stuff for the Fence to be done by a Carpenter.

Sol Says the Turff will Do yet.

The Vines are out as you Direct, you will order about Moore –

Joyce hopes you are not angry about her mencioning her Daughter's Dyet – She Says Betty Dyer had always 7s. per Week for 2 and 10s. for 3 and she never had but 6s. for 3. Poor Betty I believe Thinks now with Sorrow on her Conduct.

The Things by Captain Shepherd are come, but ['except'] the parcel with the Bed.

When you hear from Mr Lee about the Coals, you'l See how far he approves of Jo White's Conduct.

I am in great pain to know what you intimate, as my Chief Wishes are for your prosperity, Being
Dear Sir
Your Faithful
N Rowe

Rain & wind in the afternoon S.W.

Mr Brice Says had you Sent Him an account what Things had been put on Board Captain Shepherd, wou'd have got 'Em out, but now I parcel is gone to Topsham.

Since my writing the Letter I receiv'd a Melancholy one from Poor Mr Porter, That the Custom Escap'd the Fire which happen'd at Plymouth* – but fears he is a great Sufferer in the removal of his Things.

* Most of the wooden buildings in Plymouth dockyard were destroyed by fire in 1761. Mr Porter was active in Plymouth Customs and Excise.

F426

Nutwell, 4 February 1761

My Dear Sir Francis

Your Letter by Sunday's post gave me the greatest uneasiness, yours by last is some Satisfaction, But my Care & Fear for you are Ever uppermost. For Godsake Don't Let anything affect you; your Spirits are your Life, pray Support all you can – I ever Lov'd your Sister and Shall if possible exceed in it for her kind regard to you – natural affection shou'd be Concomitant attendants on so near Relations, I hope it will be always increasing between you – pray my kindest respect to Her, and Tell her She Lays me & all your Friends under the greatest Obligations, Her Care of You; pray be as much with her as possible, your Little Niece has my Thanks too, I Think I See her in her Short peticoats prattling to Her Uncle.

I won't Trouble you with anything, only Stephen as he works very hard & his 4 Men, must be weekly Supply'd.

Everything here you may Depend is Forwarded as much as possible, as I hope you'l Find at the Time you mention; I beg to hear from you, you know how I value your Welfare & not how much!
Dear Sir
Your Faithful
N Rowe

Very Fine moderate weather.

You Say nothing of General Eliot, And therefore I hope he is well, may God preserve Him for your Dear Sister's Sake!

F427

Nutwell, 13 February 1761

Dear Sir

I Beg when you are Confirm'd, you will send me the *Gazet, in memoriam rei* ['in remembrance of the event'].*

Had not the Weather hinder'd, Stephen wou'd have Finish't the Pond this week – it Snow'd yesterday & Rain'd all Day after Monday.

Stephen is gone home, But will return Sunday if the Weather is fit to work in, he has Left a Man & his Son to do what They can in his absence.

Sprye says, as I wrote you, That the Wooden Shute won't Do, I Think Selley was to blame to advise you so improperly, Says unless there is Some Thinn Sheet Lead under, it will soon Decay the Wall-plate; I don't know what to do without your Direction, So he must go on as it is – he Says the Leaden Pipes are too heavy for the Heling ['roofing']; I hope to hear this post something from you about it.

Your health is the Top of my Thoughts: Everything else is insignificant; pray Take care of yourself, Reflect on the Goodness of God, & Support yourself under Every Other Consideration.

I hope the Method you propose will Restore your health perfectly, I pray God it may.

I am Dear Sir
Your Faithful
N Rowe

It has been very Cold for Some Days, the Snow alter'd it Quite, which went off presently, it Seems now to be Mild, I hope, Tho' some Showers, it will come in good again.

*Kissing the hand of the new king, George III, would confirm FHD's position in the royal household.

F428

Nutwell, 20 February 1761

Dear Sir

I have your Several Favours, am very Glad you are Better, pray God restore you to your perfect health – I shall be rejoic'd to hear you have kiss't the King's hand.* Your Letter to the Collector will revive Him.

I can't Trouble you Just now with every Trifle: you may Depend Everything is pursu'd you Direct or is for your Service: Selley & Sprye have agreed to line the Wooden Shute with Lead which go's round the Ovice [?] of the new Building, which as they Say was absolutely necessary to preserve the Roof, & it is Done: Sprye says the Bump in the Front Roof may be mended, but there must be new ridge Tiles of an equal Size from one End of the ridge to the Other & Some of the Heling ['roofing'] rip't all along: Selley agrees to it.

Last Sunday we had a violent Storm of wind & rain which Continu'd most part of the Day & Monday at S.W., it Tumbl'd about your plantacion But no great Damage – it beat into all your Front windows, I fear the Putty is Decay'd, no news from the Painter tho' I have sent Twice to Him – the rain forc't thro' the S. Gutter of the Chapel much, so as the Plumbers were here I got 'Em to Look into it & They found it so bad, That some of the Timbers were Decay'd; it is now mended I hope Effectually, the Library gutter was Done when they were here before – I'm perswaded you won't Think much of the Expence so absolutely necessary.

The Trees from London are come & Planted as you Directed – Sol & the Men have been much Taken up about the Walks & the Edge of the pond, They are now gone about Clearing the old Nursery again, which is about half Done, tho' I assure you they are always Employ'd about one Thing or another – Sol has planted Several of the Large Trees, Says he understands what you Order and will Do it as Fast as he can: the spring being so Forward, the Shrubbs you intend to plant yourself must be soon remov'd, as they begin to Shoot out.

Your inner Stable is Finish'd, & so is the Privy all but Stucco'd –

Stephen return'd Wednesday noon & One Man, who is a Mason, offers to stone the East Ditch for 1s. 4d. a perch, which as you want Sol for Other matters, Seems for your Service. The Pond is Done, and all the Walks, but the East fill'd with what came from Thence, so the Earth from the Ditch is to supply <u>That</u>. He will Endeavour to get you some Men, if he knew how many & <u>at what Time</u>.

Sol & Stephen Think it best to defer digging thro' to the Ditch in the South Meadow 'till you See it. You will send your answer.

Joyce says She knows nothing wanting here but some pickles, and Since you are so kind to mention it, an Advertiz'd Cut Wig wou'd be a Favour.

Have wrote to Moore who promis't to go to Buckland soon after Christmas.

The Honysuckles & roses are in Leaf, the Potatoes shall be set.

You'l Send word if you'l have Sprye alter the Front Roof as he proposes.

I am Dear Sir
Your Faithful
N Rowe

A Frost a Wednesday, a stormy night – yesterday rain & windy, today will be Shoury S.W.

* See note to F427.

F429

15 July 1761

Dear Sir

I have your several Favours with the *News* & Franks – That you are so Distinguish'd is the Greatest pleasure to me, I heartily wish you a good & successful Voyage and a safe Return – and may the Royal Person prove the Delight of Her Royal Consort!* When the Coronation is over, I hope you'l have Time to Visit this Place, and to have a smal recess after so much Fategue. Whenever it is, it will be to me very agreable, But to hear you are Well, & That you are so Employ'd, however seldom I see you (For seldom I must Expect it) it will be the Highth of satisfaction: & may success in Everything attend you.

I don't know how to Trouble you with any Trifle from hence, now you are so much & so Momentously Employ'd.

Moore came here a Sunday night – it was high Time to do the Trees, being vastly shot out.

Sol has been ailing for some Time But what you direct shall be Done as soon as possible, the Weeds are great hinderance – have wrote to Stephen to forbid the Men –

As Lammas Fayr at Exeter approaches Clark & Hannah will want a Little money.

I Believe the Parson wou'd as soon venture to Greenland As to Helo[goland];** But will visit you at the Coronation. Where ever you go may God be with you,

shou'd there be a Battle before the Peace, I hope the General will come off well, my
best Wishes attend you & your sister.
    I am Dear Sir
    Your Faithful
    N Rowe

* FHD was chosen to accompany Earl Harcourt's diplomatic mission to the Elbe, to escort
George III's bride, Charlotte of Mecklenburg-Strelitz, to England.
** Rowe is suggesting that Parson Lee was too fearful to venture to Heligoland, at the mouth
of the Elbe. For his parsimony, see the following letter, and F438 and F440.

F430

17 July 1761

Dear Sir

    I wrote you last post, have Little to add – Moore is pruneing the Trees, They are
so Rank, That laying 'Em back Takes up much Time, he won't Finish 'till towards
the End of next Week; I must pay Him, & the Freight of the sashes when they arrive,
so when you send money to pay Mrs Wreyford for the Malt, you will please to order
Somewhat the More, as I must pay Harry Weekly.
    The Collector of Exeter wrote to the Farmer to come in as this Day for the Cask
of Wine, and he is gone in for it accordingly: it shall be put in your Cellar.
    They have begun about the Ditch in the South Meadow, 5 ft Deep & 10 ft broad,
with a better slope than the Other.
    It is extreme Hot & Drye, no rain. The inclosure at the upper End of the South
Meadow Must be How'd & Burnt, and as it must be done soon, he not being able to
do it, & the other Things in Time proposes to Set it out.
    I hope you are well, pray God keep you so, and enable you to go thro' what is
expected of you with the Success I wish you, and a Safe Return.
    Mr Lee is full of the Coronation, but the Expence! he Sends you his Compliments
—

    I am Dear Sir
    Your Faithful
    N Rowe

My kind remembrance to Mrs Eliot, may she have good news from Germany.
    The Jays & Magpies are so numerous they devour much of the Garden-Stuff,
Fruit &c.
    Moore thins the Fruit as he go's along, & leaves what you'l Think Enough.
    No grapes on the vines in the vines [*sic*] in the new garden, Tho' there was much
Blossome on the Biggest.

F431

24 July 1761

Dear Sir
    I hope you are well this very hot Drye weather! We have had no rain for a long Time.
    The Pipe of Wine was brought last Friday night, it was past 10, & near 12 before it
cou'd be got in, with much Trouble it was got in to your little Cellar, where it Lyes
very well, & as Joyce keeps the key, I hope very safe.

No Painter nor any Work about your house, I wrote to Selley but have heard nothing from Him about the Window in the passage.

Moore has finish'd the Trees.

We have been oblig'd to Water Everything.

Sol & Harry are about the South Meadow Ditch, but to dig it 5 ft Deep (& under will be no Fence) the ground is so hard, will be long about.

Mr Porter wrote me to Enquire after your Welfare.

As matters seem by the news to be alter'd, your going will be sooner than you imagin'd, whenever it is, I heartily wish you a good Voyage & Safe return.

I wrote you that Some money wou'd be, and now is wanting to pay the necessary here, you will please to order it with the Soonest, & it shall be only Employ'd in your Service.

Channon was here last Saturday, can't get a Vessel to bring the Timber & Slates – I wish Madam by her <u>airs</u> don't make the Man & his wife weary of the place!*

I am Dear Sir

Your Faithful

N Rowe

* Rowe fears once more that Mrs Samuel Drake will exhaust the patience of Channon and his wife.

F432

Nutwell, 29 July 1761

Dear Sir

I have yours of 25th with a Ten pound Bill, will pay Mrs Wreyford's Bill for Malt & keep the rest for what may Occur.

Will observe what you mention about Clark & Selley.

Will get Mr Brice to write you his Opinion about agreing with Selley for his part in the Farme-House.

Sol is about the Ditch, the Ground is so hard, it will be a Tedious affair: … Plank will secure <u>stand</u> 'till you come down.

I pray God send you a good Voyage & Safe return – I am very Sensible of your present Fategue, this hot Weather must Make it very Irksome; There, I hope God will give you health to go thro' with all your Difficultys.

I congratulate you on the great News, which I hope will have the Desir'd Effect. I shou'd be very Glad to sail up the Elb – in my imaginacion I shall be always with you; I Flatter myself I shall have the pleasure once more of seing you, I never Long'd more for it, God keep you.

I am Dear Sir

Your Faithful

N Rowe

I hope your Sister Eliot has good News from the General, my best Wishes to Her.

The Fruit that may be Ripe before you come down, how wou'd you have it Dispos'd of?

Mr Lee sends his Compliments.

If I pay Mrs Wreyford I can't pay Clark & Hannah any Money & Keep some to pay Harry &c.

A Thunder shower in the night.

F433

Nutwell, 19 November 1761

Dear Sir

Enclosed is William Spry's Bill, which I acquainted him I wou'd Transmit to you, who wou'd Order Mr Channon to pay it, the number of Days he work'd here between 5th & 19th for the rest is Left to you; he put in the Sky-Lights, & mending the Farmer's House Took him up near 2 Days with his Man – Says that part of your house over the Kitchen ought to be pointed next Spring.

Enclosed is a paper you Left on the Table in the Long Gallery with the Yarcomb Counterparts, which I presume you intended to Carry with you.

The Mornings have been Frosty ever since you went, Today very hard, But Seems to look like rain or Snow.

Sol Finish'd the gutter yesterday Morning, have since Transplanted the Weymouth Pines in the new Nursery, the Burgomot from the Pear garden to the place in the new Garden you Directed, are now Transplanting the Cedars & Pines to and from the great Slope.

The Hurdles I fear is not a Sufficient Fence, one of the Cows got thro', But I happening to see her prevented any Mischeifs. I wish They may Do no more –

The Thatcher has not yet begun about the Linney, only his Boy has Layd on some Wadds.

As to the Farmer's receipt you Left with me, wou'd you let me add to 'in full of all Demands' the words 'for Labour & money Laid out' –

Harriss has Look'd over the Doors which you have here, Says They are too heavy for the Coal-House, But will serve for the Farme-House, you'l have his account of the Skantlings – Says you order'd the Stuff he has Saw'd & is Sawing to be Flung into the new pond –

I shou'd Desire if you can Find Sol's account of Hannah's Time, which I sent you in the Spring, Because She gives out I have wrong'd her of 20 Days; to be the object of Such Scum, is very Disagreable, Therefore I shou'd be very Glad to have it, as in the Demand Sol brought me, as many Days (Sundays Deducted) were charg'd, as the Entire Days from 4th of April, the Time her account I sent you Commenc'd, to the 4th November Instant (viz 181 Days) and I can make it but 132½ Days which I think is her Just Due, can it be imagin'd she shou'd Loose no Time in 7 months: She & Her Fellow I fear are very Bad – as had there been no Controul, They wou'd have made that Demand on you!

Horrell the Younger came here today to know how to Direct a Letter to you, Says he hears you intend to have an Act of Parliament to alter the Road,* which will make his Estate Little worth, you will no Doubt have a Long Scrawl.

I am Dear Sir
Your Faithful
N Rowe

I wrote you last post, Hope it Found you well after your Fategue.

As I had no Letter from you this post, I am very uneasy Least any Accident happen'd to you on the Road – I hope I shall hear from next post – hard rain this morning & in the night.

---

* See Rowe's early letters from Nutwell (F270, F274, etc.) for attempts to prevent local

people's use of the path along the wood. There is no record of FHD taking this step but his successor, Lord Heathfield, lost no time in stopping up the road between Meeting House Lane and Nutwell Pound at the Devon Quarter Sessions in 1795–1796 (DHC QS/113A/217/2).

F434 [John Channon to Nicholas Rowe]

Buckland, 24 November 1761

Sir

I Received yours by William Spry.

I imagine Exeter fair will be this day fortnight & if so I shall be at Nutwell the Evening Before. I supose Sir Francis would have his Cows sold, I imagine they must be losting fless rather than gaining as they are Confin'd in a small Compas of Ground. I took all the care Immagenable in Buying good Cows for Sir Francis & if they are not well feed I hope he will Ecuse [*sic*] me if they do not make him a proper Returne for I am very doubtfull I shall find them not fatt when I come to sell them. I shall be Obleigd to the Farmer if he can get me keeping for half the sheep, if not I will Order them down againe when I come up, I hope they will not be very Offensive before that Time as it is so neare. Captain William Drake sent home a letter last week from Bell Isle & is Expect'd heare every hour. I will take care to pay William Spry's Bill as soon as it comes to my hand. I have seen Mr Wyett & his Aunt sine [*sic*] they Came home, they are Both well as I hope you are likewise.

I am Sir
Your Humble Servant
John Channon

I hope I shall not Commit any Blunder in selling the Bullocks without a punctuall Order. I am very sorry I should in sending the sheep, it was never my Intention to Disobleige Sir Francis Drake.

F435

Nutwell, 10 December 1761

Dear Sir

I have your Favour of the 3rd – I am under great Concern about you; Fear your Fateguing Journey & your Other Avocations affect you too much – I hope you interpose proper resources.

Harris had your Letter directly, he Seems to think Elm Boards won't be so profitable for you as Deals.

Channon came here Sunday Evening, he sold at the Fayr Teusday 3 of the Cows, Says they have got nothing these 6 Weeks, being Depriv'd of the Other Meadow; They are to be kep't here 'till near Christmas, & Sol with Dyer were all Day driving them to Exeter & back.

I believe had Sol 3 Men, he wou'd not be Easy without his Woman, But to me She Seems not so Necessary, & your Determination is certainly Right; he has Lay'd himself so under her influence, She'l be his ruine, She is a very impudent Woman, & he is I fear not improv'd by her Conversation.

Yesterday it rain'd from Morning to night; today very good Weather – I continually Caution Sol about Securing the Hurdles, no Breach of Late – the East Meadow is so wet, Channon has remov'd his Sheep to Withays for Change; Farmer Watts lately hurt his Leg, But is about again, I wrote Mr Carpenter about Him, a Destress wou'd Lay him under great Difficulty.

Mrs Drake has wrote me for the Key of the Closset, in return I have told Her I have not the Key, she may break open if she has Lady Drake's authority so to do – Captain William is now There –

The Men are doing out the Linney, they all Say 'tis but Bare Enough for 3 Bullocks – the Thatcher has done all but the Cob Wall.

As the care of yourself is so Essential, I beg you'l regard it.

I am Dear Sir
Your Faithful
N Rowe

Has £.s.d. sent Dr Green to Lincoln?

Harris Says had the Skyelights been set in another Frame, They'd have been above the Heling ['re-roofing'], which wou'd more Effectually keep out the wet; none came in the late hard rain; But wire Grates would Save the Glass.

Mr Porter expresses great Concern at your Late Journey. Says you'l hurt yourself by it.

F436

Nutwell, 24 December 1761

Dear Sir

My Last I wrote in great Confusion! But yours of the 15th gave me some Consolation; however not having heard from you since, I am under very great Uneasiness; I hope this will find you Quite recover'd; I Pray God give you health & many happy years.

Here has been much Close weather, But nothing Like what you mention; I remember when I was in Town it was so – we have had much rain, the South Meadow is very Wet, & the Earth which was flung out of the Ditch, that is Stoning, is much Fallen in; & the East Meadow is Like a Morass – I am glad the Tinners clear'd out the Gutter – That you Order'd in the green to be inlarg'd has answer'd the Purpose, no Water came into the Cellar, or new brick gutters the last Spring Tide, tho' high & a great Freshut & much rain.

I have seen Harris who will send you the Particular Rates he will undertake the Farm House for; wants to know Who is to draw the Timber; Suppose he was to get it Drawn by Whom he can?

Yesterday, & one Day before, the Men have been Cleaving & Sawing wood in the Coal-House; Else for the week past They have been Transplanting the Apple Trees & Digging over the new Nursery – the ground is extreme Wet, & some of the last planted Weymouth Pines look Doubtful, this winter will Trye 'Em.

Channon writes me the Captain & his People are much There. I hope the poor Man won't suffer for the <u>Expence</u>.

Lady Fanny Courtenay it's said Dy'd at Bath last Saturday.*

For Godsake Take care of Yourself & Let me hear how you are, as I am under the greatest anxiety for your Welfare.

I am Dear Sir
Your Faithful
N Rowe

Hard rain all Day yesterday.

* Lady Fanny Courtenay, wife of Sir William Courtenay of Powderham.

F437

[no document with this number in the DHC file]

F438

Nutwell, 10 January

Dear Sir

I have your Favour of the 5th, am Extremely Glad you Find yourself Better, pray God give you perfect health.

The Spanish War makes this Country very Melancholy, pray God send Peace.

Your Neighbour's passions have a Different Turne from yours, nothing but the man's utter ruine will Satisfy him* – miserable <u>morals</u>!

The Paper in the Necessary House is most Soil'd the Furthest from the Door, it is owing to the Dampness of the place.

It is a Spring Tide today, & from the frequent rain, wind high & at S., we shall see if it affects the House; hitherto it has not, so I hope your Gutters will answer your intension.

Sol has not been here several Days, he Sent Word by Dyer he has a Crick in his Back & can't Work; when he Comes will inform you where you can put the Spanish Nuts you intend to send.

Your 2 Boxes go this Day by Bird's Waggon.

I am Sorry I am oblig'd to trouble you, But Joyce is a miserable object, helpless & quite Stupid, and I fear will be always so – She is so Troublesome, That She makes Phillis very Uneasy, & what can be Done with Her I know not.

I am Dear Sir
Your Faithful
N Rowe

* As F440 makes clear, Parson Lee's father, the Exeter attorney Alderman Lee, left a bequest to his servant John Brutton, which Parson Lee was determined to reclaim.

F439

Nutwell, 15 January 1762

Dear Sir

I have Troubl'd you with Several Letters But Shall reduce it for the Future (unless anything of Moment shou'd happen) to this post only – But as the Weather has mended Since the late Storme, I have only to add what I Forgot in my last, That the Sea Wall under the Wood is Torne in many Places & much wash'd under, & to the End of Sea-Lane broke away, the End of the Field on the Other Side wash'd in greatly & a Tree on the Hedge flung Down: The Wall beyond the Lime Kiln much broke up, the End next Mr Brice's wash'd from the ground, so high Tides will come thro': The Water was so high to carry away the Cullum, which lay by the Kiln; & on the Other side of the Water much Damage Done.

Mr Channon came here a Wednesday, Says Several Men of War were in Danger in the Sound & some Ships lost: I Fear the Company will drive the poor Man away – I wish the Steward, who is gone to London may answer Expectacion. He has pass'd no accounts with Channon these 4 Years – so Lady Drake Knows nothing of her Expence.

Thomas Wyatt has had no Directions from you about the Pacquet He wrote you, he had received of Portreeve of Bere Alston, nor from Mr Carpenter to whom He wrote about it.

Channon has order'd Sol to drive the 2 remaining Cows to Moreton today, to Sell 'Em next Teusday at Tavistock Fayr; by Him I have wrote to Mr Carpenter.

I hope you are as well as I wish you.

I am Dear Sir

Your Faithful

N Rowe

Your Brother William is skedll'd & went out of the Dock 11th.

[Added in pencil on reverse]: You have not acted up to what Lady Drake cou'd wish.*

* The added pencil note, perhaps in FHD's hand, may suggest that Rowe should have mentioned sooner the failure of Lady Drake's steward to 'pass accounts' with Channon for four years.

F440

Nutwell, 21 January 1762

Dear Sir

I am extreme glad you grow Stronger, pray God give you health, this uncertain Weather pray Take care of yourself.

In the late Storme you came off much Better Than I imagin'd, & all about have – Sir William Courteney's Marshes were all overflow'd which have not been these 20 years before – But Mr Porter writes me a very Melancholy account from Plymouth of the Damage Done There. I wish at your Leisure you wou'd write the Little Man, if But a Line, he is so anxious about your health – your Brother, Mr Channon writes me, is Order'd to Portsmouth to go on Some Expedicion, it was well for Him, his Ship was not in the Sound.

The Method you propose about carrying the Pipes round the House Clark Says will Do; the poor Man's wife Lys in a Deplorable Condicion, money to Him wou'd be very useful.

There is some Defect in the Wall over your groom's Chamber window, which has rotted the Lintal, & flung down all the plaistering, it looks down to the Stair Case Window under; as Soon as the Weather is Settl'd will get it mended, at present Nothing can be Done, Every place is so Wet.

Mr Lee has recover'd from Brutton £170! besides his Cost (all paid) so the Man has Lost all his Legacy.* He [Mr Lee] Says your not Sending him the *News* as formerly, his people give out you are disoblig'd with Him about the Road, and his not having from you an answer to his Letter makes him Fear so. Enclosed is Phillis's account. She is a very careful Woman, & has great Trouble with Joyce, which with no little address I perswade to bear with Her – She is a miserable Creature indeed!

unfit for anything – is very well as to her health & as Strong as Ever, But will do nothing – no-one here will Take Her – and as for her Doctor, how he will be paid! All the Money She had of you being Gone & in Debt Too; her Daughter Ruin'd Her, & has brought so I fear.

I am Sorry to give you this Trouble
& am Dear Sir
Your Faithful
N Rowe

The Bills are from October to Christmas.

[Added on reverse]: For fear of losing £50 or £60 you have put me to 5 times the Expense.
Lady Milner informed me of this.**

* See F438 and note.
** In the addition on the reverse FHD is perhaps referring to payments made to Joyce, as mentioned at the end of the letter. Lady Milner may have advised Sir Francis on appropriate 'compensation' for servants' claims. Elizabeth Mordaunt (1726–1785) married the baronet Sir William Milner in 1747.

F441 [John Channon to Nicholas Rowe]

Buckland, 31 January 1762

Sir

This is to Informe you that the old Robert Kelly is a Bedlayer & I imagine he'l Continue so till his Death. He is very desireous to be carie'd home to Beer. Radford is very willing to take him but he wants to know whether Lady Drake or Sir Francis will Alow him anything towards a maintainance. The old man seem to claime a Right on the family to support him. If you know anything of the Affair I Beg you be so good as to Informe Lady Drake & Sir Francis of it, I have taken care not to let him want for anything the that the [sic] family affords, you'l please to Consider it must be very Mallencolly for a poor old man to lay alone such a distance from the family & very likely may be found Dead in his Bed in the end & if it shou'd happen so I should be greatly Troubl'd at it, for the Neighborwood [sic] will Reflect upon me & my Wife for leting him die alone & it's Impossible for us to keep any one Constant with him without we hire one on purpose for the Maids & my wife have more Busness all Ready then they can well performe & More Masters & Mistresis then they can well Obleige. I should think myself much happyer had I But one Mistriss to serve but at present have many to Obey.

I am Sir your Humble Servant
John Channon

F442

Nutwell, 11 February 1762

Dear Sir

Your Letter of the 4th I received with great anxiety, as you Seem to be so Uneasy, For God's Sake raise your Spirits, as I hope you have no particular Reason; I wish it was in my Power anywise to alleviate any Disagreable, But That's far <u>Otherwise</u>!

I am Sorry I am oblig'd at this Time anywise to add to your Trouble – But Joyce is so Nasty & Troublesome (She do's Everything a Bed & about the House as She Walks); and Tho' as Strong & healthy as ever She was, can go to Limston & do any Errand, yet won't do the least Thing here, even Dress herself, or make her Bed without Compulsion – Phillis will, She Says, go away unless She is remov'd, wou'd Serve you to the Utmost, But is not able to Bear with Her; I Fear no-one here will Take her; Cou'd She be got down to Buckland & put into the Gift House,* There She might be manag'd –

I hope there won't be any Occasion for the removal you mention – I refer you to my Former Letters, which I hope you will Take order about.

I am Dear Sir
Your Faithful
N Rowe

Very Stormy Hail & rain.

* In 1661 the 2nd Baronet, Sir Francis Drake, died and left £120 for the erection of almshouses in Buckland Monachorum, still known as The Gift House (see A. J. Bere, *Buckland Monachorum* ([Buckland Monachorum], 1930)).

F443

Nutwell, 17 February 1762

Dear Sir

I have your Favour of 11th which Gives me the greatest anxiety – pray Take care of Yourself, & I hope with the Grace of God you will Recover your Spirits.

I have acquainted Harris with Your Order for him to go On with the Farm House according to his proposal, which He is ready to do, But Says he can't get anyone to draw the Timber, hopes you will Let Him employ Farmer Coleman, as from Himself – whenever the Slatts & Timber come from Buckland, how are they to be got on Shore, & who is to pay the Freight, you will please to Order Both – I have paid Phillis 2 Guineas Since you went, you will please to order Some money as I have paid all away, & Clark begs to have his Bill; I Sent you an account of what was Due here Some Time ago –

I am Sorry I am Forc't to repeat about Joyce – But Phillis Says She must Leave your Service, if you don't Order her away Directly, For She is so nasty, That She can't Look after Her any Longer – She must be Sent to Buckland.

I am Dear Sir with my best Wishes for your health
Your Faithful
N Rowe

The House was never so Damp, continual wet!

F444

Nutwell, 18 February 1762

Dear Sir

I am under Continual Concern about you, and when I don't hear from you, imaginations Flow in upon me, which I can't Express, Still hope the Best, & beg if it is but a Line, Let me hear how you Do. For Godsake Take Care of yourself, and Don't Let your Spirits Sink; I hope when the good Weather Comes you will Ride much, Exercise do's great Things –

I am asham'd to trouble you so often about that Miserable Wretch Joyce – But the Short is, Either She must be put out of the House, or Phillis won't Stay, it is with the greatest Intreaty I prevail upon Her to wait your Direction – as No-one here will Take Her I wrote to know if Susannah Northmore wou'd; Enclosed is Channon's Letter about it;* when I hear from you will Send her away directly: it is the Cheapest Method, & as Buckland is her native Place, you may do hereafter as you Think Best.

Uncommon Stormy Wet Weather, never Saw the House so Damp, keep Fire daily in the Drawing room.

Sol must Carry Joyce, She is Strong but very Stubborn, the reflection on her misconduct has Turn'd her Brain, She is nasty beyond Expression.

God give you Ease & Health.
I am Dear Sir
Your Faithful
N Rowe

My Share of the Trouble with Her, I can't Name.

* Channon's letter is preserved as 346M/F20. It includes the Northmores' offer of care for Joyce provided that FHD would cover the costs. The Northmores were a long-established family at Buckland Monachorum.

F445

Nutwell, [1] March 1762

Dear Sir

This Morning I received yours with the Two Bills of £10 Each, which I will keep to Pay the Freight of the Stuff from Buckland, only pay Clark, who is very Poor.

Joyce is gone But Sol is not return'd, hope no accident with Her.

I am very Glad you Say in your Last you are Better, pray God give you health – I can say no more now But That

I am Dear Sir
Your Faithful
N Rowe

Fine frosty weather for Some Days N. & E.

F446

Nutwell, 4 March 1762

Dear Sir

I am rejoic't to hear you are Better, I hope as the Spring advances, you will be perfectly recover'd.

They are fencing South Meadow, the Farmer & Sol Seem to do it very Securely, he is very Thankful for the Favour – I am, I assure you, no advocate for the Man, Think of Him as you do, yet I am Sorry you won't employ Him, for I don't know where to apply for any Occasion; how must the Slatts & Timber be got up from the

Vessel when She arrives? Spry Says a proper person Shou'd put away the Slatts properly, wou'd you have Clark? As to the Tunnage of the Timber from Buckland, must get Mr Brice to do it.

How must the Dead & other Earth be remov'd that was cast up out of the South Meadow Ditch, it Shou'd be Done before the Meadow is Heam'd ['ploughed'] up, wou'd you permit me to Bargain with the Farmer as from myself?

Thomas Wyatt writes me That your Brother Sail'd from Thence last Friday Bound for Jamaica, in high approbation of the Voyage – he Say John Wills is so ill of the Yellow Jaundice, That his recovery is very Doubtful; a Letter from you wou'd be very acceptable to the Poor Man.

Mr Lee Seems much Crest Fallen he is not Favour'd with a Letter, the *News* he is much pleas'd with.

Sol had a great Deal of Trouble to get Joyce over the Moor; when She Found where She was going, he cou'd not keep her on the Horse, She wou'd be Continually Sliding off, She bewray'd herself Twice between Moreton Town & Merrypit, & he was forc't to get women to clean Her: She piss'd a Bed the 1st night at Buckland – a Miserable Nasty Creature!

As to the Weymouth Pines, inclosed is an account of 'Em.

Pray God send you health.

I am Dear Sir

Your Faithful

N Rowe

Fine Frost Still.

F 447

Nutwell, 15 March 1762

Dear Sir

I have your Favours of 9th & 11th last and will observe the Contents, But can only Say now That Phillis thinks, the month of March being Cool, Strong Beer may be Safely Brew'd, & Small Beer to keep the Summer, if it be <u>well Hop'd</u>.

The House is full of Wood, & much yet To be Brought in.

I wrote you we had Snow on Teusday night last, which Just Cover'd the ground, But was gone by next Day noon – none Since, So the N. E. & S. exceed W. None Lay Longer on Hal Down; & I don't hear of any on Dartmoor – when Sol return'd, There was Little or None There – I presume you have heard from Channon of the Death of Joyce, Enclosed is his Letter to me – the Wretches at Limston have Spread a report That She was ill-us'd here, and that Sending her down to Buckland kill'd her by the Journey – Scandall has no Bounds! You have been uncommonly Good to Her, & the Woman here,* I can Answer, did more than cou'd be Expected from her. The poor Wretch was happy She went off, as She was a Trouble to herself & Everyone Else.

You don't Say General Eliot is gone, I am Glad your Sister is Better, & That you find yourself so.

Pray God give you Both Health & Happiness, it is the wish of

Dear Sir

Your Faithfull

N Rowe

Fog & rain.

As I have frequent Letters from John Carpenter and Channon – I wish you wou'd Send me Some Franks.

* The 'Woman here' is Phillis Drake, formerly employed by Parson Lee, who succeeded Joyce as Nutwell housekeeper.

F448

Nutwell, 20 April 1762

Dear Sir

The Weymouth Pines were brought here Saturday Evening & planted on Monday, They were heated in bringing, Some of 'Em moldy & the roots breaking out, The Nut Sets were Budded above an Inch out, Sol Seems to doubt of 'Em.

I have given Phillis your orders, which She is Executing as far as She can, She do's not know of anything wanting here – and Since you will have me to be Troublesome, Some Strong Cloth for 2 or 3 Shirts woud be a Favour.

I wish you may Find Everything here to your Likeing, I have Endeavour'd it all I could, But can't Say have been so Successful as I wou'd.

The inclosed I received from Mr Channon on Sunday. Shou'd you write a Line to the Widow it wou'd be much Taken Notice of. Poor John will be mis't at B—n [Beer Alston?].

Sure your Mama wou'd not Forbid bare House-room – nor the Ladys Forbare a Jant [sic] to Plymouth.*

Jack Carpenter return'd here from Yarcomb on Monday afternoon, will write you this post of his affairs from Exeter, where he go's tomorrow.

Mrs Scarle Sent the Book & Brocoli from Powderham, which Sol will Sowe directly.

I heartily wish you a good Journey whenever you Come, & That I may once more have the pleasure of Seing you as well as I wish you.

I am Dear Sir
Your Faithful
N Rowe

Fine Temperate Weather, Small Showers – a Fine Spring.

Yours of 17th gives me great Pleasure, if you are well, I am Well, & all's Well.

* Rowe is once again hoping that Mrs Samuel Drake and her sister will make room for FHD at Buckland (see F419 for the situation in August 1760).

F449

Nutwell, 10 May 1762

Dear Sir

I received your Favour of the 4th with the Utmost pleasure, I could not Conceive you had been so Bad, had I, I shou'd have been under the greatest pain. God be Thanked you are got so well over it, pray God keep you so, yet you alarm me by intimating you are not Quite Sound, Lord what has been your Disorder That has Left such Effects! I Long to See you once more.

Your Man Sol has been at Work all this week, & has done more in the Garden Than for several Past; had his been a Sickness acquir'd by any means but Drunkeness, I wou'd assisted [*sic*] him to the utmost, but Such a Debauch deserv'd none, neither had he any of me: The Woman is a vile Strumpet, & has Confounded, But whether his Conduct proceeds from Stupidity or Stubborness, perhaps Both – he has not been Toward ever since you order'd her not to Work – whenever you come you won't Find anything in your garden for present use. –

Dyer is ingag'd with Several People to Look after their gardens, But he assures me you may be Sure of him 4 Days one week with another, he's a very Careful Man, has a Family & is asham'd of his Direeter [?]; when you See Him, you may observe more of his ability.

The Grafts are not come, unless a Saturday, won't it be Too Late? will send today again.

For Godsake Take care of Yourself, pray God preserve you.

I am Dear Sir

Your Faithful

N Rowe

Fine weather Still E.

I hope tho' I hav no Letter from you last post That you are perfectly recover'd.

F450

Nutwell, 17 May 1762

Dear Sir

I received your Favours of 10th & 11th Instant after I had Sent my Letter away, they were very agreable, But yet as you recover so Slowly, I am under fluctuating Turns; God is Good, I Still Flatter myself with the Best.

Mr Parker had a reccommendacion from the Lord Lieutenant, it was unanimous at the Meeting Last Thursday, but not Cordial – the Election is to be next Wednesday – the Blews drop L. C. [?] no Courtier can relish with — I have got a Milz'd ass, I hope, who had Foal a few Weeks Since, Am Sorry you want ['lack'] one – may any, Every means give you health.

When you are here, the Least Hint from you to Mrs— brings the Collector & her, you remember your kindness to an Insignificant – brought 'Em here, nothing now but what is important indeed (yourself) will bring her <u>again</u>. He is an Israelite indeed! Loves you beyond the poor Man's Expression – wou'd you write Him? I cou'd not of your Ilness.

As to the Wretch Solomon, don't Trouble yourself about Him, it is to no purpose, can the Sowe from Wash quit the Mire? I will Endeavour what I can – the Stone Hedge he shou'd Finish, he is about the pond which must be Turff't soon or too Late.

As to the Lime pit, must refer to your being on the Spot; as to your Neighbour's partiality to your Tenant, money I know not, But the Butter is Forgot – your overlooking Low life is Showing.

It is the Finest Spring here, no Wither'd Top – the wind is now W., There have been Several days at E. but no Bad Effects as I hear of – an amazing Blossome of apples & Pears <u>now Set</u>. I have Sent Several Times about the Grafts, you now Satisfy me.

My Dear Sir Francis, what is this World, if you want health; I ebb & Flowe, to your Family I may apply that to the Prophet, the Chariot & the Horseman Thereof. Pray God give you health.

I am Dear Sir
Your Faithful
N Rowe

My Compliments to Mrs Eliot, you never Said the General was gone to the West Indies.

F451

10 July

Dear Sir

I was Disappointed sending my Letter yesterday – I have acknowledg'd the receipt of all your Letters but this of the 6th.

As to the Figures in the Chapel windows, it is impossible to take 'Em out entire, the Masons before I received your Letter took down one of the Windows but in so many pieces, That being so much Leaded, & Flint into the Stone Work, are much Broke* – Bance shall Take out the rest, I hope Better – the Floor Stones were Taken up last Week, & pil'd up in the Court, There is no room for 'Em under the Arch nor in the Little room, they are so many – the Chapel Door is kept Lock'd & the Back Door Too – as they begin on Monday on the other Chimney they shall want, They say, many Skaffold Boards, as it is outdoor Work; here are none, They Took some of the Elm planks; Harris Says, he can't Spare Them, & besides they are not Measur'd & the Mortar will Spoil Them – to Stop the Side of the Barn which Fell down, Took up Every one about.

The pulpit & Top is Taken down, but where to put 'Em I know not: Eliot Says Mr Waters wou'd buy it for Bicton Church, & Mr Lee wou'd fain have the Pews for his, was you to give 'Em him, might it not be a Forerunner of the advowson? They can't be put up well in the room you mencion, But some where They must be remov'd. Will Take all the care possible of the Fig Trees – Moore prun'd the Vines as you mencion.

You may have one of the Alderny Cows from Powderham, But here is no grass, no Surrey There yet directed – Young Master won't part with his Dear For All —

Mr Lee has undertaken to manage about the Coals.

The Farmer can't part with the Gate, what is to be Done?

As to the Dogs, Nel is very Big, won't the Medicine hurt Her? Ponto don't Seem infected yet, nor She much.

There being so much Mortar wanted for your new Library, the Masons Say 20 Hogsheads, must postpone Taking down the gate at present; will endeavour to get in the Soft Bricks, they'l want many, But the Bay Horse won't Draw, They say.

As to Ciril, he will comply with your offer & to be paid Quarterly.

Dyer hopes you'l give order for the payment of his increase of wages, you have Quick revercion of … [?]

The Master nor Masons have apply'd to me for any Money.

The Farmer won't draw the Earth away now from the Meadow Ditch, Says he can't Bar up his Barn & Pound House.

11 July

Dear Sir

I have your Two Letters with two Ten pound Bills inclos'd.

I wish matters of Every kind had been Settl'd by you Before you Left the Countrey.

Clark is to come tomorrow to go about the Foundacion, if there is any obstruction, you shall know by the first post –

If the Earth is not Carry'd away by some one They can't Finish the Stone Hedge – 'till then any Men will be useless. I Dare Say Sir John Rogers wou'd readily oblige you.

I am Sorry John Slater is so insensible to his own Interest to disoblige you, sure it must be owing to the Effects of Age, Wonderful That I don't Dwindle into Stupidity! But all such Chaps have Turns of Oddity.

It has not rain'd Since you went away but once which was the 6th, except a Few Drops, & no Signs of any – exceeding Hot & Drye, all the grass burnt, Tho' the Wind at South or West.

The Brocoli & cabage are planted, I hope They will prepare against rain, whenever please God to Send it.

I hope you Take care of yourself this Trying Weather, pray God give you health – I Strive against it, But a Drye Tree no Season Favours.

I am with my best wishes Dear Sir

Your Faithful

N Rowe

I wish you may pick out what I mean, you may Depend I will mind Everything for your Interest.

The making these Chimneys will Hurt the Chapel-gutter. The Stones are very hard to get out.

* For the conversion of Nutwell Chapel into a library, see Introduction, section 3, pp. 29–30.

F452

Nutwell, 22 July 1762

Dear Sir

I hope this will Find you Better, pray Exert yourself, God give you health & let nothing Else Trouble you.

Sol is Stoning the Hedge, but the gound is So Fretted in & the Bottome so full of pits, That it is very Troublesome doing – the Man has Fail'd with his Cart, I don't know where to get one, Harvest being Begun, & the weather Fair, Everyone is Busy.

The Alderny Cow won't Calve these Six Weeks; if you wou'd let Clark pave the room within the kitchen with Bricks, Phillis cou'd then keep the Milk There clean & Cool.

The Masons will use more than the heap of Bricks, must then go to your new Ones, you will send Directions. They have Done the Chimneys, & are about the Windows, the gutter must be Mended, wou'd you have Arthur do it?

They have got a fresh Supply of Culm, so more Lime may be had, if wanted.

Clark has not begun yet about the Farme House; I have Sent to Him, the Days Shorten & the Fair Weather may alter, I wish it was Done.

The Newfoundland Land affair has made a great Breach in these parts, their Loss not yet known.*

Harris desires to know if you wou'd have the Temple Tarr'd over with Oaker mixt with it, or Solely.

I hear nothing about the Pulpit, I don't know where to put it out of the Way, nor the altar Decoracions.

I can't help Troubling you about these Things, But if you are not well, why or what do's all Signify!

Pray God give you Ease & Health
I am Dear Sir
Your Faithful
N Rowe

The young Fellow works very well.

* Newfoundland was lost to the French and then recaptured by the British in 1762, during the Seven Years' War.

F453

Nutwell, 9 August 1762

Dear Sir

I have your Favour of 3rd, am very Glad you are Better, hope you'l soon recover your Lowe Spirits.

As to the Masons, I can't understand what Ashlar work is, But they Saw & Smooth with a Chissel Every Stone they put in, & if you intend to Stucco the Face of the Side where the Windows are to be, that must then be hid. They have been about the window next the Necessary, 2 Masons & 2 Labourers, the week before & last week 1 Mason & a Labourer, & not yet Completed; most of the Time is taken up in fitting & Furbishing the Stone; unless there are more hands, the Way they go on, the 3 windows won't be done by Christmas.

The Fruit don't ripen yet, I hope you'l be at the Eating of it, For Things won't then move in a Different manner – Clark can't get any Men as yet to help him, The Stone hedge not near Finish'd, the poor Fellow I wrote you about is Dead, he was very good Labourer, & wou'd have been of Service to expedite Matters before wet Weather comes.

I can't yet get the Cart to draw away the Earth, Harvest not yet over, the Man can't attend it.

The Joyners are about the Bracketting, with what Plank Harris has Let Them have & Some Sawing for Them it will I hope do – When is the Stuff to be Taken out of the Pond? The rain & the rats have broken it up once or Twice, it is stop't for the present.

The Plumber has not been here yet, nor Eliot, who is to transact about the pulpit – Mr Lee has had the Pews away.

The Masons in the Chapel Say they shall want 15 Hogsheads of Lime more, and when they come to make the partitions, you must order 'Em to use all the old Bricks, before they have any new.

I heartily wish you Ease & Health.
I am Dear Sir
Your Faithful
N Rowe

Fine rain Saturday, Sunday & Some today.

F454 [continuation of F453]

10 August

I was Disappointed Sending my Letter a Monday, Since a Labourer from Exeter has offer'd himself, which is upon Trial; he work'd with the young Fellow that is Dead, But won't under 8s. a Week; Dyer Says the Same and I don't Find any Care to, as your Work is uncertain; at present a man is much Wanted, to help get in the Stones for Clark, & Bricks for the other Masons, as they are going about the particion Wall. As the Farm-House is built on Such uneven Ground, it will Take a great Deal of Earth to Level the inside, which must be brought from the Ditch in the Meadow. I expect the Man to draw it away today.

The Sash Lines in the one pair of Stairs rooms in the new Buildings are mostly Broke; wou'd you have any from Exeter, or Send 'Em from London?

As I Find you intend to Face the Side of the Chapel next the green with Smooth Stones, you'l Find it will Take much Time; the Sides of the Windows and the rest to be rub'd over as They Say, to do which a Stone cutter is Coming, who may be more adroit – There's a Chimney runs up in the Side of the Window, which has formerly been much us'd, & another on the other Side of the Chappel; They must have more Lime now, having us'd very near all they have, So they'l want 30 Hogsheads at Least in all.

Selley came here this morning & Stay'd 'till Evening – the Exeter masons had today 15 Hogsheads of Lime; you will send word what Quantity you shall want for the plaisterers.

I don't know whether your Groome Told you, But the Plank in the Inner Stable is all rotten; Selley says if the Stalls were Layd with hard Brick, it wou'd Do; Something must be Done before you can put your Horses There.

F455

Nutwell, 13 August 1762

Dear Sir

I have your Favour of 7th and as you Say Nothing to the Contrary, I hope you are Better, I wish you So.

There are some of the Weymouth Pines Look but indifferent – Sol is so Obstinate, Stubbourn & Stupid That I can't Say much about Him – He don't mind anything I say, But the Contrary. As he has 2 men to help, I shou'd hope the Stone Hedge may be done next week, if the weather don't hinder, But the various Things Take Dyer off often; Wednesday he was Drawing Bricks for the Masons in the Chappel, & Clark wanting Stones I was oblig'd to take the Man's Cart all Day to bring Them; it is impossible with the Parson's Cart to bring enough for Him, and when the Bricks are to be brought from the Brick Field (which will be Soon, As they have near us'd the heap) the Man's cart with 2 Horses must Fetch 'Em, as Mr Lee's with one Horse can't, & yours won't Draw.

Ciril is now going over the Old Nursery, he has a particular Charge about the Bare-Bind ['bindweed'] there – the pond don't Leak now.

What is to be done for Scaffold Boards for the Plaisterers, & where are Laths & Lath nails to be had? Mr Brice has no Laths.

Here is a Stone cutter come, hope will give Dispatch to the Stone-work. A Bricklayer is carrying up the particion Wall.

Phillis has found out That your Workmen & the Masons as She believes have got into the Cellar where the Strong Beer was, thro' a hole under one of the Windows in the Chapel, where a Chimney was & Drunk several Bottles of October; They deny it but the Suspicion is Strong against 'Em – Such Fellows don't mind Such pranks, But They are not to be Trusted.

The Farmer has been Serv'd with a process from Mr Heathfield the proctor for not paying the Tyths of all the Estate which he formerly rented, without regarding what you have Excepted by your Last Lease, which He hopes you'l Excuse him from.

I am Dear Sir
Your Faithful
N Rowe

Fine rain yesterday afternoon, wind S.E.

F456

Nutwell, 18 August 1762

Dear Sir

I Congratulate with you on the Birth of a prince, a Joy to all Faithful Subjects.*

Mr Waters came here last Saturday with a Carpenter to look on the pulpit, who Told Him it was too Big for his Church; as Wills, who was here yesterday, has order'd his people to take up the remaining Stones in the Chapel, I was oblig'd to get the Pulpit remov'd into the Hall, the only place capable of receiving it; they have Finish'd at Last the Window They first begun upon, & are going to break out another; by the Fall of the Scaffold with the Man the White Fig Tree is much Hurt, I am afraid the others won't Fare much Better; Tho' they are often Caution'd, they are very odd Fellows, and as the garden lys open to 'Em, they will Steal the Fruit, Tho' I Threaten & Watch Them all I can.

The Fruit begins to ripen, what wou'd you have done with it? It's a pity it shou'd Rot under the Trees.

Clark can't get any Men to help Him, Only one Mason beside Himself; I am oblig'd to hire a Cart to bring Stones for Him – Mr Lee's when I can have it, is Taken up to carry Bricks & Sand for your new Building: There are 2 Masons, one Stone cutter & 6 Labourers Sawing Stones, & Tending Them. The two Joyners are making Brakets for your new Chamber & getting rafters ready.

The Greenland ship is arriv'd, have caught 5 Whales, next week the nasty boyling the Blubber go's on, which will poison Us – I am glad you are not here, it wou'd be Intollerable to you.

Sol is getting the Earth out of the Meadow; to Level the Inside of the Farm-House Will Take a great Deal – Clark desires you'd Spare Him Ten pound, won't Trouble you any more, 'till the work is Done, the Window Frames will be up this Week.

I wish you Ease
& am Dear Sir
your Faithful
N Rowe

Channon came here a Sunday about the cow, which He will Take care about.
Some rain a Saturday.

If there shoud not be Enough of the ordinary Stone for your Farme House, may They use some of the worste of the Lime-Stone?

* The prince born in 1762 was the future George IV.

F457

Nutwell, 28 August 1762

Dear Sir

I hope you are well. I have been for Several Days very Mawkish, whether it was from the Stench of the Boiling the Blubber, or as it is not very healthy here just now; I am very glad you are not here!

As to the going on of your alterations in the Chapel, I can't Say much – they are now making the Window next the Door, in breaking out of the Walls there is much Trouble – Here has been a Stonecutter 9 Days in fitting the Stones, he has been absent some Days, & is now wanted again, I presume he'l come next week; the two Walls are Done as Far as they can at present.

The Joiners are now altering the Gutter to Communicate with your Water Closset, they have Taken up the Lead, & the plumber is Sent for.

The Stone hedge is Just Done, the Man is return'd again, he went away on account of his Father's Illness; as Everything is very Backward, I will keep Him 'till you come down, you will then order as you think proper.

As to Clark, he goes on but Slowly, he can't get any Men; you will send your Directions how you will have the Oven done, as it Stops the Work on that account; to have it with Daverton Stones He Says is most for your advantage, I have been oblig'd to buy Scaffold ropes for Him, as they can't part with any for him.

They are now carrying out the Earth from the Meadow, it is very Fine Weather; as the Expence Encreases by the additional Man, and for the Cart &c, you will please to Order Some more money, as your last is Just gone; and the £10 for Clark.

I am so Feint I can Scarse write, you will Excuse what's amiss.

I am Dear Sir

Your Faithful

N Rowe

F458

Nutwell, 31 August 1762

Dear Sir

This is your Birthday,* I wish you many with health & happiness – on Such Days People use to Confer Favours when it is in their power, permit me Sir to ask one of you; the Farmer is a Brutal Man, I am no advocate for him, But I beg you wou'd be so far Reconcil'd, as to let him have what necessary repairs are immediately wanted; the stormy weather, we have had, has blown away the Thatch over his Cellar, that it rains in upon his Cask, & rots his hoops, wou'd you be pleas'd to let him mend it?

As to your building in the Chapel, Selley, who is often here, will acquaint you whether the Masons do you Justice, they are here Early & late – they will want hard Bricks to cast an arch over the recess at the great Window, I hope soft ones will be found to Close up the Window; the Labourers are very Troublesome, won't pick up the pieces, which wou'd Do, I have much Difficulty with 'Em.

Clark go's on as fast as he can, he wants hard Bricks to turn arches over the Windows, he & Harris Both Say it is for your Service to have 'Em as they will be so much expos'd to Weather, & he has no Stuff for Lintals; he will want Brick for other uses, I hope you will order about it, & for the Daverton Stone for the <u>Oven</u>; he can't well go on 'Till he knows your pleasure.

Phillis is much out of Order, & I have had a Cold & a Touch of an ague, which has much weaken'd me, But I hope I shall weather it, being Better.

Sol with his 2 Men promises to expedite Everything.

Pray God give you health.

I am Dear Sir

Your Faithful

N Rowe

It [is] now Fine Weather.

* FHD's birthday was actually 29 August.

F459

Nutwell, 24 December 1762

Dear Sir

I have your Favour of 18th, am Sorry you have got such a Bad Cold, hope you are Better, & that you won't Risque your health – Tho' the weather is Extrcme mild. Neither will I Flatter myself with any so agreable an Expectation.

I think you have Scrv'd Newman &c very Justly – Such a Man ought to be so Treated, he'l Soon cry *peccavi* ['I have sinned']. The Spillers deserve no Favour.

I wrote you of the 3 £10 Bills coming Safe by the return of the post, have paid Mr Lee £10 5s., Evans's Bill, and at the End of the Month you shall have an account of the rest.

Thc Thatcher has been with me today again to know if you approve of his proposal, Harris Says he's ready for Him, & Clark the Same; his Bill includes the Quenching of Lime, which is £3 of the amount – whatever may happen for the Future shou'd be given in Every Month, Every article may be then without any Difficulty known & Settl'd.

Harison the plumber will Finish the Water Closset today, & put up the pipes after the Holy Days. Selley came here a Thursday & Staid most part of the Day to assist about it, I Desir'd he wou'd Let you know what Further he had to do – the Mason Finishes today for the present.

The Chimney piece is Brought.

Clark go's next week for the Sand for the Plaisterers. Here are no Scaffould Boards as I have wrote you, nor any paper Lights.

I have paid Dyer the Extra you order'd, hopes you'l Consider him for Last year.

Phillis met Sol at the Lime Kiln last Wednesday, he Told Her he had his ague Every Day this month past, he look'd miserable Every Way, yet won't Forsake Hannah, 'Till she do's Him.

With the Compliments of the season
I am Dear Sir
Your Faithful
N Rowe

Your gardiner is pruning the plumbs & Cherries & Dyer digging the ground, can't get the Dung yet.

F460

Nutwell, 7 January 1763

Dear Sir

I had no Letter from you by Last Post, nor have anything to Trouble you with Particular from hence.

But Mr Porter writing me That General Eliot arriv'd at Plymouth with Admiral Pocock last Friday, & as he Sat [sic] out that Day, hope you Saw him a Sunday – I Truly Felicitate you all on his Safe arrival, with my best Compliments to your Sister, with Whom I sincerely Sympathise.

Poor Jack Carpenter is in no Small Pain, Least any Letter from you about the Yarcombe affair shou'd have miscarry'd, as he writes me, he had not any from you by Last post.

I hope you are well, pray God keep you so.

The Same Close Weather, wind Still East, not so Cold, no Frost. The Gardiner not return'd.

I am Dear Sir
Your Faithful
N Rowe

Your Man Solomon is Still with Hannah, She came here yesterday to Complain he has nothing to help Himself & is, as She Says, Dying of a Dropsy, having not been able to work these Five weeks.

F461

Nutwell, 15 January 1763

Dear Sir

I am greatly Oblig'd for your Concern, I Thank God, I bear up. I received yours of 8th with pleasure to hear you are well – the hard Frost you have at London is very Surprizing here, having had very Little since the 4th, But Close & very cold East wind, & so it Continues! The pond was froze a little on the Edge, But no Ducks or Widgen, only one Snipe – Dyer has Finish'd the gutters, & is Digging the ground in the Wilderness, has never been hindred but 2 Days. Moses is battening the middle water Closset, the Stuff for the paper windows is not yet come from Exeter, believe must Send for it.

Wills the Mason has brought me his Bill, the Enclosed is my observation on it. I believe the Time is Just, But can Say nothing to the rate per Day, or Extra, which I presume he agreed with you.

As to Farme-House, that is at a Stand at present, expect the Thatcher every Day, But it is so Cold people don't care to go on high out of Door Work.

Nicholas has behav'd very Bad about the Bricks, in the inside of the Kilne he has pack't away abundance of Broken Batts – Clark desires to know if he may use Them to brick-noggen the partition between the Brewhouse & the Kitchen, as he fears they'l break thro' soon Lath & plaistering.

I am glad you received my Letter owning the Receipt of the two ten pound Bills; as I receive & Send my Letters by the Exmouth Carryer, it is Sometimes 2 or 3 Days before they Come to my hands, But I am punctual in Sending answers to any of Consequence. I hope you are well, & don't go Late to Castle Bear.

Sir George Pocock's Fleet was said to put into Silly.

I am Dear Sir

Your Faithful

N Rowe

I believe the papers Mrs Martyn Sent you are of no great Consequence now, the Counterpart of your Father's marriage Settlement is that among Them?

Mr Lee is Qualify'd at Last after 3 journeys.

I hear nothing of Mr Carpenter. Is Mr Newman in Custody?

The Gardiner is not return'd from Buckland.

Two Covers with your Letter of the 8th came Together.

No Plumber yet.

F462

Nutwell, 11 July 1763

Dear Sir

I have your Letter of 5th. I sent you by the Same post Two Other Covers and in one of 'Em a Letter, which I hope you have now received.

I have acquainted Phillis with your Orders, She Says as the House is so Dirty, She can't keep Things so Clean as She wou'd, will do her Best; as to airing the Bed & Carpets, the weather is so uncertain & wet they can't Safely be air'd Just now, will in drye Weather – have Told her your order, That She let no One See the House, and to the Gardiner That he let No-one into the Gardens. I Fear no Devonshire woman will be Such a House maid as you Expect.

The Gardiner Says the Wet weather has made the Myrtle Shoots so Tender, it won't be Safe to venture Cuttings, 'till it is Dryer; as to his work in the pear Garden, he has clear'd the ground from the Trees, is filling up the holes, & that at the End where the hedge was pull'd down; now the ground is so wet he intends to plow the upper part of the pear Garden, and the green if you approve of it – he has pull'd Down the Wall & Thorn hedge as far as you directed, & remov'd the Stones among the Elms, a Large parcel, he Follows the workmen duly: Last week's Expence came to £3 19s. 6d.

The Joiners have put up the Glass Door going into the Garden, they want a Lock for it, are now about the upper part of it, Moses do's what They put him upon – the Stonecutter has not Sent out any Men yet, tho' I have Sent to him often; They want to have the passage Layd & the Chimney piece to be put up; have Sent for the Glazier to put Glass into the Window in the yew Room, & to Elliot to paint it & the Door. The plaisterer is doing about the window in the back Stairs, & other Jobbs as they Occur. Clark is about the Pillars in the Back Court, will do the Buttrace at the End of the House; wou'd you have the grates Taken away under the Common parlour Floor?

It is now a Spring Tide, but as no Freshot, hope it won't be very high – it will soon be Time to repair the Breeches in the Sea Walls. I expect the plumber this week to put up the remaining Pipes, the Joyners Say They have directions how the Water is to be carry'd away.

We have had Several hard Showers for these 2 or 3 Days past, and windy at S.W., I wish one of the Elms, by the necessary house don't Fall, as the ground is so wet; it now Looks as if we shou'd have Showers, it blows fresh at S.W.

The Weather is very Sultry between the Showers, uncertain Hay Time; I hope you Take care of yourself, I have got an uncommon pain in my Gumms, which is very Troublesome; as your house is so open, I can't be Easy, but when I am up & about which is very Early – pray God give you health, pray remember me kindly to your Sister Elliot, none wishes Her Better.

I am Dear Sir
Your Faithful
N Rowe

Mr Lee is about Stuccoing his Chancel if Mr Perritt & He can agree about the Charge.

F463

Nutwell, 20 August 1763

Dear Sir

Your Last Letter gives me great Uneasiness, I Long to hear from you –

I won't Trouble you with anything now, will Do the Best I can in Everything.

We had yesterday from 3 in the Morning to Noon violent Thunder, Lightning, and hard rain at South, very Sultry, afterwards good Weather. Today it is very Fair & hot at West, hope it will Continue for the Good of Everybody.

Nanny Waits your Orders.

I pray God give you health & Spirits.

Mr Lee Sends his Compliments, he Fends off the Evil Day where Expence is the Case, 'Till he Sinks with his money into Oblivion! He Says he will write you.

I am Dear Sir
Your Faithful
N Rowe

Pray Take Care of Yourself, Use Exercise, & See your Sister Often.

F464

Nutwell, 5 September 1763

My Dear Sir Francis

Your Letters Confound me – may the Day be Ever propitious – is my Daily wish, to you & yours. Job's black Soliloquy can be nowise Extenuated but, That he was oppres't by the Devil, & a vile vixen a Wife! But God be Thanked for Every Other

Frailty That don't so Far affect Us – as They are Trials for better Consequences – I am Taken off from further Expatiations by the Trifles of This World.

Captain Pulling brought here a Saturday in his own Boat your Bed, & the Packidge of China very Safe for what appears; the Bed has been air'd, & so Shall Those you Direct.

The Joiners will Finish the great Parlour & Withdrawing Room as Soon as They can; it wou'd have been Done before, But the Wainscot Boards were not Drye Enough to Lay.

It is now very Fine Weather, I Long to See you, hoping the Change of Air, & your place, which now Looks well, will Contribute to what I pray for.

I am not able to Say more But to Wish you Every happiness.

I am Dear Sir

Your Faithful

N Rowe

F465

Nutwell, 7 September 1763

Dear Sir

I received yours of 1st with much pleasure, That you are Better, & That I shall Soon See you.

It is now Fine Weather & hope it will Continue so – I have Forgot Horace – There is Something Like it – *non Semper imbres* &c ['not always showers'] *neque Semper Arcum tendit Apollo* ['nor does Apollo always keep his bow drawn']. Don't Laugh at me, as you have Him at *unguem* ['fingertips'].

But what I aime at, is That we must not always Expect Sun-Shine in our Uncertain Island, yet God be Thanked we have not Suffer'd in the great Calamitys.

Nanny is very Industrious about the Bed: in honour to your Grandfather you preserve it, at an uncertain Expence; But it was his wedding Canopy, which produc'd &c &c &c. She will put the Carpet under the new Table in the Library as you Direct.

You won't Find the Joiners so Forward in the Withdrawing Room & parlour as you Expect, They have but Just Lay'd the Floors in the New Library & Bedchamber; have not heard from Mr Dixon, want the Carv'd work for the Chimney piece in the new Library.

The Plaisterer Sets out tomorrow, his Last Job was Stuccoing the Iron Closset. I have paid him & you £55 13s.

I won't Trouble you further, but when I know his Charge, will be more particular.

I am Dear Sir

Your Faithful

N Rowe

Jack Carpenter writes me about Edmunds' Lease for East Sherford, That he Sent to you, before you went away. I know nothing of it: did not you Take it up in your Box? he has got the gout, so has Mr Collector, Man is Borne to Trouble, as the Sparks fly upward!

F466

Nutwell, 9 December 1763

Dear Sir

I have been in Fear you was not well, am very Glad you are Better, For Godsake take care of yourself.

I am very Sorry you have so much Trouble about your Trust, your not parting with any money must be your only Security – the Scotch Merchant will do anything to come at That, & much good may his Bargain Do Him, hope you'l soon get Clear – Small Encouragement for Generous actions.

Lady Drake I Felicitate, you all Sympathize, and I hope the Captain Will make all the Returns in his power to the Generous Woman.

You will greatly oblige your Constituents, in your Endeavours about the Cyder affair, whether *Mutatis vel Mutandis* ['changes having been made or needing to be made'].*

God be Thanked we have had no further Repeticion of the Storm I wrote you, it was N.E. I believe Wednesday night, as it brought Down the Trees in the Middle Culvery Hedge, But the Violence all Thursday was at S. or S.S.W. Had it been at the Highth of the Spring it wou'd have Terribly affected this place, Especially if more to the West. We have had Little rain since But, for the General very good Weather, yesterday an Uncommon Fine Day, Mild as Midsummer, today a Moderate Hoar, in the Morning, but very fair & calm at N. all the rest of the Day.

The Meadow is so Wet, the wood can't be well got out yet, Shall as Soon as possible.

Hill Sent word there is a Collyer in the River, But They won't Sell any Coals under 16s. 6d. a Quarter. You don't intend to buy any at That rate, by your Letter; perhaps cheaper, when the Greenland Ship comes in.

The Men have Clove up the Motes, they did not get 10d. a Day, I have paid Them the Guinea as agreed, They Complain it is very hard Bargain: The Same Men have begun the Hedge at 3s. per rod, But as you don't Say what highth, your Gardener imagines you approve of his proposal of 4 ft & half High.

The Joiners have finish'd the Dado in the new Library, are now about the Architraves to the Doors, & the Window Shutters – Moses as by his paper, & is Still about The new Kitchen.

Elliot's Man primeing the new Library.

The Glass is up in the new Kitchen Windows, it Looks very Light; I hope you'l Overlook Jackson's neglect, He's very poor.

Harris is Sawing the Elm in the Green, as you & Hawkins direct.

Ley's Man is Heling ['roofing'] the new Building, with Mill-Hill Stones, which Seem very Good, has brought Everything but Sand, which as there was Some on the place, he must allow what you Think proper for it; he Seems to do his work very well; Hawkins Says when he has done, which will be next Week, Clark must come directly to Close up the Sides of the roof with Brick.

When the Greenland Ship comes in, you will Send your Orders, how much & at what price you will have any Coals.

You will please to put in the Margin of the inclosed Paper what you woud have Done in Each particular & return it; I do it in this manner, That there may be no Mistake, & to Save you as much Trouble as possible.

Pray God give you health.

I am Dear Sir
Your Faithful
N Rowe

Hawkins Says the Bars for the window Shutters in the New Library & Bed Chamber will Do very well.

* The Cider Bill of 1763 was a proposed measure to put a tax on the production of cider. This was strongly resisted in cider-producing regions such as Devon. See Introduction, section 5, p. 58.

F467

Nutwell, 16 December 1763

Dear Sir
  Though I have no Letter from you, Since that of 22nd Ultimo ['last month'], I hope you are well –
  As today is the highest of the Spring Tide, tho' it blew Fresh at South, there being Little rain, yet it made a high Tide, But being no Freshot, it did Little Damage, no Water came into the Cellar: and the air-holes are so high, no rain Water can ever Fill the Gutters so high to reach Them. No more Trees blown Down, Harris has Taken away Those that were Fallen on Those Standing, Least They Shou'd bring more Down, & to Ease those They Lay upon. He is now Sawing the Elms in the green.
  The Enclosed I received from Channon about Stacey, I have wrote to Mr Porter to assist what he can, it not being in my power to do him any Service with Mr Moreshead; you will Send your Directions, if you Think proper to Employ Stacey here: whenever Channon comes up here, if you wou'd Let him have the great Bay horse to break Him, he might Then be of Service, But he is so Frekeish now, That Dyer is affraid to Deal with in Harness, and he breaks down the Hurdles, so Fear he'l get into the other Meadow.
  Your Gardiner has almost Done pruning, he Says there is much bad wood in the Wall Trees, which He has cut out; he waits for what Seeds &c you intend to Send Him – Says is Sure, was you to have been here you wou'd not have Dislik'd his Employing so many Men to Clean the ground, whilst it was good Weather, before he did anything Else – He never Shall have any Consent of mine to do anything without your immediate Order.
  Old Horrell's Wife is Dead; by the Enclosed it is Long Since the Leases were granted & Agnes still Living.
  The 3 Joiners are gone to the Fair at Exeter, their Work the Same – Hawkins is Cleaving up the Motes, & Dyer getting wood for the House. All the Bills you Left money for I have paid – Enclosed is my account of the rest.
  I am Dear Sir
  Your Faithful
  N Rowe

Your Cousin is Lady Pocock at Last to Mr Porter's no Small <u>Joy</u>!*

* Admiral Sir George Pocock (see also F460, F461) married Sophia, widow of Commodore Digby Dent, and daughter of FHD's uncle George Drake of Madras.

F468

Nutwell, 26 March 1764

Dear Sir

I sent in to Exeter a Saturday, Nothing Come by the Waggon, They very often Fail, which Occasions much Trouble.

The Gardener, as the rest have Done, Wants more Dung; I Think as you do, But be the Case how it will, none is to be had, and when you Come down, you will Settle it with him, how much you will allow – he will do as you direct about the Tubyroses &c when They Come.

One of The half Hogshead of Beer is Bottl'd, and the Timber, which is Left of the Salting Trough will make Three more, which the Cooper is now about, so only One is wanted, which may be Borrow'd, & Save you Buying any.

The Joiners have wrote to Mr Dixon for hinges for the Water-Closset, I inclos'd his Letter to you last post, They have near Done their work about it.

I sent in to Mr Wills a Saturday, he was not at home, so had no answer, But hear he has Said, he won't Do anything about the Cistern, unless he is paid for it; you will order as you See Proper – Workmen are all Selfish.

Mrs Drake being Ty'd by the Leg keeps her at Buckland – it's a Disorder of Long Continuance Some times.

The Cask will be made this Week, & Next Nanny will Brew the Beer, & hopp it well as you Direct, She Supposes you wou'd have but 3 Bushells to a Hogshead as formerly – She will ask Mrs Richards' assistance.

There has been Some Small rain Saturday & yesterday, But nothing to Signify – today it is Close but no rain, wind N.E. I hope you receiv'd no Damage by Going out, & that you will be very Cautious of Catching Cold.

I have got Some Cattle from Farmers Coleman & Creedy, hope to get it Eat Down soon, But as the Ruffit, as they call it, is so rotted, believe must have Some Sheep, after the Bullocks, to Eat it as Lowe as possible; the South meadow is much hurt, by its being Left so Long.

I heartily wish you a perfect Restoration to your Health and Strength
& am Dear Sir
Your Faithful
N Rowe

F469

Nutwell, 25 April 1764

Dear Sir

I should have acknowledg'd Your Favours of 17th & 19th But I imagin'd you was Soon Coming Down. There was no Occasion, as I was Daily in Expectation of Seing you.

The Beds are air'd, the House Clean'd, a Bushel of Wheat ground, the Two Girls Come, & Mrs Coleman has promis't to assist all in her Power. No Fowls to be got hereabout.

Poor Nanny is Gone, She's an Object of great Misery – very helpless! I have paid her the account you sent me and Taken her Receipt, & what was Due to Her here; her Last words with Tears & a Letter She Left for you, were That you had been the Best of Masters to Her, and if you wou'd but please to Forgive Her, She Cou'd Suffer

Every Other Misfortune. Indeed She is a True Penitent & moves Compassion – For my part She has in her Agonys Greatly Shock't me – But my Dear Sir Francis, I don't pretend to interfere in your Family affairs – I was quite unacquainted with Her Mad Letter, had I known it, She shou'd never have given you the offence.

I am very Sorry your Brother is Relaps't, hope there is no Danger.

The Pantry is Finish't, & Everything shall be put in the Best Manner for your Reception; as I have no Letter by this post, presume your next will Fix the Day of your Coming.

I hope you are well, pray God keep you so.

I am Dear Sir

Your Faithful

N Rowe

I have Sent Several Times about the Beans, none Come by Coach, or Waggons – Fine Weather tho' hoar Mornings, Wind East.

F470

Nutwell, 19 February 1765

Dear Sir

I had not Time to answer your Favour of the 12th in my Last.

I will pay Pridham the remainder of his Bill when I see him.

I have inform'd Mr Brice, who will Thank you Himself.

Dyer will get ashes as you Direct for the South Meadow, Which shall be Eat up in the Best Manner Can be.

I am Glad the Turkeys pleas'd you, Sarah was affraid they wou'd not Feed upon the Buckwheat; They boil the Milk for the Dogs as you direct, But now the Two Cows are Drye, Milk must be Bought for Them, as They are 4 in Number.

Miss Mugford is brought to Bed of a Boy, They Say She'l Lay it to Andrews, Wish Mr Dixon had Sent for Him before you went away, Especially as he Still Continues here, & the parish may put Him to his Trumps.

Hawkins Sends you an account of his Thoughts inclos'd. He has had Directions from Mr Dixon about the Box for the writings, he has Seen Mr Turney* and Talk'd with Him about the Mahogany, who will come here & advise about Sawing it.

Mr Channon came here yesterday, & went away this morning; his Business to the Fair at Exeter tomorrow is to buy Nets; he has advis'd Dyer what he is to do, Says the Green must be plow'd as Soon as the Frost is gone, which at present is very hard & has been so these 2 or 3 Days, at E. and Like to Continue; when Channon came over the Moor a Deep Snow – the weather pierces me Thro'. I can't Bare it as I us'd, But hope when the weather grows milder, I shall be able to Struggle with it. I am under great uneasiness about you, hope your Cold is Better, pray Take Care of Yourself, & don't trouble Yourself about me. I am Extremely Thankful for your kind regard, which is much to my Consolation, Tho' I was never press'd harder, Tho' I Thank God I have been Enabled to go Thro' it, & Trust I Shall; my head is so Confus'd you must Excuse my inconsistancys.

The 3 Joiners are all about the Brewhouse, Tucker about the Dog-Houses; pray where are They to be put when Finish't? Shall get Collars & Chains for the 2 Newfoundland Dogs.

When the ground in the Green is plow'd They Say the 2 Cart Horses must have Some Oats, it being so hard.

Inclosed is the account Of Cash, the Bills when paid is a Separate One.

Dyer & Horsey are Cleaving Wood, & Hedging.

Everyone Likes the Last Dog Mr Sparks Sent, if you Shou'd have another by Mr Withall, Channon begs you wou'd Spare him that you don't Like, must They have nothing But Buckwheat?

A Letter directed for you Comes under Another Cover by this post.

The Rats & Mice abound & Eat Everything, Even the Drye Fish! I shall send for Some Ginns & Traps, There's no Living for 'Em, They are Seen 10 or 12 Together, Rats.

You Say nothing about Mrs Scott's Bill, it is of Long Standing – The Things had by Nanny.

I am Sorry to Trouble you about Such Trifles, But am Determin'd never to pay your money without your immediate Direction.

Pray God give you health.

I am Dear Sir

Your Faithful

N Rowe

The Gardiner Still about the Espaliers, wants Some help to dig the Ground in the Kitchen Garden,

Things wou'd be very Forward if the Frost did not Cheque them, the Buds breaking out &c.

* Reading of the name in this and in several subsequent letters is uncertain: Turney/Tumey?

F471

Nutwell, 5 April 1765

My Dear Sir Francis

I was afraid you was worse than you wrote me, Hope you are Better as you Say, pray don't incommode yourself by writing to me, Two words that you are well, Will be sufficient, pray Take care of Yourself – That is all.

I have given Mr Lee a hint, Hope he'l write you, he has promis't to speak to his Friends in behalf of Mr Harison, but a line from you to Him to shew to Them, wou'd be of great Service to the Man.

Some Barly from Wimple shall be got, all say Kerton is too Rich Land. Trefoil shall be sown with it, and the Clover you mention in the green; it is Time the Culvery shou'd be Fill'd – But the ground is so Wet, Every One is Backward. Mr Carpenter writes me, they are almost drownd with rain, can Sowe no Lent Corn yet. He is going into Wales the 10th of This Month, can't be at Yarcombe till the 22nd. Desires I'l send the Leases you Left, to Matthews's against that Time. He comes here in his way Back.

Dyer will get the Scotch Firs you Direct, & Do the Rest; he and John Coleman are Digging Ground in the Garden – the Gardener is very Busy. He desires to return you his humble Thanks for your goodness in Curing Him of his ague, he is quite Well; He begs you wou'd please to Let Him have Ten pounds, being much in Want to

Buye some Things. You are pleas'd to mention warme Weather, here has been None since you went Nothing but <u>rain and Wind!</u> The Frost & wet has kill'd the grass seed sowne in South Meadow, That by the Necessary is the only Flourishing.

Hawkins has finish'd the Box, put on handles & hinges from Exeter, desires to know if you wou'd have a Lock put on it, & Rings to the Drawers, whether you have any? He has got some Mahogany from Topsham, Is going about the Sideboard Tables – Moses is righting the Window Shutters in the Hall, he seems to have Little to Do, unless you have anything Further – Enclosed is his last Week's Time.

I am Glad you have wrote to Mr Channon about selling your sheep; Farmer Coleman I hear wou'd buy 'Em, your keeping won't make 'Em Better. The Lower Culvery shou'd be Leas'd of the Stones, & shou'd not the Mud be Beat abroad & the Stones & sticks in the Middle Culvery be pick't up?

Sarah desires to know if you'd have any of the Hens set abrood. Expects your Order about it, Their Wings are Cut, & They are kept in, in the Poultry Court.

Your Newfoundland Dogs are Chain'd up & put in their Houses in the Court by the House Door, They are so Fierce, They are not to be Ventur'd Loose, Till your Gates are secur'd, & some Door to the Drying Ground, as the Hedge is all Coming Down, and was They or Either of Them to sieze any Person, they'd pull Them to pieces. Mr Lee's Dogs are Nothing to 'Em.

Tucker is making the Fence to the Hay-rick, all the Ground about it is Quite a Swamp, he has been up at Farmer Creedy's, but as the Farmer was not at home, he did not see what was wanting, will Let you know in my next.

Yesterday was pretty Good Weather, it has rain'd all this afternoon a Fog at S.E. Lord have mercy upon us & send Better Weather.

The Rats abound. Like the plague to Egypt, They come into the Bed-Chambers & Eat the Victuals from the Tables, they run about the House like Tame Rabbits; I hope you'l give your Consent to have a Cat, There's No Living with Them, I am in Daily Fear of Worse Consequences.

Pray God give you Health.
I am Dear Sir
Your Faithful
Rowe

Since my writing part of my Letter yesterday, the Gardener was Taken ill again, I wish it mayn't be a Return of his ague.

6th, 9 in the Morning

We had hard rain last Night & wind But a Moderate Freshot, a very high Tide, no Damage done to the House, or Trees. It blows hard now at West, & Fair as yet.

The Gardener is about again, so believe he won't have <u>his Ague,</u> is making the Melon Ground.

F472

Nutwell, 3 June 1765

Dear Sir

I have your Favour of 28th past, I have paid your Gardiner £6 17s., with what I paid him before makes £10. I have Discharg'd John Coleman; he says there is business for 2 Men, Watering Takes up much of the Time, But as it is your Pleasure, must Do as well as he Can – indeed hitherto to get down the Weeds, was very Troublesome, he is much Taken up about his Frames & Glasses, and I observe whatever station They were in before, they all Talk of Dukes & Lords, and tho' they come Bare, as soon as they get some of your money, They pretend to be Considerable. When you'l see how this Man has manag'd, the pond wants to be Clean'd out, the Docks & Weeds in the Green to be Taken up, Last night there was a Shower, which made no impression, today very hot wind South.

I Discharg'd Moses on Saturday night and paid him £9 14s. – in full of all Demands – Hawkins has made the Stand for the Chest of Drawers from Buckland, wants to know Where you wou'd have it put; when he has made the Little Side-Board Table, & Finish'd the 2 Great Ones I don't see what he has more to do. Inclosed his measure of the Stairs.

Ash the Mason came here this morning to work again, with 2 Men; he wants Harison to put in a pipe, who is Sent to do it, Hawkins Says you agreed how it shou'd be.

Allen came here today, the first Thing is to paint the Gates, which so much Want it – Desires to know what Colour you wou'd have the Stair Case, he thinks a Stone-Colour; the Outside Windows want much to be Painted, the putty all Crack't, & the Oil Exausted – he says 'tis the Custome, when They work in the Countrey at this Time, now the Days are so Long, to work 7 Days for 6. You will Let me know, if you approve of it, as till then he won't.

Sarah has 4 Brood of Chicken, expects more Soon, do's not know what to do with 'Em, what with the Masons & the Rats – I think the Man has Lessen'd Them – and Old Ash undertakes to Clear 'Em; if he do's, he Deserves your Encouragement.

I am very Glad you intended a Visit to Hillingdon, hope you found the Captain & Lady Well;* if she advances so Quick, there may be Representatives Enough, Since you won't have any of your Own – I hope you'l have your health, the Rest in due time.

This weather will hasten the Cutting of your Meadows, I hope you'l be Down to See that Operation; the Clover must be soon down, I wrote to desire your Directions, where to make a Rick of it – your Cart-horses don't like the Grass in the middle Culvery, it is too Long & Drye – whenever there is rain, wou'd you have the new ground in the Two Meadows Weeded, there is a great Deal of Trash in 'Em.

I am Dear Sir
Your Faithful
N Rowe

Mr Harison came here after I had finish'd my Letter, inclos'd is Hawkins's & his Determination about the pipe to go from Receiver into the Brew-house & about the Tubs, in what Condition They are in.

The Great Gates last made must be painted Twice at Least, They are so shrunk.

* FHD's brother William and his new wife set up house at Hillingdon. Rowe hopes for 'representatives' through their offspring, since FHD will not have children of his own.

F473

Nutwell, 11 February 1766

Dear Sir

I have your Favour of the 4th. My Back is Still Bad, I am Oblig'd for your kind regard –

I have Lost poor Dutchess, a Wednesday I had her Out, was as Usual, a Thursday she was in the House, & Friday & Eat her Meat, But on Saturday Morning after I had sent away my Letter, I went to take her out as the Snowe was gone, and to my great Surprize & Trouble found her Dead; I had an uncommon Fondness for her, She was my Companion in all my Solitary Walks, I sensibly Miss Her, & my Concern is so great, That I shall never Regard any of Her kind more – the Raven & the Rest are as Usuall – had I 100 Dogs I coud have parted with all, rather than Her.

Will enquire about Tiles for the Coach-House. Those are gone which you had of, there are some to be had at Honiton's Clist, which They say are Better; if any are to [be] had there, who is to put Them up?

The Seeds shall be sent for.

The Bacon Dyer has Smoak'd, & They Think Enough.

Sarah returnd on Saturday night.

The Surgeons on opening Chowne's Wife reported She had not been poison'd, But the Women don't Think favourably of him.

Mr Lee is highly pleas'd, he has got rid of his House; when I see Him, will acquaint Him of your Congratulation.

The Hens begin to Lay.

It begins to Thaw, a Fresh wind at West.

Inclosed is Dyer's Time last week, he is now making up the head in the Ditch next the Bridge.

Mr Turney comes here frequently, he has put Tucker to Sawing the Fir-Timber, he is so modest, Tho' he spends whole Days, That he will neither Eat, or Drink here, Tho' I Constantly press Him, nor won't unless you Desire Him, at any Time. I will endeavour to get something for Him, I Expect Him here today, he was yesterday at Combe Farme, & intends to go There before he Comes here.

You will Excuse my inlarging, as I write in great Pain. I hope you are well, and Take Care of Yourself, under your present Fategue.

I am Dear Sir
Your Faithful
N Rowe

Your Gardiner is preparing Ground for the Seeds you sent me the account of, he is always doing Something, Mr Turney will bring Them Out.

3 in the afternoon.

Dear Sir

After I had finish'd my Letter Mr Turney brought me your Favour of the 8th. I am very Sorry you are out of order.

The Gardiner I ask't who wants nothing beyond what he gave you & the Turnip Seed –

Dr Gely won't part with his Dung.

The ground shall be got ready for the Potatoes, But Dyer must have some one to help Him.

The Receipt for the Sheep shall be prepar'd.

Mr Turney will Look over the Pollards Taken down as also the Ash & give you his Opinion.

Pray Take Care of Yourself, I can Scarse write This, Stooping is so Painful.

Yours

NR

Mr Turney is gone to Combe Farme, will write You next Post.

F474

18 February 1766*

My Dear Sir Francis

Mr Turney has Just now brought me your Favour of 15th. Poor Dutchess gives me more Concern, Than I care to Owne. She wanted for no Victualls, but I could not go out with Her as usuall, which is now my Great Concern. I have bury'd Her in the wood Deep where I shall Think of Her as often as I go There.

Pray Excuse my inlarging now, I will observe Everything as well as I can – I am not Sick, I want Nothing, But intreat you to give yourself no Trouble about me, I hope it won't be Long so. I have a Due Sense of all your Favours, you Say nothing about yourself, I hope you are well, I always pray for Your health & Prosperity, pray God Continue it to you.

I am my Dear Sir Francis as I ever have Been

Your Faithful Friend to serve you whilst

N Rowe

Dyer shall give Mr Turney an account how many Elms are wanting.

Enclosed is his Time for Last Week.

Mr Porter wrote me lately That he had sent you a Basket of Fish by the Coach, But had heard nothing from you about it.

Your Gardiner is pruning & Dyer Digging the ground for the Potatoes.

3 in the afternoon, now very Fair & wind W blows hard – & at 4 rains so uncertain.

* Date on the reverse, perhaps in FHD's hand.

F475

Nutwell, 13 May 1766

Dear Sir

Last Sunday between 10 & 1 a noon There fell violent showers of Hail & rain, I was in it both going to & coming from Woodbery Church, Thoroughly Wet; Here was a Flood, but it did not Come over from the Mote. But the rain Cover'd the Green.

Your Garden is very Clean & full Crop't, and 2 parts Trench'd for hereafter; your Gardiner told me, That if he Continues so Weak, he must go to London, For he is not able to do anything – he has had, Sarah Says, all along a good Stomach to his Victuals, he Told me if he had not Fear'd to have Dy'd in the Waggon going up, he shoud have gone when first Taken Ill – Sarah Begs me to acquaint you, that as Everything is so Dear, Beef 4d. & Mutton 3d. halfpenny a pound, hopes you'l Consider Her. Wheat 5s. a Bushel, Every Particular has been so Ever Since you Went.

The Gardiner Says the Seeds you Sow'd are mostly Come up, & the Roots, he keeps 'Em Weeded, the Wheat is very Rank – the Blast on the wall Trees is a Calamity indeed!

Bence the Glazier desir'd I wou'd Send you the inclosed memorandum, which I Took from Him.

Your Directions to Dyer shall be Observ'd, But as the Green is so wet, Nothing can be Done there as yet, only John Coleman is to assist Him There.

Dame Crabb shall be Talk'd to about Howing the Shrubbery, But the Wheat is Generally so Full of Weed, That the women are Entirely Taken up on that account, when the Weather permits.

No Boys haunt now your Wood, & if they do in the Shrubbery it must be by Night, or they woud be Seen; Dyer Says he will watch 'Em, But this Wet Weather has been a great Detriment to Breeding – you have very Few Chicken.

The Green before the Drawing Room windows wants much to be mow'd, I have Told 'Em of it, & it will be Soon Done.

Mr Harison I have Sent to.

Mr Curtis has been Spoken to; They are affraid, if they work the Kilne, they must pay rent for it, I assur'd Them not, But that don't Satisfye 'Em, unless They have it from you.

The Weather is so Bad, it keeps Mr Turney away.

I am very much Oblig'd, for your kind wishes, I hold out Surprizingly, But I must Expect an Alteration, God knows how Soon, his holy Will be Done to

Your Faithful

N Rowe

Dyer was all Day Yesterday marking out the Willow Bed, & 5 have undertaken it, to go on Directly.

Your Gardiner says now he is Better, & hopes he Shall get the Better of his Disorder; I wish your Trees may of <u>Theirs</u>.

3 in the afternoon, S.W.

It rain'd hard yesterday & this Morning, it is now Fair & very windy, how long it will Continue is uncertain – Mr Turney this Moment is Come here, he sends his Compliments to you & desires I wou'd Let you know, that the Carpenters had Disappointed Him, But as soon as the Weather is Settl'd will come out, & overhawl the Stuff to See what is Wanted to go on with the Barn.

F476

Nutwell, 16 May 1766

Dear Sir

Mr Turney brought me your Favour of 13th this afternoon.

As to your Neighbour, as you call Him, he is Below your Notice, as to wheat it shall be Weeded, But I beg you won't Think of hurting That, for the Sake of a Sordid Lowe Creature not to be alter'd – Your Contempt will be a Sufficient Mortification.

I am very Glad you have got your Brother a Ship, I wish he had ¼ of your Sense, That would be a means to make him Think properly – as the Ladys a too Long Virginity turns their Facultys as well as their Nature to a Stoppage of Every Regular.

The Gardiner is much Better, & is very Thankful for your Goodness, hopes he shall get over his Ilness without any Further Trouble – Your Garden is full of Everything, he is always doing Something – the Blast Mr Turney says is a General Calamity, I hope your Wall-Trees will get the Better of it.

They have mow'd the Grass before the Great Parlour, it was High Time; Several of the Filleray, Lankest[er]inas Cypress's, & Some of the other Shrubbs are Blasted, but will recover again; Don't you intend to have the Walks of the Wilderness Cut, When They come to Clean the Borders in the Shrubbery by the pond &c won't They trample the Grass.

The new planted Evergreens all Shoot, only the Cypresses look very red, So they do thro' out, But as it is now Fine Weather hope they will recover too.

The Grass grows Surprizingly in Both Meadows, a Vaste Deal of Blossome on all the apple Trees, Espaliers & Standards; as much Blossome among the Strawberries.

The Lawne Before your House looks much the Larger, now it is Levell'd – Hope 'twill Soon be finish'd & Sow'd.

In July Everything will Court your Company, By that Time I hope you will be able to visit this place, which much wants your inspection to complete, what you only can Do.

The Men have begun on the Willow Bed which will be an additional Expence.

Harison has mended the Gutter, which I am very Glad of, as it begun [sic] to Stain the paper in the old Library.

Pray God give you health, you'l overlook the Folly of the World, I'm going out of it.

I am Dear Sir
Your Faithfull
N Rowe

17th in the Morning

The Fine Weather still continues, hope it will; Glass at Set Fair almost tho' the wind S.E.

Sarah begs you Consider Her these Dear Times – the Gardiner has a good appetite, Expects Nesessarys, as he Calls Them, which She is not able to Supply at her present allowance.

Pray overlook the Weakness of the priest, *quo Semel* &c ['where once'].

F477

Nutwell, 15 June 1766

Sir

Your Gardiner being Old, Poor, & in Distress I had a Compassion for Him, and wou'd not Trouble you with his bad Behaviour, as to Drinking, Being in hopes that he wou'd amend: as he kep't the Garden Clean & Stock't, hoped he would make up for what he had Done amiss. Mr Turney Thought as you wou'd be Soon Down, to Leave him to your Pleasure – But Yesterday Morning he Broke out into Madness, & So Continues; at Intervals he is very Sensible & Says he is not able to do your Business, so Desires to go Directly, & will trye to get up in the Waggon – He desires two Guineas to bare his Expences, & my Letter to you; in it I can't Say much in his Favour, only that when he did not Break out, he was up Early at his [Wor]k, but 3 or 4 Times he was out Late; Particularly last Friday night and Since then his insanity has appear'd – Whatever you intend by way of reprimand, or Otherwise, when he waits upon you, must be left to your Goodness – I fear some great Trouble attends Him.

Mr Carpenter call'd here this Morning, he is come up, about his Client Butter's affair.

The Overseer of the Poor told me today, That next Saturday, the Justices at Topsham will put an apprentice on Nutwell Barton; I Told Him, I had wrote you about it, & Desir'd he wou'd get it put off, 'Till I heard from you; said That it was your Turne, and Depended on the Justices' Determination – Shou'd they Fix one, what is to be done with it? I hope I shall have your answer –

The Gardiner gives me great Trouble, he Frightens Sarah so, That I am oblig'd to have Dyer in the House, I hope I shall never See the Like, must Send him away as Soon as possible.

I hope you are well.
I am Dear Sir
Your Faithful
N Rowe

F478

Nutwell, 28 June 1766

Dear Sir

Wednesday at 3 in the afternoon it began to rain, which held on the rest of the Day, & Thursday it rain'd most part of the Day; Yesterday it was Fair, & They got up the Hay in the Little Culvery, and if it holds Fair today, will rick it; it was very Fair this morning, it is now overcast at South, I hope it won't rain, if it don't between this & Monday, shall get in this & the other Culvery too – and then go about the Meadows – But none will work without Cyder, So Some must be got: Everyone is so Busy, the Difficulty is to get People, are oblig'd to have Dyer, Coleman, & Crabb & his Wife, can get no other; You will order some Money for this Extraordinary Expence, & for the Brick-maker, They could not Work the Two wet Days.

Mr Turney has not been here Since Teusday, nor the Carpenters, nor Sawyers, So the Barn is at a Stand. I acquainted Mr Turney that you Desir'd him to buy Oak for posts for the Pale Gate in the Sea Lane.

As to the parish apprentice, Farmer Coleman will Endeavour to get a Boy, and I should hope, if you will ask Him, he will Take it as he did the rest.

The Gardiner Dyer Left at Exeter Wednesday Evening, in a very Bad Way, but how he will get to London is a Doubt; I Let him have, as I wrote you, Three Guineas: he is a miserable <u>Creature</u>!

There have been great Rejoiceings at Exeter for Lord Buckingham, who was there Several Days.*

I hope you are well, & will be soon here.
I am Dear Sir
Your Faithful
N Rowe

Am oblig'd to have Dyer Lye in the House for Security's Sake.

* Lord Buckingham, formerly Hobart, lord of the manor of Bere Alston.

F479

Nutwell, 26 January 1767

Dear Sir

I hope this will find you Safe & Well and as the Weather was good, you had a good Journey up, which I shall be glad to hear.

Moses did not know how you wou'd have the Pales that were Taken down by the new Stable, Clos'd up again, becaus of the Gutter; has only fasten'd it up for the present, 'Till your Direction is known about it, he has done all he can to the new Cart at present.

John Denty says you order'd him if there were Stakes Enough, to frith ['fence'] up all from One End to the Other of the Sea-Wall, and as far as the Stakes are Sufficient, he has Stak't it accordingly; But I apprehended by you, it was only to be frith't ['fenced'] where the Breaches were, and you had mark't it out so; it will now take up some Time to fill it up with clay & gravel and as Lewis is much the handyest, it is best to Continue him about it Till all is finish't.

Moses and Mr Andrews have Cover'd the Stern of your Boat.

I see by your written Directions Mr Lee is to pay the Work-people, but you have not Said in what Manner.

Enclosed is the Account of the Last money I Receiv'd & paid to your Use, you will please to Compare it with the Other Sent you, & Let me know if there is any Mistake, I have Vouchers for everything.

I heartily wish you health & am
Dear Sir
Your Faithful
N Rowe

Denty went away a Saturday at Breakfast to go to Exeter to receive his pention [*sic*], so the Boy was in his room.

F480 [brief note]

The Boy says he can't ride out the Coach-Horses, as their Shoes are so Bad.

The Cart horses go tomorrow to plow the Field at Southton. Shou'd not they have Some Oats? You've ordered None.

F481

Nutwell, 28 January 1767

Dear Sir

I hope you got well to Town. I wrote you by Monday's post, & sent you my account.

They cou'd not Finish the Bents in the Sea-Wall on Monday, Lewis not being There, & no more Furze Brought – yesterday it rain'd most part of the Day, Coleman

& Lewis went home again, as They coud not Work, Dainty dig'd a Little, & Will went to Plow at Southdon, but was oblig'd to Leave off. Dainty Says he is to have 8s. a Week <u>Wet & Drye</u>; it's a pity nothing can be Contriv'd, when it rains, I know of Nothing but Cleaving Wood, & there is no ax, or Hook – is he to have the Key of the Tool-House, in Wet Weather it wou'd be Convenient for him – it now rains & I fear little can be done today – next Week you shall have an account of what is Done in this.

There is no Wood or Fagotts for the Maid, how will you please to order it?

The Cart Horses must have Oats now they plow, & indeed always Hay, as there is no Grass for Them.

I wish you health, & happiness.

I am Dear Sir

Your Faithful

N Rowe

F482

4 February

Dear Sir

After I had wrote my 2nd Letter, I read your Favour of 29th past.

I understood you, when you went away, That you would Consult General Eliot about Shoeing Your Coach-Horses, which was the reason They were not; having Lost Some of their Shoes, They could not be rode out, Both shall now be done.

As you directed they had 2 Bushels of Oats last Week, now you Say they are to have none, but when They work, and as to hay to give them each Twenty pounds a Day, & Likewise to give them Barly Chaff, when there is any; this method will Take up Time Every Day to do it, one of the Men must assist, and it must be done with your little Beam.

I don't wonder Lady Drake declines in her ... [left edge clipped off] having so long Confin'd herself. I am very Sorry for her, as I am That you have got Such a Cold, pray Take care of yourself.

It never was so hard with me as now, as I can't Walke but with great Pain.

I am Dear Sir

Your Faithful

N Rowe

As to the Cart horses, when the Middle Culvery is Dress't, there is onely the higher one for Them to go in, & there is no Grass in the Field; They must have hay, and Should have Some Shelter at nights.

F483

Nutwell, 4 July 1767

Dear Sir

I have your Favour of 29th past, & Sarah Last night brought me That of 1st – I can't Express my Concern for you, I Conjure you for Godsake, your own & your Friends, That you will Take particular Care of yourself; I am perswaded Good Mrs Eliott will Show the Good Sister, pray my best Best Compliments to Her, the

General & pretty Miss, She will help to Nurse her Dear Uncle – pray don't Think of Taking so Long a Journey, 'Till you have got Strength, and Safely able to bare it.

The Hay-rick is Thatch't, in good Order.

The Green shall be mow'd, the Grass is Burning away.

Farmer Creedy brought a Cow & Calf this Morning.

The Things you mencion to have Sent by Captain Minifie, Shall be Taken Care of as you direct, if they Come before you, But as your Two Men are Both Bad, must Desire to get Them brought ashore by Mr Brice.

I hear Nothing of the Brick-maker nor have had any Directions from you about Him; the Furze is all Brought in, & Rick't, They Should be Thatch't, if you don't use Them this Year.

It has been very Stormy & Showry these Two or Three Days, which Tumbles about the Wheat, That Ears well.

Pray Take Care of Yourself, when Hercules* Comes will acquaint Him with what you write, he must Board himself, Martha can Scarse do for Here.

Let me have but a Line, when you can, how you Do, for myself *n'importe*, Tho' your Kindness I am very Thankful for.

I am Dear Sir
Your Faithful
N Rowe

* Hercules More, the pruner, who was required to provide his own food.

F484

Nutwell, 31 July 1767

Dear Sir

Mr Turney brought me your Favour of 25th, Who will write you – I Constantly write you Every Wednesday & Send the Sherborne Paper, & Shou'd oftner, did anything particular Occur, & Your Ilness made me unwilling to trouble you – I am extreme Glad you are so well, hope your Strength will increase Daily, & your health perfected, which I heartily wish.

Hercules More is not Come yet, Neither have heard of Moses, have Desir'd Mr Turney to See Him.

Your Wheat is much Beat down, whenever it is fit to be reap'd, I hope you will desire Farmer Creedy to reap it, as he did That Last year at Southtown; the Barly is very Full of Hoar Oats, Else pretty well – as I presume you intend to put the Wheat in the Barne, the Floor must be righted, before it is put in, the Planks are Started so much.

Your 3rd Hay-rick is Thatch't in good Time, the Weather is so uncertain, Yesterday it rain'd hard Showers Several Times, blew fresh S.W.

It blew very hard this Morning at N.W. with a Smart Shower at 4 morning, another at 11. Fair Till 3 when Mr Turney brought me your Favour of 28th.

Your Directions about the Herbs & Distilling Martha Says She believes She can Do, But here is no Charcoal, have Desir'd Mr Turney to get Some.

You Say Nothing about the paying the Brickburner Weekly for Moulding the Bricks, I Beg you will Let me have your particular Orders; as the Moulders don't belong to Him They must be paid Weekly, and as they do their Work very Well, They must be Encourag'd.

If the Wheat Shou'd be fit to Cut next Week, must ingage Farmer Creedy to do it. Your Barly won't be ripe These 3 Weeks.

I am perswaded Mrs Eliott will Take great Care of her Dear Brother, pray my Compliments to Her, the General & Miss, and I hope you won't Venture Such a Journey as here 'Till you are perfectly Strong & Well, which I heartily wish you & am

Dear Sir
Your Faithful
N Rowe

The Rabbits increase & Eat your Flowers in the Shrubery, as do The Birds your Beans, pease &c.

F485

Nutwell, 3 December 1775

Dear Sir

I have your Favour of 30th past with the Several Letters inclos'd, which are Sent as Directed.

Jenkins shall have your Directions about Comb Farm.

Your Sheep have got another Disorder – the Foot Rot; a man by Channon's Order has been here & Look'd Them over, & Left Stuff for the Skab, and will Send Something for the Other, don't Doubt of Curing Both, it is not gone Far; They are Chang'd, the Sound in South Hill, the Others in 7 Acres, I hope it won't go Farther. Your Gardiner will give you a more particular Account.

The weather is very Mild, the ground Excessive Wet, hope it will Turne out Fair yet.

Channon when here Said He would write you about the Bullocks, of which you Say nothing.

I hope you are as well as I wish you; as you Say nothing to the Contrary, I conclude so, pray God give you health.

I am with Respect Dear Sir
Your Faithful & Oblig'd
N Rowe

Your Cat is very well, we Converse often Together.

THE LETTERS III

From William Hudson to Sir Francis Henry Drake, 1767–1778 (Devon Heritage Centre 346M/F166–F195, re-ordered 1–29, followed by DHC number)

1–F166

20 September 1767

Sir

I am sorry to acquaint you that yesterday there arived an Express with an Account of the Death of the Duke of York at Monaco on the 17th instant.* It is immagined that his Illness was brought on by over fatigue; as he had travel'd near 500 Miles from Fryday to Monday when he arived at Toulon where it is said he danced all night and then embarked for Genoa but went to Monaco in order to see some Roman Antiquities &c. He found himself but very indifferent on his arivel. He was receiv'd with great politeness by the Prince and at Supper complain'd of being sick and desired to have something in private which was granted but when it was brought him he was not able to eat anything and insisted upon embarking the next morning for Genoa, tho perswaided to the Contrary by the Prince &c, but he was determined to get there if Possible. But after he had been out some time he found himself so ill that they put back again immediatly. Upon his arival they sent away for Physiciens both from Nice & Turin. His disorder turned out a Milliery fever and as he did not find himself better in ten or twelve days he insisted upon taking Dr James's Powder, which accordingly he did & it had its usual effect. It is said that the Eruption struck in & fell upon his bowels and brought on a mortification in his stomach & bowels of which he died the day after, viz the 17th instant. He was ill 13 days – This is what I have been able to learn of this Melancholy affair for I have not been able to see My Mother [?] (who had letters) as they were in such confusion and hurry – Lord North is appointed Chancellor & W Ellis succeds Lord North.

I am sir your oblig'd humble servant
W Hudson

* See Introduction, section 5, p. 61, for the sickness and death of the Duke of York, a younger brother of George III.

2–F167

London, 9 January 1768

Sir

I this Day received the favor of yours and am glad to hear you have got the Ducks all safe. Before you turn out your Ducks I would advise you to cut their wings, otherwise you may stand a chance of Loosing them as happened to a Gentleman this

Autumn who bought half a dozen. Three of them flew away into a river which was near his house and he never could get any inteligence of them afterwards, only that they had been seen there. After once they become acquainted with the Place there is no danger of their going, it is only at the first. The Weather has been so severe that I durst not venture to send the Turkeys but as it now begins to thaw shall send them by the Waggon this day Week if I hear nothing from you to contradict it. The Glass has been as low as 8 Inches & as I have got a diary of the weather I have sent you a few Days account of the Thermometer.

The remainder of the changes are now likely to take place, tho much against the inclination of the Duke of Grafton & Lord Chatham, particularly Lord Weymouth's & Lord Sandwich's.

The whole conversation for some time has been engrosed by Lord Baltimor.* I make no doubt but that you have seen the account in the papers which, tho most part of it was swore to by Miss Woodcock, yet from what appear'd before Lord Mansfield it seems to be quite a Canning affair.

The following is what I received from Mr Dayrolles who dined with his Lordship and heard him tell viz that her Father applyed to him for a Habeas Corpus, which being granted Lord Baltimore was serv'd with it and sent word that he would wait upon his Lordship immediatly; and accordingly he went with the girl in his hand and when he came there, the Father & several other Friends of the Girl were waiting. She past by them without taking any notice of any of them. They were shown into Lord Mansfield where after the common Compliments were over Lord B was desired to walk into another room as he must examine her alone; which he did. Lord M asked her how long she had been with Lord B, what she answer'd about ten days. He then askd her whether she went on her own accord or was carried by force. She answered the former. He then asked her whether she thought herself Lord Baltimore's Prisoner. She said no & that she was ready to go back with his Lordship. Upon her saing this Lord M askd her her age, she told him she was 24. He said she was then at years of discretion and he had no power over her. He then asked her by what means she came acquainted with Lord B. She desired to know whether she was obliged to answer that or no. Lord M told her not; then she said she did not chuse to do it till she had seen her father. Lord M told her she might see him as he was then in the house; she was shewn to him and after having about half an hour's conversation she was sent for again, and was ask'd the same question which she answer'd by saing that she now looked upon herself as Lord B's prisoner and demanded to be released. This surprized his Lordship much and it appearing so very extraordinary that he order'd his door to be thrown open and a number of People who were waiting were desired to walk in, when his Lordship told them what she had said to him but that since she had seen her Father she had altered her opinion and left them to judge of the afair. 'As for you Madam you are at liberty to go where you please'. Accordingly she went along with her father and immediatly to Mr Feelding** and swore a Rape &c against Lord B. He granted his warrant for apprehending him. Lord B hearing what was done absconded, for which he is blamed by Lord Mansfield, who said it was in the Power of a Lord Chief Justice of England to grant Bail even in cases of High Treason.

I am Sir your obliged humble servant

W Hudson

January	1	at 8 in the morning	27
		at eleven Night	24
	2	Morning	22
		Night	19
	3	M	15
		N	17
	4	M	22
		N	22
	5	M	10
		N	19
	6	M ½ past 8	13
		Night 11 o. Clock	19
	7	at 20 Minutes past 8	8 ½, this was the lowest

I have Not yet received the remandor from Mr Shad…

* The notorious Lord Baltimore was tried for rape in 1768 and acquitted in the absence of adequate proof that Sarah Woodcock had resisted his advances. He went abroad, travelled with a 'harem', and died in Italy in 1771.
** The blind magistrate John Fielding (1721–1780) was a younger brother of the novelist Henry Fielding (1707–1754). Each in turn became London's chief magistrate, and both were renowned as champions of the poor.

3–F183

[Autumn 1768]

Sir

I have this day sent you the Tea, cinnabar of Antimony & extract of Hemlock as I should think she should continue it a little longer & to Purge her two or three times with salts or any other purging medicine and wash (with bran & water strain'd or thin water gruel) the sores twice a day.*

I am sory I had no roots to send you, indeed I have had little time this autumn to look after plants. I expect some soon from Yorkshire & if they come fresh you may expect some of them.

I have heard nothing yet from the Captain.

We have little or nothing stirring, the cheif conversation runs upon is Elections. Sir J Lowther it is almost Certain will loose Cumberland, Curwen being 1000 & Fletcher 500 upon the Canvas ahead of him. He has offer'd to compromise with Curwen which he refused with contempt. Lord J Cavendish is likely to loose Lancaster by not declareing himself sooner. Sir H Harper will undoubtedly loose his Election tho I am sory to say Lady Caroline has prevail'd upon the Ministry to influence some in his behalf and letters have been sent about, beginning as I am well inform'd: <u>By order of the Chamberlain</u> &c. Yet even this won't avail – it is said Sir Robert & she are parted upon the occasion.**

The King went to the house this day – and I hear the first thing they are to go upon is Mr Dempster's breach of Privilage. Lord Chatham does not come to Town yet, but will be at Hayes soon; J Mires [?] it is said will succed Hewet – Mr Norris who succeds to his Father's Place for <u>Life</u> viz Usher to the Customs, said to be a nominal 1000 but beleived to be worth 7 or 800 £ a year, rather than not be in Parliament & to oppose, has resign'd it; which perhaps will be more than he'll get should the oposition come in –

Since my last we have tryed the Aple Juice.*** It acts very slowly upon lead for after standing two days it won't colour. The Iron did a little. So that from the small quantity of Lead about the presses and its acting so slowly upon it are sufficient proofs that the colick does not arise from it. However in order to remove that objection Tin may be used in its stead as I don't find Cyder will dissolve it, for after standing 3 week it won't show the least alteration with the Gipsum soil water and I much doubt after all, that should no Lead whatsoever be used in the making the Cyder that they will find the distemper just the same provided they continue to drink the crude juice –

I am Sir your obliged humble servant

W Hudson

* See Introduction, section 5, p. 67.
** Hudson is reporting here on the elections in his native regions, Cumberland and Lancaster. Lord John Cavendish (1732–1796) withdrew one week before the 1768 Lancaster election, which was won uncontested by Sir George Warren (1735–1801). For Sir George's domestic arrangements, see below 21–F170. Lady Caroline Manners (d. 10 November 1769) was the mother of Sir Henry Harpur, 6th Baronet. After becoming a widow she married, on 17 July 1753, Sir Robert Burdett (d. 1797), from whom she is here said to have 'parted' on account of her efforts on behalf of her son.
*** See Introduction, section 5, pp. 59–60.

4–F186*

[20 September 1768]

Sir

I have just received the favor of yours & and am sorry to hear your Magnolia tree died. As to the Hypericum I would not have you disspare as the stalks generally die down and the root remains good and shoots out next spring.**

I should think the first thing to be done for the woman is to let her have an Issue cut at the knee & then to give her a dose or two of Hiera Picra or any warm Opening medicine so as to get two or three stools & then give her some Pills prepared with equal Parts of Gum Ammoniacum & Soap, twelve Pills to be made out of a dram, and to take four night & morning for three weeks.***

I have been a good deel hurried for this week past having patients out of Town where I have been obliged to go every day which has prevented my getting the roots so soon as I intended but will send them by next Fryday's Coach if Possible –

I saw Dr Thomas today who told me that Lady Drake is very ill. He was out of Town when she was taken ill and so they sent for Dr Addington; but from Dr A's account of her Thomas thinks she will not be able to get over it and I don't find that Dr Addington has much hope.

We have nothing new here; all the conversation runs upon the King of Denmark. I hear the King intends entertaining him at Richmond on Tuesday next –

I am Sir your oblig'd humble servant

W Hudson

* Dated from added pencil note, 20 September 1768, and from mention of Lady Drake's severe illness.
** See Introduction, section 4, p. 37.
*** See Introduction, section 5, p. 67.

5–F187*

[November 1768]

I was much surprized today to hear by Miss Thomas, Dr Thomas's daughter, that Lady Drake had been dead some time, especially as I had applyd to the Dr to get some account of her illness as you desired and having heard nothing from him nor seen him since made me inquire if she knew anything about her when she gave me the above information –

I have inclosed you a few seeds which I have just received from Bath, viz the Glastonbury vetch which wee looked for in vain, the Bath one & what they call Thlaspi hersutum found near Weymouth but which I take to be the Allysson hirsutum –

We have nothing new here worth mentioning; Lord Chatham's Letter to the King & likewise to the Duke of Grafton are got into some few hands and are call'd very spirited ones but as yet I have not been able to get a sight of them.

I am Sir your obliged humble servant

W Hudson

* Dated on internal evidence of Lady Drake's death in early November 1768.

6–F168 [continuation sheet of a letter]

17 November 1768

I yesterday received a letter from Captain Andrews informing me that the things must be onboard this day as he sail'd in two or three Days at farthest. I immediatly went to Mr Ayliffe's to see if the chairs were ready and was told they were not made & could not be sent so soon.

As to your wheat I wrote a person, a friend of mine, to get it for me & send it to town. He inform'd that he would purchase some of the Best sead wheat he could get at Kingston. If there was not in the markitt good enough he would get it from some of factors who attends the markitt & send it to London. In consequence of the captain's information I wrote to him yesterday to desire if he had got it to send it immidially, if not to let it alone till such time he heard from me again. I have not yet received an answer which makes me apprehens[ive] you won't have it by this opportunity nor the chairs. I shall not do anything about the wheat should it not come till I hear from you about it. I should think you might get good out of Dorsetshire or some of those counties nearer you, should no opportunity offer of sending it by sea.

This night Dr Hill was put to the Ballot for a member of the Royal Society at a very full meeting – for him 14, against 82. Alas poor Hill!*

What Mr Symour's Motion is I can't learn from the absence of the members at the Royal Society. I suppose the House was not up. Some say it's about the Letter, others the Duke of Grafton, others Corsica & others the C[ommons] list. Tomorrow will unravil the mystery.**

I am Sir your oblig'd humble servant

W Hudson

* For Dr John Hill (1706–1775), see A. D. Morris, '"Sir" John Hill, M.A., M.D. (1706–1775): Apothecary, Botanist, Playwright, Actor, Novelist, Journalist', *Proceedings of the Royal Society of Medicine* 53 (1960), 55–60.
** The mystery was unravelled as Corsica.

7–F184*

[after 10 January 1770]

Sir

I received the favor of yours, and have the pleasure of informing you that I have got rid of my fever &c.

I have not been able to call upon the Grocer but shall see before the next post, I beleive he told me he had no lump nor any to be got at that price – he was to have enclose'd Bill of Parcels in the Cash –

We have strange work heare, they were going to send Lord Chatham to the Tower on Wednesday. He said that Lord Cambden had been much favorized for his Vote in Parliament, Lord Marchmont took them down and was very warm upon them. Lords Rockingham, Suffolk, Shelborne, Duke of Richmond said the same. After several debates they wanted to adjourn for they found they cou'd do nothing with them, upon which Lord C got up & said he stood their culprit & that he would go out while they debated it but that if they adjourned it should be with his protest upon which Lord Weymouth moved to proceed – you'll see the results in the paper.

Monday is expected to be a worse day in the Commons, what will be the event I don't learn. Each party are violent, the minority I hear intend to publish a Manifesto which by all accounts will be a very extraordinary one – the Lords it's expected if they enter upon it will protest &c.

Miss Eliott is very ill with the fever which we have had for some time, she was much better this morning & continues better this evening but yet I don't think her out of danger yet –

I hope you'll aprove of your gardener, he lived with Lord Frederick Cambel & since with the Duke of Northumberland –

I am Sir your oblig'd humble servant

W H

* Dated on internal evidence: the threat to send Lord Chatham to the Tower was made on 10 January 1770.

8–F189

[16 January 1770]

Sir

I received the favor of yours and am sory to hear you are so indifferent – if your purging continues I would encourage it by taking a few grains of Rhubarb, and repeat it occasionally and take after it is gone off twenty grains of Mithridate with ten of Contrayerva – and the contrayerva without the Mithridate in the morning – if you are feverish with your Rhumatism two or three drams of Mindereri Spirit with the above – *

We have strange work here, nothing but turning out – Lord Cambden, Huntington, Willoughby, Coventry – Grandby – the Dukes of Manchester, Beaufort – & Bolton – the last is supposed will be turn'd out with the rest – the Attirney Generall and several others are talked of. The Lords yesterday adjourned till Monday. Lord Rockingham inform'd the House that he had a motion of great consequence to send on Wednesday and hoped they would concurr with him in ordering summones to the Lords to attend that day, upon which Lord Weymouth got up and moved for the adjournent [sic], which was opposed and occasion'd a warm debate but was carried by a great majority. In the minority were Bolton, Couventry & another court Lord who I have forgot. The Commons were yesterday upon the Corn bill which is continued, I hear, but with a Clause giving the King & Concile a power of opening the ports as they shall see occasion. The House broke up early as the Speaker was still but indifferent.

Sir Richard Banfield desired that he might have leave to differ his motion till this day as his collegue was not able to attend, it is expected he will make it today with regard to Dr Musgrave at the Request of the County – **

The debates were so high lest week that they had like to have sent Sir George Savile to the Tower*** and likewise Rush & Glyn – had they sent any of them Sixteen others were ditermin'd to have accompanyed them. The purport of what was said has been in papers – Conway got upon in order to make excuses for Sir George and said that many gentlemen said thing in their heat and passion which they were sory for afterwards – Sir G said he was much obliged to that Gentleman for making excuses for him but that he was neither worn or in a passion and to shew that he was not either he repeated it again, that that House of Commons had betray'd the trust reposed in them by the Freeholders &c or words to that effect –

You are happy to be out of these squables – werse debates are likely to happen daily.

I hope to hear you are better and am Sir

Yours &c W H

* See Introduction, section 5, p. 68.
** Sir Richard Bampfylde, member for Devon, presented an address for his constituents on 16 January 1770. The subject of the address was the allegation of the Devonian Dr Samuel Musgrave (1732–1780) that the peace signed in 1763 had been sold to the French by persons of high rank (see *ODNB*; also **10–F182**).
*** The threat to send Sir George Savile to the Tower was made on 11 January 1770.

9–F181

[January 1770]

Sir

I have the pleasure of informing you that Miss Eliott continues mending and if the Weather would but alter I should hope she would be able to get out the beginning of next week.*

This day they had a common hall, the result you'll see in your Paper, tho not a true one in every particular from what I have heard.

I have not been able to see Mr Miller having been so hurried that I have not had time to go to Chelsea.**

Captain Minifee call'd today to tell me that he sails on Saturday but as I have not seen Mr Miller I could do nothing about the Tiles.

Scheffer's *Insects* is by much the Most genneral work & the best I have seen.*** I have not had time to look over it but saw it at Nourse's and the few plates I examined, they seem'd exceedingly well done and as exceedingly Expensive. There are four Volumes, two are his *Elements* – and the letter press of it is in German. The other two are The *Icones insectorum* and contain 100 plates, several Insects on each, the letter press in Latin but no references or descriptions, but they will be very useful as Linneus has refer'd to a great Number of them at the end of his *Systema*, Vol 1, part 2. I should like to have them provided I could get them from abroad at a cheaper rate for I am certain at nine Guineas they must at least get 3 – If I can find any way of getting them I will write to Scheffer's for two or three sets as there can be no doubt of dissposing them –

I am Sir your obliged humble servant

W H

* For Miss Eliott's illness, from which she was now recovering, see 7–F184.
** Philip Miller, director of the Chelsea Physic Garden and author of *The Gardeners Dictionary*. See Introduction, section 4, pp. 39, 40, 41.
*** Jacob Christian Schäffer's *Icones insectorum* was published in Regensburg between 1766 and 1769.

10–F182*

[23 January 1770]

Sir

I have got the Roots & shall send them by Thursday Coach if possible.

Mr Dyson desired I would let you know that he has been but very indifferent or he would have wrote to you. He has got the Rheumatism – but is rather better –

The Duke of Grafton resigned yesterday and this morning wrote to the Treasury board to acquaint them that the business of the day would be transacted by Lord North who they must now look upon as first Minister. Tho he has resigned yet I don't think his power at an end – he is still to continue of the Cabinet counsel and to advise the Treasurers and Lord North to Nominal Minister. This will not Last long for they can't find People to fill the Vacancies – his retiring in this manner seems <u>fear</u>! –

Yesterday Dr M[usgrave]** was before the House for four hours, and gave a very circumstantial account and came off with a great character for his abilities – but his information treated as you'll see by the inclosed motion – He gave an account how he came by his information which is as follows: that he was in company with a

Scotchman, an Irishman & a French Com[t]e – that they disputed upon the goodness of the peace and that the dispute run high when the Frenchman who had said nothing before said that the peace had cost the French dear enough – This occasion'd further conversations with him and in one of them he told him that 8000000 Louis had been given for it, that half was given to a great Lady & the other divided between Lord Bute & Holland & that he could prove it. This he inform'd Lord Hertford who was then Minister & it was treated slightly by him as appea[red] by their Letters which were read. He came over to England and menti[oned] it to Drs Blackston & Dean at that time, offering to impeach some persons of selling the Peace and what he had told. Fitzherbert, Sir G Young are agreeing with what he had heard at Paris. That he went immediatly and acquainted Lord Hertford of it and advised him to send for Dean which the other would not. It appear'd that Dean offer'd to impeach the Princess Dowager of Wales, Lords Bute & Holland. They were mention'd by name in the House – that the princess had half which was paid into the Hands of the brother of a maid of Holland meaning Vansiter and the other Half between Lords Holland and Bute – I have not time to tell you more, only that in a conversation with the late Duke of Newcastle when he was told that Lord Holland had as above the Duke said he beleived Lord Holland was rogue enough to do enything but not Fool enough to do that. His sons were both in the House when this was mention'd. Lord Northington is not dead –

* Lord Grafton resigned and Lord North became Prime Minister on 22 January 1770.
** For Dr Musgrave, see **8**–F189 and note.

11–F180

[Autumn 1770]

Sir

I should have wrote to you sooner but that I have been obliged to attend Miss Dyson at Hampstead, who has been extreamly ill having been in constant Hystericks for ten days or more but now is got much better and came to Town today in order to go to Stoke tomorrow.*

The Messenger is returned from Spain as you'll see by the Paper but has brought no answer. They are to send one by a Messenger of their own.

Mr Dyson intended sending a Parcell to me for you which I'm to send by the Coach along with which I will send your shoes.

I am Sir your oblig'd humble servant

W H

* Mr Dyson's home, where Hudson often visited him, was at Stoke in Surrey.

12–F192

[March 1771]

Sir

I just sent you an account of the Books and should have wrote to you on Saturday night but was obligid to be out and did not return in time for the Post. The Books I got for you are as follows:*

360 [W] Turner [*A New Herbal*] a very fine copy, £1 16s. od.

526 Belon's *Observations*, 539 Bel: *Hist Cys*. I did not receive your letter in time for; the first is at the end of Clusius.

540 & 541 put up together, £1 2s. 0d., a tollerable copy.

550 [Conrad] Gesner: *Historiae Animalium*, 5s. 0d.

564. Cixtius *de Arb. Con:* 2s. this is a scarce Book.

574 *Magnol: Bot. Mons*, 2s. 0d. – Clusius's other peices are in his great work.

595 Oxted: £1 13s: 0d., very dear but very scarce.

603 Van R. H. Leydens, 10s. 6d. Cheap being very scarce, may comiss[ion] from abroad. Gower is, I understand, about publishing a New edition.

624 *Fl. Lapp*, £1 1s. dear indeed.

627 *Fauna Suec*, 6s. 6d., cheap, out of print.

658 Bad Copy.

642 very Bad & imperfect, sold only for 6d. on that account.

The two Books on agriculture I bought on account of Mr Strange as they were books lent by him to Mr Stillingfleet.

635 sold for £2 16s. 0d. and supposed to be the first book printed on botany.

Dr Pemberton's Books will begin to be sold the 24th and will last 18 or 20 Nights, shall send you the catalogue.**

The House sold for £435.

No fresh news from Denmark.

Sir J Mawbey Has been distilling Wheat, they made a seizure on Saturday and had it not been for the excisemen the Mob had pull'd down his House.

Mr Dyson is much better tho still troubled with the Head Ache in a morning –

Mrs Elliot has been for some time getting better. I intend'd to have call'd today but was prevented. The last time I was there which was Fryday she went on mending. They wonder'd they had not heard from you.

The Princess would not see the Duke of Cumberland.*** He went to Carleton House but was refused, he is shamed for going: he should have sent as it was disstressing her to give a negativum.

We have had quite a Spring day.

Lord Ossery can't get a divorce.**** The Commons refused to a 2nd divorce as she was a Whore when he married her and is no more now –

I am Sir your oblig'd humble servant

W Hudson

* The books listed in this letter demonstrate Hudson's expertise in the areas of interest that he shared with FHD (see Introduction, section 4, pp. 36–7), and his business acumen. Benjamin Stillingfleet, botanist and author (1702–1771), was an important mentor of Hudson's, and is sometimes credited with having written the introduction to Hudson's *Flora Anglica* (see *ODNB*).

** Dr Henry Pemberton (1694–1771), FRS, was an eminent physician and a writer on medical subjects (see *ODNB*).

*** Henry, Duke of Cumberland was a younger brother of George III. The king did not consent to the duke's proposed marriage to Mrs Horton (see **14**-F194–F195).

**** For Lord Ossery's continuing difficulties in extricating himself from this marriage, see **16**-F193.

13–F179

[late March 1771]

Sir

You would see an Account of what is going forwards here in the papers. Where this will end, God knows. It at present seems as if it would be worse than the M[iddlesex] Election.* This day the King went to the House and the Greatest crowd I ever say [*sic*] upon the occasion, his first going not excepted, and nothing but his howling & all the contemptable noises that could be thought of. It was said that stones were thrown at him but as I walked by the side of the coach from St James to the Horse Gaurds [*sic*] I think I should have seen it had their been any, for I kept my Eye on the Coach all the way –

Mr Charles Fox's sulky was broke and he obliged to take refuge in a coffee house. His sulky is a charriot which Holds only one and the highest carriage about town so that I think he may be oblig'd to them for breaking it, at least had it been mine I should have [*sic*] ashamed to have be seen in it –

The City are all in a bustle and are determin'd to support their Lord Mayor & aldermen. Petitions, … [?] and a run upon the Bank are talk'd of, the first is more than probable will take place. What you see in the paper about Mr Townsend is fact, he mention'd the Princess Dowager often in the House – **

I will send you the Books, they will go best by the Waggon. I have not had time to look out your seeds but will send them next week.***

We have as severe weather as any this winter, snow, wind and frost and still continues as at present Tho the Wind is inclinable to get into the south –

I am Sir your oblig'd humble servant

W H

* The Middlesex election affair followed John Wilkes's expulsion from the House of Commons in February 1769 on grounds of seditious and obscene libels. While in prison, Wilkes was returned unopposed for Middlesex at three by-elections, which the Commons declared void. The Hon. Henry Lawes Luttrell was given the seat (see note on **14–F194–F195**).
** James Townsend's criticisms of the Dowager Princess of Wales were made in late March 1771.
*** The books to be sent were probably those listed in the previous letter.

14–F194–F195

[October 1771]

Sir

I received the favor of yours, and am glad to find you give so good an account of yourself.

Mr Dyson is tolerably well. He had a return of the Gout in his right hand upon coming to town, which is now in a great measure gone; not so much as to be able to write, otherwise he would have done it before now, but as soon as he gets the use of his fingers he will do it – he desires his Compliments &c.

I find by Mr Wiston that except you have somebody in Holland you are liable to be imposed on as they don't scruple sending instead of those kinds mention'd their very worst. He has no correspondance there, therefore despere getting them this year but will look out for someone who is going abroad next year to get some. I see some of oure seedsmen are getting into the same method of selling them in sorts at so much per dozen or hogshead. Marché in the Haymarket has got several sorts but I beleive they are dear if one may judge by their names –

I promised to send you an acount of the Duke of Cumberland &c by this Post.* So much as I have heard I will mention – from what I can Collect I have reason to think that he sent express for Sir J Deleval from Seaton Deleval who came to town as he dared not go to the King alone. I understand he took him along with him On Saturday morning to Richmond and were near two hours along [sic] with his Majesty, and before his going there he, I beleive, sent a letter to the Princess. His reception I suppose was not a very agreeble one as he set out immediatly along with his Lady & Sir John for Callais and so to Switzerland. The King immediatly came to town to the Princess – who was very much shocked and being ill at the same time it was thought it would have been attended with fatal consequences which was agravated by the Account of the Duke of Glocester.**

When the whole of this affair comes to light I make no doubt but it will apear a very dark one & Lutterel the Member a principal actor in it. I make no doubt but that they took the advantage of his being in Liquor and by Bullying forced him to marry Mrs Horton.

The account of the Duke of Gloucester you'll see in the Papers & tho he is better for the present yet I shou'd not be surprized to hear of his death by the High Messengers. However there is little probability of his returning to England. The Princess is better than she was & her case is look'd upon as not so dangerous as at first but nevertheless sooner or latter her present complaint will be her death, if what I hear about her is true, tho it may not happen so soon as the generality of the People wish. Lett her faults be what they will, she is greatly to be pityd and I most sincerely feel for both her & the King – if one looks forward this marriage is a very serious affair, more so then at first it appears to be –

But as both Marriage and divorces are now in fashion I will mention two of the former, one is of Lord Tyrrawley to a Miss Carter, the other is Lord Montford to Miss Blake.*** This last is a very extraordinary affair as follows. Captain Scawen had made love to Miss Blake for some years and had labour'd long to get his father's consent but to no purpose. At last he met with him in a good humor and obtain'd it with a promise of £400 a year. Away he flew to acquainte Miss Blake with it who in the mean time had seen My Lord. When he came he acquainted her with his success, she told him she was sorry he had given himself so much trouble as she had alter'd her Mind – that she was ditermin'd to have Lord Montfort. He made use of every argument he could think of to make her change her mind but without effect. He left her and Lord Montford paid his addresses and all was agreed on when they made a party at Newmarket last meeting, where Miss once more saw Captain Scawen and relented. She went home and wrote a letter and desired her sister to see it conveyed to him. She remonstrated against it but to no purpose, when she agreed to send it, but instead of that the family had consultation upon it and it was agreed to be burnt. She hearing nothing from him for a day or two got it out of her sister that it had not been sent. She then put on her hat & Cloak and tho nine o'clock at night set out for W. M… near a mile and went to the house where she … … known by the name of Hell and inquired for the Capton. When he saw her he was surprized and desired to know what brought her there. She desired to speak to him alone, he told her she could not do it there without loosing her Character but th[at] if she would return home he would come and speak to her in the morning. Accordingly she went back and found the Family in alarm at her absence. She told them where she had been, they upbraded her but notwithstanding she went to Bed and fell fast asleep at the same time. The next morning he came according to his appointment and she told him that she had changed her mind and hoped he would forget what was past as she was now ready to marry him whenever he pleased, to which he answer'd that she could not suppose that his father would give his consent a second time, neither would he be at the trouble to ask him for it and therefore beg'd to be excused. In the meantime Lord M came in and upon seeing them together was surprized but it was soon explain'd to him. He said had he known she had been engaged or even had proposals made from any others he should not have thought of paying his addresses to her but that as she had a prior engagement he should wish her a good morning. Upon this she said it did not signify, she was determined one or other should marry her. Captain Scawen beg'd to be excused – but Lord Montfort said if that was the case he would marry her and accordingly they are to be married next week – she for his Title, he for her fortune which is 10000 or 14000 –

I am Sir your oblig'd humble servant

W H

Dr Jebb and Mr Adair are I hear going to the Duke of Gloucester

* The marriage of the Duke of Cumberland to Mrs Horton took place on 2 October 1771. Mrs Horton was the daughter of Simon Luttrell, Baron Irnham, and the sister of Henry Lawes Luttrell. Father and son were both MPs. Hudson's reference to 'Luttrell the Member' is probably to the son. (See also note on 13–F179.)
** The Duke of Gloucester, a younger brother of George III, recovered and lived until 1805.
*** The marriage of Lord Montfort to Miss Blake took place in 1772.

15–F169

16 November 1771

Sir

I just mention'd at the Bottom of the paper that you might give Mrs B some milk or flower of sulphur, which will take off the effect of mercury sooner than anything else I know. She should take a sufficient quantity night & morning so as to give her one or two stools a day, and to discontinue it a few days before she begins her Pills again; if she can go into a tub of Warm Water twice in a Week it will then be giving this method a fair trial and by opening her pores the mercury will be less liable to affect her mouth – *

Mr Dyson continues mending and has once more got the use of his hand so that you'll have a letter from him I suppose next week. His health I hope will be much mended by this fit of the Gout, he looks clearer and is freer from those hypochondriacal symptoms he used to complain so frequently of than I have known him. He goes out every day and by means of the Bark and exercize I hope we shall set him up for the winter.

The different people who collect the Taxes and Rates for your house in John Street have call'd upon me for Payment. As you did not mention it to me I did not know whether you would have me pay them for you or not, I pay'd one which was the only one I happen'd to be at Home when they call'd, viz the common sewers, which is charged upon the Landlord. It is 14s. – shall I pay th'others when they call again?

As the Gentlemen don't like to be long out of the Fashion and as the Ladies have set the Example by eloping, the Duke of Kingston has set the example to the rest of Husbands by eloping from his Dutchess not with a companion as the Ladies do but by himself and it's supposed he's gone abroad.** The reason of his going is because he could not live any longer with her.

I have just got your Tickett No. 10873. I did [not] purchase it myself having had such bad luck but got Mrs Otway to do it for me.***

I am Sir your oblig'd humble servant
W Hudson

* For the treatment recommended for Mrs B, and for Mr Dyson in the following paragraph, see Introduction, section 5, pp. 52, 55, 67.
** The Duke of Kingston-upon-Hull married Elizabeth Chudleigh in 1769. She had previously married Augustus Hervey, later 3rd Earl Bristol, and was convicted of bigamy in 1776, after the Duke of Kingston's death.
*** On reverse of letter, perhaps in FHD's hand: '1771. Nov.16. Mr Hudson with an account of Lottery-Ticket.'

16–F193

[January 1772]

Sir

I received the favor of yours and am glad Mrs B is better – *

I call'd this Day on Mr Shelton and pay'd him the money. He says you may alter the second hand with your fingers as it may be moved to point to any division without hurting it.

I am glad the yellow W[ood] Anemone flowers,** in all probability you'll have plenty next year – I have inclosed you two seeds of a new English melica, which was lost formerly out of the letter. I had but four, & I have likewise inclosed a few seed of the Welsch Cerastium which I hope will succeed. I have not yet received any of the Plants from Mr Aiton.***

We have had no Brocoli here worth a pin. Cucumber, Sparrow grass & Radishes are plenty tho the two former dear. As for anything else except smal sallet we are destitute. Dandilion has been the only sallet I have eat this winter, and still continues as I think it the Best for the bitterness improves by eating the same as olives do.

Since my last what I mention'd is now come out – two more Ladies and I should not be surprized to hear a dozen more. I beleive I mentioned three, the other two are Lady Rodney and Lady Ossery. The first was caught at a Bagnio with Mr Aston by Sir George who went thither upon the same errand but unfortunate for his Lady was introduced into a Room where he met with his Lady's schawle or Capuchine with her name on the Neck of it which put it out of doubt – The last it's said has had an afair with her buttler, this is descending with a Witness from a Duchess to a Countess and now she may be a buttler's wife should his Lordship proceed. But it's doubted if he has sufficient proof – and therefore like the two other Lords says there is nothing in it –

I am Sir your oblig'd humble servant
W H

* This follows on from the reference to Mrs B in the previous letter.

** Wood anemone being likely to flower in the early months of the year, this letter probably dates from early 1772.
*** William Aiton (1731–1793), director of the Royal Botanic Gardens at Kew. See also 25–F173.

17–F177

[January 1772]

Sir

I sent to Roper and they had no double flowers left. I have try'd several shops but can't get any Hyacinths but what are very dear, a shilling a root. I can get you Double Narcissus cheeper than what he sold them at 8s. per Dozen and Tuleps almost at what price you please according to their goodness – they tell me some fresh Hyacinths are expected, but they can't be certain of them – If you'll let me know what I am to get, will send them immedially.

Mr Dyson has had a periodical Headach with fever but is now got better of it, the Headache having left him some days but he still continues the Bark, and must do so some time longer. He is much stronger than he was, but can't bear Much business yet –

I am sory to tell you that I here Mrs Eliott is but very indifferent and is in a good deel of Pain at times, from the maid's account of her, and I much doubt if she will … better of her complaint.*

By letters received yesterday from Dr Jebb the Duke of Gloucester is recovering from his flux, his pulse was not quite so quick nor the heat of his flesh so great. His legs still continues [*sic*] to swell at Night and his stools are more natural than they had been, he had Roud out the 14 & 15 and bore it very well, but I don't find that he's one bit better in regard to his pulmonic complaint so that there is no probability of his Recovery – the last letter was dated the 16th.

The Princess continues ebbing and flowing but not the least better.**

The extraordinary account you'll see in the Paper from Stockwell is every tittle of it true.*** Mrs Otway's son was there today and knows the People, most of them of credit and above deceit, two of them keep their Carrages – How to account for it they are at a loss. I know several myself of those mendion'd [*sic*] in this extraordinary account and besides the Parson Mrs Golding was so much afrighted that her fit were so strong as to occasion her too black Eyes, or at least by the Account they brought me she has a large black circle under each Eye –

We know nothing new else worth mentioning.

I am Sir your oblig'd humble servant

W Hudson

* FHD's sister Anne Eliott died in February 1772.
** The Dowager Princess of Wales died on 8 February 1772.
*** Hudson fell for the story of the Stockwell ghost hoax, for which see Mary Golding, *An Authentic, Candid, And Circumstantial Narrative of the Astonishing Transactions At Stockwell … Surry … the 6th And 7th … of January, 1772* (London: Partridge, 1809).

18–F185

[Spring 1772]

Sir

I received the favor of yours inclosing a Draft for Mr P's Bill which I paid them and have return'd the Bill. I shall not be able to send you the Pulv. Contrayerv. C. till next week and that towards the latter end of it, as I am promised a share of a small quantity of the true Root brought from Portugal, for I have not at present more than 4 oz left of the old sort.* What this kind they have brought I don't know but if I have it I find I must pay for it very dear, after the rate of 500 per Cent, but there is no remedy.

Mr Dyson continues tolerablily well, & I think goes thro the business of the House much better than he did any year since I knew him, tho I beleive he does not think so.

The story of the Treatment of the Opera dancer is in great part true tho not quite so bad as the paper Mentions, for she danced three or four days after.** The affair was transacted at a Mr Willims, a Chapman oposite the Opera House, and both the Women & man are gone to France.

We have little here besides what you see in the Papers –

It is said Lord Melbourne is broke up and that his House in Putney is to be sold &c, occasion'd by a demand made on him by Lord Waldgrave. His Friends say it's no such thing, that it's only a Tale propagated by one Laws who my Lord is going to prosecute.

Five or six more Lords, it's said, either have or will stop payment very soon. Many of inferior Rank are expected to do the same. Private Credit was never so lo as at present. Several of my Patients complain that Tradespeople are so thespe [?] that they won't let them keep any money. Many Families don't come to Town upon that account as they left their bill unpaid last year and find they will be oblig'd to discharge them on their coming as well as find difficulty in getting Credit for more, so the Town is likely to be empty. When credit will be reestablished God only knows for when Capital Bankers, at a time when every King seems to be over, are Raising all the Money they can upon their Estates in order to answer any demands that may be made upon, looks as if they expected soon capital strike took. It is generally thought the Air Bank won't stand more than another year or two at the most.***

Sir W Medals sold amazingly each about £500, his prints not quite so well being in too large lots for private purchasers. As soon as the descriptive Catalogue comes out will send it you –

The Princess of Wales's Jewels &c are to be sold on Monday at Christie's. I have not yet seen them nor shall I be able to go as they begin selling on Monday.

I am Sir your oblig'd servant

W H

* See Introduction, section 5, p. 62.
** The treatment of the opera dancer could possibly refer to the Betsy Fox affair reported in *Harris's List of Covent Garden Ladies 1772* (London, 1772).
*** Great distress in the City was reported in the *Gentleman's Magazine*, June 1772.

19–F190

[August 1772]

Sir

I should have wrote to you last week to have inform'd you of the fate of your Ticket which is come up a £20 prize. I wish I could have added three more cyphers to it – but even that is more than I had expected, having had five blanks before in this Lotery and twelve the two preceeding ones without one prize –

We are in great distress in the City as you'll have seen by the papers. Where it will end, God only knows. No private credit nor any business carried on without money –

I hope you continue free from fever &c.

Mr Dyson continues tolerable, not quite free from complaints but upon the whole much stronger and better than last Year –

The Town continues very thin, but rather sickly, but no dangerous dissorders in particular.

I must conclude with wishing you many happy returns of the season.*
and am Sir Yours
W Hudson

* FHD's birthday was on 29 August.

20–F178

[Autumn 1772]

Sir

I should have answer'd your favor and thanked you for the Cockles, which were most excellent (indeed I don't know whether I do not think them better this way than Oysters), but that I was in hopes I should have been able to have told you when I should have been able to have left Town, but at present I am far from being able as I have several Families who in passing thro Town make some days stay and as one goes another comes. However, I must still desire you will let me meet you upon the road as it will be loosing so many days my coming to Nutwell, and I am fearful that I should not be able to be above a week absent at a time.

In regard to Seales, they are not to be got at present. There is so great a demand for them and they doubled there [sic] price for them. However, you may do I think very well with those you have, for the full weight of G[rain]s is five penny W[eight] nine grains, and all prior to George the 3d must only want six Grains, those of George 3d three grains, Half G[rain] in proportion, so that the two Dram weight which is five penny weight and three Grains does for the former & six Grains for the latter.

Wee have nothing here new.

If you mean the salt of Lemons for taking out Iron moulds I will get you a Powder which does infinitely better, if it is for Punch then that will do but cream of Tartar full as well, having tasted both.

Captain Corbet is gone off with Lord Bute's fourth daughter.* His Lordship seems to be particularly unhappy in his family, I pitty him much –

We have had very fine weather here.

I am Sir your obliged humble servant
W Hudson

* Captain Corbet eloped with Lord Bute's fourth daughter in 1772. Their marriage took place on 26 July 1773: see J. Burke, *A Genealogical and Heraldic Dictionary of the Landed Gentry*, 2 vols (London: Henry Colburn, 1846), vol. 1, lineage of Corbett of Elsham and Darnhall.

21–F170

30 October 1772

Sir

I was prevented last night from writing being sent for out.

I went yesterday to have bought your Ticket but they are so much upon the rise that they advised me to waite a little as there are but few sold. I much doubt myself if they will be much cheeper except it is just before the drawing. However I shall be in the City on Monday and if I find upon enquire they are not, will purchase it then.

Last night sent you the Cocoa. It is very good. I could have had some much cheeper but then it was mixed with Burnt Beans &c.

I have got the Trap & Cage but they would not send it Both home.

I should think you might have it full as cheep by the Waggon. I have wrote for the Screen, and wil send the Trap to Stanton's Wharf.

We have less sickness at present than any time this summer, a few fevers and colds, the fevers most of them are of the putrid kind.

Mr Dyson is come to Town but I much doubt if the Hurry of business he seems to be getting into does not thro him back again.

Sir G & Lady Warren are got together again and everything is to be forgot & forgiven.* She gives up her Family and Friends and has promised to be a dutifull wife and Sir George beleives her. She is most thoroughly humbled.

They sell Scheffer's *Icones insectorum* for 10 Guineas which cost me under five, they are determin'd to get rich in a hurry. Clerk's Book which sels for 15 Guineas is a most miserable work notwithstanding what Linnaeus says of it. I have seen many halfpenny prints much better coloured.

The City business you see in the papers. The India dividend from what I can collect is likely to be only Six Per Cent which will reduce the stock to 130 or 40, if not under.

I have just seen Mr Lee who sent the Things last Wednesday –

I hope I shall be able to send you some seeds this next spring and will get some of the Cabbage Seed from Sir Robert. He & Sir Charles are about setting out for Bath but shall see him upon his return.

I am Sir Your oblig'd
Wm Hudson

* Sir George Warren, member for Lancaster (see 3–F183), married as his second wife Frances Bisshopp, maid of honour to Queen Charlotte.

22–F171

19 December 1772*

Sir

I sent the Things you disired by Stanton's Wharfe and they were to go by the *Hopewell* &c and should have answer'd your letter before, but that it had slipt my memory.

I have just examined your Ticket which is still undrawn. You certainly have a right to a prize this year for I have purchased three Blanks already out of 5 Tickets. Yours and another remains undrawn.

In regard to the person you mention, I think you had best give him a Dose of Rhubarb or two, and then give him Two tea Spoonfulls of Tincture of Bark in a Cup of Strong Camomile Tea with some Ginger in it twice a Day, and drink Ginger tea for common drink to half a Pint, of which he may add if necessary two Spoonfulls Brandy, if drunk as punch or instead of wine. If as common drink then only one Spoonfull to a large half Pint and sweeten it to his taste, by which means he will get the better in a great measure of his indigestion &c and perhaps bring on a fit of the Gout. He should occasionally take a dose of Rhubarb with a few grains of Ginger with it.**

We have nothing new here worth mentioning.

Mr Dyson is better than he has been of late. Having got Cold some time ago together with too much business brought on his headach &c but they are now much abated.

I am Sir your oblig'd humble servant

W Hudson

* The date, 19 December 1772, is added at the end of the letter, perhaps in FHD's hand.
** See Introduction, section 5, p. 63.

23–F172

Epsom, 20 August 1774

Sir

I have got so far on my road to Mr Dyson's before I recollected that Yesterday I received a note from Malcolm that the Plants were sent by the Waggon on Wednesday and had forgot to direct them to give you notice of it at the Bottom of the Paper –

Mr Dyson has not been so well for these few days Past & has desired to see me, otherwise could ill spare the time as I am obliged to return tomorrow morning.

I have given up my Hampshire Ichen* therfor this year, unexpected business prevents me.

I shall next week send you some seeds which I have received from Jamaica.**

& I am Sir your obliged humble servant

W H

[sketch: 3 sides of square, divided into rectangles, circle within, measurements]

* Hudson had perhaps been planning an excursion along the River Itchen in Hampshire. We are grateful to Irene Derczynska for recognizing the river in Hudson's 'Ichen'.
** The despatch of the seeds from Jamaica is recorded in the following letter.

24–F191

[late summer 1774]

Sir

I did not receive yours till Sunday or should have wrote to you by Saturday's post, occasion'd by my being at Mr Dyson's who has had a return of his bilious laxness &c, but I lefft him this morning better and I hope near well of it.

I have only sent you half a Pd of Bark* as it is so extravagently dear and likely to be much more so if some don't arive soon. Contrayerva except the bastard kind is likewise scarce and Russia Rhubarb more than either. As to your Patient, I should think you should give him another vomit and then a dose of Rhubarb and then the Bark again so as to prevent a return.

I hope you have received the Plants safe. Some of them I rather went higher than was mention'd in the List, particularly the Gardenia, for those of 5s. were very small.

I have sent you some seeds from Jamaica for your store** – along with the Bark &c this night –

I have not been able to get out of Town yet nor shall I now this year.

We have had for some days past a good deel of Rain but as the Glass begins to rise I hope it won't continue –

I am Sir your oblig'd humble servant

W Hudson

* See Introduction, section 5, p. 57.
** For seeds from Jamaica, see the previous letter.

25–F173

20 July 1775

Sir

I have this evening sent the thermometer &c to the Inn so that you'll receive it by the first A & R's Waggon. I could not send you a Peice of Guaiacum Wood as it is difficult to get except from the Turners who ask much more than the whole of the Shavings come for.*

Mr Dyson came to Town yesterday morning in order to see Dr Heberdon and returned this morning. He is very well and indeed as much so as he will be, could he be brought to think so, but unhappily he has taken a different turn and finds out complaints which don't exist, and distresses himself so much that I only wonder he is so well as is. He is dissatisfied with himself and everybody else – indeed he makes himself truely miserable –

I have not heard of Mr Aiton's being yet come from the sea.** I fancy he will return next week along with a Patient of mine who he went with – and as I set out upon my Tour on Monday I much doubt if I shall see him till after my return – which will be in about three weeks or a Month for I have not yet been able to get the better of my complaint tho I have made little excursions about Town. I mean to go thro Yorkshire and return by the Lancashire road, Which I think will take me near a Month for my Poney won't cary me above thirty miles per day without my fatiguing myself too much, for if you put them above a certain pace it becomes uneasy & my strength will not yet bear it, but I hope before my return I shall be able.***

I hope you have had no return of your Feber.

I am Sir your obliged humble servant

Wm Hudson

* See Introduction, section 5, p. 62.
** William Aiton, director of the Royal Botanic Gardens at Kew, as above in **16**–F193.
*** Hudson's projected tour on horseback would take him to his native region in the north of England.

26–F174

30 August 1776

Sir

I am at last got back from my Tour thro North Wales and, thank God, find myself much mended by the Journey – *

I was as successfull as usual in regard to Weather for two Days that I was at Llanberys out of three were remarkable fine, particularly the day I went to Snowdon and they told me they had not had two such days so near together for six Weeks. Some company had waited upwards of ten days at Carnarvon to go to the top of Snowdon and were obliged to depart without seeing it –

I was equally successfull with regard to Plant as I found all the Plants mention'd to grow there and some few others, some that had not been found since Richardson's and Brewer's time** – tho searched for by several – and I got roots of most of them which are now at my Freind's in Yorkshire and if he suceeds shall be able to furnish you with some of them.

I have inclosed you a few seeds which I picked up and which are rather ornamental plants for a garden – particularly the Campanula patula – some of which you had better sow this winter and the remainder in the Spring – as well as of the Vicias –

I was at Mr Dyson's since my return who is just as usual teazing himself and everybody about him about nothing – I have just received a letter desiring me to go down again – which I shall on Monday –

We have nothing new, no news from the Howes, the end of next week or the begining of the week following is the time they expect to hear of them and I much doubt if it will not be such another as Sir P P [?] – As to Burgoyne, the best thing he could do would be to return for they will be too many for him. They have thrown into Ticondirago 8000 besides what was there before and more are marching that way so that he will have warm work of it indeed. It's well if they are not all cut to peices   ***

I hope you have escaped your fevers this summer.

I am Sir your obliged humble servant

Wm Hudson

I have just received the *Flora danica* and the last No. of the fourth Volume is expected soon. I have received no books from Mr Paine –

A new and lush Volume of Scheffer's *Icones insectorum* &c is come over but I have not been able to get one yet for you but some are expected and likewise Gmelin's *Historia fucorum*.

* This tour, one year later, took Hudson to North Wales, where he had been with Joseph Banks in 1768 (see Introduction, section 1, p. 13).
** Richard Richardson (1663–1741), a native of Yorkshire, and William Brewer (1670–1743), who moved to Yorkshire to work with Richardson, were well-known botanists and collectors.
*** Admiral Lord Richard Howes and General William Howes headed the British peace commission in America. The fort of Ticonderoga in New York State was abandoned to the British General Burgoyne the following year, on 6 July 1777, so on this occasion Hudson's pessimistic prognosis was not borne out by the facts.

27–F188

[early September 1776]

Sir

The reason you had none of the other plants was that most of them are at such pricies [*sic*] that I did not think you would give it and secund not to be met with and other not for a store, the Plumeria fabulsa very scarce and the very smallest plant £2 2s., the other somewhat cheaper. Gloriosa C not to be had and the Clitoria, except some has been raised from some seed I had two years ago. The Antholyza lyries &c are dear, Pentapetes I hope to have some seed, Sea Pancratia I beleive you have, Giant Asclepias not to be got except as extras: pr: Cereus grandiflor. & flagellis. I don't know how they sell Gladiolus & Leonarus.

The Jassamines, I will see if I can get. The Heliotr[opium] Odoratum as desired he would put up is a sweets[cented ?] flower and which continues a long time –

Mr Dyson continues, I hope, mending.* I had a letter today and shall see him again tomorrow and return on Monday.

I have no Franks or should have wrote to you more fully about the plants – Vallis I beleive will be the best place to get the Jassamin for they frequently have them over.

I am Sir Yours &c
W H

* Here, Hudson's optimism was not borne out. Dyson died on 16 September 1776.

28–F175

17 December 1776*

Sir

I this day received the favor of yours and am sory to hear your Bowels are so indifferent. I would advise you to try bark in small doses, about ten grains, and some Nutmeg – and Mithridate at night while the laxness continues, but the Bark I would continue twice a day for a Month.

As to the Person you mention, the best thing to be done is Poulticies of bread and Milk and the skin to be oil'd with a Feather to prevent the Poulticies sticking as greasy things do very seldom. With ulcers of that kind he should keep his leg up as much as possible and at the same time, if much inflamed, hold it over the steam of warm-water, the water should not be too hot – and the steem should be confined by a Cloath thrown over the Leg &c at the time of steeming it, and then to apply the Poulticies. His body should be kept open – but I doubt if you will be able to heel them intirely – **

No news yet from the Howes.***

Lord Petersham was this day elected for Westminster. Sir Watkin Lewis came too late after the Books were closed and demanded a Poll but not granted. He threatens a Petition as they did not keep the Books open the time alowed –

I am Sir your obliged &c
Wm Hudson

* The date is given by Hudson at the beginning of the letter, and repeated at the end, perhaps in FHD's hand: 'Dec.17.1776. Sir Fr. D.'
** See Introduction, section 5, p. 64.
*** For the Howes, see **26–F174** and note.

29–F176

6 January 1778*

Sir

I am sorry to hear you have got so troublesome a complaint. I hope it will not be of long continuance – I would advise you to take a dose or two of Physic such as will give you two or three stools and to rub your Loins with some volatile liniment and to keep a flannel to them – and likewise to take some contrayerva with some weak whey to promote a gentle Perspiration. If the contrayerva & Physic does not relieve your Pain I would then advise you to take two drams of oil of almonds or olive & ten grains of salt of Hartshorn and some mint water with a little sugar and to take it three times in the day – and if restless ten or twelve drops of Laudanum added to night draught or you may take twenty grains of Mithridate.** I hope soon to hear you have got rid of your Pain – without any further aid –

I forgot to mention that the plant you sent me was a new one. I don't recollect to have seen it before. It is a diadelphia plant.

I am sory to tell you that your ticket is a Blank if I took down the No. right – ***

Nothing new from America – stocks fall and a French war talked on as unavoidable – it is said that Franklin is acknowledged at the court of France & have no doubt about the treaty being signed which is mention'd in the papers –

I suppose we shall see you the end of this Month.

I am Sir Your obliged &c

W Hudson

Many happy returns of the season.

* The date is given by Hudson at the beginning of the letter. At right angles in the right lower margin is a note, perhaps in FHD's hand: 'Jan. 6. 1778. Sr. Fr. D. Rheumatism in his Loins.'
** See Introduction, section 5, p. 68.
*** A last mention of lottery tickets.

BIBLIOGRAPHY

Alexander, J. J., 'Bere Alston as a Parliamentary Borough', *Transactions of the Devonshire Association* 41 (1909), 152–178.

Andrews, H. C., *The Botanist's Repository for New and Rare Plants*, 10 vols (London: for the author, 1797–1811?).

Archer Briggs, T. R., 'Some Devonian Stations of Plants Noted in the Last Century', *Journal of Botany* 22 (1884), 168–174.

Baker, G., *An Essay, Concerning the Cause of the Endemial Colic of Devonshire* (London: Hughs, 1767).

Bashin, M., E. Dietrich-Daum, and I. Ritzmann, 'Doctors and Their Patients in the Seventeenth to Nineteenth Centuries', *Clio Medica* 96 (2016), 39–70.

Bere, A. J., *Buckland Monachorum* ([Buckland Monachorum], 1930).

British Pharmaceutical Codex (London: The Pharmaceutical Press, 1923).

Burke, J., *A Genealogical and Heraldic Dictionary of the Landed Gentry of Great Britain & Ireland*, 2 vols (London: Henry Colburn, 1846).

Burnby, J. G. L., 'A Study of the English Apothecary from 1660–1760 with Special Reference to the Provinces', PhD thesis, University of London (1979).

Cartwright, J J., ed., *The Travels Through England of Dr. Richard Pococke* ([London]: for the Camden Society, 1888).

Chanter, J. F., 'Exmouth – Sir John Colliton', *Devon & Cornwall Notes & Queries* 11(1) (1921), 146, 209, 260–261.

Charlton, R., *An Inquiry into the Efficacy of Warm Bathing in Palsies* (Oxford: Clarendon Press, 1770).

Cheyne, G., *The English Malady or a Treatise of Nervous Diseases of all Kinds* (London: Strahan, 1733).

Cheyne, G., *Essay of Health and Long Life*, 9th edition (London: Strahan, 1745).

Childs, J. R., 'Sir George Baker and the Dry Belly-Ache', *Bulletin of the History of Medicine* 44 (1970), 213–240.

Coleridge, B. J. S., 'The Parliamentary Boroughs of Devon', *Transactions of the Devonshire Association* 30 (1898), 25–41.

'The Colleton Family in South Carolina', *South Carolina Historical & Genealogical Magazine* 1(4) (1900), 325–341.

Corfield, P. J., 'From Poison Peddlers to Civic Worthies: The Reputation of Apothecaries in Georgian England', *Social History of Medicine* 22(1) (2009), 1–21.

Crawford, C., 'Patients' Rights and the Law of Contract in Eighteenth-Century England', *Social History of Medicine* 13 (2000), 381–410.

Crellin, J. K. 'Anton Störck (1731–1803) and British Therapeutics', in E. Lesky, *Wien und die Weltmedizin* (Vienna: Böhlau, 1974), pp. 27–31.

Crellin, J. K., 'Dr James's Fever Powder', *Transactions of the British Society for the History of Pharmacy* 1(3) (1974), 136–143.

Crellin, J. K., 'Domestic Medicine Chests: Microcosms of 18th and 19th Century Medical Practice', *Pharmacy in History* 21 (1979), 122–131.

Crellin, J. K. and J. R. Scott, *Glass and British Pharmacy 1600–1900* (London: Wellcome Institute of the History of Medicine, 1972).

Darley, G. W., 'Court Leet' (2004, rev. 2016), huttonlehole.ryedaleconnect.org.uk.

DeLacy, M., *The Germ of an Idea: Contagionism, Religion and Society in Britain, 1660–1730* (Basingstoke: Palgrave Macmillan, 2016).

Desmond, R., *Dictionary of British & Irish Botanists and Horticulturalists* (London: Natural History Museum, 1994).

Digby, A., *Making a Medical Living: Doctors and Patients in the English Market for Medicine, 1700–1911* (Cambridge: Cambridge University Press, 1994).

Dix, R., *The Literary Career of Mark Akenside* (Madison, NJ: Fairleigh Dickinson University Press, 2006).

Dix, R., 'A Newly Discovered Manuscript Dedication by Mark Akenside', *Medical History* 53(3) (2009), 425–432.

Donn, B., *A Map of the County of Devon* (London: published according to Act of Parliament, 1765).

Dyson, J., ed., *The Poems of Mark Akenside, M.D.* (London: Bowyer, 1772).

Emery, A., *Greater Medieval Houses of England and Wales, 1300–1500*, 3 vols (Cambridge: Cambridge University Press, 2006).

Fissel, M. E., *Patients, Power, and the Poor in Eighteenth-Century Bristol* (Cambridge: Cambridge University Press, 1991).

Fuller-Eliott-Drake, E. D., *The Family and Heirs of Sir Francis Drake*, 2 vols (London: Smith, Elder, 1911).

Geach, F., *Some Observations on Dr Baker's Essay on the Endemial Colic of Devonshire* (London: Baldwin, 1767).

Gerarde, J., *The Herball or Generall Historie of Plantes (Enlarged and Amended by Thomas Johnson)* (London: Norton & Whittakers, 1633).

Golding, M., *An Authentic, Candid, And Circumstantial Narrative of the Astonishing Transactions At Stockwell ... Surry ... the 6th And 7th ... of January, 1772 ...* (London: Partridge, 1809).

Gray, T., *The Art of the Devon Garden* (Exeter: The Mint Press, 2013).

Gray, T., *The Garden History of Devon* (Exeter: University of Exeter Press, 1995).

Gray, T., *Lost Devon* (Exeter: Mint Press, 2003).

Gray, T., 'Their Idols of Worship: Fruit Trees and the Walled Garden in Early Modern Devon', in S. Pugsley, ed., *Devon Gardens* (Stroud: Sutton Publishing, 1994), pp. 28–41.

Gray, T., 'Walled Gardens and the Cultivation of Orchard Fruits in the South-West of England', in C. Anne Wilson, ed., *The Country House Kitchen Garden, 1600–1950* (Stroud: Sutton Publishing, 1998), pp. 114–128.

Gray, T. and M. Rowe, eds, *Travels in Georgian Devon: The Illustrated Journals of the Reverend John Swete 1789–1800*, 4 vols (Tiverton: Devon Books, 2000).

Harris, B., 'Lottery Adventuring in Britain, c. 1710–1760', *English Historical Review* 133(561) (2018), 284–322.

Harris's List of Covent Garden Ladies, 1772 (London, 1772).

Hart-Davis, D., 'Sir Francis Drake', in *Buckland Abbey* (Swindon: National Trust, 2014).

Heath, S., *The Story of Forde Abbey: From the Earliest Times to the Present Day* (London: Francis Griffiths, 1911).

Heberden, W., *Antitheriaka: An Essay on Mithridatium and Theriaca* (n.p., 1745).

Hinde, T., ed., *The Domesday Book: England's Heritage, Then and Now* (London: Hutchinson, 1985).

Hiscocks, R., 'Francis William Drake' (2016), https://morethannelson.com/officer/francis-william-drake/.

Hoskins, W. G., *Devon* (Chichester: Phillimore, 2003).

'The Household below Stairs: Clerks of the Green Cloth 1660–1782', *British History Online*, https://www.british-history.ac.uk/office-holders/vol11/pp403-407.

Hudson, W., *Flora Anglica* (London: Nourse & Moran, 1762).

Hume, D., *The Philosophical Works of David Hume*, 4 vols (Edinburgh: Adam Black and William Tate, 1826).

Huxham, J., *Dissertation on the Malignant, Ulcerous Sore-Throat*, 3rd edition (London: Hinton, 1759; 1st edition 1757).

Huxham, J., *An Essay on Fevers, and their Various Kinds, as depending on Different Constitutions of the Blood; with Dissertations on Slow Nervous Fevers; on Putrid, Pestilential, Spotted Fevers; on the Small-Pox; and on Pleurisies and Peripneumonies* (London: Austen, 1750).

Huxham, J., *Observationes de Aëre et Morbis Epidemicus*, vol. 1 (London: Austen, 1739).

Huxham, J., 'A Small Treatise on the Devonshire Colic which was very epidemic in the year MDCCXXIV', in *The Works of John Huxham*, 2 vols (London: Bent, 1788), vol. 1, pp. 5–51.

Huxham, J., 'Two Remarkable Cases in Surgery, by Mr. Francis Geach, Surgeon in Plymouth', *Philosophical Transactions* 53 (1763), 231–237.

Huxham, J., *The Works of John Huxham*, 2 vols (London: Bent, 1788).

Irvine, S., 'Surgeons and Apothecaries in Suffolk: 1750–1830', PhD thesis, University of East Anglia (2011).

Jenner, M. S. R. and P. Wallis, eds, *Medicine and the Market in England and Its Colonies, c. 1450–c. 1850* (Basingstoke: Palgrave Macmillan, 2007).

Jones, J. P. and J. F. Kingston, *Flora Devoniensis* (London: Longman &c, 1829).

Jump. H., 'Mark Akenside and the Poetry of Current Events 1738–1770', DPhil thesis, University of Oxford (1987).

Kanefsky, J., 'Railway Competition and Turnpike Roads in East Devon', *Report and Transactions of the Devonshire Association*, 109 (1977), 59–72.

Langford, P., *A Polite and Commercial People, England 1727–1783* (Oxford: Oxford University Press, 1998).

Lease, O. C., 'The Septennial Act of 1716', *Journal of Modern History* 22(1) (1950), 42–47.

Leong, E., 'Collecting Knowledge for the Family: Recipes, Gender and Practical Knowledge in the Early Modern English Household', *Centaurus* 55 (2013), 81–103.

Leong, E., 'Making Medicines in the Early Modern Household', *Bulletin of the History of Medicine* 82 (2008), 145–168.

Levitin, D., '"Made up from Many Experimentall Notions": The Society of Apothecaries, Medical Humanism and the Rhetoric of Experience in 1630s London', *Journal of the History of Medicine and Allied Sciences* 70 (2015), 549–587.

Lewis, W., *The New Dispensatory* (London: Nourse, 1753).

Loudon, I., 'The Nature of Provincial Medical Practice in Eighteenth-Century England', *Medical History* 29 (1985), 1–32.

Loudon, J. C., 'Notices of Some Gardens and Country Seats in Somersetshire, Devonshire and Part of Cornwall', *Gardener's Magazine* 19 (1843), 238–250.

Louis-Courvoisier, M. and A. Mauron, '"He found me very well; for me, I was still feeling sick": The Strange Worlds of Physicians and Patients in the 18th and 21st Centuries', *Medical Humanities*, 28(1) (2002), 9–13.

Lowe, M. C., 'The Turnpike Trusts in Devon and Their Roads: 1753–1889', *Report and Transactions of the Devonshire Association*, 122 (1990), 47–69.

Lysons, S. and D. Lysons, *Magna Britannia*, vol. 6: *Devon* (London: Thomas Cadell, 1822).

Mackintosh, A., *The Patent Medicine Industry in Georgian England* (Basingstoke: Palgrave Macmillan, 2018).

The Magic Tree (Exeter: compiled by NCCPG group, 1989).

Major, E., *Madam Britannia: Women, Church, and Nation 1712–1812* (Oxford: Oxford University Press, 2012).

Mauchline, M., 'The Cistercian Foundation', in *Buckland Abbey* (Swindon: National Trust, 2014).

Maxted, I., 'Cider and Eighteenth-Century Evidence-Based Healthcare: A Devon Pamphlet War' (1996), Exeter Working Papers in Book History bookhistory.blogspot.com/2007/02/cider.html.

Maxted, I., 'John Huxham's Medical Diary: 1728–1752', *Local Population Studies* 12 (1974), 34–37.

McConaghey, R. M. S., 'John Huxham', *Medical History* 13 (1969), 280–287.

McConaghey, R. M. S., 'Sir George Baker and the Devonshire Colic', *Medical History* 11(4) (1967), 345–360.

Meller, H., *The Country Houses of Devon*, 2 vols (Crediton: Black Dog Press, 2015).

Meller, H., 'Tour of the Abbey', in *Buckland Abbey* (Swindon: National Trust, 2014).

Miller, P., *The Gardeners Dictionary*, 8th edition (London: for the author, 1768; first published 1731).

Moore, T., *The History of Devonshire from the Earliest Period to the Present*, 2 vols (London: R. Jennings, 1829–1833).

Morgan, M., 'The Suppression of the Alien Priories', *History* 26(103) (1941), 204–212.

Morris, A. D., '"Sir" John Hill, M.A., M.D. (1706–1775): Apothecary, Botanist, Playwright, Actor, Novelist, Journalist', *Proceedings of the Royal Society of Medicine* 53 (1960), 55–60.

Munk, W., 'Biographica Medica Devoniensis; or Collections towards a History of the Medical Worthies of Devon', *Western Antiquary* 6 (1887), 258–262.

Noyes, R., Jr, 'The Transformation of Hypochondriasis in British Medicine, 1680-1830', *Social History of Medicine* 24(2) (2011), 281–298.

Perman, E., 'Samuel Tissot: Patient Compliance in the 18th Century', *Hektoen International: A Journal of Medical Ethics*, 3 (2011), https://hekint.org/2017/01/30/samuel-tissot-patient-compliance-in-the-18th-century/.

Peters, T. J., L. Payne, and N. J. Level, 'The Life and Times of Francis Geach MD, FRS (1730–1798), Senior Surgeon to the Royal Naval Hospital, Plymouth (1778–1798)', *Journal of Medical Biography* 23(2) (2015), 63–73.

Pevsner, N. and B. Cherry, *The Buildings of England: Devon*, 2nd edition (Harmondsworth: Penguin, 1989).

Polwhele, R., *The History of Devonshire*, 3 vols (London: Cadell & Davies, 1793–1806).

Porter, D. and R. Porter, *Patient's Progress: Doctors and Doctoring in Eighteenth-Century England* (Cambridge: Polity Press, 1989).

Porter, R., *English Society in the Eighteenth Century* (London: Penguin, 1990).

Pulteney, R., *Historical and Biographical Sketches of Progress of Botany in England*, 2 vols (London: Cadell, 1790).

Renbourn, E. T., 'The Natural History of Insensible Perspiration: A Forgotten Doctrine of Health and Disease', *Medical History* 4(2) (1960), 135–152.

Rhea, N. 'When Sheep Were Big Business', *Darlington & Stockton Times*, 22 January 2016, https://www.darlingtonandstocktontimes.co.uk/news/14224382.when-sheep-were-big-business/.

Risdon, Tristram, *The Chorographical Description or Survey of the County of Devon* (Plymouth: Rees and Curtis, 1811; 1st edition 1714).

Roberts, W., *The Book-Hunter in London* (London: Elliot Stock, 1895).

Robertson, J., *An Essay on Culinary Poisons* (London: Kearsly, 1781).

Robinson, N., *A New System of the Spleen, Vapours and Hypochondriack Melancholy* (London: Bettesworth, 1729).

Schupbach, W., 'The Fame and Notoriety of Dr John Huxham', *Medical History* 225 (1981), 415–421.

Smith, D. C., 'Medical Science, Medical Practice and the Emerging Concept of Typhus in Mid-Eighteenth-Century Britain', *Medical History*, Supplement 1 (1981), 121–134.

Smith, E., *The Life of Sir Joseph Banks* (London: John Lane, 1911).

South Carolina Historical & Genealogical Magazine

Stirling, D. M., *The Beauties of the Shore* (Exeter: W. Roberts, 1838).

Stobart, A., *Household Medicine in Seventeenth-Century England* (London: Bloomsbury Academic, 2016).

Waldron, H. A., 'James Hardy and the Devonshire Colic', *Medical History* 13 (1969), 74–81.

Weston, R., *Tracts on Practical Agriculture and Gardening. Particularly addressed to the Gentlemen-Farmers in Great-Britain* (London: S. Hooper, 1773).

Williams, R. M., 'Two Unpublished Poems by Mark Akenside', *Modern Language Notes* 57 (1942), 626–631.

Worth, R. N., *A History of Devonshire* (London: Elliot Stock, 1886).
Wyndham, H. P., ed., *The Diary of the Late George Bubb Dodington* (Salisbury: E. Easton, 1784).

Websites consulted

The Cullen Project: The Medical Consultation Letters of Dr William Cullen, www.cullen-project.ac.uk.
Historic England, historicengland.org.uk.
History of Parliament, www.historyofparliamentonline.org.
Munk's Roll: Lives of the Fellows of the Royal College of Physicians (1861–), munksroll.rcplondon.ac.uk.
Oxford Dictionary of National Biography (2004), www.oxforddnb.com.

INDEX

This is a select index of people, places and ships named in the letters, with sub-entries that include some themes and topics.

For major themes and topics, see the relevant sections of the Introduction (which is not indexed): section 2 for Bere Alston elections, section 3 for Buckland Abbey and Nutwell buildings, section 4 for Nutwell estate planting, section 5 for medical matters.

Members of Bere Alston's Court Leet are listed individually – this being a Devon history project. Many Members of Parliament mentioned in the Hudson letters, and Parliament itself, are not included in the index. Rather, see www.historyofparliamentonline.org.

For some London personalities and events, see notes to the Hudson letters.

The overall scheme of the index is alphabetical, but within entries it has at times seemed more helpful to proceed chronologically.

References to page numbers 73–285 are to Rowe letters, 289–311 to Hudson letters.

DEVON AND CORNWALL
RECORD SOCIETY PUBLICATIONS

Previous volumes are available from Boydell & Brewer Ltd.

A Shelf List of the Society's Collections, ed. S Stride, revised 1986

New Series

1 *Devon Monastic Lands: Calendar of Particulars for Grants 1536–1558*, ed. Joyce Youings, 1955

2 *Exeter in the Seventeenth Century: Tax and Rate Assessments 1602–1699*, ed. W. G. Hoskins, 1957

3 *The Diocese of Exeter in 1821: Bishop Carey's Replies to Queries before Visitation, Vol. I Cornwall*, ed. Michael Cook, 1958

4 *The Diocese of Exeter in 1821: Bishop Carey's Replies to Queries before Visitation, Vol. II Devon*, ed. Michael Cook, 1960

5 *The Cartulary of St Michael's Mount*, ed. P. L. Hull, 1962

6 *The Exeter Assembly: Minutes of the Assemblies of the United Brethren of Devon and Cornwall 1691–1717, as Transcribed by the Reverend Isaac Gilling*, ed. Allan Brockett, 1963

7 *The Register of Edmund Lacy, Bishop of Exeter 1420–1455, Vol. 1*, ed. G. R. Dunstan

8 *The Cartulary of Canonsleigh Abbey*, ed. Vera C. M. London, 1965

9 *Benjamin Donn's Map of Devon 1765*, Introduction by W. L. D. Ravenhill, 1965

10 *The Register of Edmund Lacy, Bishop of Exeter 1420–1455, Vol. 2*, ed. G. R. Dunstan, 1966

11 *Devon Inventories of the 16th & 17th Centuries*, ed. Margaret Cash, 1966

12 *Plymouth Building Accounts of the 16th & 17th Centuries*, ed. Edwin Welch, 1967

13 *The Register of Edmund Lacy, Bishop of Exeter 1420–1455, Vol. 3*, ed. G. R. Dunstan, 1968

14 *The Devonshire Lay Subsidy of 1332*, ed. Audrey M. Erskine, 1969

15 *Churchwardens' Accounts of Ashburton 1479–1580*, ed. Alison Hanham, 1970

16 *The Register of Edmund Lacy, Bishop of Exeter 1420–1455, Vol. 4*, ed. G. R. Dunstan, 1971

17 *The Caption of Seisin of the Duchy of Cornwall 1377*, ed. P. L. Hull, 1971

18 *The Register of Edmund Lacy, Bishop of Exeter 1420–1455, Vol. 5*, ed. G. R. Dunstan, 1972

19 *A Calendar of Cornish Glebe Terriers 1673–1735*, ed. Richard Potts, 1974

20 *John Lydford's Book: The Fourteenth-Century Formulary of the Archdeacon of Totnes*, ed. Dorothy M. Owen, 1975 (with Historical Manuscripts Commission)

21 *A Calendar of Early Chancery Proceedings Relating to West Country Shipping 1388–1493*, ed. Dorothy A. Gardiner, 1976

22 *Tudor Exeter: Tax Assessments 1489–1595*, ed. Margery M. Rowe, 1977

23 *The Devon Cloth Industry in the 18th Century*, ed. Stanley D. Chapman, 1978

24 *The Accounts of the Fabric of Exeter Cathedral 1279–1353, Part I*, ed. Audrey M. Erskine, 1981

25 *The Parliamentary Survey of the Duchy of Cornwall, Part I*, ed. Norman J. G. Pounds, 1982

26 *The Accounts of the Fabric of Exeter Cathedral 1279–1353, Part II*, ed. Audrey M. Erskine, 1983

27 *The Parliamentary Survey of the Duchy of Cornwall, Part II*, ed. Norman J. G. Pounds, 1984

28 *Crown Pleas of the Devon Eyre 1238*, ed. Henry Summerson, 1985

29 *Georgian Tiverton, The Political Memoranda of Beavis Wood 1768–98*, ed. John Bourne, 1986

30 *The Cartulary of Launceston Priory (Lambeth Palace MS. 719): A Calendar*, ed. P. L. Hull, 1987

31 *Shipbuilding on the Exe: The Memoranda Book of Daniel Bishop Davy (1799–1874) of Topsham, Devon*, ed. Clive N. Ponsford, 1988

32 *The Receivers' Accounts of the City of Exeter 1304–1353*, ed. Margery Rowe and John M. Draisey, 1989

33 *Early-Stuart Mariners and Shipping: The Maritime Surveys of Devon and Cornwall 1619–35*, ed. Todd Gray, 1990

34 *Joel Gascoyne's Map of Cornwall 1699*, Introduction by W. L. D. Ravenhill and O. J. Padel, 1991